"This important book broadens the scope of comparative capitalism in two dimensions. It goes beyond the limits of the traditional 'firm-based' varieties of capitalism approach to analyse a novel model of capitalism characterized by close state-business relationships. This book also pushes the usual geographical boundaries of the genre, and focuses on usually neglected though increasingly important emerging economies (Brazil, India, China, South Africa). A must read for any scholar of comparative capitalism."

— **Bruno Amable,** *Professor of Economics at the University of Geneva, Switzerland.*

"This is a challenging book. While mainstream economists continue to put all their coins in the market, four political economists show that fast growing emerging economies adopt a state-permeated capitalism. I oppose the successful developmental capitalism of China and India to the unsuccessful economic liberalism of Brazil and South Africa – the four countries studied in this book. State-permeated and developmental capitalism are the same thing – an economic system where the market coordinates the competitive sectors, while the state, the non-competitive industries and the macroeconomy. Or, in the words of the authors, a system where there is an "informal cooperation between individual national capitalists and representatives of state agencies".

— **Luiz Carlos Bresser-Pereira,** *Emeritus Professor at the Getulio Vargas Foundation and former Minister of Finance of Brazil.*

"The research team has developed an eclectic and viable framework for a study of emerging market economies based on, but going beyond, the Comparative Capitalism perspective, by adding in important historical and comparative dimensions. Their method also transcends the firm-level focus of the regional varieties of capitalism approach (VOC) and its more macro-foundations framework will be warmly welcomed by scholars in political economy, development studies, sociology and international relations. It is a timely and useful intervention in the context of the rapidly changing balance of economic power in the contemporary world economy through focusing on the key characteristics of the capitalisms of the larger and varied market economies of the Global South."

— **Vishnu Padayachee,** *Distinguished Professor and Derek Schrier and Cecily Cameron Chair in Development Economics, School of Economic and Business Sciences, University of the Witwatersrand, South Africa.*

"This ambitious work takes the BRICS beyond an investment option to a systematic political and economic examination. The analysis ranges widely across careful country studies while adding in the international political economy usually lacking in the "varieties of capitalism" framework. Deftly organized and deeply researched, this book greatly advances theoretical debates on comparative capitalism in developing countries."

— **Ben Ross Schneider,** *Ford International Professor of Political Science and director of the MIT Brazil program.*

"Every so often you come across a book which imparts the smack of something original and important enough to rank as a "must read" for a long time. This is such a book. It stands on the shoulders of three main fields of knowledge about "the wealth of nations" – varieties of capitalism, comparative politics, and international political economy; and paves the way for lots of follow ups. Believers in neoliberal philosophy may not approve of much of it, but they should read it first and then pick a fight."

— **Robert H. Wade,** *Professor of Global Political Economy, London School of Economics, UK.*

State-permeated Capitalism in Large Emerging Economies

This book systematically analyzes the economic dynamics of large emerging economies from an extended Comparative Capitalisms perspective. Coining the phrase 'state-permeated capitalism', the authors shift the focus of research from economic policy alone, towards the real world of corporate and state behavior.

On the basis of four empirical case studies (Brazil, India, China, South Africa), the main drivers for robust economic growth in these countries from the 2000s until the 2010s are revealed. These are found, in particular, in mutual institutional compatibilities of 'state-permeated capitalism', in their large domestic markets, and beneficial global economic constellations. Differences in their institutional arrangements are explored to explain why China and India have been more economically successful than Brazil and South Africa. The authors highlight substantial challenges for the stability of state-permeated capitalism and assess the potential future growth, sustainability and likely pitfalls for these large emerging economies.

Opening further avenues for empirical and theoretical research, this book raises questions for the future of the global economic order and should appeal to academics, graduate students and advanced undergraduates in politics, economics, economic sociology and development studies. It should also prove a worthwhile and provocative read for development practitioners and policy-makers.

Andreas Nölke is Professor in International Political Economy/International Relations at Goethe University Frankfurt, Germany.

Tobias ten Brink is Professor of Chinese Economy and Society and director of the China Global Center at Jacobs University, Bremen, Germany.

Christian May is Senior Researcher at the Department of Political Science at Goethe University, Germany.

Simone Claar co-leads the research group 'Glocalpower' at the Department of Political Science at University of Kassel, Germany.

RIPE Series in Global Political Economy
Series Editors:
James Brassett, *University of Warwick, UK*,
Susanne Soederberg, *Queen's University, Canada* and
Eleni Tsingou, *Copenhagen Business School, Denmark*

The RIPE Series published by Routledge is an essential forum for cutting-edge scholarship in International Political Economy. The series brings together new and established scholars working in critical, cultural and constructivist political economy. Books in the RIPE Series typically combine an innovative contribution to theoretical debates with rigorous empirical analysis.

The RIPE Series seeks to cultivate:

- Field-defining theoretical advances in International Political Economy
- Novel treatments of key issue areas, both historical and contemporary, such as global finance, trade, and production
- Analyses that explore the political economic dimensions of relatively neglected topics, such as the environment, gender relations, and migration
- Accessible work that will inspire advanced undergraduates and graduate students in International Political Economy.

The *RIPE Series in Global Political Economy* aims to address the needs of students and teachers.

Power in North-South Trade Negotiations
Making the European Union's Economic Partnership Agreements
Peg Murray-Evans

Informal Economies and Power
Anna Danielsson

The European Periphery and the Eurozone Crisis
Capitalist Diversity and Europeanisation
Neil Dooley

State-permeated Capitalism in Large Emerging Economies
Andreas Nölke, Tobias ten Brink, Christian May and Simone Claar

Japanese Resistance to American Financial Hegemony
Global versus Domestic Norms
Fumihito Gotoh

For more information about this series, please visit: www.routledge.com/RIPE-Series-in-Global-Political-Economy/book-series/RIPE

State-permeated Capitalism in Large Emerging Economies

Andreas Nölke, Tobias ten Brink, Christian May and Simone Claar

Routledge
Taylor & Francis Group
LONDON AND NEW YORK

First published 2020
by Routledge
2 Park Square, Milton Park, Abingdon, Oxon OX14 4RN

and by Routledge
605 Third Avenue, New York, NY 10017

First issued in paperback 2021

Routledge is an imprint of the Taylor & Francis Group, an informa business

British Library Cataloguing-in-Publication Data
A catalogue record for this book is available from the British Library

Library of Congress Cataloging-in-Publication Data
Names: Nölke, Andreas, 1963– author. | Ten Brink, Tobias, author. | May, Christian, author. | Claar, Simone, author.
Title: State-permeated capitalism in large emerging economies / Andreas Nölke, Tobias ten Brink, Christian May, Simone Claar.
Description: 1st Edition. | New York : Routledge, 2019. | Series: Ripe series in global political economy | Includes bibliographical references and index.
Identifiers: LCCN 2019027061 (print) | LCCN 2019027062 (ebook) | ISBN 9780367203696 (hardback) | ISBN 9780429261145 (ebook)
Subjects: LCSH: Government corporations—Developing countries. | Government business enterprises—Developing countries. | Developing countries—Economic policy. | Industrial policy—Developing countries. | Developing countries—Commercial policy.
Classification: LCC HD3850 .N65 2019 (print) | LCC HD3850 (ebook) | DDC 330.12/2091724—dc23
LC record available at https://lccn.loc.gov/2019027061
LC ebook record available at https://lccn.loc.gov/2019027062

ISBN 13: 978-0-367-77770-8 (pbk)
ISBN 13: 978-0-367-20369-6 (hbk)

Typeset in Times New Roman
by Apex CoVantage, LLC.

Contents

Figures

Tables

Author biographies

Andreas Nölke is professor in International Political Economy/International Relations at Goethe University Frankfurt, Germany. Among others, his research specialization includes comparative capitalism in larger emerging markets, multinational companies in the Global South, financialization and the political economy of European Integration.
https://orcid.org/0000-0002-0357-9682

Tobias ten Brink is professor of Chinese Economy and Society and director of the China Global Center at Jacobs University, Bremen, Germany. He teaches and conducts research on global political economy, China and large emerging countries as well as on comparative politics and social theory.
https://orcid.org/0000-0002-2892-3742

Christian May is senior researcher at the Department of Political Science at Goethe University, Germany. His research and teaching focuses on comparative capitalism, political economy of finance, corporations and the political economy of India and Brazil.
https://orcid.org/0000-0001-7550-8747

Simone Claar co-leads the research group 'Glocalpower' at the Department of Political Science at University of Kassel, Germany. Her research interests include capitalism, green economy, development and trade, class analysis, labor and renewable energy transitions with a regional focus on emerging markets and Sub-Saharan Africa.
https://orcid.org/0000-0001-5999-3711

Acknowledgements

This book has developed out of a research project on the nature of capitalism in Brazil, India, China and South Africa at Goethe-University, Frankfurt, Germany. Conducting the research and writing the book was supported by the German Research Foundation (DFG) under grant numbers NO 855/3–1, NO 855/3–3 and TE 1069/6–1.

A whole host of individuals supported us with the analysis and observations in this project. We had the opportunity to share insights from our research with our project advisory board (Robert Kappel, Stefan Schmalz, Heather Taylor-Strauss, Reinhard Wolf), but also in various conferences and guest lectures all over the globe, for instance at Institute of International Relations Prague, Hungarian Academy of Sciences, Koc University, University of Cambridge, University of Stellenbosch, University of Lucerne, Sun Yat-Sen University Guangzhou, the New School for Social Research in New York, University of Sussex, Warsaw School of Economics, International Studies Annual Convention (San Diego, Toronto, San Francisco), Annual Conference of the Society for the Advancement of Socio-Economics (Chicago, London), Rising Powers in the New Global Political Economy (Nottingham), 8th Pan-European Conference on International Relations of the European International Studies Association (Warsaw), Global Norm Evolution and the Responsibility to Protect (Frankfurt), the German Political Science Foundation (Bonn), Finances, 'Financial Crises' and Political Responses (CAS Leipzig), the Institut Québécois des Hautes Etudes Internationales (Université Laval), the World Interdisciplinary Network on Institutional Research (Hong Kong) and the World International Studies Conference (Frankfurt).

We are very grateful for inspiring and thoughtful comments at various stages of the work process, in particular from Caner Bakir, Moises Balestro, Cornel Ban, the late Uwe Becker, Patrick Bond, Renato Boschi, Antonio Botelho, Luiz Carlos Bresser Pereira, Ian Bruff, Jan Drahokoupil, Peter Draper, Matthias Ebenau, Beata Farkas, Magnus Feldmann, Eli Friedman, He Gaochao, Tamas Gerocs, Keith Hart, Roger Haydon, Marcel Heires, Anne Henow, Alexandre Henriksen, Robert Kappel, Lena Lavinas, Sebastien Lechevalier, Carmen Ludwig, Boy Lüthje, Eric Magnin, Surajit Mazumdar, Christopher McNally, Daniel Mertens, Franziska Müller, Martn Myant, Natalia Naqvi, Ziya Onis, Morten Ougaard, Vishnu Padayachee, Jaya Prakash Pradhan, Ryszard Rapacki, Judit Ricz, Carlos Santana, Stefan

Schirm, Stefan Schmalz, Ben Ross Schneider, Tim Shaw, Daniel Sitera, Matthew Stephen, Oliver Stünkel, Ngai-Ling Sum, Miiklos Szanyi, Heather Taylor-Strauss, Alexandra Dienes-Vasileva, Hugh Whittaker, Reinhard Wolf, Axel Wölk, Mustafa Yagci and Patrick Ziegenhain.

Our cooperation and interview partners in Brazil, India, China and South Africa gave us tremendous support during our field trips, and we would like to thank our hosting institutions: the University of Brasilia, University of Sao Paulo (FEA-USP), the Institute for Development and Reform of the Pearl River Delta at Sun Yat-sen University Guangzhou and the Human Economy Program at the University of Pretoria.

For valuable research assistance, we are deeply indebted to Manisha Döbler, Sabine Englert, Hauke Feil, Sahil Matur, Sebastian Möller, Michael Schedelik, Vanessa Endrejat and Zheng Mian. Johannes Petry, Amanda Schimunek, Tobias Schottdorf and Peter Volberding helped with editing the manuscript. For most valuable help in preparing the manuscript, we would like to thank Brigitte Holden and Karoline Schäfer.

Finally, we highly appreciate the advice given by the three anonymous reviewers. At the same time, we would like to thank the editors of the Routledge RIPE Series in Global Political Economy, Claire Maloney and the Routledge publishing team for their most valuable support and inspiration.

Introduction

When Goldman Sachs coined the acronym BRIC in 2001 to promote an alternative investment portfolio (O'Neill 2001), very few would have thought that countries such as China and India would be in the driver's seat of the global economy only a decade later. Within that decade, BRIC became the BRICS – not just through the incorporation of South Africa, but because these countries began to form a political alliance of their own. The perception of these five countries changed from being seen as underprivileged emerging markets into veritable global players that Northern policymakers and international institutions would have to pay attention to. Today, the annual BRICS meetings receive considerable global public attention. Notably, the 2015 BRICS meeting led to the launch of the New Development Bank (NDB), which is the first global development bank established after the World Bank. Hence, many observers interpreted this as a challenge to the Bretton Woods Institutions, which are dominated by the rich countries of the Global North.

Yet, much is still unknown about how these large emerging economies, some of which are now indeed global players, actually work. Obviously, the strong role for the state in the economy distinguishes the BRICS economies from their developed counterparts, but terms like "state capitalism" used so far serve as labels rather than as explanations for the growth dynamics in these large emerging economies. Moreover, economic turbulences since the mid-2010s have led observers in the business world to conclude that we are now witnessing the end of the rise of emerging markets, or perhaps even their "melt-down" (Talley 2016). Stock market volatility, falling growth rates and capital outflows are indications that even the Chinese economy is now facing serious challenges. In India, the Modi government is struggling against many hurdles in order to implement its economic reform program. Brazil encountered first a massive recession and then the breakdown of its whole economic model, while the South African economy seems as "fragile" as ever. And the NDB has made very little impact so far, funding only a small number of renewable energy projects.

Nevertheless, the economic rise especially of China, India and (if to a lesser degree) Brazil from the 1990s to the early 2010s marked a key global trend. Let us put this into perspective: Between 1995 and 2011, China increased its share of world GDP from 3.5% to 17%, whereas India increased its share from 3% to

5.6%. Together with Brazil, these three countries now rank among the top 10 in terms of global manufacturing value. Comparatively speaking, the global financial crises of 2008–2009 hardly affected the economic dynamics of the largest emerging economies. Thus, beyond the alleged hype initiated by the Goldman Sachs BRIC(S) studies, large emerging economies were in fact responsible for a fundamental long-term shift in global economic dynamics. Were it not for these economies, the growth prospects of the world economy would have been much bleaker than they even have been after the financial meltdown of 2008.

Whereas growth in Brazil and South Africa has been slowing down, or even moved into recession from the early 2010s onwards, China and India still continued to fare relatively well. For many Western observers, what is puzzling is that the more liberal emerging economies (especially South Africa) perform worse than the 'state-led' ones. It is also a conundrum for those observers, who assert that the quality of inclusive economic institutions is the most important factor for long-run economic growth (e.g. Acemoglu and Robinson 2012) as the country with the most exclusive institutions – China – has so far outpaced more inclusive, democratic emerging countries. In order to make sense of these puzzles, we have to resort to alternative explanations. This book aims to solve some of the puzzles surrounding the rise of large emerging economies. In particular, we want to find out to what extent large emerging economies share common institutional features, and if so, whether an "economic model" encompassing these features would be able to explain the socio-economic performance of these economies.

The economic dynamics of Brazil, India, China and South Africa call for explanations that cannot be provided by any single theory. In order to identify the relevant institutional commonalities and differences, we build on an eclectic analytical framework that is based upon a 'Comparative Capitalisms' heuristic. However, we go beyond it in important ways. On the one hand, we account for the historical evolution of national capitalisms; on the other hand, we place national systems of capitalism in their transnational contexts, thereby reducing an artificial split within the political economy tradition by combining concepts from comparative political economy with international political economy. In order to systematically compare these four emerging economies, we examine a number of crucial institutional spheres of capitalism: corporate governance, corporate finance, industrial relations, education and training, the pursuit of innovations, the role of domestic markets and international economic integration. In contrast to the earlier 'Varieties of Capitalism' research (Hall and Soskice 2001), we avoid an exclusive focus on microeconomic rationality but complement it with compatible analytical tools from critical research in development studies, sociology and comparative politics.

The book is the first systematic attempt to analyze the economic dynamics of large emerging economies from a Comparative Capitalisms perspective. It goes beyond existing approaches that mainly focus on regional varieties of capitalism, such as in Asia (Witt and Redding 2014) or Latin America (Schneider 2013). We also move beyond purely quantitative approaches, which use cluster analysis to identify varieties of capitalism and which treat the properties of capitalism as linear variables (Becker 2013d; Buhr and Frankenberger 2014). Rather, we employ a mixed-method approach in order to develop a theoretical and empirical understanding of capitalisms in large emerging economies. We draw on quantitative indicators based on international and national data sources and complement these with secondary sources and expert interviews using detailed country case-studies. We conducted 62 interviews with civil servants, business representatives, economists and politicians between 2012 and 2014 in China, South Africa, Brazil and India.

Based on these country case studies, we develop a model of capitalism that covers the most important features of emerging market capitalism. We argue that state actors and a close relationship between state and business play a crucial role across all institutions in these economies. However, in contrast to the popular idea of 'state capitalism', we maintain that the state is not an all-powerful, centralized steering bureaucracy (as in the classical developmental state model of Japan or Korea). Rather, its activity is based on close cooperation and competition between various state and domestic business coalitions at the national and subnational levels. For this reason, we speak of 'state-permeated market economies' (SME). Such an economic model is held together by reciprocal mechanisms of loyalty and trust between individual members of these (competition-driven) state-business coalitions. It thus differs from other economic models, where there is either coordination by the market and formal contracts (liberal economies), or formalized networks and associations (coordinated economies), or hierarchies within multinational enterprises (as in dependent economies).

Our research focuses on the 2000s up until the early 2010s and on industrialized regions of large emerging economies. For this period, we are able to reveal many surprising commonalities between the institutional foundations of capitalism across the four countries under study, despite their very different geographical locations and historical trajectories. These foundations include strong state-permeation in corporate governance and corporate finance, segmented systems of low-cost though comparably well-educated labor and increasing innovation capacities. Furthermore, in each of these economies, a pro-indigenous business policy stance supports national development, provides access for indigenous companies to large domestic markets and defends firms against foreign competition. The mutual compatibility of these features, which gained stability over time via private-public economic growth alliances, made for an institutional 'fit' that helped establish a dynamic growth regime during the 2000s. Against the background of their coherent internal institutional architecture as well as a rather selective integration into the world economy, China, India and Brazil weathered the global slump better than South Africa, for instance. More significantly, while other large developing economies may share some of the characteristics of state-permeated capitalism in any single institutional sphere, the overall concurrence of these features (especially in China and India) established remarkable *and* stable economic dynamics in place of patrimonial structures in important sectors of the economy. This growth potential has been realized through a specialization on the production of medium-tech goods for the domestic market.

We maintain that large emerging economies can continue their growth trajectories if they adhere to the model of state-permeated capitalism notwithstanding serious challenges, external shocks and other contingent global economic conjunctures. To be sure, this is a very complicated task. As our comparative analysis shows, these economies have moved towards, but also deviated from, this particular model over time: While South Africa has arguably never really embraced the model and Brazil has gradually moved away from the SME ideal type since 2013, India – despite major changes in the political economy – has moved closer towards the model we outline.

From our perspective, challenges to state-permeated capitalism are mainly of a social and political nature. The state-permeated type of capitalism relies on close, informal cooperation between individual national capitalists and representatives of state agencies, with socio-economic inequality embedded into the system. This makes SMEs vulnerable to public charges of corruption and social exclusion. Especially the (lower) middle classes are likely to become politically vocal when growth slows down and limits their consumption capabilities. The resulting demands for more political influence and transparency will then eventually clash with a 'cronyist' economic coordination mechanism at the heart of SMEs. Thus, the paradox of state-permeated capitalism lies in the fact that the very success of this model sows the seed for its own destabilization. Thus, over the long term, SMEs will eventually 'exhaust' themselves, and thus, similar to other types of capitalism, they too are stable only for a short period in time.

The book develops this argument in three main steps. First, we introduce our analytical framework and situate it within a discussion of the existing discussions. Our framework builds on the Comparative Capitalisms tradition, but we extend this approach by taking into consideration the integration of national capitalisms into the world economy, the various roles of the state in economic development and the different forms of economic coordination. In a second step, we present four empirical case studies of the individual countries. Based on extensive field studies in Brazil, India, China and South Africa, as well as a mix of qualitative and quantitative methods, we analyze the institutional pillars of each economy, charting the different paths of their emergence. In a third step, we compare, evaluate and synthesize our findings. To this end it highlights the commonalities and divergences between the four economies with a view to substantiate our claim of a common model of capitalism that would account for the four cases. Moreover, we look, on the one hand, at their comparative advantages in order to understand the economic dynamics of these countries and, on the other hand, at differences in their institutional arrangements to explain why China and India have been more successful than Brazil and South Africa. In doing so, we also identify dysfunctions and paradoxes of state-permeated capitalisms both within the economic and in the political realms that may bring an end to their high-growth dynamics. In the conclusion, we not only develop novel empirical and theoretical research perspectives, but we also discuss the economic policy implications of our model while analyzing the implications of the emergence of this type of capitalism for global economic institutions. We thereby contribute both to extending research in the field of political economy and also to complementing existing research on the rise of emerging powers in the discipline of international relations.

In selecting the countries for our case studies, we decided to focus on the most prominent and economically successful emerging economies of China and India. But by choosing for comparison Brazil and South Africa in addition, we seek to argue that state capitalism is not an exclusively Asian phenomenon. Brazil has become the sixth biggest economy globally after the 2000s and was widely perceived to be the growth engine of Latin America, at least until the recent economic downturn. South Africa still is the second largest African economy, although, as we show, its economic growth has recently slowed down significantly due to its hybrid institutional architecture. We deliberately exclude Russia as it may be neither considered an 'emerging' economy nor particularly interested in national development. Instead, it can be seen as a predominantly rent-seeking economy with limited economic development outside of the natural resources sector. This is different from Brazil and South Africa, which both have a strong primary sector, but both attempt (more or less consequently) to integrate it into an overall industrial and development policy. It is hardly surprising that Russia, though being strongly state-led, shares few commonalities with China, India, Brazil or South Africa. The mere fact that Jim O'Neill from Goldman Sachs included Russia in the BRIC category does not warrant its inclusion in a comparative analysis, as it would be an ill-suited case for comparison as we have argued here.

Exploring the commonalities and differences between the capitalist institutions of emerging economies, understanding the prospects for their further development and addressing some of the international implications of such an analysis constitute currently among the most important challenges for comparative and international political economy. Recent academic and popular debates about the qualities of state capitalism as well as the de-legitimization of Northern economic models following the global crisis has only increased the importance of such an exercise. Although 'state capitalism' in large emerging markets has of late become a very popular topic, it has so far received more of a popular treatment (e.g. Bremmer 2010) than a scholarly one. Our contribution demonstrates that state-permeated capitalism has established itself as a viable alternative to liberal market systems. The fact that some of the countries we have studied either found it difficult to keep within the SME model or withdrew from it altogether allows us to differentiate between those features of state capitalism that are necessary and those that are sufficient in order to yield sustained economic growth and development.

1 Extending Comparative Capitalisms

A framework for analysis

The study of capitalisms in large emerging economies has grown in comparative political economy scholarship over the last years. Based on analytical concepts derived from Comparative Capitalisms (CC) approaches, scholars have started to highlight the commonalities and differences of economic institutions in the Global South (section 1.1). Starting with some smaller empirical studies, the field has considerably matured and produced a number of major edited volumes, special issues, monographs (Bohle and Greskovits 2012; Walter and Zhang 2012; Becker 2013b; Schneider 2013; Benney 2014; Musacchio and Lazzarini 2014; Witt and Redding 2014; Rougier and Combarnous 2017; Demirbag and Wood 2018; Vasileva-Dienes and Schmidt 2019) as well as a first comprehensive review essay (Feldmann 2019).

While recent studies have very much contributed to our knowledge about the nature of capitalism in emerging economies, we identify three major shortcomings and use these for further conceptual development. First, CC scholarship on emerging markets does not pay sufficient attention either to the particular international situation in which the economic institutions in these countries have developed, or to the significant role of domestic markets for economic growth, especially in large emerging economies (section 1.2). Second, we argue that existing CC scholarship on large emerging economies does not pay sufficient attention to the central role of the state for the organization of these economies, although a rich body of research on the state in development exists (section 1.3). Third, recent CC scholarship does not pay sufficient attention to the modes of coordination that support (or not) growth in large emerging economies, particularly alliances between state and business (section 1.4). Based on these considerations, we formulate a framework that guides our analysis in the remainder of the book (section 1.5).

1.1 Capitalist diversity and emerging economies

Recent debates in comparative political economy constructively engage with the canonical 'Varieties of Capitalism' approach (VoC; see Hall and Soskice 2001). In a nutshell, the VoC approach identifies two ideal types of capitalism, liberal (LME) and coordinated market economies (CME), based on the distinction of central institutional spheres in capitalist economies and their mutual complementarities. However, as it has increasingly been criticized on a number of accounts, this section assesses whether the recent wave of Comparative Capitalisms (CC) scholarship on large emerging markets is able to master the analytical challenges identified in the critical debate on VoC (see Hancké et al. 2007; Bohle 2009; Streeck 2010; Bruff et al. 2013; Ebenau et al. 2015). It starts with summarizing this debate, before turning to recent scholarship dealing with capitalism in Latin America, Eastern Europe and Asia.

1.1.1 The Comparative Capitalisms research program[1]

While its antecedents date back to Gerschenkron (1962), Shonfield (1965) and Polanyi (2001), the CC research program established itself during the 1990s. Important in this regard has been the work by Albert (1993), Hollingsworth and Boyer (1997), Crouch and Streeck (1997) as well as Dore (2000). However, the VoC approach as developed by Peter Hall and David Soskice (2001) had the most forceful impact in the academic discipline. Distinguishing between LMEs and CMEs, they provided a very parsimonious but powerful approach for understanding the major differences within contemporary capitalism. Instead of using indicators on the macro level such as economic aggregates or public policies, it went down to the company level in order to study how capitalism works on an everyday basis. In contrast to many critical approaches, it did not focus on the crises of capitalism but rather tried to explain its growth dynamics and relative stability. The concept of institutional complementarities has been crucial in this explanation as it logically combines a number of important institutions of contemporary capitalisms (e.g. corporate governance or industrial relations), that have hitherto been analyzed only in singular, sectoral studies. Moreover, VoC has been implicitly normatively motivated, as it presented an alternative to the then-current hegemony of neoclassical economics and neoliberal economic policies that both maintained that there is one "truth" about good economics (Coates 2015, 19).

Since VoC has been proved as an effective framework of analysis, subsequent analyses branched out into the study of electoral systems (Cusack et al. 2007), comparative public policy (Höpner 2009) or the macro-economy (Amable and Azizi 2011). Yet, a huge number of further studies in the VoC tradition tried to apply this framework to countries beyond the United States, Europe or Japan – on which arguably most VoC work centered. Another important path for the further development of VoC tackled the static picture it presents of capitalism and developed concepts to analyze institutional change within the VoC framework (Streeck and Thelen 2005; Deeg and Jackson 2007). Arguably, many criticisms of the VoC approach have been addressed by works that are definitely part of the CC program but not VoC. Bruno Amable (2003) developed a typology of capitalisms based on a rather inductive analysis of quantitative data which is more inspired by Regulation Theory. Equally, scholars in the field of business studies identified national business systems through empirical efforts (Whitley 1999). Although coming from diverse theoretical backgrounds, these approaches all highlight a number of similar features yet disagree about their origins and importance.

Gregory Jackson and Richard Deeg (2006) identified three broad commonalities that all CC approaches consider important. First, all CC approaches share the notion that economic action is embedded in institutional arrangements which are important for coordinating economic behavior. Basic social coordination mechanisms such as markets, associations or hierarchies thus have become an important point of departure for studying capitalist systems. Second, a key focus of CC approaches is to associate institutional configurations with certain measures for economic success, such as growth or innovation. More precisely, they argue that particular institutional configurations have 'comparative advantages' to achieve certain advantages (or disadvantages). Hence, one of the main objectives of CC research is to explain the differences among capitalisms and why particular forms of capitalisms produce particular outcomes. Third, all approaches are more or less specific as to which institutions characterize (national) economies. Though often not considered as equally important, they usually comprise the institutions of *corporate governance* (i.e. different forms of stakeholders relations in companies), *finance for investment*, *industrial relations* (i.e. the relations between capital and labor), *education and training* (such as the different emphasis on skill creation through vocational training or general education) and *innovation* (for example, incremental or radical).

The extent to whether these institutions provide compatible functions is epitomized in the notion of institutional complementarities between features of these institutional spheres. This concept helps to "explain why suboptimal organizational arrangements are sustained and how particular institutions are supported, constrained or exist in tension with the presence or absence of other specific institutions" (Deeg and Jackson 2007, 153).

Especially in its institutionalist foundations, CC shares common ground with other approaches, most notably Business Systems studies, Social Structures of Accumulation and, above all, Regulation Theory (RT). The latter especially shares many similarities with the CC approach that makes it sometimes hard to distinguish between the two when it comes to analytical strategies. 'Classic' regulationists address five institutional areas: monetary relations, the wage-labor nexus, forms of competition, the state and the insertion in the international regime (cf. Boyer and Saillard 2002; Boyer 2005). It shows how institutional analysis can be used for different analytical purposes: while many CC scholars are interested in how institutional configurations yield economic growth, the RT approach wants to understand 'merely' the stability of economic regimes despite the tendencies of capitalism for cyclical dynamics and crises. Due to its focus on the temporal nature of 'accumulation regimes', regulationist analyses are critical for an understanding of Contemporary Capitalisms.

1.1.2 Recent controversies about Comparative Capitalisms scholarship

The VoC research program has been criticized on many accounts and from various backgrounds. One strand of critique comes from within the institutionalist camp

(Crouch 2005; Streeck and Thelen 2005; Jackson and Deeg 2006; Hancké et al. 2007; Bohle and Greskovits 2009; Streeck 2010); another major strand of critique is rather exogenous, often stemming from critical or Marxist scholarship (Radice 2000; Peck and Theodore 2007; Bruff et al. 2013; Ebenau et al. 2013; Bruff and Ebenau 2014; Ebenau et al. 2015). Some of these criticisms are targeted against the version of VoC by Hall and Soskice (such as the oversimplifying duality of CME and LME, its conflation of ideal types and empirical cases or their neglect of crisis and change, thereby leaning towards neoclassical equilibrium models). Other criticisms, in turn, criticize institutionalist CC research altogether. One of the most central points of critique is the historically and spatially limited application of the CC research program. As almost all of the models in CC research relate to OECD economies in Western Europe, the USA and Japan, there are good reasons to doubt whether CC would actually make for an appropriate approach to study capitalisms as such – also beyond the core of the world economy. This is important because the choice of its research objects already reflects a very specific perspective on capitalism. As many of the CC pioneers have their intellectual background in the analysis of (neo-)corporatism in the early 1980s, they tend to overemphasize formal industrial relations, with formal employer organizations and unions, neglecting the informal sector at the same time. As a consequence, informal labor relations and informal linkages and networks (in contrast to formal organizations) more generally have been underestimated. Similarly, at least the original VoC approach as developed by Hall and Soskice neglected the role of the state for steering the economy. This quickly had to be rectified, e.g. for the analysis of the French or Italian economy (Hancké et al. 2007). The regional divergence of the Italian economy between North and South also points to the problem with considering national economic models as homogeneous spaces.

Furthermore, many institutionalist CC studies suffer from a relatively short horizon. Especially recent studies on institutional change tend to analyze merely one or two decades. This not only leads to an overestimation of 'change' but compromises the explanatory power of an institutional approach (as institutions, if understood adequately, are relatively persistent and slow to change). Moreover, it neglects the historical foundations and evolution of institutional patterns and the particular historical conjuncture in which processes of growth and development occurred – not least because different timings involve different ways of insertion into global and transnational economic dynamics.

Because, inter alia, this ahistoric tendency of institutionalist CC, many historical materialist or critical scholars argue to transcend the institutionalist confines of the CC program (also see Streeck 2010; Ebenau et al. 2015). From this perspective, VoC focuses too much on specific elements such as companies or national economies, while neglecting the systemic dynamics in capitalism as such. These include, amongst others, the tendency to expand across national boundaries, where the transnationalization of capital makes the international analysis less and less fruitful (Bruff 2010). Critical scholars also criticize the functionalist tendency within CC. Institutions, as they would criticize, are explained by way of the functions they fulfill in the capitalist economy but not as results of power and class struggles (Bohle and Greskovits 2009; Bruff 2011). VoC and CC, they would argue, share an overly positive perspective on capitalism as such, with economic growth and innovation as a desirable goal of economic activity while constantly neglecting the distributional aspects of different forms of capitalism.

One response to these criticisms was to discard the institutionalist study of CC altogether. The suggestion, then, is to turn to alternative, critical theories and to focus on general characteristics of capitalism in the singular (Coates 2014; Jessop 2015). However, such response precludes the possibility of fruitful cross-country comparisons of capitalist formations, leaving us only with basic distinctions between core and periphery or dominance and dependence.[2] Another option, which we pursue in this book, is to adopt a 'critical institutional analysis' approach to the comparative analysis of capitalist institutions in non-Western countries (May and Nölke 2015). A critical institutionalist analysis acknowledges the criticisms outlined earlier and retains an institutionalist perspective while extending the range and scope of institutions to be analyzed. It allows to build on previous analyses and conceptualizations while also looking at the insertion of emerging economies into the global political economy, to highlight the relevance of the state and political power as well as of distributional effects that come with particular capitalist formations. There is no inherent tendency of institutional analysis to be ahistorical or functionalist; it depends much on how institutions and capitalist relations are understood.

1.1.3 The developing field of emerging economies' comparative institutional analysis

One obvious reaction to the critique regarding the too-narrow focus of the VoC approach – but also to the fact that considerable economic growth happened in countries which are not close to CME and LME ideal types at all – was to extend the study of national capitalist institutions towards countries beyond the OECD. One reason is the high rate of growth in large emerging economies since the early 2000s, another their relevance due to their growing weight within the global economy. From an institutionalist perspective, these countries must feature some institutional advantages, for otherwise their continuous growth would be a miracle, given that they are not understood as cases of known "successful" capitalist varieties. In the following, we discuss the most relevant accounts of capitalism in emerging economies over the last few years from a critical institutionalist perspective. Strikingly, when it comes to capitalist modeling, these are rather of a regional character (East Asia, Central and Eastern Europe, Latin America),[3] whereas global comparisons are relatively rare.

Bruno Amable (2003) has been one of the pioneers in including emerging economies into a comparative capitalist analysis. As he inductively modeled five types of capitalism, he also included a meso-corporatist Asian model that finds its expression, for instance, in South Korea. However, this Asian model hardly applies to all Asian emerging economies (let alone beyond Asia) because it hinges strongly upon the features of East Asian developmental states, especially the strong role of public managers. Research on the diversity of East Asian capitalism has been further advanced by Carney et al. (2009) and by Witt and Redding (2013, 2014).[4] Coming from a national business systems approach, they make a strong argument for the distinctiveness of different Asian forms of capitalism when compared to Western types of capitalism. Again, this approach is largely limited to Asia and remains within the more narrow confines of VoC theory. Other CC models have been developed by McNally (2012) and ten Brink (2013a, 2019) in order to explain the Chinese variety of capitalism. Here, some limitations of the traditional VoC approach have been transcended by taking the historical evolution of Chinese capitalism and transnational influences into account. Their frameworks highlight how, historically, top-down state-centric modes of governance have interacted with bottom-up networked modes of entrepreneurship and how domestic as well as international market forces create a highly original capitalist dynamic. Characterizations such as 'Sino-capitalism', however, remain limited to China. They also do not use the full analytical potential of CC, i.e. the distinction between the various institutional spheres and their complementarities which would yield more explanatory power.

The second region where CC scholarship has flourished is Latin America, not least due to the ardent work of Ben Ross Schneider (Schneider 2009; Schneider and Soskice 2009; Schneider 2013). Over the last couple of years, he has developed a model of Hierarchical Market Economies (HME) as a third basic variety of capitalism. In contrast to markets (LME) and negotiations (CME) hierarchies, he argues, is the central coordination mechanism in Latin American capitalism. While sticking to the analytical instruments of VoC, he has modified the purpose of this research program. Unlike the traditional preoccupation with the success of coordinated and liberal capitalism, he uses the approach in order to explain the muted economic development in Latin America. His model highlights the importance of diversified business groups, multinational corporations, low skill levels and atomistic labor relations. According to this model, hierarchies are pervasive not only within business groups and multinational corporations that are controlling the access to capital, technology and markets, but also in labor market regulation, union representation and employment relations (e.g. by weakening broad-based labor movements). As a result, the model highlights the importance of a 'low-skill trap', i.e. low levels of investments in skills and training, based on various negative institutional complementarities. Policy recommendations, therefore, center on overcoming the HME status and on moving into the direction of a CME or LME.

The HME model received considerable criticism from a critical perspective. Besides the pessimistic tendency and a strong leaning towards modernization theory, critics argue that the model focuses too strongly on the national institutional context and ignores the strategies of multinational corporations (Ebenau 2013; Fishwick 2013). Nevertheless, the HME model sparked a fruitful debate on the nature of Latin American capitalism, particularly on the value of institutionalist approaches for the question of development. As many authors from the Southern Cone region develop this debate further (e.g. Boschi and Gaitán 2009; Bizberg

2010; Boschi and Santana 2012), we might speak of an emerging 'Latin American school of Comparative Capitalism'. Although it has not (yet) amounted to a general 'emerging market model of capitalism', it delivered some important interim conclusions, for instance on the important role of close cooperation between business elites and the state for development policies that could overcome the negative complementarities formulated by the HME model. In fact, the role of the state is the main point of contention between Schneider and Boschi and his associates, with the latter assuming the ability of the state to remedy the deficits highlighted by Schneider within a national development project of inclusive development (Ebenau et al. 2013, 223).

Schneider has furthermore developed some original notions about institutional complementarities between corporate governance, education and industrial relations that can be applied to emerging markets in other world regions. In this way, his HME framework is a very sophisticated and convincing addition to the original CME/LME typology. Other important institutional spheres identified within CC, however, are neglected, such as the sources of investment finance and of innovations, thereby limiting the explanatory power of his argument about complementarity. While Schneider caters for some of the requirements of the post-VoC debate, such as the importance of multinational corporations, of the informal sector and of political struggles, others are being excluded, such as the role of the state for directing technological upgrading and of large domestic markets for demand-driven economic growth. These shortcomings may be of limited relevance for medium-size Latin American economies but are more important for Brazil as the most dynamic economy in the region. Schneider himself highlights the possibility that Brazil breaks out of the low-skill trap, based on its large domestic market, on an increasing demand for higher skills and on state intervention (Schneider 2013, 168–74). In a more general way, Schneider's arguments underestimate the crucial role of the state and of informal state-business networks.[5] While this is understandable – as Latin American political economy scholarship had strongly focused on the state for decades – this turn to business and business associations may be an over-reaction, just as with the original Hall and Soskice model which was justly criticized by Schneider himself (2013, 189).

The third region of enhanced CC scholarship is Eastern Europe. Some 15 years after the end of the cold war, an increasing number of scholars came to the conclusion that the phase of transition from communism to capitalism has come to an end and wondered which kind of capitalism had developed in the region. A first set of studies simply applied the CME and LME typology to countries in the region, to find out that the countries do not fit and can be considered as 'hybrid' capitalisms (e.g. Feldmann 2006; Buchen 2007; Mykhnenko 2007; Drahokoupil and Myant 2015). A more radical departure from VoC sharing basic features of a broader CC research program is the model of 'dependent market economies' (DMEs) in East Central Europe. According to Nölke and Vliegenthart (2009), a completely unique type of capitalism has emerged in the Czech Republic, Hungary, Poland and Slovakia. Similar to Schneider, they identify hierarchies as a crucial mode of operation in Eastern European capitalism. Yet, they locate these hierarchies within the organizational structure of multinational enterprises that dominate these economies thoroughly. As a consequence of the dependence of these economies on the strategic decisions in multinational headquarters (in the capitalist centers), they have been able to combine the explanatory concepts of institutional CC and dependency theory, which culminate in the model of 'dependent market economies' (DME). There are some intriguing parallels to the concept of HMEs, but the DME type indicates an even more radical implementation of hierarchy as central coordination mechanism, as national business groups are largely absent and the role of multinational corporations is pervasive. The DME form of capitalism could emerge in the particular historical situation of post-communist transition: while the old bureaucratic elites have been sidelined and a domestic capitalist class was lacking, foreign direct investment and the integration into globalizing production networks have been welcomed by all means. This model proved to be successful over the 1990s and 2000s, but yet, it will not prove sustainable in the middle or long run. Crucial economic decisions are made outside of the country (without the ability to include foreign capital into potential national growth projects) and the need to attract foreign capital comes with relatively low tax rates, which makes the financing of comprehensive education, innovation and social security systems difficult.

Bohle and Greskovits (2012) provide the most comprehensive treatment of capitalism in Eastern Europe. They agree on the characterization of East Central Europe as DMEs but highlight the importance of a multitude of new capitalist models in the region (Bohle and Greskovits 2012, 12). In order to cater for the latter, they strongly depart from the CC research effort: they not only forego the parsimony of a very limited number of ideal types but also highlight the importance of political agency for any understanding of East European capitalism. Since they find it impossible to build upon the CC research effort for this purpose, they turn to a Polanyian triad of self-regulating markets, social protection and the political institutions mediating between the two with a certain degree of autonomy. Subsequently, all East European regimes are located between ideal types of neoliberalism, welfare capitalism and democratic corporatism. Their separation between theoretical ideal type and empirical country cases is convincing, the integration of political developments magisterial and the treatment of country cases comprehensive. Yet, this radical departure from the VoC research program sidelines many advantages of the latter, such as the detailed study of institutional spheres and mutual complementarities. Similar to many VoC skeptics, Bohle and Greskovits seem to throw out the baby with the bathwater. While offering an interesting analytical alternative to conventional CC scholarship, they have lost many of the microeconomic insights of the CC approach. The same can be claimed for most of the field of "Varieties of Transition" that primarily focuses on the formerly planned economies of the Soviet Union and the national particularities of their transition processes (e.g. Lane and Myant 2007; Myant and Drahokoupil 2011; Demirbag and Wood 2018) and for recent attempts to comprehensively cluster all types of capitalism in developing countries according to quantitative indicators (Benney 2014; Rougier and Combarnous 2017).

A similar judgement applies to the systematic study of the BRICS economies from a comparative political economy perspective, as led by the late Uwe Becker (2013a, 2013b). While providing the most comprehensive global treatment of the issue so far, Becker and his associates share some fundamental traits of Bohle and Greskovits's study of Eastern Europe, including the absence of systematic discussions of institutional complementarities at the company level and the preference for a clear separation between ideal types and real country cases. Based on the relationship between state and economy, respectively capital and labor, Becker develops – similar to Amable – five ideal types: liberal, statist, corporatist, meso-communitarian, and patrimonial. Applied to Brazil, China, India, Russia and South Africa, it shows that patrimonialism features strongly everywhere, although declining over the last two decades, as did statism. Liberalism, in turn, has only grown slowly. On the whole, all four countries represent hybrid cases in his typology, which combine patrimonialism, statism and (limited) liberalism, as well as a hint of corporatism in the case of Brazil.

The research effort by Becker and his associates are undoubtedly impressive both with regard to the theoretical rigor of the models and to the empirical analysis by way of quantitative data. Yet, it does not yield a coherent model of a 'large emerging market model of capitalism', although some parallels between these economies are identified. As it rather emphasizes the diversity among large emerging economies, the question of why in this particular period many of them are suddenly growing and prospering remains unanswered. Moreover, as a loosely coordinated research effort, there are some necessary limits to the internal coherence of the outcome, as Becker himself (2013c) highlighted.[6] Moreover, Becker's approach represents a clear break with the firm-perspective in CC, thereby limiting its utilization for an extended CC research program.

1.1.4 Towards an extended Comparative Capitalisms program for emerging economies

Putting aside the objection that the comparison of country-specific political economies is misguided by methodological nationalism, comparative political economy analyses of emerging markets seem to branch out into two major streams: On the one side is a CC research program that builds upon the advances made by the microeconomic VoC research program, and on the other side is a return to the critical pre-VoC debate within comparative political economy, with its more macroeconomic orientation and related discussions of corporatism or political regime types.[7] We think, however, rather than discarding one of the strands altogether, there are good reasons to further develop CC scholarship, also through eclectically integrating elements of the critical research strands. Correspondingly, we will use an extended CC framework as a heuristic device, building upon recent advances made in the wider field of comparative political economy. Thus, we look for alternative models and coordination modes, beyond the CME and LME dualism and the HME or DME types, since they do not seem to fit the reality of very large emerging economies. Moreover, our focus will be on the industrial centers of these economies, acknowledging that there exists regional heterogeneity which cannot easily be submerged into national 'containers'.

Based on our notion of critical institutionalism, we likewise incorporate the analytical advances made by critical studies and see three major fields where we need to complement the CC framework. *First*, we need to study the specific form and timing of the insertion of a given economy into the global economy. Is the economy inward-looking (based on a large domestic market) or outward-looking (export-oriented industrialization)? Is it inserted into the global economy during a period of stable growth, or in a period where transnational capital is desperately looking for profitable investment opportunities? To what degree does a government of an emerging economy have to give in to the demands of transnational actors? *Second*, we need to clarify the function of the state. Given that the state obviously plays a central role in the development of emerging markets, does it resemble the familiar East Asian developmental state, or does it carry different features? *Third*, what is the basis of economic coordination in emerging markets, and in which ways do they differ from Western modes? The next three sections will review this literature in order to develop some more specific analytical instruments for our empirical analysis with regard to these three theoretical issues.

1.2 Extending Comparative Capitalisms research: insertion into the world economy, external pressures and internal capacities

In order to develop a CC framework for the analysis of emerging economies, we also draw inspiration from the broader field of international political economy (IPE) and critical development studies. Astonishingly, these literatures have not substantially been integrated into the analysis of emerging capitalisms, although developing countries' attempts to 'catch up' and the associated problems and rigidities have been analyzed extensively from such perspectives.[8] In particular, two aspects of the rise of emerging economies call for a reconsideration of these works: *First*, developing countries always experienced the tension between autonomy and dependency from external pressures in the global economy. Historically, these included international organizations, world market structures and transnational forces, which arguably are of great relevance for the development ambitions of emerging economies. Emerging economies addressed these challenges by either focusing on import substitution strategies (ISI) or export-oriented industrialization strategies (EOI). *Second*, the world economy, into which emerging economies integrate, is itself highly unstable and fluctuating. Unlike models that portray the world economy as an abstract entity with universal characteristics (as in much trade theory), its character changed considerably over the last decades and thus provides different pressures and options for developing countries at different times. The internal-external relationship, therefore, depends a lot on the properties of the international context, which then deserves closer attention by CC scholars.

1.2.1 Autonomy, dependency and transnational relations

In their strife for industrial catch-up, developing countries always had to decide about how and how much to engage with the (Western-led) world economy. Liberal theorists regularly make the Ricardian claim that increasing trade with the world economy would bring economic growth. Yet, scholars mostly from Latin America recognized that trade according to the principles of comparative advantage does not generate as much growth as expected because their revenues from trade tend to decrease (Prebisch 1950). Furthermore, free trade would keep developing countries stuck in low productivity sectors such as primary goods and simple manufacturing. Higher income, however, would be feasible only with higher levels of productivity, which in turn would require a process of industrialization. As the world economy, from a Southern perspective, hampers the development of countries in the South, two theoretical routes to overcome this situation have been devised: on the one hand, theories of *dependencia* that analyzed the structure of Southern engagement with the global economy; on the other hand, theories of industrial development that argued for the feasibility of ISI strategies to achieve *self-reliance*.

Dependencia theories argued that the assumptions of economic theory about a single economic system in which neoclassical recipes work uniformly was questionable. Instead, global capitalism produces the stratification into two economic systems that work according to different rules: center and periphery (Prebisch 1950). Moreover, these two economic hemispheres are characterized not just by different growth dynamics but, more importantly, by a relation of dependence. The global economy, in other words, is not only an economic system but also a system of domination, which some observers labeled imperialism (Galtung 1971; Rhodes 1971; Senghaas 1972). Starting from these premises of a systematic connection between national development and international dependency, *dependencia* theorists inquired about the different modes in which developing countries are inserted into the world economy and how this insertion affects the domestic capabilities of the state, classes and political factions (Cardoso and Faletto 1979).

To be sure, reconsidering key insights and shortcomings from the *dependencia* debate reminds us to go beyond one-sided explanations for the success (or failure) of national development strategies that either focus on the structure of the world economy or on domestic institutions alone. This is even more important in the light of the increasing transnationalization of the world economy, which affects emerging economies in particular through the activities of transnational corporations (TNCs) and global financial flows. Early examples of this were provided by Peter Evans (1979), for instance, who highlighted the crucial role of TNCs in the Brazilian development trajectory; and by Jeffry Frieden (1981), who pointed towards the increasing role of external private credit for the pursuit of industrialization strategies in the South. The extent to which countries are open towards foreign firms or capital has huge influence on how much they can achieve by means of economic policy.

Based on the assumption that the relations of developing countries with the world economy are always characterized by different degrees of dependency, some theorists attempted to provide feasible theories to achieve industrialization with a maximum of national independence from external pressures. Here, we refer to the classic accounts of ISI and national self-reliance. They all follow a broadly Listian strategy that seeks to achieve industrial catch-up by establishing appropriate domestic structures (Gerschenkron 1962; Hirschman 1968; Senghaas 1977). However, such strategies can be successful only if domestic industries are protected from external pressures exercised by global market forces and transnational investors. In other words, attempts to achieve a national development program eventually meet the resistance of external forces that push for liberalization and opening of national economies. For countries that seek to follow a particular path of development, it seems that the relation between the domestic and the international is usually conflictive. Whether motivated by the strife to overcome dependency or to protect the national industrialization project, developing countries regularly seek to achieve autonomy from external pressures.

However, previous trajectories by developing countries faced a number of problems. Classic ISI strategies often reached a stage of exhaustion at some point, where growth could not be achieved within the domestic economy alone anymore but only through exports or by fueling the economy with external credit. Developing countries regularly borrowed on international credit markets, thereby creating a new form of dependency – this time of a financial kind. By the end of the 1970s, Southern economies followed less an import substitution, but rather an indebted industrialization (Frieden 1981). With this shift, the original decoupling of Southern economies through an ISI strategy became obsolete: by the 1980s, Southern countries were deeply entangled in the international financial circuits regardless of their industrial strategies. Moreover, they were almost exclusively borrowers and therefore dependent on the goodwill of their lenders. While the influence of TNCs could be minimized through ISI, the pressure of transnational finance capital became ever more visible. With the debt crisis of the early 1980s and its aftermath, many developing countries replaced dependency on external trade for financial dependency. Similar to liberal accounts, which saw free trade as the best way to achieve growth, this new financial dependency has been supported by neoliberal theories which promoted general economic openness, capital mobility and open currency regimes (Williamson 1990; Sachs and Warner 1995; Haggard and Maxfield 1996, 210–11). Unsurprisingly then, EOI became ever more relevant.

Apart from the respective causal claims made by different theories about the insertion of developing countries into the world economy, we advocate a closer look at the relations of large emerging economies with the Western-led world economy. The large emerging economies' development strategies are highly dependent on their embeddedness in global economic structures that provide decisive barriers and options for particular growth trajectories. No successful project of industrial catch-up took place in a monadic, isolated fashion but relied on a careful balance of internal and external dynamics. Furthermore, many development projects have been victims of external shocks and ruptures, most dramatically through a number of currency and fiscal crises. The relation between domestic and international institutions has to be studied accordingly, not least because states are well advised to minimize their vulnerability against such shocks to protect their capitalist institutions. An important strand of research in IPE has been the work by Peter Katzenstein (1978a) and Peter Gourevitch (1978) on the reaction of Northern countries to the external shocks of the 1970s, followed by Gourevitch's inter-temporal comparison of three major economic crises. Basically, they found that reactions were different between countries because domestic structures 'channeled' external shock effects. Since states can manage these structures for a good part, countries are not equally subject to external ruptures. Instead, domestic structures explain why foreign economic policies differ across similar countries:

> The international economy presses on individual countries, and it does so through working on domestic actors. It is these domestic actors who are affected by changes in international market conditions and who, as a result, seek changes in national policy.
>
> (Gourevitch 1986, 235–6; see also Fioretos 2001)

Arguably, the increasing transnationalization of the global economy renders the clear domestic-international distinction less valid because external forces are able to work on domestic economies directly, without being mediated by domestic actors. However, transnationalization itself constitutes an external pressure, and domestic actors devise strategies to deal with it. As the classic work of Susan Strange (1986) demonstrated, it was domestic actors that changed economic policies in a way to accommodate the emerging options arising with transnational investment and credit.

1.2.2 Export orientation, domestic markets and the control over external flows

The strategies of contemporary large emerging countries to cope with external pressures can be compared with the experience of East Asian developmental states. Historically, East Asian economies represented comparably successful cases of industrial catch-up (see also section 1.2.3). Over time, states such as Japan, Korea or Taiwan moved from import substitution to an export-oriented industrialization strategy. While the ISI strategy proved to be of vital importance in the early stages of development, it also displayed negative effects. In Korea, for instance, the protection of domestic markets from external competition and imported products led to the domination of local markets by a small number of enterprises. In the 1960s, the Korean government implemented an export-oriented model on top of the existing model that came to fruition due to large Western buying power (Chibber 2014).

However, in our view, the reactions of large emerging countries to external pressures should be different from the East Asian developmental states because their industrial development started later. Large emerging economies developed in a phase of advanced transnationalization coinciding with a comparatively stronger opening of the economy. Thus, in conjunction with the timing of emerging economies' growth phase in the 2000s – with a world market more integrated than ever – differences might be spelled out with respect to both the historical strategies of import substitution and export-led industrialization.

Moreover, in opposition to East Asian developmental states, the domestic markets of China, India, Brazil and, to a lesser extent, South Africa are bigger. Looking into the domestic market dynamics and into state managers' reactions towards global pressures therefore is a prime target of this research. CC scholarship on European economies has recently turned to demand side institutions in the context on debates on various 'growth regimes', which itself is inspired by RT and various schools of heterodox macroeconomics (Stockhammer 2011; Armingeon and Baccaro 2012; Becker and Jäger 2013; Regan 2013; Jessop 2014; Stockhammer et al. 2014; Baccaro and Benassi 2015; Baccaro and Pontusson 2015; Johnston and Regan 2015). Our suggestion is to incorporate these concerns into the debates on emerging market capitalism as well.

The demand side and domestic markets did not play an important role in economic development debates during the last decades because of the small market size in most developing countries. Although Brazil, China and India were sometimes identified as having large domestic markets (Frieden 1981; Tybout 2000, 13–14), their role so far did not enter the debate. Large domestic markets, however, are relevant not only with regard to the demand they can create for domestic companies, but also with regard to the countries' external negotiation position, for example with regard to foreign investors. Rob van Tulder (2010) has sketched such a novel development path that systematically includes the institutional effects of large domestic markets. This development, in a nutshell, should first show a tendency towards net inward investment, while later turning towards net outwards investment. Typically, this takes the following stages:

(1) Selective opening towards inward FDI (for modernization of technology, to prevent overly strong rent-seeking, and the accumulation of capital), accompanied with significant entry conditions and beneficial deals for domestic companies (e.g. forced joint ventures).
(2) Some foreign entries find it difficult to sustain their operations given the difficult conditions offered by host governments and due to cultural and institutional differences; this leads them to subsequently sell off their subsidiaries to local companies that gain an oligopolistic position on these local markets.
(3) Governments of emerging economies encourage outward FDI by companies with large domestic market shares – first in the field of natural resources (accompanied by direct government support, bilateral investment treaties, etc.), but later followed by industrial firms.

Throughout the whole process, large emerging countries, according to this model, should remain less penetrated by inward FDI than HMEs, DMEs, LMEs and CMEs. Thus, only the very largest countries are able to act along these lines: their size, particularly large populations, rapid and sustained economic growth as well as their powerful governments make them attractive potential markets for OECD firms, but also powerful negotiation partners (van Tulder 2010, 53, 68). From there, it follows that in contrast to more dependent economies in the Global South that are under the heel of the Washington Consensus, large emerging economies may become strong bargainers vis-à-vis foreign firms and states.[9]

1.2.3 Integration into an unstable world economy

It has already been noticed in passing that there is not just variation on the domestic side, which shapes the domestic-international nexus. The international context, i.e. the world economy, changes as well. This in turn must have consequences for foreign economic policy preferences of large emerging economies. Instead of a neoclassical perspective that views integration and liberalization as unequivocally beneficent for emerging economies, it is important to inquire when and which sectors of an economy integrate with the global circuits and how the national and the international capitalist systems are constituted at a particular time. To fully understand external relations of large emerging economies, however, requires looking more closely to the development of the global economy as a whole. As most scholars of IPE would agree, the world economy of the 1960s has been very different from that of the 1990s and 2000s. As a consequence, insertion into the world economy has different forms and implications at different times. While Prebisch saw an unfavorable pattern for developing countries through the integration into global trade, these countries have arguably suffered more from the integration into global credit markets. Likewise, this particular insertion into global credit flows was possible only because foreign banks sought lucrative investments for an increasing amount of Eurodollars (Strange 1986, 122–5; Frieden 1991). This credit-driven development trajectory pursued by Southern countries thus has been possible only since the 1970s, not earlier. Similarly, the success of export-oriented growth strategies depends on a considerable demand in world market 'niches'. However, EOI strategies become rather difficult to manage in floating currency regimes because changes in foreign exchange relations heavily determine the competitiveness of export goods (Fernández Jilberto and Mommen 1996; Amsden 2007). On another plane, the monetary expansion of the 1980s, which spurred the growth of global financial markets, quickly found its way into the Global South and provided financial opportunities for firms in emerging economies that did not exist before.

Here, the work of critical IPE scholars on global finance comes into play. In particular, the process of financialization has been not just an expansion of finance and credit, but also a qualitative shift in the global political economy (Helleiner 1994; Strange 1998; Krippner 2011). It involves the emergence of new economic actors on the political economy stage such as investment funds, hedge funds or rating agencies that fundamentally shift the 'balance of power' in the financial sphere towards private actors – which are hardly supervised or controlled by public bodies. Other actors and institutions have been around before but play a much more significant role since the 1980s, including central banks, investment banks and stock markets. Foreign economic policymakers increasingly have to account for these actors, which work beyond the structures of economic diplomacy. Perhaps more fundamentally, financialization also entails the increased power of new capitalist logics. The finance-driven accumulation regime follows different rationalities from those of the industrial regime that dominated until the late 1970s (Stockhammer 2004). It finds expression in the advent of standards for the valuation of economic activity such as shareholder value or fair value accounting, which have become almost hegemonic in the business sector (Lazonick and O'Sullivan 2000; Perry and Nölke 2006). Finally, financialization tends to produce rentiers, which proves especially problematic in less developed countries (Lapavitsas 2009; Piketty 2014). Thus, developing economies have to deal with, for example, higher profit expectations by creditors and higher exit-options for foreign investors, just to name two practical implications (J. Becker 2014a).

We therefore have to expand the CC literature that emphasizes the national diversity of economic systems and their path dependency over time, because it tends to underplay the pressures induced through the forces of global capitalism. We have to include insights from studies that are concerned with the analyses of global capitalism, its development in distinct historical phases and how this affects national economic and political actors. Such an inter-temporal account of the world economy not only complements national and comparative approaches (such as in Gourevitch 1986), but it also stresses the dynamic character of the global political economy.

Perhaps most useful for this purpose is to orient (again) towards Regulation Theory (RT) and some important work by heterodox economists (Mandel 1980; Brenner 2006). The backbone of RT was in fact the close analysis of the Fordist accumulation regime, which has been a period of stable growth after decades of economic and political turmoil (Aglietta 1979). As we saw earlier, the analytical tools of RT are compatible with institutionalist CC, although the two approaches have different analytical goals. For RT, crises and recovery of capitalist systems are at the heart of the approach's endeavor, and as such it necessitates an inter-temporal perspective. Some authors argue that RT is actually merely a theory of Fordism because it fails to present a veritable theory of "what follows Fordism" (Jessop 2001; Dannreuther and Petit 2006). However, we think that RT is better equipped than many competing approaches to make analytical sense of neoliberalization and financialization (as successors to Fordism) from a critical institutionalist point. Of particular importance is its notion of institutional hierarchies (Amable 2003). Capitalism is not simply a collection of institutions. Rather, these institutions are arranged in a particular hierarchy in any accumulation regime. While the wage-labor nexus has been on top of the Fordist institutional hierarchy, contemporary capitalism is dominated by the regime of monetary relations. This means that any capitalist period is broadly characterized by the logic of the most dominant institutional sphere. For CC, this means that some institutions are more important than others at different points in time.

As we mentioned earlier, RT identifies the 'insertion into the international regime' as one of the crucial institutional conditions of capitalist diversity. However, "[a]n international regime does not determine the mode of growth of a country by itself; everything depends on relationships established between that regime and the country's other institutional forms" (Boyer and Saillard 2002, 40). Thus, the international economy can and should be analyzed from an institutionalist perspective (and not to be left to an IPE that mainly engages with the 'global' economy), but it must be done in a relational fashion. Only by specifying the relations between the international and the national institutional forms of capitalism does the picture become accurate. As we argue, this is, despite transnationalization and global integration, a valid assumption especially for large emerging economies, where the institutions of capitalism are very much of a national character – not least due to the strong position of the state.

1.3 Extending Comparative Capitalisms research: the role of the state in emerging economies

In the following, we try to gain insights both from the rich historical experience of economic state activity and from the general debates on the state in CC research for our analytical purposes.

1.3.1 Historical varieties of state activity

Back in the 1960s, the state served as a pivot in Andrew Shonfield's three models of capitalism – liberalism, statism and corporatism (Shonfield 1965; also see Gerschenkron 1962). It subsequently dropped out of view, only to be brought 'back in' since the early 1980s, when analyses highlighted the autonomous role of state institutions in the restructuring of national economies in the face of economic crises. However, the role of the state has historically been central to debates on industrial development, beginning, among others, with the work of Friedrich List in the 19th century, and continuing in the writings of the workers' movement (e.g. Lenin or Gramsci) and in the Historical School of economics (e.g. Gustav Schmoller).

The first wave of state-led development consisted mainly of attempts at industrial modernization and protection of national domestic industries. By a range of state policies, Germany, parts of Scandinavia, the United States and later Japan helped to upgrade their economies vis-à-vis the liberal hegemon Great Britain. Special emphasis was thereby put on state subsidies and protective tariffs. Domestic firms were given myriad concessions to reduce their input costs, or to increase retained earnings – through cheap credit and land as well as through preferential tax policies. In addition, domestic firms were protected from advanced foreign competitors through the erection of tariff walls. Moreover, the development of central banks enhanced the state's ability for macroeconomic policymaking and to mitigate the pressures of external economic shocks. Especially since the economic instabilities of the 1870s, the states expanded socio-economic, technological and human resource infrastructures of production as well as legal regulations and their enforcement (Kromphardt 1987; Bairoch and Kozul-Wright 1996; Mann 1998; Hobsbawm 1999).

After a period of liberalization, which followed the state-led war economies of the First World War, a second wave of state capitalism materialized in the course of the Great Depression. With the war economies in the fascist regimes of Europe and following the New Deal in the United States, a new phase of 'state-capitalist' regulation was introduced as a result of the global economic crisis and the arms race (Pollock 1975). State capitalism did not retreat after the Second World War. Rather, it took several shapes – ranging from a permanent arms economy in the United States, with the military-industrial complex representing the second largest planned economy on earth, to leftist Keynesianism in Scandinavia. State capitalism also expanded geographically – leading to different varieties of developmental states in the South, and most successfully in East Asia, experimenting with import substitution and later export-led attempts at industrial modernization.[10]

Thus, although the basic aims of state engagement – industrial development by any means deemed necessary – have remained more or less consistent in the first two waves of state capitalism, its instruments and its scope have not. While earlier state activity merely manipulated the background conditions in which firms operated (e.g. through tariffs), state actors in the second wave also strove to influence the final investment decision of firms. State instruments thus shifted from influencing investors indirectly to manipulating investors directly.

1.3.2 Industrial strategies of the East Asian developmental state

Although the state began to fade away in Western debates in the 1990s – on the background of the processes of globalization and regionalization – state action was vigorously analyzed in debates on East Asian economic development (Haggard 1990; Wade 1990; Evans 1995; Kohli 2004). In its attempts at steering investors and with recourse to different industrial planning policies, the East Asian developmental states in all probability represented the most articulated variety of state capitalism in the 20th century. In contrast to liberal or coordinated capitalisms, their governments much more openly focused on industrial policy in which the rationalities of private firms have been frequently constrained by the priorities of industrialization. Therefore, they are often portrayed as blueprints for emerging economies (Baek 2005; Balestro 2014).

In order to "govern the market" (Wade 1990) in the interest of national industrial expansion, theorists of late development – arguing persuasively against neoliberal visions of East Asian growth in terms of the economic benefits of a restricted state, trade liberalization and private entrepreneurship – stressed the necessity for joint projects between political elites and domestic entrepreneurs (Gerschenkron 1962; Evans 1995). The imposition of discipline on capitalists and the abolition or subordination of other powerful groups such as landlords was a major precondition for this.[11] Yet, as less successful developmental projects after 1945 show,[12] this was achieved only in countries where other preconditions were also met, in particular the development of efficient institutional state capacities.

Key capacities in the case of the East Asian developmental states were fiscal capacities, i.e. the creation of a tax regime that channeled state revenues to infrastructure and firms, which would increase both the speed and scale of investment and was supported by detailed planning. Next to state revenue being put to developmental uses existed a certain level of bureaucratic cohesiveness (Haggard 1990; Wade 1990; Evans 1995). As Chibber (2014, 4) put it, "no state-led industrialization is possible if its institutions are vulnerable to capture, or if bureaucrats fail to follow the duties attached to their station". Pilot agencies stood on top of such a functioning bureaucracy. These supra-ministerial institutions, such as the Ministry of International Trade and Industry (MITI) in Japan, the Economic Planning Board in South Korea or the Council on Economic Planning and Development in Taiwan, provided coordination and monitored and directed the performance of other state agencies (Johnson 1982; McNally and Chu 2006). Consequently, this led to positive effects in implementation. Last but not least, this was complemented with dense networks between state institutions and domestic enterprises to foster the exchange of information about investment priorities, developmental goals and a firm's commitment to follow bureaucratic directives (Chibber 2014). For Evans (1995), the key to macroeconomic success was to be found in a balanced relation between the state and domestic business. The state had to retain a degree of autonomy while still being embedded into the business environment. Only then the state would not necessarily become a rent-seeking predatory state but could efficiently engage in "midwifery" or "husbandry": strategies of assisting domestic business to develop and pursue growth-bearing initiatives.

1.3.3 Comparative Capitalisms approaches on the state

How is the state integrated into comparative political economy? In critical CC scholarship of the late 1990s and early 2000s, which focused on Western economies and the (uneven) effects of liberalization, the state was sometimes seen as a relevant actor that constrained converging tendencies arising from the pressures of globalization and thus fostered national divergence (Amable 2003; Streeck 2010). As has been lamented repeatedly, it has been downplayed in the VoC approach, not least as a consequence of its firm-centered perspective. Within this paradigm, no systematic attempt has been made to sufficiently analyze the (albeit changing) role of the state for the organization of capitalist economies, except for the much more vaguely conceptualized notion of "Mixed Market Economies/MME" (Hall and Gingerich 2004, 35). Notably, countries that did not fit into either the LME or CME ideal type – countries that, according to Hall and Soskice, would probably get into economic trouble sooner or later because of lacking institutional complementarities – were all countries in which the state played a very active role, such as France or South Korea (see Schmidt 2009).

Consequently, in the attempts to transfer insights from the VoC approach to non-Western economies, the problem of the state is circumvented. Schneider, for instance, in his research on Latin American economies, argues that the state is of course relevant in many instances, but "the fact that states are crucial to the emergence and functioning of any capitalist system does not in itself create an analytic imperative to incorporate state features or aspects of relations between business and government into typologies of capitalism" (Schneider 2013, 31). Yet, Schneider refers to cases of "political capitalism", where "states in some developing countries so overwhelm the economy that it is less appropriate to use an ME (market economy) suffix to describe them". However, to classify very different types of capitalism such as rentier states, petro-states or developmental states into one single variety of "political capitalism" paints over crucial differences within state capitalism(s). Apparently, in the 2000s state-led capitalisms of the Chinese, Indian, Brazilian or South African kind had relative economic advantages and therefore deserve closer inquiry from a CC perspective. Indeed, we agree that extreme cases of natural resource rent economies (rentier or petro-states) make for state-dominated economies. But, similar to predatory states, they should be analytically separated from the specificities of large emerging economies. An important difference between the different types of economies with a strong role for the state lies in the central coordination mechanism, to which we turn in the following.

1.4 Extending Comparative Capitalisms research: coordination of state-business relations in emerging economies

The various institutions characteristic for capitalism must be connected with each other to deploy their productive capacities. On the institutional level, this is analyzed by the degree of complementarity and the mutual 'fit' of institutions. However, this does not properly address the question of how institutions translate into routinized practices of economic agents and vice versa. For this reason, different mechanisms of economic coordination are crucial to understanding the stability of a capitalist system. Within the respective models, economic coordination in LMEs is dominated by market mechanisms, while CMEs are coordinated by reconciliation and bargaining (Hall and Soskice 2001, 15). Schneider (2013, 22) further distinguishes the 'German-type' from the 'Japan-type' CME, the latter being essentially a prime case of a trust-based "network market economy".

But what about state-led capitalisms, especially in large emerging economies, in which central state actors often have limited capacities or incentives to dominate economic relations? Much depends on the analytical perspective. One can address the relation between the state and business on a macro level, in particular the different power resources both try to invoke in shaping the economy. Another possibility is to look for the relation between state and business on the ground, i.e. where individual firms interact with state agencies and agents (Haggard et al. 1997, 45–8). We broadly follow the latter option, not least because "we still possess relatively little knowledge about [business] actors and how they interact with the wider institutional set-up" of state capitalism (Storz et al. 2013, 227). We neither solely find continuous power struggles between state and business in large emerging economies, nor do we find sufficient evidence that it were particular economic policies or macroeconomic incentives set by the state that would explain growth in countries such as China, India, Brazil or South Africa. Instead, we assume a joint developmental approach by both the state and business on the micro level of individual firms and agencies.

In the recent past, such joint coordination by states and businesses in emerging economies has been referred to as "crony capitalism" (Kang 2002; see also the discussion in Mazumdar 2008a). Initially, this has been blamed as one major cause of the Asian financial crisis of the 1990s because it was said to have encouraged actors to engage in 'moral hazard'. According to this argument, economic agents took unbearable risks because their decisions rested on personal connections rather than on the rules of law of markets (Kang 2010, 15; Bose 2012). Yet, there is more to 'cronyism' and of allegedly detrimental economic effects of close state-business coalitions than is widely assumed (see Maxfield and Schneider 1997). Not least, such 'cronyist' relations have been extensively debated in the discussion on the developmental state. A Weberian perspective was at the heart of the classic argument by Johnson (1982), for whom the existence of a strong, meritocratic bureaucracy was central for the success of the Japanese model. What made these bureaucracies efficient, however, were their informal internal and external networks. Informal relations based on shared educational background provided coherence within the bureaucracy, while external networks that connected the state with business elites were even more important (Evans 1989, 573). The importance of such "developmental alliances" (Chibber 2005, 132) led observers to the conclusion that the success of the developmental state resulted "not from its own inherent capacity but from the complexity and stability of its interaction with market players" (Richard J. Samuels, cited in Evans 1989, 574).

Such an interpretation of the developmental state as an amalgamation of bureaucracies and private elites (Chibber 2003) obviously raises doubts about the perception of the state as primarily an authoritative allocator of resources in developing countries. Rather, it indicates that economies with a high degree of state activity in economic affairs are regularly coordinated through close state-business relationships supporting national development projects. In a recent assessment on the characteristics of Asian capitalisms, Zhang and Whitley assert that these are less characterized by the form of the state but by the different type of "dominant coalitions" between state and business actors. Yet, state activity in the economy and business coordination remain two separate things (Zhang and Whitley 2013, 302). As a common feature of studies on the state-business relationship in developing countries, Evans's (1995) notion of "embedded autonomy" is also based on the idea that an autonomous state apparatus is nested in a business environment and that successful late-developers have to achieve a well-balanced connection between the state and business interests. Similarly, Schneider's (2009) analysis of business power in Latin America assumes that business organizes in groups before it articulates its interests vis-à-vis the state. In most accounts, state and business remain clearly separated, although at least Asian capitalisms demonstrate the coordination of economic affairs by way of state-business alliances. Yet, these instances of mutual state-business coordination are not yet sufficiently translated into appropriate theories about politico-economic coordination on their own. In most cases, these are presented as special cases or deviations from analytical models assuming that states and businesses have initially different interests. This might hold true for OECD countries, but in developing economies, both state and business may have a similar developmental interest and therefore need to adjust their activities on a macro and micro scale.

1.4.1 State-business relations in modern capitalism

One early way to grasp state-business relations was the concept of "policy networks" (Katzenstein 1978a). Successful economic policy relies on the existence of such networks that span both the public and the private sector (Katzenstein 1978b, 308). These networks are in turn conditioned by "the centralization of state and society and the differentiation between them" (Katzenstein 1977, 894). Though this makes for a clear conceptual framework, empirical comparison at this level of abstraction is a difficult endeavor. Atkinson and Coleman (1989) therefore transposed this concept to the meso-level of sectoral economic policies. They identified different types of policy networks along the pluralist-corporatist division based on three factors: state autonomy, concentration of power within the state and mobilization of business interests. When state autonomy and business organization are both high, they speak of "concertation networks" as the dominant form of state-business interaction. This type is relevant for the question of coordination in large emerging economies. In such networks, "it is business, and usually just a single element of fraction of business, that shares policy-making responsibility with the state" (Atkinson and Coleman 1989, 58).

However, what makes concertation in developing countries different from developed ones is the nature of business organization. Concertation in the former is based on centralized organizational structures, which requires business to establish strong associational structures (Lehmbruch 1984). In large emerging economies (but also in some East Asian states), where business associations are weak or absent, such centralized structures are rather found on the individual firm level. In other words, states seeking to devise developmentalist policies are confronted with a business sector which is strongly organized along corporate principles – not least in state-owned enterprises. In such a 'firm-based concertation', bureaucrats have to cooperate with individuals from businesses rather than associational representatives.

How can we conceive of those concertation networks on a general scale? More importantly, what it is that provides stability to such networks in order to make them efficient mechanisms of coordination? Clearly, we are well advised to look for the particular types of coordination in political economies beyond the narrow confines of inter-firm relations. One way to think of coordination that is able to incorporate the state level is formulated by Bruno Amable. He finds the internal coherence of diverse capitalisms resulting from the existence of relatively stable power constellations (Amable 2003, 2005; Amable and Palombarini 2009). Institutions do not only have to be more or less complementary in order to constitute a stable political economy, they also "need to be supported by a socio-political bloc reflecting common interests and agreement over a political strategy" (Amable

2003, 11). Hence, not only do institutions need 'external' coordination; this coordination is also deeply political. In contrast to the ideal-typical mechanisms of coordination prevalent in CC research, this notion introduces central political modes of coordination, namely conflict and compromise, into the debate about different types of capitalism. Capitalisms feature not only different complementarities among institutions but also particular institutional hierarchies. Social groups struggle not only over the design of institutions but also about their placement in the institutional hierarchy. Dominant social groups are able to locate those institutions that serve their interests higher in the hierarchy in order to receive more attention by economic policymaking. So while industrial relations had a high priority within the OECD during the 1960s and 1970s, other social groups, in particular those associated with finance capital, were able to place monetary relations on top of the institutional hierarchy. The extent of institutional change, therefore, depends on the vested interests of the dominant social bloc (Amable 2003, 68–9; Amable and Palombarini 2009).

Dominant social blocs have a basic coordinating function: they ensure that institutional configurations are not torn apart by socio-political conflict. This emphasizes the requirement of internal coherence among different socio-political fractions in order to establish relatively stable power constellations. This might take on the form presented by Amable for OECD democracies (through the organized articulation of interests by powerful groups), but in fact, such coherence could be achieved by various means.

Following our earlier discussion, there are good reasons to assume that in emerging economies this bloc constitutes less of a broad formal socio-political agreement but rather consists of informal small-scale coalitions and alliances. One reason for this lies in the particular structure of fragmented state power in these countries and different forms of business organization; another in the observation that popular classes in emerging economies are excluded from economic policy considerations, such as the peasantry and the working class. The idea of a social bloc can be understood either in a pluralistic (as Amable does) or corporatist fashion (see Cox 1987, 70–82). Concertation networks instead are strictly elitist: they limit themselves to leading operational figures within bureaucracy and business, excluding both representation of political parties and labor.

Importantly, this does not mean that a broad bipartite alliance of the state and business is controlling the economy. This picture is misleading because capital is usually fractioned: the business sector is almost always divided along major fault lines (Gill 1990; van der Pijl 1998). Often, one capital fraction is externally oriented, while another focuses on the domestic economy. Where financial markets play a stronger role, capital is usually divided between a finance- and an industry-oriented fraction.[13] As a consequence, the business sector has no single, unified interests but is characterized by competition among capital fractions.

There are at least two reasons why fractions should be central in emerging economies: historically, the state incorporated industrial and internally oriented capital into its developmentalist projects, thereby frustrating other capital fractions, such as merchant capital (Chibber 2003). Hence, there is always competition for the access to the resources that the state provides. Another reason lies in the liberalization movements in the developing world during the 1980s and 1990s. Externally oriented capitalists became more powerful through their transnational linkages and tried to achieve access to the state apparatus themselves. Governments, in turn, reconsidered with which capitalist fraction they would ally – in particular in the light of balance of payments problems that many developing countries suffered from.

As business associations are less developed and concertation takes place at the firm level, we may assume that class fractions often manifest in the dominant position of single big businesses in the political economies of emerging countries. The (looming) competition among fractions of capital would be an important corrective against capturing: state-business alliances can change when new emerging capitalists are more promising for the envisaged developmentalist goals; often, they compete with each other and prevent political economies from turning into rent-seeking regimes.

1.4.2 Economic coordination through interpersonal relations

The kind of economic coordination through "developmental alliances" (Chibber 2005), "growth alliances" (Abdel-Latif and Schmitz 2010; ten Brink 2013a) or "growth coalitions" (Silva 1996; Bräutigam et al. 2002) has been analyzed empirically for a range of developing countries in Asia, Africa and Latin America. However, these diverse accounts are often presented as temporary phenomena but not as a general feature of emerging economies. As a consequence, it has not been dealt with appropriately either in the theoretical discussion about the developmental state or in the comparative analysis of emerging market capitalism. The previous discussion should indicate, however, that alliances are rather a phenomenon embedded in the structural properties of the state, businesses and underlying class structures.

To recapitulate: the Asian developmental state has been characterized by the existence of informal relations between bureaucrats and business elites. This renders the strict division between state and business in terms of economic coordination rather useless because it is the amalgamation of those two domains that is essential to understand developmental projects – not only of the East Asian kind. Furthermore, the characteristic mode of joint coordination by state and business can remain 'balanced': the state must not become subsumed to narrow business interests, nor is the corporate sector necessarily dominated by state control. This balance, which proved to be fruitful for the success of several developmental projects, can be attributed largely to the competition of different capital fractions within and among such growth alliances.

Such alliances are not merely ad hoc arrangements. They are supported by social and economic sources of long-term continuity. Firms in emerging economies are organized into long-standing and durable corporate structures and most firms are embedded in business groups, often led by families. Obviously, this should support the stability of state-business alliances: Not only does the strong concentration of the corporate sector make it easy for state officials to target the 'right' allies, but the dynastic structure of big corporations in emerging economies makes sure that business complies with the joint developmental project as a whole. Families and other interpersonal communities are therefore central to the coordination of political economies through closely knit growth alliances.

This mode of coordination, however, is regularly framed as morally wrong: "The attachment to the family becomes nepotism. The importance of personal relationships rather than formal legality becomes cronyism. Consensus becomes wheel-greasing and corrupt politics" (Economist 1998). Such a schematic view is clearly beyond the point, especially if it combines the role of families in almost any economy with the existence of corruption. Similarly, Kang (2002) treats "cronyism" and corruption synonymously, though these are two different things: if transactions are based on personal relationships such as family and other reciprocal ties, there is actually no need to "buy" the other party's approval through bribes and other favors. Begley et al. (2010, 284) are much more specific on that point: "For cronyism to exist, four conditions must be satisfied: (1) no immediate return of favor, (2) something of value exchanged, (3) shared network membership, and (4) at a third party's expense". Here, the first condition already indicates that the relation between the coordination through networks and the problem of corruption is not a straightforward one. Particularly the third condition of membership underlines an important aspect that distinguishes cronyism from corruption. It refers to a somewhat 'communitarian' dimension to coordination which we would draw even a bit further: the logic of membership is based on common ties, loyalties and interdependencies among members which neither markets, hierarchies nor networks possess.

Relations between firms and state agencies may provide access to the resources provided by the state, such as credit, market access or licenses for production. If such access relies on credible personal relationships, these create in-groups or communities that are able to control the flows within the economy. This exclusivity nourishes much of Western criticism of cronyism (or how one wants to call it): the coordination by interpersonal relationships makes it very hard for outsiders to gain access to crucial resources (that is, the fourth criterion mentioned). The processes, by which access becomes granted, are slow and steady, since they involve establishing personal, empathic relationships – that might often be of more than just an economic kind. Interpersonal alliances, therefore, are not just means of coordination for the economic realm but permeate a range of socio-political institutions as well.

Overall, these remarks are intended to shed more light on the likely nature of economic coordination, especially between state and business, in large emerging economies. Rather than occasionally lobbying the state, business engages in relatively durable and predictable relations with it. Yet, these relations are institutionalized not in the same way as, for example, in CMEs (by strategic consultation of peak organizations), but rather through soft interpersonal ties. These ties may be as efficient as other forms of coordination in keeping together the institutional setup of emerging market capitalism.

1.5 Comparative Capitalisms extended: a framework for the analysis of economic dynamics in large emerging economies

The previous sections highlighted a number of 'routes' for understanding the dynamics of large emerging economies. In our view, these analytical traditions are mutually compatible – not because we wish to herald analytical eclecticism as the best way to pursue academic research, but because some of these traditions address aspects of political economies that others sometimes neglect. Although we work with a decidedly CC approach, we agree with the shortcomings identified by numerous scholars. As Clift (2014, 199) noted, "VoC may not offer the same explanatory purchase over the emerging market economies" and "a 'VoC of the BRICS' research program has not developed" yet. However, we think that by a more accurate determination of their national/international nexus, by incorporating a more precise analysis of state action and through an investigation of their distinct mode of coordination, an extended institutionalist CC analysis that includes and transcends VoC can fill this gap (see also Boyer 2005; Hancké et al. 2007; Hall 2007).

We propose an extended analytical CC framework to understand and explain the advancement of capitalism and capitalist growth dynamics in large emerging economies. In the next part of our book, we substantiate our analysis through examining a number of questions in detailed empirical studies, both country-specific and comparative ones. We do not construct a model deductively from theories that tell us how capitalism should in fact work if the theoretical assumptions are met (such as Becker 2009). The aim, rather, is to find out the degree to which large emerging economies share common institutional features, and if so, whether this 'model' is able to explicate the socio-economic performance of these economies. These features are not determining the course of existing capitalisms (Hall 2007, 39–40), but they can illuminate how some economies have become more dynamic than others without resorting to simple economic policy analysis or a purely historical narrative (Djelic 2010). Our aim is not simply to typologize large emerging economies, as to add a missing piece in the puzzle of global capitalist diversity. Instead, we look at a number of factors that helped to explain differences in the economic performance for OECD capitalisms and assess whether these can also explain the growth of China, India, Brazil and South Africa. Some of those factors stem from a rationalist, others from a more historical and structural institutionalist background, but they have complementary explanatory power.

In order to be able to compare these economies, each of the subsequent country chapters will focus on a set of factors that proved crucial for the explanation of comparative (dis)advantages in OECD economies as well as of particular industrial development strategies in emerging economies. In the following, we will summarize how we use the various analytical instruments provided by the theories surveyed in this part of our study for structuring the country chapters. Our analysis roughly spans from 2000 up to the early 2010s. The main purpose of the country studies is to explain the extraordinary growth phase of the 2000s, not the most recent developments in individual countries (which are dealt with in Chapters 6 and 7).

Correspondingly, we are not pursuing the Weberian approach of constructing ideal types. We rather followed the strategy pursued by Hall and Soskice (2001), i.e. by constructing a model both by ideal-typical, deductive reasoning (from an action-oriented version of institutionalism) *and* based on empirical evidence. Given the wide acclaim for the Hall and Soskice strategy and its ability to stimulate hundreds of successor studies, we think that this is a particularly successful avenue for research, even if it does not comply with the demands articulated by Weber (or by the late Uwe Becker, to name a contemporary colleague working on emerging markets). We are also following the strategy pursued by Hall and Soskice as far as the number of coherent models of capitalism is concerned. We assume that the latter is limited. However, given the economic dynamism demonstrated by large emerging markets during the first decade of the new millennium, there should be at least two coherent models of emerging market capitalism (the other being the model of dependent market economies). Of course, there are more models of emerging market capitalism, but these models instead focus on negative complementarities, such as the model of hierarchical market economies developed by Ben Ross Schneider, or models of patrimonial capitalism.

1.5.1 Historical conjuncture

One debate in CC is about the appropriateness of considering capitalisms in the plural, rather than taking capitalism as essentially one socio-economic system (Peck and Theodore 2007; Bohle and Greskovits 2009; Lane and Wood 2009; Bruff 2011). We understand capitalism as a historically specific form of economic organization in which growth occurs systematically through a particular mode of production. Capitalist production generates surplus value on the basis of labor exploitation and involves the systematical accumulation of profits as capital. This process is socially and politically organized: through the state, which shapes the dynamic of accumulation (Jessop 2002); and through other social structures that define, for example, the conditions of labor vis-à-vis informal and household work, or the distinction between public and private. Overall, we assume that capitalist accumulation exists next to non-capitalist forms of economic activity. The analysis of capitalism, in our view, requires a firm perspective – no matter which definition of capital we might apply, it is usually a kind of value that is systematically deployed by private entrepreneurs in order to spur accumulation. Hence, in order to understand capitalism, we need to know what capitalists are actually doing.

Thus, while we do not deny that capitalism entails an essential core of accumulation which is central to every capitalist economy, we nevertheless want to stress that capitalism never occurs as an abstract system of capital accumulation but comes in concrete ways. That is, real existing capitalism is always related to specific instances of time and place. Since these instances vary, capitalisms do, too. It is therefore important to put capitalism in large emerging economies in its historical and international context because, as we argued earlier (in section 1.2), it defines the parameters in which development can take place. The potential of any economy depends in a large part on its position in the world economy. Consequentially, this insertion into the world economy constitutes an important determinant for the dynamics of particular political economies, and therefore this has to be taken into account in our analysis. For this reason, each country chapter starts with a historical discussion of this insertion.

1.5.2 Mode of coordination

As a core hypothesis throughout CC scholarship, economic coordination is more effective when a particular logic of action is valid across all institutions because equivocal rationality principles reduce uncertainties and risks for economic actors (May and Nölke 2015).[14] This isomorphism is part and parcel of CC approaches that are broadly rationalist: the acronyms of LME, CME, DME or HME refer to such overarching system coordination mechanisms. Such mechanisms (e.g. markets, associations, dependency, hierarchy) are in fact defining characteristics of these ideal-typical models of capitalism, and as such, they are able to explain a good deal of the coherence of each type of capitalism (Hollingsworth and Boyer 1997). RT, in turn, is more explicit about the defining role of these mechanisms or "overall logics" in shaping the institutional forms of capitalisms (Boyer 2005, 22).

It would be easy to depict the state as the sole authority to define these principles in so-called state capitalisms of large emerging economies. However, as discussed in section 1.3. contemporary state capitalism is more than a simple command economy; it is therefore improper to treat the state as the sole dominant 'coordinator' of economic life in large emerging economies. Departing from previous analyses of state-business coordination in developing countries (section 1.4), we assume that the precise nexus between state and private business is key to understanding economic coordination in China, Brazil, India and South Africa. Broadly, we assume that thick ties between state personnel and business actors, on an interpersonal level, are crucial for the overall effectiveness of contemporary state capitalism. This requires us to think outside of the box: cronyism, hitherto analyzed as detrimental to effective coordination, may be in fact a very efficient mechanism of economic coordination – under the specific socio-economic conditions in these countries. Thus, we look at these instances not as deplorable exceptions but as the rules of economic life. This, of course, runs counter to the established strict (analytical, but also normative) separation of the economic and the political in Western societies but is more appropriate to deal, in a sober way, with the economic realities in large emerging economies. If cronyism (or interpersonal coordination, to use a less derogative term) were in fact poisonous for economic growth, it would be a miracle how, especially, China and India were able to achieve considerable economic growth. For this reason, we look at the individual countries to find out about the specific characteristics of these interpersonal and reciprocal connections. If these connections are thick and stable, the institutions of capitalism are more robust. It also leads to the establishment of a dominant 'social bloc', which resembles a cadre or a managerial class.

1.5.3 Institutional domains

In contrast to the broad body of research on developing economies that hitherto focused especially on economic policy and the state as facilitators of economic growth, we choose a more firm-oriented approach for the study of emerging economies. The firm is the primary locus of capital accumulation and, therefore, is a prime point of reference to understand and explain capitalisms. Apart from Business Systems Theory (Whitley 1999), the VoC approach was perhaps the most explicit in following a firm-based perspective (Hall and Soskice 2001), but essentially, most institutionalist Comparative Capitalisms work with a range of economic spheres in which institutionalized relations among firms and stakeholders are essential for the efficiency of economies (Boyer 2005; Jackson and Deeg 2007). In line with our discussion of the appropriateness of CC in general and for the study of large emerging economies in particular, we broadly adopt these categories to our countries in focus.

For some of these categories, however, less information from previous studies is available than for OECD countries – mostly for reasons of data availability. We know relatively much about the area of *corporate governance* in emerging economies, especially with respect to pyramidal ownership and parastatal hybrids (Estrin and Prevezer 2011; Claessens and Yurtogu 2013; Musacchio et al. 2015). Since many of these works come from a business perspective, they often focus on efficiency, firm strategy and deficient institutions. Yet, a political economy approach that aims to understand the control over the resources for accumulation can still derive a lot from them, and we will make repeated reference to this body of research in the country chapters.

Less is known about the ways and means that firms use to secure *funding for new investments*. Still, we can use macroeconomic data, e.g. on investment flows, and validate these through selected examples at the firm level. Generally, this area is closely associated with the area of corporate governance: as we will see, firms with a closed governance structure are able to keep their resources within the corporation. Their little openness with regard to corporate governance reflects a low exposure to external credit for investments (see Chapter 6). More is known about the role of large banks in these countries (see de Paula 2003; Sáez 2004; Minella 2007; DB Research 2012; Kidwai 2012; Zheng and Zhu 2013). One of the important questions, then, is whether large emerging economies show similarities in financing patterns with traditional bank-based systems like in Japan or Germany, or whether they follow a distinctly separate path.

There are numerous studies on *industrial relations* in the four countries, although they often focus on either business or labor (Harriss-White 2003; Clarke et al. 2004; Gallagher 2004; Chen 2009; Bowles and Harriss 2010; Balestro 2014). This is not least due to the fact that large emerging economies' industrial relations differ greatly from those in OECD countries. As the country chapters illustrate, a system of industrial relations that is straightforwardly comparable to developed countries is mostly absent (Schneider 2013; ten Brink 2013a). Additionally, they show capital-labor characteristics that in turn are usually less relevant in the North (e.g. informal labor). Yet, this does not mean an application of CC instruments is implausible. Rather, as the country chapters show, an analysis of the capital-labor nexus is indispensable for the explanation of large emerging economies' performance.

There is less to be drawn from existing studies on *education and training* in emerging economies, and there is also a limited applicability of established instruments on non-OECD countries (but see Pilz 2012; Benson et al. 2013). Arguably, this area is a staple in CC research because of the German case. Scholars largely agree that the dual system of vocational training as a means to increase the value of human resources has been a crucial element of the success of Germany's post-war economy and an important factor for Germany's advantage in incremental innovation of high-quality goods. Although this particular system could never have been transferred to other countries to yield the same level of efficiency, as a blueprint it helps to understand the role of education and training in different capitalisms. However, studies on this field in emerging economies are few and usually not related to the effect on these economies' comparative advantage. From a comparative perspective, these countries are usually seen as not having functioning systems of schools, vocational training and higher education. Yet, these countries have been able to grow – which leads us to take a deeper look at their education and training systems, which indeed have matured lately (although to different degrees).

Innovation usually plays an important role in CC research, whether as an outcome of particular institutional configurations (Hall and Soskice 2001, 38) or as an element of diversity through different national systems of innovation. At the heart of most CC research lies the thesis that innovation is indispensable for growth. Theoretically, this is a plausible statement, but empirically, it is difficult to specify the precise effect of innovation – institutions that fail to transform innovation into profitable products can mitigate its beneficial effects and other, powerful factors could be responsible for growth in the first place. This is important to keep in mind because capitalism in the Global South also thrives because of oligopolies, theft and clientelistic patronage – factors against which developed countries established legal measures. It points to the problematic ideal type of the firm in modern capitalism that underpins much thinking about innovation in capitalism, going back to the work of Schumpeter and others. However, we have to be careful with assuming the existence of 'the modern corporation' in countries like China, India or Brazil from the outset; not least because the idea of this corporation usually does not entail any role for the state – again, maintaining a strict separation of the economic and the political, which is unsuitable for the countries we are dealing with. A second staple of CC with regard to innovation is the distinction between incremental and radical innovation. Here, too, this dualism stems from the limited set of countries from which the analytical tools have been developed, and we are careful to simply adopt these to large emerging economies. For instance, a common thread in the discussion about innovation tends to equate innovation with R&D and higher technology intensity. Moreover, making technological "leaps" would require venture capital because radical innovation is risky and costly (Hall and Soskice 2001, 40; Jackson and Deeg 2006, 20) while incremental innovation helps to maintain competitiveness in, for example, capital goods. In large emerging economies, this archetypical form of innovation is relatively weak (Scerri and Lastres 2013). We find, however, some indication that innovation is to be found not in the technological sophistication of products and production processes, but rather in the ways firms react to market demands (Radjou et al. 2012).

In all of these institutional domains, *the state* plays a crucial role in defining the rationalities for economic actors across the board. Yet, there are reasons to take a closer look at the precise mechanisms in which state actors exert their influence on these domains. On the one hand, the state usually has a wide range of measures at its disposal, including direct ownership of firms, legal limitations and options for particular groups of actors and a high degree of discretion about who is to benefit from policy measures. On the other, we assume that state capacities in large emerging economies are rather fragmented and decentralized. As will be shown, state action does not always feature the amount of cohesiveness of 'strong' central state institutions that are normally assumed to make for successful catch-up development – as, for instance, in the classical developmental state sense. Certainly, internal differentiation among the four countries studied comes to the fore as well: Some countries are better able to exert influence on institutional domains, although state capacities may be located at different bureaucratic levels. Thus, we aim at moving beyond schematic and simplified pictures of 'state capitalism'.

Importantly, an institutionalist analysis does not automatically mean that the growth of large emerging economies can be explained only from within. No modern capitalist economy is able to thrive in complete isolation, as the history of auto-centric development in the Southern Hemisphere shows. Yet, we also know that emerging economies that completely succumb to global market forces were doomed to fail as well. Therefore, analyzing China, India, Brazil and South Africa from a CC perspective requires a closer look at their *global insertion*, because their integration into Western-dominated global markets differs from established Western LME or CME capitalisms which largely adopted the same liberal and open stance towards free trade and, usually, capital movement (with the exception of Japan).

Neither the mode of international insertion nor the importance of domestic markets have traditionally played a role in CC scholarship – a development that has only recently been reversed in the context of the Eurozone crisis (Nölke 2016). If we start with the idea that capitalism in large emerging economies is a type of state capitalism, we should pay attention to the 'switch' that regulates the internal-external nexus, because here the state becomes the single most important actor. It is the state that decides about the openness or closure for particular flows of goods, capital or credit. In other words, the picture of contemporary state capitalism becomes more nuanced if we not only look at the direct involvement of the state in business – such as in state-owned enterprises (SOEs) – but also take the regulatory domain into account. In contrast to much international relations (IR) scholarship about the economic policies of states, which predominantly focus (from inside out) on how these policies influence the international economic order, we are more interested in how regulating the intrusiveness of external economic flows shapes the nature of the *domestic economy* (from outside in). According to this hypothesis, the integration into international economic relations must be well managed in order to bring about beneficial effects for economic growth (see section 1.2, including the creation of demand and the protection of domestic markets. From our perspective, domestic markets potentially are very important for growth in large emerging markets. Correspondingly, we address the size, dynamic and protection of the domestic market in each of our country studies as another institutional domain.

1.5.4 Complementarities and comparative institutional clusters

Last but not least, single institutional domains do not work in isolation but are always embedded in a set of other institutions. Within interdependent systems, institutions ideally have to 'fit' to each other. This is because institutions provide blueprints, shortcuts and routines for action. Firms, banks, ministries and bureaucrats require some certainty that minimizes the risk of choosing the 'wrong' plan for action. As a consequence, routines and habits are established, which cumulate into economic 'cultures' that are held together by overarching principles of coordination. For this reason, there is also a tendency for the development of isomorphism across institutions: logics of action in one institutional domain usually (or allegedly) work as well in another. This is an important feature of institutions that cannot be stressed enough: Institutions require some degree of overarching cohesion in order to work productively. Cohesion means that the logic in one institutional domain does not interfere negatively with the logic in another institution and, therefore, frictions or contradictions between practices are minimized. A uniform mode of coordination across institutions, as argued earlier, is an indispensable source for cohesion. Another one is the notion of "institutional complementarity", which is one of the explanatory backbones of CC for which strong empirical and theoretical support exists (Hall and Gingerich 2004; critically, Deeg and Jackson 2007, 165–6).

Complementarity usually refers to situations in which the existence of one institution amplifies the performance of another. This has been subject of considerable debate (cf. Höpner 2005; Morgan 2005; Deeg 2007; Crouch 2010).[15] One prominent argument states that Hall and Soskice's complementarities are actually isomorphisms, and as a consequence, the theoretical conclusions might be skewed (Amable 2005, 372; Bohle and Greskovits 2009, 360). We argue that this is completely plausible from an institutional CC perspective as we find more theoretical and empirical support for the productive effects of isomorphism than of institutional bricolage or incoherence (see Crouch 2005).

In the end, it is difficult to empirically assess whether it was institutional complementarity or isomorphism that brought about a particular effect anyway.

For this reason, we propose a modest distinction between 'strong' and 'weak' complementarities. *Weak complementarities* exist when institutions do not contradict each other or diminish the organizational function of any of them. We can speak of *strong complementarities* when an institution provides incentives to invest in a particular mode of action that has an added value in another institutional domain as well, thereby amplifying institutional effects – through efficiency gains, but also through the reinforcement of particular principles of rationality that are inhibited in institutions. This adds a qualitative dimension to the idea of overarching coordination mechanisms, covering both instances of complementarity and isomorphism (see also Boyer 2005, 35). Complementarities, therefore, are necessary but insufficient conditions for economic performance (Deeg and Jackson 2007, 169). Moreover, strong complementarities between particular institutional domains can create compatible *institutional clusters* that are crucial for the reproduction of capitalisms. As will be shown in the following parts, some emerging economies have indeed formed such clusters; in particular, a corporate governance/investment finance cluster and a labor/education/innovation cluster. In the end, we construct an institutional model (if tentative and limited) that can explain the performance of large emerging economies. In this model, institutions are not simply 'collected' but causally linked to one another. Furthermore, these are contextualized not simply to limit the model's scope conditions, but to specify how its explanatory power depends on the historical and spatial context.

In the next chapters, we will compare capitalist institutions in China, India, Brazil and South Africa. We order our country studies not only according to the extent of economic growth from the 2000s to the early 2010s, but also to the extent that they represent the ideal type of state-permeated capitalism that will be developed in Chapter 6. As we will demonstrate, China's economic institutions are most similar to our ideal type, followed by India, Brazil and South Africa in that order, with the last two showing the greatest deviation from the ideal type.

Each of the four country chapters will be structured in a similar manner. The introduction gives a short assessment of the development of capitalism in the respective country followed by a section on the historical development of the economy within its global context. A second section investigates the country-specific mechanism of general economic coordination. The third section engages with the various economic institutions as highlighted by our extended Comparative Capitalisms framework, while the fourth section concludes with a special emphasis on the comparative advantages and disadvantages as well as institutional complementarities and contradictions in each of the four economies.

Notes

1 The following three sections further develop arguments originally articulated in Nölke and Claar (2013).

2 For the latter, see the typology in Ebenau et al. (2013, 230). A rare exception of a historical-materialist comparison of country-specific modes of capitalism – with remarkable parallels to the CC research program – is Coates (2000).

3 Applications to Africa are still quite rare and mostly limited to South Africa (Nattrass 2013; Padachayee 2013a).
4 Also see Walter and Zhang (2012), who develop another typology of East Asian capitalism.
5 Thereby, somewhat ironically, falling short on his own excellent work on this topic in Maxfield and Schneider (1997); also see Schneider (2004).
6 Some elements of Becker's work are taken up in Dienes-Vasileva and Schmidt (2019), without, however, developing a more systematic model of emerging market capitalism.
7 Typical cases for the latter are, e.g., Becker (2013d) and Bohle and Greskovits (2012).
8 But see Suau Arinci et al. (2015).
9 On bargains in IPE, see Strange (1988, 39–42).
10 Some authors include the states of the Eastern bloc and Maoist China in this development, as they represented the most extreme form of state intervention. Castoriadis (1988) describes these economies as "bureaucratic capitalism", because in the Eastern bloc, as in Western capitalism, all means were used to ensure the unlimited expansion of dominance over nature and society and the unlimited development of productive forces.
11 See Amsden (1989). South Korea's and Taiwan's comprehensive agrarian reform and abolition of landlordism were significant factors in their subsequent successful industrialization compared with Latin American states; see Kay (2002).
12 On the contradictions of the Indian catch-up process before the 1980s, where an enduring 'joint project' did not prevail on the background of an import substitution strategy, see Chibber (2003); Kohli (2004).
13 See van Apeldoorn (2002) for the European case and Claar (2015) for the South African case.
14 In contrast to, e.g., Amable (2003) who defines institutions as "political-economic equilibriums", we adopt a more sociological approach to institutions because it is able to link the micro-level of individual firms and the macro-level of economic systems. Obviously, some institutions are indeed established to reconcile conflicts among divergent interests, but these are not sufficient for the cohesion and performance of capitalist systems.
15 Some of the problematic goes back to different notions of institutions. While we advocate a more socio-theoretical understanding, others support a more political version of institutions that reject the definition as problem-solving devices (Amable 2003, 10; Höpner 2005). The latter, however, is theoretically more narrow and, as such, limits the applicability of institutionalist reasoning to settings, in which there is open conflict about the direction of an institution or between two alternative institutions.

2 China

A success story in economic growth

China is the most dynamic economy in our study. Although enormous diversity exists in this continent-sized economy, the system is characterized by a *unity in diversity*, by a heterogeneous assortment of socio-economic and political institutions under a state-permeated regime.

It is by now a truism that China has emerged as the world's second largest economy, biggest trading nation and largest exporter, with an average GDP growth rate of 9.6% from 1978 to 2010 (Laurenceson and Rodgers 2010, 325–7; for the 2010s, see ten Brink 2019). Supported by a unique institutional architecture, accompanying inequality and a range of favorable external contingencies, China's GDP growth has surpassed that in every other growth period in the history of modernity. Despite the fact that the increasing significance of market institutions in economic life is indisputable today, the People's Republic of China (PRC), which is a pivotal part of a world economy organized by neoliberal precepts, retains nonetheless its specific character.

In contrast to liberal observers (cf. Bremmer 2010), who do not distinguish between the contemporary Chinese economy and older varieties of state capitalism, we analyze China's economy here as a novel form of capitalism with strong state activity at different administrational levels and refurbished forms of development planning. It is based on close, competition-driven operations between various state and domestic business alliances at the national and subnational levels, rather than on an all-powerful, centralized steering bureaucracy. The emergence of this economic regime has underpinned a relative societal coherence, especially from the mid-1990s into the 2010s.[1]

While China exhibits a degree of continuity in its political and social institutions (including the ruling Chinese Communist Party, CCP) and still features vestiges of a bureaucratic command economy, capitalist imperatives function in all of its main institutional spheres. Thus, China's economy cannot convincingly be treated as a simple hybrid that combines 'capitalist' and 'socialist' principles (McNally 2012). Such a description would apply only if one defined these terms narrowly by viewing socialism merely as a form of economic modernization, as the current Chinese leadership does, and capitalism simply as a synonym for markets. Rather than proving its capitalist-socialist character, China's economic arrangement points to the reality of a complex set of competition-driven relationships between ‘private’ and ‘public’ actors as well as between various vertical and horizontal decision-making structures – a distinctive capitalist constellation that, so far, has been kept in check by central power elites as the authority of last resort in moments of crises.

The extent of state interventionism in corporate governance, its support for a firm’s external transactions as well as the role of the CCP make for a special form of capitalist modernization with a communist ‘façade’. Furthermore, China’s comparatively successful response to the global crisis in 2008–2009 has reinforced the belief of its power elite that this success justifies their economic system, their strategy of utilizing both market mechanisms and macroeconomic instruments (while only selectively integrating into the world economy) as well as many of their other industrial and administrative policies. Moreover, China was able to prosper at the expense of other countries and to benefit from supportive economic dynamics in East Asia, from the activities of overseas Chinese and from an increasing over-accumulation of capital in the Global North. Besides distinctive domestic institutional complementarities, these favorable transnational complementarities helped to advance China to the position of the most successful large emerging economy. Nonetheless, it should be kept in mind that China’s apparently unstoppable political economy is confronted with problems and severe challenges that are also addressed in this chapter. Against the background of falling growth rates, societal polarization and diminishing returns from erstwhile successful institutional complementarities, the Chinese government currently faces some difficult choices.

2.1 Contemporary Chinese capitalism: global context and historical evolution[2]

An understanding of Chinese capitalism must include its historical evolution and the specific form and timing of its selective insertion into the global economy. In the following, we first introduce the roots of state-led development in China after the 1930s and under Mao. Second, we turn to the Post-Maoist reform era that led to the adoption of the current growth model. Three phases of gradual reforms will be roughly identified: the periods from 1978 to 1989, from 1992 to 2002 and from 2003 onwards. During these periods, a ‘functional fit’ of institutions gradually emerged in an uneven process. Years of reform were at times jeopardized by both the pace of change, which differed from region to region, and by crises-driven U-turns. Third, we demonstrate the success of a *selective* economic opening after the 1980s, largely guided by preferences for autonomous national development, which led to a differentiated matrix of deep integration into global trade and production networks, on the one hand, and shallow integration into global capital markets, on the other.

The emergence of the Maoist command economy after 1949 was itself the result of path-dependent development based on industrial and other economic arrangements that arose during the Republican era under the Nationalist government and under the pressure of war. When the Nationalist government retreated into the interior of China in the late 1930s, wartime pressures led to the development of a 'government-sponsored' economy. By the early 1940s, "of all industry in unoccupied China, state-run firms accounted for 70% of the capital" (Naughton 2007, 49). While many large enterprises were state-led even before the Maoists took power, a newly established legal framework for industrial relations, along with state-corporatist tendencies and paternalistic practices, also helped to establish the preconditions for the "socialist" workplace (*danwei*) system (cf. Bian 2005; Chan and Unger 2009). In addition, the former economic integration of China into East Asia and the world economy, for instance, via colonial Treaty Ports, was replaced by an autarkic import-substitution strategy.

In the 1950s, after gradually isolating itself both from the US-led international economy, and then increasingly from the Soviet Union's sphere of influence, a strategy of *big-push industrialization* was implemented. Based on the suppression of consumption for the sake of development and the resulting exploitation of the countryside to benefit heavy industry, it paved to some extent the way for an industrial take-off in the 1980s (ten Brink 2019). Bizarre images of Mao as some kind of "utopian ruralist or twentieth-century peasant rebel have now been laid to rest: he was a super-industrializer and an empire-builder of the most ambitious kind" (Arnason 2008, 406). At the center of this growth model was the state that intervened on a large scale into the economy towards a broadly diversified industrial structure, flanked by an appeasement of capital by way of planning and of labor by way of CCP-controlled unions. The union leadership urged workers to distinguish between "short term" and "long term" interests and thus to sacrifice immediate economic benefits for the greater "good" of the nation (Friedman 2014, chap. 2). Overall, despite the enormous human costs of this big-push strategy, its economic effects are now widely regarded as rather positive. Liberal-institutionalist economists such as Barry Naughton acknowledge that industrial output grew at an average annual rate of 11.5% between 1952 and 1978 (Naughton 2007, 56). Investments in basic human capital, education and health grew rapidly, too.

During the period of the Cultural Revolution, however (1965–1975), the Maoist command economy ran into serious crises and political instability. Facing the ruin of the Cultural Revolution, important factions of the power elite acknowledged that whatever policies would increase national output had a valid place. The resulting gradual movement away from Maoist planning occurred as a crises-driven process of institutional change.[3] It entailed the transition from a bureaucratic, authoritarian-developmental dictatorship to a regionalized state-capitalist arrangement in which domestic market competition played an increasing role. While the party-state leadership insisted they were not abandoning egalitarian Communist ideals, in the future "everyone would get rich, but some would get rich first" (Andreas 2009, 274).

When factions around Deng Xiaoping took power at the end of the 1970s, tensions within the political elite resulted in a conflictual process of a 'trial and error' mode, which led to an enormous success of 'experimentation' with markets and entrepreneurialism. The accumulation drive in China was achieved in an environment, where economic rights of disposition and control shifted from state authorities to the management of numerous state-invested, hybrid, or de facto privately run companies. While the resilience of the party-state prevented more radical transformations, the tentative strategy of "crossing the river by groping for stones" enabled adaptive informal institutions to play a vital role in the process of change (ten Brink 2012). When confronted with the urgent need for new development strategies, an increasing orientation towards East Asian developmental states could be observed. By the late 1970s, Japan and South Korea had industrialized at a break-neck pace, and the Guomindang regime in Taiwan was not far behind. This led to the realization that greater wealth through strengthening market mechanisms could translate into internal legitimacy and power (on the question of legitimacy in China, cf. Gilley 2008). In addition, a new geopolitical setup, e.g. more friendly relationships with the United States, helped to open the economy towards the West from the 1980s onwards.

The *first phase of reform* from 1978 to 1989 already included the 'reform and opening' (*gaige kaifang*) of the economy towards foreign capital as well as the establishment of 'special economic zones' and the entry of FDI (rather than portfolio capital) into selected Chinese spaces. However, there was still no deep integration into global capital markets, which is why China was among the few economies in the Global South that were not affected by the debt crises of the 1980s. While China increasingly opened its economy towards trade and production, integration into global capital markets remained significantly restricted.

Notably, China's opening originated at a time in the 1980s when the prolonged global post-war boom period had come to an end. But in contrast to other 'state socialist' societies, China profited from the onset of globalization in trade and production. Indeed, the global signs of stagnation in the real economy from the 1970s on put more pressure on the Soviet Union and its vassals than on China and "contributed to the destruction of [its] productive capacities [. . .]. This is much less the case in China [. . .], where the agrarian sector remained dominant through the whole socialist epoch" (King and Szelényi 2005, 209). Despite big-push industrialization, China was still comparably under-industrialized and could exploit this situation while profiting additionally from its geographical location in East Asia.

The further development of the Chinese 'miracle' can thus be explained partly with reference to external factors such as increasing FDI and its attendant export orientation. Geographical factors and good timing also favored economic growth. As an investment location, China was in the immediate vicinity of the East Asian growth region and benefited from the networks of the overseas Chinese. The East Asian growth dynamics were a decisive external factor in China's successful selective integration into world markets. For instance, one of the initial reasons for high foreign investment in China was to target other Asian markets from China (AHK 2007, 20). In this process, a special link was forged between parts of coastal China, Hong Kong and Taiwan. From the 1990s on, a transnational economic region – the 'China Circle' – was thus established. As time passed, the networks of overseas Chinese merged with the mainland China ones. While most Western and Japanese entrepreneurs were still criticizing the investment climate in China, overseas Chinese were able to become the key source of FDI during the first phase of economic reforms thanks to their familiarity with Chinese customs and language.

The *second phase of reform* roughly took place from 1989–1991 to 2002 – from the 'Tiananmen Intermezzo', followed by a series of course reversals to the regaining of power by Deng Xiaoping, the rule of Jiang Zemin, up to the coming into power of Hu Jintao and Wen Jiabao. It was an era of intensified liberalization of the domestic economy, henceforth endorsed as a 'socialist market economy' by the CCP. It was characterized by path-breaking company reforms that allowed private firms to become serious competitors in domestic markets, flanked by accompanying reforms in the financial sector, in labor relations and in the education and science system. Thickly embedded private capitalists and 'red capitalists' – mainly private entrepreneurs, who were CCP members – came to be critical factors in the second phase of transition. Last but not least, it was only after 1992 that the selective integration of China into the world economy accelerated. Tariffs were reduced and the government opened some domestic sectors for foreign participation, e.g. producers were granted rights to sell their goods. However, the Chinese State Council, certain ministries such as the trade ministry MOFCOM, the central bank and local governments controlled important capacities to regulate the process of opening the economy while helping domestic firms to keep pace with TNCs. The government generally supported foreign investments in the country, but even after joining the WTO in 2001, it controlled the criteria that regulate market access while limiting access to certain key sectors. Currency policies and control of the exchange rate also helped to prevent a 'sell-out', which was feared by some factions within the power elite.

As an emerging economy, China benefited from another global economic factor. From the 1990s onwards, transnational capital was desperately looking for profitable investment opportunities (Brenner 2006; Hung 2008). Authors who single out low labor costs as 'pull factors' for FDI to explain China's rise (Lardy 2002, 61) overlook a fundamental 'push factor' for risky investments: an over-accumulation of capital due to a capital investment crisis in the traditional production centers. To some extent, the initial FDI of overseas Chinese thereby eased the way for the wave of FDI from Western and Japanese transnational capital, first and foremost in the electronics industry. Thus, the two engines of the world economy, the United States and, to a lesser extent, China, achieved growth via two different, complementary and mutually dependent paths. Whereas large chunks of US GDP growth consisted of debt-financed consumption rather than productive investments, the Chinese boom was precisely the opposite. Investments continued to grow massively from around 30% of GDP in the early 1990s to nearly 40% after 2000 (Hung 2008). Large amounts of liquid assets in the North helped secure the supply of investments and stoked the boom even further. In this situation, the old centers acted as end consumers of Chinese exports, including those by foreign producers assembling in China. All this was assisted by an undervalued RMB, in stark contrast to Brazil, for instance, where an overvaluated currency hampered export competitiveness (see Chapter 4). Still, the end of the consumer boom in the

United States and other countries was bound to trigger a crisis in those Chinese sectors geared to Western consumer markets. It also fueled the conflict between the United States and China, notably by US allegations of China's 'currency manipulation', i.e. keeping the value of the RMB below 'market levels'.

The *third phase of reform* from 2002 into the 2010s demonstrated the persistence, and even strengthening, of non-liberal institutional dynamics in China. An incoherent mix of rival state agencies held loosely together by the party at the beginning of the reform period turned into a much more coherent institutional architecture. The background of a competition-driven form of governance in China should not lead to the premature conclusion that the central state is growing weaker (see, as an example, Goldman and MacFarquhar 1999). In fact, it was precisely its instability in the first phase of reform, culminating in the crises of 1989, which lent the central government and the rule of the Party new legitimacy to reinforce power. One important precondition of this was the rise in its extractive power: particularly since the tax reforms of 1994, the central state has been able to recentralize resources to a considerable degree.[4] Moreover, in terms of its own modernization, several waves of bureaucratic restructuring led to strong (supra-) ministerial institutions such as the Ministry of Commerce MOFCOM and the National Development and Reform Commission NDRC, which since 2003 has been a hub for industrial development organization.

The hope, often expressed in the West, that China was on its way to becoming a liberal market economy accompanied by high hopes for China's democratization prospects were premature at best (see, as an example, the special issue "Will China Democratize?" in *Journal of Democracy*, 9(1), 1998). The paramount leaders of China between 2002 and 2012, Hu Jintao and Wen Jiabao among others, and later the administration led by Xi Jinping (see Xi 2014), were utilizing statist instruments to "rebalance the economy". This was due to the perceived export dependency, on the one hand, and deficient domestic demand, on the other (ten Brink 2013b). It included the very large economic stimulus set up after the global financial crises in 2008. Measured against GDP, this stimulus program represented the biggest rescue package in the world. Although further liberalization of parts of the financial system, in some industries and the *hukou* residency system continued, this was selective "strategic liberalization" (McNally 2011, 25) limited to some subdivisions of the whole economy. Development planning remained essential to affect reforms in areas such as industrial upgrading, infrastructural construction, science and technology, human resources, education and social welfare. Nevertheless, this was a new-style development planning, which was aimed at planning "with and for markets", including ample room to adjust long-term plans in cases of emergency as well as mid-course plan evaluations and policy reviews that allow planners to escape rigidity traps of earlier development planning (Heilmann 2011).

As will be illustrated in the following, these high levels of state-permeation were also largely in the interest of Chinese business, which forged close alliances largely with local state managers over the course of the reform period.

2.2 Coordination in the Chinese political economy

The Chinese socio-economic landscape has changed considerably over the last decades, making it difficult at first sight to understand the model of capitalism that emerged. With change as the only apparent constant, how might it be possible to conceptualize a coherent and stabilizing mode of coordination in China? Moreover, how can a CCP-dominated party-state coexist with a rising private sector in an economically efficient way in the light of recurring debates on corruption and rent-seeking? In our view, such a coordination mode can indeed be found in the PRC from the 2000s to the early 2010s. It worked both in favor of economic growth and societal stability. In particular, private-public growth alliances at the local level worked as stability 'anchors' to weather substantial institutional changes and helped in the development of characteristic institutional compatibilities. The Chinese economy is coordinated by closely interwoven private-public alliances grounded on informality and reciprocity, *guanxi* in Chinese. It is different from market coordination in LMEs, industry- or group-based strategic coordination in CMEs and hierarchy in DMEs. To put it crudely, China's dynamic rests on the dominance of a "social bloc" for growth (Amable 2003), comprised of party-state elites and a new class of state, hybrid and private capitalists. These private-public alliances and thickly embedded private capitalists transcend a purely corrupt setup (for early evidence, see Walder 1995). Rather, productive 'crony' reciprocal relations reduce uncertainties in a quickly changing economic environment. At the same time, special features of China's non-liberal mode of coordination such as a strong central state prevented divisions between domestic class fractions from spiraling out of control.

Over the course of the last decades, the explosive growth of the private sector has enabled a rags-to-riches rise of some individual businessmen. At the same time, The *Hurun Rich List*, a Chinese equivalent of *Forbes*, reveals that up to one-fifth of those listed had "been appointed to significant government advisory posts, handing them a powerful platform in a business climate that values official contacts" (Hurun 2010). This has also been a trend for the medium echelons of the private sector. Many entrepreneurs, including businessmen working in the most marketized regions such as Zhejiang Province, either belong to or have close ties to political bodies (e.g. the local People's Congresses and People's Consultative Conferences), or take part in village elections (Chen 2015). All in all, one-third of the Hurun Rich List is estimated to be made up of CCP members.

The Hurun Rich List exemplifies the dominance of close public-private relations in China. Both the party-state elite and businessmen have an interest in joining these networks. Indeed, the "larger the 'sales revenue' of a firm, the more likely its owner is a Party member" and the more likely that Party organizations exist in their firms. Capitalists operating the largest firms often "are the most likely to be involved in the political arena. Indeed, most of them [. . .] are more likely to support the [. . .] existing authoritarian political system rather than pose a direct challenge to it" (Dickson 2007, 852). "Co-opted" entrepreneurs state in surveys that the main reason for joining the party is the economic advantages and connections to the political sphere. Close relations between firms and state agencies provide access to the resources provided by the state, whether credit, market access or land (see Dickson 2016).

The prevalence of closely interwoven growth alliances reflects a process that can be termed *unity in diversity*. Although China is a heterogeneous country, this dominant form of coordination based on informal and non-transparent personal relations aligned through the common interests of national economic growth, acted as a pillar of unity and stability. Achieved through a temporal taming of labor, it was largely unchallenged by wider social unrest in the 1990s and 2000s. Moreover, it was flanked by a comparably strong central state able to regulate competition among local alliances and domestic class fractions (see below). In other words, this dominant private-public bloc has coordinated, and thus fostered, the rise of China. At the same time, local alliances between state managers and entrepreneurs also created the space for the aforementioned experimentation policies as long as GDP growth rates remained high. It equipped the ruling elites to cope with the hazardous path of muddling through complicated reform processes into what one may call an almost hegemonic rule of the 2000s.

What made these alliances work? Shared social backgrounds is often thought to be a factors supporting intra-elite coherence in China (Li 2010; McNally et al. 2007). Stemming from blood ties or friendly exchanges, reciprocal *guanxi* networks add to this and result in intra-family 'work partition' (e.g. husband as local official, spouse as well-connected entrepreneur) and friendship ties (cadres who have strong ties to entrepreneurs from their hometowns). In addition, shared political backgrounds often create legitimacy for the prevalent statist and long-term-oriented developmentalism. Hence, proactive industrial policies and a preference for patient capital have a high status, even among formally private entrepreneurs, compared to OECD countries. This is exemplified by individual private entrepreneurs caring "about the overall development of the private economic sector and the development of specific industries" (Chen 2015, 624). It should therefore come as no surprise that even representatives of Chinese 'venture capital', usually skeptical about the state in the West, generally accept the dominant institutional arrangement.

Thus, "communist" party-rule and Chinese-style entrepreneurship have not undermined one another. Rather than seeking autonomy, many local (private or state) capitalists have pursued a combination of institutional and affective ties that "thickly embed" them with the party-state (McNally and Wright 2010). The increasing socio-economic mobility of entrepreneurs has to an extent been facilitated by their ties with the regime, so they have had little reason to criticize it. On the contrary, the common interests of the party bureaucracy, the state and capitalists frequently lead to common viewpoints.

> In contrast to the popular perception that privatization is leading inexorably to democratization, [. . .] survey data suggest that [businessmen] are increasingly integrated into the current political system. [. . .] This again suggests

> that the growing shared interests of government and business are creating an environment that supports the status quo.
>
> (Dickson 2007, 852; also see Dickson 2016)

Notably, in contrast to CMEs, economic coordination in China is not provided primarily by formalized business associations. Business associations such as the *All China Federation of Industry and Commerce* for private entrepreneurs exist and have become more vital and autonomous from the party-state after the 1990s (Kennedy 2011), but they are less significant compared to the role of informal, personalized relations between individual entrepreneurs and state managers at different administrational levels. Thus, existing class fractions such as China's predominantly private export-oriented and predominantly state-invested, domestic-oriented capital did not organize themselves in associations or political organizations. Rather, their preferences are articulated through informal networks between company representatives and state agencies, which makes large-scale organization of business associations redundant. Firm-based concertation in China, mostly within particular industrial sectors in which policymakers cooperate with individual businessmen rather than associational representatives, also points to the relative insignificance of strong inter-company relations in China. Additionally, large business groups are mostly dominated by SOEs, which function as hierarchical conglomerates rather than as networked business groups without a dominant member (as, for instance, in Japan; see Witt 2010).

To be sure, the prevalence of state-business growth alliances has not prevented large-scale institutional change. They have rather channeled reforms into a process that is characterized by *continuity in change*. Institutional change did not lead to the radical replacement of one institutional arrangement with another, but to new combinations and layering that brought about significant processes of institutional conversion (Tsai 2006). The rise of private capitalists exemplifies this process of adaptive change. In the 2000s, these privately run companies were viewed by state managers as allies for development, rather than as rivals of state-owned enterprises, especially when they reached a certain size (Naughton 2007, 361). State officials changed their approach to private enterprise, exemplified by the legalization of party membership for entrepreneurs (2001), the constitutional amendment on assurances for private property (2004) and the announcement on property rights (2007) that formally gave the same protection to both private and public property.

Continuity in change thus signifies substantial institutional continuity based on the interests and policies of local growth alliances despite incremental or adaptive institutional changes. The goals of industrial growth via the market *and* the party-state, of steering the economy and of long-termism have not been stalled by novel, liberal institutions. Despite serious legal changes in industrial relations and new tripartite consultation bodies, the low-wage regime with a malleable workforce has persisted over time. Last but not least, regardless of selective liberalization and opening of the economy, nationally controlled firms remain dominant in most sectors.

In the course of the reform process, the power configuration between industry and government changed, with corporate strategies exerting greater influence on the behavior of local political bodies (Chen 2015). Greater dependency on the activity of entrepreneurs is manifest in a new kind of competition: "Previously, citizens competed to enter officials' patronage networks. [. . .], now officials also compete with each other for links to larger private companies, with successful ones becoming shareholders and managers" (Wank 1999, 198). The result is not the emergence of an autonomous civil society but rather authoritarian, semi-autonomous network communities of public and private actors. Newly founded institutions at the local level, like chambers of commerce and other non-governmental entrepreneurial civic associations, exemplify this trend.

Among the special features of China's mode of coordination, three stand out: (1) competition pressures between local alliances and managerial capacities of state actors, which also impinge on the problem of corruption; (2) the significance of an enduring strong central state to minimize socio-economic disparities and divisions between capitalist class fractions; and (3) the largely favorable role of foreign capital.

(1) Although state-business growth alliances are analyzed here as representing a non-market mode of coordination and as mechanisms for capitalist reproduction in their own right rather than just 'market distortions', these alliances themselves are subject to competition with other alliances. Since the subnational political levels in China have assumed the role of local developmental states, they attempt to build settings conducive to success by creating incentives to stimulate economic efficiency in 'their' territories. Good examples of this are the major investments in local infrastructure, the development of 'supply-chain-cities' and specialized single-product clusters. Competition between local alliances vying with each other to attract investors stimulated economic development. In this process, government officials often act entrepreneurially and are, therefore, depicted as 'state managers'. Their frequently creative commercial activity is in a way reminiscent of the Schumpeterian entrepreneur, but in a novel 'state-capitalist' sense. Although local state-business alliances lend the Chinese economy a high degree of particularized coordination, they occur within the confines of a competitive society. As part of the growing monetization of social relations, these alliances do not, as assumed by neoclassical theory, constitute a gradual transition to a 'pure' market. Instead, they are themselves a form of state-permeated marketization.

Competition among state-business alliances is at the same time an important corrective against state-capturing and harmful types of corruption. In opposition to media coverage in the West, the overall setting in China is not predominately patrimonial. Local governments in prosperous regions especially share with their business partners the overall goals of development, upgrading and innovating to such a degree that they reduce forms of corruption, which are detrimental to economic growth (this is not to say that they prohibit such corruption; see Wedeman 2004). The opportunity to successfully join in local 'crony' growth alliances makes local politicians take entrepreneurial risks. Likewise, it fosters individual careers in the political system and within the CCP. The system of cadre-evaluation, essential for individual career paths, is based mostly on economic indicators, although some social indicators have been included. More than 70% of the annual evaluation points are directly linked to economic growth (Naughton 2011, 81). As an interviewee from the German Chamber of Commerce remarked, there may be different kinds of bribery in investment and development projects, yet in contrast to "purely-corrupt environments, in the end, these projects are conducted and finalized" (Interview AHK, 3 January 2013). In a way, then, some types of 'cronyism' have facilitated economic growth. Perhaps this constellation can explain the apparent paradox of "the coexistence of corruption and high economic growth" in China (Zhu 2018, 318).

(2) Although local competition is of utmost importance, it still remains largely *competition under hierarchy* in the last instance. There was a transition from the incoherent mix of rival agencies held together by the CCP at the end of the 1970s to an increasingly coherent central state apparatus from the late 1990s onwards. It represents the second special feature of Chinese-style coordination. With regards to the central state, the government did not just adopt capitalist growth policies and individual entrepreneurialism (ten Brink 2013a; Yang 2004). There was and still is another central-state role that is not to be underestimated: the provision of an overarching institutional architecture that accommodates competition among local alliances. One political strategy regularly used by the regime to gradually initiate reform was to introduce change in only a few test areas, e.g. de facto privatizations in Wenzhou or in Guangdong Province, followed by a wider introduction of the policy when the test proved successful. Despite the fact that experimentation procedures have been delegated to local authorities, the central administration in Beijing played an indispensable role in universalizing local innovations, thereby generating further coordination into the Chinese policy cycle. In other words, although local governments and local alliances clearly feel more confident and sheltered today in making local choices, this has not "eliminated the weight of hierarchy and ad hoc central interference", especially in times of crises (Heilmann 2008, 11; cf. Zheng 2010).

The relative autonomy of the central government, in a way, enabled it to often adopt policies that advanced the interests of the entire power elite without degenerating into clientelism. This is reflected in continuing debates among central policymakers and planning experts revolving around how the state could limit clientelism and corruptive oligopolistic groups with vested interests. Additionally, central anticorruption campaigns, especially the very large one under Xi Jinping after 2012, have proved effective in preventing the expansion of harmful corruption (Zhu 2018).

(3) Regarding the role of foreign capital, coordination has to take the power of international capital into account, but in a qualitatively different way from that of dependent market economies and other large emerging economies such as South Africa. The economic integration of China did not lead "to box domestic firms out of most dynamic manufacturing sectors" (Schneider 2013, 82). Although TNCs play a significant role, they were not able to influence coordination to the detriment of Chinese alliances. Rather, they have tried to become part of domestic

alliances, mostly on equal footing. This particularly holds true for Taiwanese and Hong Kong entrepreneurs, defined as "patriotic capital" in the PRC. Many overseas Chinese have thereby been deeply integrated into the mainland economy. On another level, TNCs induced competitive pressures that also prevented strong rent-seeking, at least in coastal areas.

Does all of this imply an analysis of China as a smoothly coordinated and governed entity? Not at all. However, it contributes to an understanding as to why recurring internal tensions and conflicts, between political factions ('populists' versus 'elitists') within the party-state, or between China's private export-oriented and its state-invested, domestic-oriented capital fractions over currency issues[5] did not erupt as severely as in 1989, or in other emerging countries, where such alliances for growth could not be forged. As factions and capital fractions mostly share the fundamental goals of domestic socio-economic stability, the survival of CCP rule and its enhanced global role, a system of checks and balances has kept conflicts mostly under control. In a way, non-liberal coordination in China created the framework within which the market-oriented state capitalist, the private entrepreneur and state managers could effectively operate, at least up until the early 2010s.

2.3 The institutional foundations of Chinese capitalism

2.3.1 Corporate governance

Ownership of Chinese companies is highly concentrated, and the control of big firms rests with insiders. Matching the rather decentralized political structure of the country, various state levels (e.g. central, province and city levels) own, control and invest in companies. A complicated system of mostly decentralized state ownership with important segments dominated by private property thickly embedded in the (local) political scene has emerged, including competition among state-owned firms and various forms of state involvement in business operations. Foreign firms dominate some important industrial sectors, but this has so far not created high levels of external dependency. In most sectors, national capital in different guises prevails. All in all, these features are conducive to long-term development strategies.

Many large Chinese companies are exchange-listed and usually dominated by state block-holders (see Table 2.1). Firms are controlled by various governance hierarchies, as according to the 2005 Company Law different types of companies may have different corporate governance structures. In contrast to the Maoist era and previous versions of state capitalism, there is neither a classical top-down control, nor is there a single guiding enterprise model such as Chaebols and Keiretsu in South Korea and Japan, respectively. Rather, restructured forms of profit-oriented and competition-driven state-controlled enterprises such as China Mobile, Baosteel, and Sinopec have emerged. Additionally, private firms such as Huawei or Geely and public-private hybrids like Lenovo have also been able to play a significant role in economic development. Personal unions rank high

Table 2.1 The 20 biggest companies of China, by turnover, 2012

Name	*Origins of owners*	*Activity*	*Central Huijin Investment*	*China Investment Corporation (CIC)*	*Private*	*Limited state control*	*High state control*	*Majority state-owned*	*Strong family ownership*
China Petroleum & Chemical Corporation (SinoPec)	CHN	Petroleum & Gas						x	
Petrochina Company Limited	CHN	Petroleum & Gas						x	
State Grid	CHN	Electricity						x	
Hon Hai Precision Industry (Foxconn)	TWN	Electronics			x				
China Mobile Limited	CHN	Telecommunications						x	
Noble Group	HKG	Diversified		x		x			
China State Construction Engineering Corporation Limited	CHN	Construction						x	
Industrial and Commercial Bank of China Limited	CHN	Finance	x					x	
China State Construction Engineering Corporation	CHN	Construction						x	
China Railway Group Limited	CHN	Railways & Construction						x	
China Railway Construction Corporation Limited	CHN	Construction & Engineering						x	
Saic Motor Corporation Limited	CHN	Automobiles						x	
China Construction Bank Corporation	CHN	Finance	x					x	
China Life Insurance Company Limited	CHN	Insurance						x	
Agricultural Bank of China Limited	CHN	Finance	x					x	

China Southern Power Grid	CHN	Electricity					x
China Faw Group	CHN	Automobiles					x
Bank of China Limited	CHN	Finance	x				x
China North Industries Group	CHN	Diversified					x
China Communications Construction Company Limited	CHN	Construction & Engineering					x

Source: Fortune Magazine 2012; SASAC 2012; ACFIC 2012; company websites.

Note: In *private companies*, the state holds less than 10% of the firm shares. However, in many firms, *controlling families* hold the bulk of the private shares. *Limited state control* refers to companies in which the state (through direct or indirect holdings, such as pension funds or distinct state-controlled firms) holds at least 10% of the voting shares and is able to act as a minority shareholder, within the range of legal options that apply in the respective countries. We speak of *high state control* when the state holds at least 30% of a company's shares. In such companies, the state can effectively dominate firm strategies because it makes rivaling private shareholder initiatives very difficult to impossible. *Majority state-owned enterprises* are companies in which state actors hold 50% (or more) of all shares. Private investors then act only as additional sources of capital without any substantial control over the strategies of the firm.

across firm types: the CEO is often not only the top manager or a member of the board of directors, but also the party chairman. When asked about potential conflicts between the party and company interests, the CEO of Haier, Zhang Ruimin, answered bluntly: "I appointed myself party secretary of Haier. So I can't have any conflicts with myself, can I?" (McGregor 2010, 194).[6]

Although regional and sectoral heterogeneity make for an opaque system of corporate governance at first glance, the saliency of national control is astonishing. At the 'top tier', refurbished SOEs continue to retain their influence, especially in sectors such as petrochemicals, telecommunications and electricity (for a comprehensive picture, see Li and Xia 2008; Pearson 2011; Lüthje et al. 2013). As Table 2.1 shows, the biggest companies in China are mostly majority state-owned. Many of the large, centrally controlled state enterprises were drawn together from 2003 onwards under the new State Asset Supervision and Administration Commission (SASAC) and have preferential access to capital resources such as loans (via commercial state and policy banks), land and subsidies. On the central level, SASAC administers government holdings and supervises around 100 of the biggest national firms. Quasi-trustee control of the SASAC as well as that of regional SASACs that are dispersed all over the country, however, does not correspond to that of a classic planned system authority into which companies pay money.[7]

In the 'middle tier', where there are no natural monopolies, less strategic concerns prevail. These include machinery, automobiles, chemicals, and electronics as well as environmental, energy and other 'emerging industries'. SOEs here coexist with big public-private hybrids such as Lenovo and private firms such as Huawei or Geely. Such large non-state firms are also considered as 'national champions'. Beneath those two dominant tiers, a great variety of small and medium (mostly private) firms exist, for instance in light manufacturing and export-oriented sectors.

Because of the strategic role of government, developments in the financial sector do not follow the notion of a simple adaptation of prevailing global models. Stock markets in Shanghai and Shenzhen are no liberal markets for corporate control, although shares are partly traded. There is rather an 'insider'-dominated mode of corporate governance, as Chinese listed companies regularly have very big shareholders (more so than in CMEs) who are able to control the company without taking into account the influence of other shareholders. Dispersed shareholding is rare, and minority shareholders are typically disadvantaged. Trading and the issuance of shares is rather motivated by the desire to reorganize shareholding, to consolidate companies and firm groups and to raise new capital. Potential minority shareholders in China may hope for a lucrative return on investment, but they cannot aim to exercise control. Hence, minority investors cannot easily force the company management to pursue investor-friendly policies. The management of major companies is also fairly independent of short-term fluctuations on the stock markets in China.

Historically, China's corporate governance system has not had an LME, CME or DME trajectory. Despite some liberalization and deregulation, state and hybrid capital still prevails. In a way, the state stepped back in the 1990s, only to return forcefully in the course of the 2000s, albeit in a transformed way. The rapid expansion of the official private sector "from below" (Nee and Opper 2012) and the whole or partial privatizations "from above" (Oi 2011), especially medium and small enterprises owned by cities or urban districts, has not fundamentally challenged this. Due to their close connections to state authorities, many privately owned enterprises, on the one hand, cannot be regarded as classic private enterprises in the liberal sense. They often continue to incorporate state shareholders or private shareholders embedded in the local party-state. Private property remains politically embedded, as demonstrated in the case of 'management buy-outs' by local party and state functionaries. In the 1990s, many former political cadres chose the path of 'red' capitalism, an option made possible in a clause of the Corporations Act of 1994 that permitted the reforming of 'public' companies as private 'limited liability companies'. On the other hand, many restructured large SOEs have become success stories over the course of the 2000s and early 2010s, with rising profit rates in the late 2000s (McNally 2011; Naughton 2011).

Last but not least, the role of foreign multinationals is key to understanding China's capitalism. Although TNCs have substantially increased their prominence in the Chinese economy since the 1990s, this is far from the kind of domination they exert in DME economies (see Chapter 1). With some notable exceptions, for instance in the IT industry (see "Computers, electronic and optical products" in Table 2.2) which is deeply integrated into global production networks and markets, most industrial sectors are not dominated by foreign multinationals but by national state-controlled, hybrid and private capital.

Note that in Table 2.2, Sino-foreign joint ventures such as in automobiles ("Transport equipment") as well as investment from Hong Kong and Taiwan are included in the Foreign Investors category. If investors from Hong Kong and Taiwan were excluded (i.e. actors that have been integrated into Chinese capitalism to a large degree), the picture would be even more obvious. The figures also show that over time, the market share of foreign investors has even decreased in some industries. Additionally, in marked contrast to DMEs, there is no clear sharing of tasks between TNCs (e.g. higher technology, complex manufacturing) and local companies (e.g. commodity, simple manufacturing). Rather, as the case of the IT industry illustrates, even in foreign-dominated industries, large Chinese firms have emerged as competitors for established Western and East Asian firms.

Moreover, foreign firms only very rarely increase the contestation of economic policymaking, as exemplified by M&A activities. In the mid-2000s, inbound acquisitions of domestic companies increased, reaching almost US$20 billion in 2006. The main aim was to increase domestic market access. Eventually, M&A has entered the public debate in China, and as a result, new regulations on mergers and acquisitions by the Ministry of Commerce and other state bodies became effective, though the NDRC still relied on its own internal M&A guidelines and policies. This allows the prohibition of foreign acquisitions of 'leading' local companies (e.g. Xugong Group Construction Machinery Company). While Western business associations emphasized "significant new barriers to foreign M&A activity that directly discriminate against foreign companies in normal acquisition

Table 2.2 Market share (%) of foreign investors (FI) in China's largest industries, 2001–2011

Ratio of FI gross industrial product/total gross industrial product	*2001*	*2002*	*2003*	*2004*	*2005*	*2006*	*2007*	*2008*	*2009*	*2010*	*2011*
Extraction of petroleum and natural gas	7.50	7.80	7.30	–	7.80	7.40	7.30	7.60	7.30	6.80	6.30
Textiles	33.90	33.60	35.00	–	25.50	24.80	24.00	22.90	21.90	21.30	21.10
Fabricated metal products	35.70	35.9	34.90	–	36.50	34.90	34.80	30.90	25.10	25.30	24.40
Food and beverages	23.60	23.40	23.70	–	23.60	25.30	25.00	24.20	22.70	21.10	20.90
Chemical products (incl. pharmaceuticals)	22.00	22.10	22.80	–	25.20	26.30	26.80	26.90	26.70	26.60	25.50
Machinery and equipment	19.90	21.50	22.50	–	26.10	26.70	27.2	26.30	23.30	23.80	22.80
Transport equipment	30.90	31.80	40.40	–	42.80	46.10	45.50	44.80	44.40	44.40	44.00
Computers, electronic and optical products	53.60	53.20	56.10	–	61.00	59.90	60.70	58.30	55.00	54.40	53.10
Production and supply of heat and electric power	17.70	18.30	18.10	–	10.60	8.80	8.50	8.30	7.70	6.60	6.60
Non-metallic mineral products	19.10	18.80	17.00	–	18.30	18.30	18.40	17.00	14.90	14.20	13.10

Source: China Economic Information Network, http://db.cei.gov.cn/.

transactions", such as restrictions on M&A activity in "key industries" (AmCham 2007, 30), no substantial conflict followed.

Finally, some caveats about potential malfunctions in Chinese-style corporate governance should be mentioned. They range from claims about soft budget constraints leading to the support of 'unproductive' state-owned firms, to assumptions of decreasing SOE profitability in recent years and expectations about foreign competitors increasingly outcompeting Chinese firms (Meissner et al. 2015; Shambaugh 2016; Shih 2015). Certainly, the passionate debate on whether this system is economically reasonable (generally denied by liberal observers), or whether it is superior in the long run despite economic deficiencies at the plant level (emphasized by heterodox economists), is far from over.

2.3.2 Finance for investment

From the 1990s onwards, most large companies in China remained relatively unaffected by short-term volatilities on global capital markets and from the profit expectations of foreign investors. They raised investment capital mainly through internal savings and loans by national banks, enjoying preferential support by the state. This promoted a rather strong role for patient capital and accommodated long-term strategies of firms. In opposition to CMEs, domestic banks and capital markets are more state-controlled. In contrast to LMEs, CMEs and DMEs, state regulation of the credit sector also limits the influence of foreign capital and thereby maintains the concentration of capital particularly within domestic fractions. This constellation has served the Chinese growth strategy well in the 2000s in actively allocating capital to investments in industry, in real estate and, increasingly, in services.

What is the most important source of investment in the PRC? It is not the domestic capital markets, which have grown to become the second largest in Asia (Walter and Howie 2011). But as often with China, absolute size conceals the significance of many other phenomena. By international comparison, the Chinese stock and bond markets have been hardly dynamic (Allen et al. 2011). Two-thirds of all shares on Chinese stock exchanges are non-tradable and mostly held by the state. About 80% of all listed companies are state-controlled enterprises. Significant price fluctuations of shares, such as in 2007–2008 (or in 2015), therefore, did not affect the real economy seriously because stock markets are not markets for corporate governance. Moreover, the party-state protected crippled banks and (mostly state-owned) companies in times of instability, even though capital markets are not the primary source of investment for large firms (Li and Zhou 2016).

Global capital markets do not play a big role in the country's economy, either. The institutional characteristics of nationally controlled enterprises and a rather closed financial system[8] create incentives in which foreign investment and stock market capitalization play a minor role in the investment regime, thus diminishing the pressure emanating from foreign share- and bondholders. Although a severe crisis of the banking sector in 2000–2001 led to proposals to liberalize the financial sector (also in order to fulfil WTO obligations), further reforms failed to meet the expectations of Western financial experts (Walter and Howie 2011). Indeed, global capital markets are tapped selectively in order to modernize the domestic economy. While the Chinese productive sector has been integrated into global product markets, the financial sector remained largely isolated. The latter was thus kept relatively independent of external finance with the exception of FDI (typically in fixed investment, as the state also restricts the inflow of foreign portfolio capital). Partly because of this peculiar structure, the financial sector came through the 2008–2009 global financial crisis comparatively well. Instead, national firms primarily use internal funds and bank credit for their operations. Due to the prevailing corporate governance structures in China, the use of *internal funds* controlled by national (local) capital is significantly high. This facilitates autonomous and often long-term business strategies that would be more difficult to follow if firms were to rely more on (foreign) shareholders.

Large domestic firms usually raise capital for investments via *bank credits*. The banking system is made up of competing commercial state banks, dominated by the 'Big 5': Industrial and Commercial Bank of China, Agricultural Bank of China, Bank of China, China Construction Bank and Bank of Communications. They are complemented by regional state, semi-governmental and city banks, along with both independent banks and credit cooperatives. In addition, state-controlled 'policy banks' (China Development Bank, Export-Import Bank of China, Agricultural Development Bank of China) have been established. Approximately 85% of external loans for very large firms come from the Big 5, other commercial banks and city banks. National state-controlled firms are usually able to tap loans from the Big 5, while local SOEs have greater access to provincial and city banks (NBS 2012; Interview SYSU, 17 December 2012; again, the size and heterogeneity of China makes for a much more complex reality than that covered here). Foreign banks never represented more than 2% of the Chinese banking sector in the 2000s and after (CBRC 2012), unlike the more dependent economies in the Global South.

This was conducive to long-term strategies, mostly for large firms.[9] While short-term loans doubled between 2005 and 2010, long-term loans more than tripled (NBS 2012, Table 20–2). Besides lending practices on paper, bank loans to enterprises are in fact often state credit lines, which create strategic advantages over global credit markets due to longer credit maturities and/or lower interest rates. Official interest rates on loans of financial institutions in China were high in the 2000s, ranging from 5.04% to 6.57% for short-term loans and 5.76% and 7.8% for long-term loans (see NBS 2012). Similarly, this gives state institutions a certain 'grip' on companies. Other direct and indirect state support, especially at the local level in terms of cheap land, informal preferential credits and tax rebates contributed to very favorable financing conditions.

A Chinese peculiarity that sets the system apart from CMEs such as Germany and Japan is the fact that banks usually do not own shares of enterprises. Banks, therefore, have few means to enforce their interests. Because of the long tradition of passively accommodating state lending policies, banks have less capacity to monitor enterprise performance (Naughton 2007, 320). Although firm groups were assigned to a bank as part of the efforts to emulate the Japanese model, the "systems work quite differently. [. . .] whereas Japanese main banks are performing (ex ante and ex post) monitoring, this is only limitedly the case in China" (Conlé 2011, 27).

All in all, this investment regime, in opposition to liberal perceptions (cf. Huang 2008), served well the national development strategy of supporting domestic growth by all possible means and of creating 'national champions' for industrial development, while also increasing their transnational influence. Reform policies thereby also included loans for Sino-foreign joint ventures (e.g. in automobiles) and private firms (e.g. in real estate or IT). The decisive criterion has changed from "SOE or not" to "is the firm profitable or not and does it have the capability of paying back" (Interview SYSU, 17 December 2012). When compared to companies from liberal economies, Chinese enterprises are safeguarded against short-term financial turbulences both domestically and globally, as was evident during the global crisis of 2008–2009. The crisis was mitigated by short-to-medium-term public measures, in particular by additional bank credits and domestic demand stimulation aided by the Central Bank's high stocks of currency reserves (US$3.1 trillion by 2011) to protect the local currency in order to prevent external financial disturbances.

However, state-permeation also created considerable problems. What proved capable of managing macroeconomic instabilities in 2008–2009 has created obstacles to correcting the imbalances that developed as a result of China's growth model. China currently deals with the economic consequences of its expansionary credit policy since 2008. The party-state used two main instruments to come to grips with the global slump. First, the huge investment stimulus relied on the structure of the CCP which was used to mobilize local governments to invest. Second, it was "the financial system – especially the state-owned banks – which had been ordered to provide credit to finance these investment projects" (Naughton 2010). As a result, since 2010 problems resulting from bad loans and over-investment have emerged that cannot be easily contained. (See Naughton 2016 for the "Supply-side Structural Reform" policies to address these problems; also see Shih 2015; Song and Wei 2018. For recent attempts at re-regulating the financial system, see Naughton 2017.) Rising local debt and a housing bubble in urban markets are indicative of these problems. Moreover, the investment regime did not back a more equitable distribution of economic resources (ten Brink 2013b).

2.3.3 Industrial relations

Industrial relations in China are not easy to compare to LMEs, CMEs, DMEs or HMEs. They are regulated at the firm level, which is very different from the sector-corporatist CME model. There are parallels to LMEs and DMEs/HMEs, which also feature firm-level regulation, yet there are differences with respect to lower wages, less worker protection and a larger informal sector. This regime was supported by a continuous supply of cheap rural labor power and de facto state preservation of low wages, often through the selective non-enforcement of labor regulations which remain at times only on paper. State institutions arrange for the preservation of a low-wage regime, very often by *not* intervening in business misconduct.

China's industrial structure is the product of its gradual transformation into a party-state-mediated, class-divided society (So 2005; Chan 2015). A low-wage regime, based on segmentation and segregation of the labor force, proved a key motor of accumulation and made for significant labor cost advantages. It resembles a neoliberal utopia: "The Party state has created a rough approximation of the neoliberal ideal whereby a disorganised mass of individuals is forced to confront the hegemonic power of state and capital *as individuals*" (Friedman and Lee 2010, 530). Obviously, Western TNCs producing in China also benefit enormously from this system.

Generally, labor markets are fragmented between a comparatively well-paid segment of workers and a semi-informal segment of (mostly migrant) workers. Several SOEs as well as joint ventures in the auto sector (at least at parent plants) and TNCs act as grounds for a comparatively well-protected segment of technicians and highly skilled workers. The same holds for a number of leading private and hybrid Chinese companies such as Huawei and ZTE as well as "fabless" companies, which do not operate production facilities under their own name, but rather focus on the design of hardware and components (Fan 2011, 845; Lüthje et al. 2013). A much larger segment of the workforce has significantly lower wages, whereas basic wages amount to only 50% of total wages. In 2007, only about 50% of all firms had signed contracts with their employees, and the rate for migrant workers was even lower (Friedman and Lee 2010, 509). Although the 2008 Labor Contract Law changed this, it is still common for workers to sign short-term contracts with a duration of less than one year (Lee 2016). Hierarchical wage systems combined with little influence on product management policies, company restructuring and production relocations have resulted in a high degree of insecurity. Board-level employee representation is virtually non-existent.

The workforce is, therefore, highly polarized between the low-wage mass workforce in most areas of manufacturing and well-paid employees in technical, engineering and service professions (Lüthje et al. 2013). While huge differences between industrial sectors prevailed into the 2010s (for instance, between the textile and automobile industries), enormous differences within sectors also continue to exist. Recently, the growth of various kinds of informal and precarious labor, including student interns and 'dispatch' workers directly employed by contracting firms, many of which are owned by local labor bureaus, has enhanced flexibility for employers. In industrial production, healthcare and the service industry, 30% to 50% of the workforce is often made up of interns and dispatched labor (Interview SYSU, 8 January 2013).

On top of this segmented wage organization comes the *segregation* of urban and migrant workers. The household registration system (*hukou*), which ties an individual's social benefits to a particular place, is very detrimental to migrant workers and "is obviously central to the current system of sustaining super low-cost Chinese labor in the international market" (Chan and Buckingham 2008, 604).[10]

Although fairly sophisticated labor laws exist, their actual implementation is weak.

> Millions of collective contracts have been signed in the last few years, but in reality, wages and other labor standards remain low and unstable. Rather than being the result of effective bargaining, the majority of collective contracts are signed, either as a way for enterprise unions to fulfill the official quota of upper-level trade unions, or as a perfunctory effort of employers under the pressure of local labor administration. Accordingly, many collective contracts contain only general principles or legal terms, instead of any substantial statements or quantitative figures on labor standards. [. . .] In practice, workers are usually excluded from the process, enterprise unions are unwilling or unable to make any resistance, and consequently collective contracts are virtually in the hands of employers. At the same time, coordination at above-enterprise level, e.g. regional or industrial bargaining, is largely absent.
>
> (Luo 2011, 67; also see Gallagher 2017)[11]

Importantly, the size and heterogeneity of China (with even lower wages in interior provinces) allows employers to exploit divergent conditions of accumulation. Moreover, the fact that wages are regulated mainly at the firm level stems from a lack of collective and cross-sector regulation of labor and social standards. Chinese unions do not work strategically at branch or sector level, as in CMEs, in order to curb competition between employees.

Chinese workers were not only comparatively cheap, but also more productive. Increases in productivity compensated for wage increases during the 2000s. A combination of low wages, heavy capital investment, positive infrastructure and transportation network externalities, new management systems and investment in human capital (see the next section) led to a historic increase in labor productivity. As illustrated in Table 2.3, its rise surpassed the rise of unit labor costs, i.e. the average cost of labor per unit of output. Indeed, China has been increasing labor productivity much faster than Brazil, South Africa, India or any OECD country since the 1990s (Herr 2011; Leung 2011). Only since the early 2010s has labor productivity no longer outpaced the increase in wages.

The three main actors in labor relations (state actors, employers and trade unions) have established a particular kind of functional relationship with one another. The *state*, though not as dominant as in the Maoist period, remains influential through indirect political steering, particularly via the juridification of work relations (Gallagher 2017). Moreover, the state has established industrial consultation by tripartite bodies at different levels, consisting of the relevant local state institutions, trade unions and employers (Shao et al. 2011). The objective is clearly the institutionalization of statutory and regulatory norms governing wage labor. At the local level, however, state actors only selectively enforce labor regulations, while serving as the authority of last resort when strikes and other forms of resistance emerge. The *employers* mostly act as individual lobbyists. Although employer associations are relatively insignificant, businessmen have developed a

Table 2.3 Labor productivity and labor costs

Year	*Hourly labor productivity (dollar/hour)*	*Unadjusted Unit Labor Cost*	*Adjusted Unit Labor Cost*
1999	2.06	0.263	0.106
2000	2.52	0.241	0.097
2001	2.93	0.232	0.093
2002	3.36	0.221	0.088
2003	4.13	0.203	0.081
2004	4.88	0.191	0.079
2005	5.09	0.190	0.080
2006	6.29	0.183	0.080
2007	8.05	0.177	0.084
2008	11.02	0.169	0.093
2009	11.01	0.185	0.103

Source: www.ceicdata.com, Estimates from CQMM research group of Xiamen University 2011. Adjusted unit labor cost according to purchasing power of China.

remarkable awareness of common interests on many issues and act in their 'class interest', regardless of many differences in opinion, mentality and conduct. Last but not least, the *trade unions* largely act as a tool of co-management and aim to pacify social conflicts. The All China Federation of Trade Unions (ACFTU), with more than 200 million members, is officially the largest union in the world. However, it cannot be regarded as an independent trade union since it is largely controlled by the CCP and does not function as an independent advocate for wage earners. "Chinese unions think of themselves as, and behave like, government agencies" (Friedman and Lee 2010, 522). Trade union officials are also usually administrative functionaries in the companies. Still, the ACFTU is the sole national trade union organization formally represented with its subdivisions at nearly all levels in provinces, local districts and firms.

To conclude, instead of downright inordinateness in industrial relations, a quasi-corporatism came into existence in the 2000s. However, a collective representation of worker interests that is typical of most developed capitalist systems is conspicuous by its absence. Therefore, China's quasi-corporatist structures remain fragmented and partial. As trade unions have not become independent from the CCP, a fourth party is in practice added to the usual tripartite corporatism: a working class with minimal union representation. The working population, albeit largely outside the existing consultation systems, is influential through their own initiatives and opposition. A series of widespread strikes in the summer of 2010 has even been interpreted as the harbinger of the end of the Chinese model of labor subordination (Butollo and ten Brink 2012; CLB 2014).

Overall, then, although Chinese media commentators have declared that the era of low-wage labor has come to an end, this has certainly not been true for large parts of the workforce in the 2010s (Lee 2016; Gallagher 2017). Even though material conditions for particular segments of workers are better in relative terms, the Chinese labor system constitutes a delicate institutional equilibrium because it is grounded in the suppression of labor demands (Friedman 2014).

2.3.4 Education and training

The quality of 'human capital' and its institutional fit with other segments of the economy are decisive criteria for socio-economic development. Among the countries analyzed in this book, China is probably the most prominent case of the *economically efficient* provision of human capital from the 2000s to the early 2010s. Representatives of foreign chambers of commerce have noted that low labor costs are not the only advantage that China has. In comparison to other emerging countries, it also "offers a workforce that is relatively well-educated, hardworking, eager to learn skills, and reliable. This combination is hard to beat" (AmCham 2005, 24).

China has developed an education system in which the vast majority of the working population now receives a secondary education of nine years or more (see Table 2.4). Since Chinese state-business alliances show greater concern about long-term national development than in DMEs or HMEs, they have supported the creation of a relatively advanced skill formation system (compared to other emerging countries). This even accounts for the migrant workforce with an average level of education of 9 to 10 years of schooling (Friedman and Lee 2010, 516). Complementary to the institutional realm of industrial relations, we find a fragmentation between small groups of highly qualified labor and a much larger group of less qualified labor with a focus on general skills. Well into the 2010s, this has matched the demand for mostly medium-level skills.

Although the central government's aim in 1993 of achieving 4% GDP spending on education by the year 2000 has been achieved only in the 2010s, investments in education have led to overall advancement. However, though there was a rise of spending across the board, it is most pronounced in higher education, exemplified by China's important engineering faculties (Andreas 2009). Since the 2000s, the PRC has the largest number of higher education students in the world. Moreover, based on rich historical traditions that were only temporarily interrupted during

Table 2.4 Education level of industrial workers, in percent

Year	*More than 12 years of education*	*12 years of education*	*9 years of education (secondary)*
1985	2.9	23.6	73.5
1995	5.7	34.1	60.2
2004	11.4	32.9	55.8
2006	14.9	26.6	58.5

Source: NBS 2008.

the Cultural Revolution, the system of technical schools and colleges (which young workers attend after nine years of regular school education) has been reorganized. It is now mostly focused on general skills of medium-level quality (for a critical evaluation, see Vickers and Zeng 2017).

Education and spending on training is to a large degree decentralized, with large regional variations. While Shanghai is rated among the best in international PISA comparisons, for example, the situation is rather different in interior provinces. Importantly, local state-business alliances have become key players in selective and often informally organized support for vocational training. Close relationships with local state institutions have given firms the option to select interns from vocational schools, and to compatible training in areas in which allied companies are operating. Beijiao Professional Technical School in Shunde, a district in the city of Foshan, Guangdong Province, provides a good example. The students there complete a three-year training period after nine years of previous schooling. The contents of courses are aligned with Shunde's industry structure, and the school has close cooperation with local companies like Midea and Galanz (both home appliance manufacturers) to ensure that the school provides graduates with skills that fit easily into production lines. In fact, the school has even become integrated into factory operations with an apprenticeship program. Some students spend their final year on the factory floor, working full-time but being paid as interns (Interview Foshan, 13 December 2012).

On the whole, education is highly segmented, allowing for only a low level of class mobility (Lin 2011; Woronov 2016). From early on, children of migrant workers, children of workers with an urban *hukou* and upper-middle- and higher-class children live in different worlds. While the urban youth spend their first nine years of education in public schools that might be respectable by international standards, most migrant worker children go to separate 'private' or 'non-government schools'. These private schools should not be confused with the luxurious private schools in higher education that are now flourishing in China. In terms of educational quality and student-teacher ratio, they belong at the lower end of the system. An added difficulty is that these persisting divisions among children from different backgrounds in different types of schools is almost impossible to overcome after the sixth grade.

Regarding incentives, especially in terms of higher-level skills, the central state strongly aims at upgrading the skill formation system. Yet, this is not always implemented at the local level. A very big obstacle to stronger employer *and* employee incentives to significantly upgrade skills is the high turnover rate in Chinese industries. Employee loyalty ranks among the lowest worldwide. Chinese workers would certainly invest more in training if there were higher returns, but due to their short-term employment relations, most industrial workers are not incentivized in this way. Informality and short-term work contracts thus discourage investment in skills.

Such fluid labor markets (a similarity to LMEs) are complemented by a training system that continues to focus on general skills because companies are unwilling to invest in advanced apprenticeship programs "imparting industry-specific skills where they have no guarantees that other firms will not simply poach their apprentices without investing on training themselves" (Hall and Soskice 2001, 30). Some companies have started their own training programs, but only for small groups of employees in need of specialized, high-quality skills. Many other firms utilize only short on-the-job training schemes, which has become a trend even among German employers.

To summarize, the Chinese education and training system functionally benefited the industry demand for low- and medium-level skills well into the 2010s. Nevertheless, it is under stress. Increased efforts and substantial reforms are necessary to cover the growing demand for higher-skilled labor. Moreover, there is an oversupply of academic white-collar workers vis-à-vis qualified personnel from vocational education. In order not to remain stuck in a medium-skill equilibrium so prevalent in Latin America (Schneider 2013), huge challenges have to be met. Even though the Chinese government has more power than DMEs/HMEs to make substantial investment in skill upgrading (local growth alliances may be more concerned about long-term development), the lack of business and worker incentives to upgrade skills are a serious obstacle to China's further economic development (also see Benson et al. 2013; Vickers and Zeng 2017).

2.3.5 Innovation

Ideal-typically, innovations in LMEs are mostly spread via markets, whereas innovation in CMEs is based on inter-company cooperation, and in DMEs it is based on intra-firm transfer in multinational firms. The Chinese system of innovation transfer represents a state-permeated variety. In the 2000s, it included technology transfer and reverse engineering through a relatively weak patent rights system and mostly incremental technological innovations through public support in selected sectors, in spin-offs as well as in other thickly embedded national firms.

For a long time, China's innovation activities concentrated on labor-intensive 'imitative innovation', i.e. innovation which is new to Chinese firms but imitative in nature. The literature on innovation in China has documented the successful introduction of existing global technologies in domestic firms since the 1980s. This externally induced innovation was achieved through technology/knowledge transfer via FDI or joint ventures with multinationals (Fu and Gong 2011; Fu 2015). China's technological development has been inseparable from the expansion of global production networks and the relocation of production stages, including R&D.

In this process, state managers played a crucial role in providing the setting for progress in innovation and technology transfer.

> China's innovation policies favor domestic Chinese entities through tax incentives; government procurement policies; standards setting and requirements; security regulations; subsidies; and competition law policy. A combination of policies forcing technology transfer and China's failure to effectively enforce protection of foreign intellectual property rights (IPR) are also seen by many

> as strategic moves to give Chinese firms time and access to proprietary intellectual property (IP) in order to develop competitive domestic alternatives.
>
> (AmCham 2011a, 64)

Since TNCs are not willing to share technology, this led to conflicts about the protection of intellectual property rights. Chinese actors remained strong antagonists in these conflicts. Although year after year foreign commentators applauded commitments laid out by the State Council on strengthening IP protection, it appears that the Chinese side was deliberately slow in implementation. In the late 2000s, foreign firms and associations complained about IPR infringement and an increase in the volume of counterfeit products produced in China.

> Protection of intellectual properties such as copyrights, brands and trade patterns have been the main concern for foreign companies . . . Even if WTO entry implied a comprehensive modification of its patent and trademark legislation, in 2007 – six years later – the application of these standards seems insufficient.
>
> (AHK 2007, 26)

With regard to competition law and policy, a "lack of transparency and clarity" has caused special concern. According to the American Chamber of Commerce, China's Anti-Monopoly Law "does not clarify the distinction between legitimate and abusive exercise of IPR" (AmCham 2011a, 78).

Most studies conclude, however, that technology transfer did not lead to fundamental progress in Chinese domestic innovation capacities.[12] This has motivated the Chinese government to substantially increase its public innovation policy efforts at the national and local levels (Altenburg et al. 2008; Gu et al. 2009; Bresnitz and Murphree 2011; Schüller and Schüler-Zhou 2015). R&D spending has risen to almost 2% of GDP in the 2010s. The Ministry of Industry and Information Technology and the National Development and Reform Commission have sponsored incentive and benefit programs to promote R&D investment and expanded funding at local levels for basic and applied research in priority areas. To the dismay of TNCs, "while in October 2010 China announced it would begin to allow foreign companies to participate in these funding programs, to date, the majority of funds has been almost exclusively funneled to Chinese enterprises" (AmCham 2011a, 68).

Consequently, there is increasing evidence that China is capable of going beyond imitative innovation and moving into real innovation (Fu 2015; Prud'homme 2016). Although some authors argue that the causal effects of government innovation funding remain unclear, it has also been demonstrated that the effectiveness of R&D subsidies is improving (Guan and Yam 2015). Regarding the quality of 'indigenous' innovation, incremental improvements of existing technologies in existing markets, often emerging out of customization and 'really new' innovations (innovations that embody new, yet not radical new technologies or new markets) are on the rise. While media coverage has sometimes focused on rather isolated success stories in high-end technologies such as the Tianhe-1A, a supercomputer, Chinese firms are global technology leaders in very few sectors. Their main advantage in innovation is at home in meeting the demand for medium-tech products that do not require radical innovation (see the next section for the role of domestic markets). Some spin-offs from state-run research institutes are among firms that have become innovation leaders in China. Lenovo, originally a spin-off of the Chinese Academy of Sciences, was definitely not the only example. Others include: Fiberhome Telecommunication Technologies, founded by Wuhan Research Institute of Telecommunications; Datang Telecom Technology, from the Telecommunications Science and Technology Research Institute; and Shanghai Shyndec Pharmaceutical, from the Shanghai Institute of Pharmaceutical Industry.

At the local level, heterogeneity in innovation capacity building must be taken into account. Recent studies have identified positive developments in regions with proactive local states, party organizations and state-business alliances (cf. Li et al. 2008; Bresnitz and Murphree 2011; Yang 2014), like the technologically advanced Pearl River and Yangtze River Deltas. There is also evidence that policies at the local level (e.g. subsidies, investment and tax policies as well as market creation policies) have contributed to innovation capacity building in "new strategic industries" (e.g. in nanotechnology and in the photovoltaic and LED industries; see Butollo and ten Brink 2018; Gruss and ten Brink 2016; Huang and Wu 2012).

Given the demand for mostly medium-tech products, are domestic firms willing to invest in innovation at all? Indeed, firms are frequently comfortable with adapting foreign innovations for domestic markets, without seeing the necessity to invest in cutting-edge innovation. Imitation or smart adaptation suffices. At the same time, R&D spending increasingly shifted from state authorities to large (state-owned, hybrid and private) companies over the course of the 2000s. Under increasing competitive pressures, induced partially by TNCs striving to enter domestic markets, firms have increased their innovation efforts substantially, largely aiming at 'incremental' or 'really new' innovations. Some, like Huawei or ZTE, are sustained with almost no direct public support.

> Based on the experience and innovation capability accumulated from initially simple, but later sophisticated imitative learning, Huawei was able to transform itself further into an innovator. Today it has joined the established firms to generate emerging technologies in advanced countries. Not only has it been the domestic leader for patent application in China since 2002, it also became the fourth-largest global patent applicant in 2007, following only Matsushita, Philips Electronics NV, and Siemens.
>
> (Fan 2011, 835)

Notably, the diffusion of technology does not stem from inter-firm linkages, like in CMEs, as Chinese experts confirm as well (Interview PRD, 30 January 2013). Moreover, particular segments of the higher education system have been an important precondition for innovation. This is especially true for engineering.

Huge innovation potential results from the fact that Chinese companies can take advantage of a vast supply of mid-level engineers to increase the quality of human capital (Simon and Cao 2009). As mid-level engineers are relatively low cost in terms of salaries, they enable firms to "industrialize the innovation process" (Williamson and Yin 2014).

Given the benefits of technology transfer as well as proactive state support, combined with competitive pressures to upgrade innovation capacities, China has put in place the most developed innovation system among large emerging economies. Its long-term viability, however, is far from guaranteed. Several dysfunctionalities in the Chinese system create challenges: Many companies neither benefit from technology transfer nor have successfully developed innovation capacities on their own. A weak IPR system works increasingly to the detriment of Chinese firms, as shown by the fact that most civil IPR litigation involves Chinese rights holders suing other Chinese. The fact that the quality of innovation capacity building is measured by (the indeed very high) output in terms of articles in scientific journals or patents is highly controversial, since this may exaggerate China's actual innovation capacity. Notably, in order to increase the efficiency of the science system, several reforms in the 2010s aimed at structurally improving the innovation system (Jefferson et al. 2014). The objective to close the innovation gap between science and industry is high on the agenda of the Xi Jinping administration and is reflected in the "Made in China 2025" plan to create an innovation-driven economy.

2.3.6 Domestic markets

A very large and thriving domestic market is of particular importance to understanding capitalist dynamics in China. It was not feasible for the Chinese government to implement an autarkic import substitution strategy (ISI) after the 1980s (in a world market more integrated than ever), nor has economic development been simply reduced to a straightforward repetition of the export-led model, for example, as in South Korea. In addition, as compared to East Asian developmental states, Chinese domestic markets are far larger. While Chinese state managers selectively brought competitive pressures home, market protection and proactive support of national capital persisted. Furthermore, indigenous firms developed comparative advantages in their domestic institutional environment vis-à-vis foreign companies in the production of 'good enough' products which do not require the highest levels of technology. The rise of consumerism and increasing demand for intermediate goods led domestic firms to successfully occupy large market segments, especially in medium-tech and/or medium-range markets. Nonetheless, there is still leeway in terms of domestic market growth which is hampered by social inequality.

Perhaps somewhat surprisingly for standard analyses, which focus primarily on China's efforts at opening its economy and at its export achievements, Chinese domestic industrial firms on average sell three to four times more goods on the domestic market than abroad. Given the particular structure of China's domestic markets, increasing production of medium-tech goods for domestic consumer needs is a suitable strategy, a segment in which domestic firms enjoy strategic advantages due to their proximity to home markets, knowledge about consumer preferences and state support. In earlier periods, it was mostly low-tech industries that contributed to Chinese GDP growth. However, in the 2000s, more medium-range segments of the market have emerged as drivers of economic growth.

Rather than orienting themselves towards Western markets, indigenous firms developed comparative advantages in the production of 'good enough' products. For instance, these medium-tech or medium-range markets accounted for two-thirds of Chinese TV sales, while the premium range, dominated by foreign firms, accounted for a market share of only 13% (Gadiesh et al. 2007). In China, practical utility determines the decision to purchase a particular product more than in high-income OECD countries. For this reason, many Western multinationals failed for a long time to sell products to new Chinese consumers because they did not design their products to meet the consumer's specific demands, and Western products were still too expensive compared to products from domestic companies. In the Chinese auto industry, which is characterized by a relatively high share of foreign capital and a dominance of joint ventures, domestic producers such as BYD and Geely have gained a larger share in medium segments of the market. This trend was even more evident in other utility vehicle markets such as wheel-loaders or excavators (Brandt and Thun 2010, 1562–70). Furthermore, domestic Chinese component suppliers have also been strengthened. One important end-consumer market is the one for home appliances. Midea, the sixth largest private enterprise in China in 2012, with a focus on air conditioning and other white goods, is an archetypical example of a competitive medium-tech firm. While Midea is present in other developing economies thanks to its domestic success, its home market accounts for more than two-thirds of total revenue. According to firm representatives, the domestic market net profit rate was well above the sector's global average until the early 2010s (Interview Midea, 28 December 2012). While foreign competitors such as Siemens are able to serve the Chinese high-end market, Midea successfully aims at the middle of the home appliances market, and local state managers proactively function as efficient 'service-providers' for the company (Interviews Shunde, 2012–2013).

Where is demand located? Certainly, the Chinese luxury markets have become the world's largest in some respect. However, what accounts for greater economic growth is the rise in mass consumerism, resembling consumption patterns in the Fordist era of the 1950s and 1960s in the West. Consumption in China grew from around US$650 billion to almost US$1.4 trillion from 2000 to 2010. Regardless of its relative percentage of GDP, China's consumption has been growing faster than any other large economy in absolute terms. In addition, China's household income is huge, currently above US$5 trillion a year, with a high amount of unreported income (Woetzel and Towson 2015). In particular, the new middle class is pushing domestic demand, thereby reflecting the vast need for durable goods, ranging from textiles to white goods and mobile phones, as well as the desire to travel: tourism has recently become a multibillion-dollar RMB business. To be sure, inequality is large across China. Although the government has not provided an official Gini coefficient since 2005 when it stood at 0.42, a survey by a university in Chengdu put the country's Gini coefficient at 0.61 in 2010. Although Gini readings above 0.4 are typically interpreted by analysts as an indicator for potential social disturbances, this degree of inequality has also spawned some important factors that fostered growth. Consumption in China still grew strongly in absolute terms, despite a relative GDP wage share decrease to about 40%. While for migrant workers and rural laborers, average real income had indeed risen until the 2010s, this was even more the case for the growing middle classes. Overall, despite increases in inequality and high saving ratios arising from poor Chinese households paying a large share of health, pension and education expenses, the rise in absolute wealth levels has made possible a new mass consumerism. "Encouraging consumerism is, after all, the new party line" (Gerth 2010).

Next to end-consumer demand, rising demand for intermediate goods, consumed as production inputs ranging from office equipment to computers, vehicles and plant machinery, has been important. Due to China's investment boom, domestic firms producing intermediate goods are flourishing. Construction is an important sector as well, representing the single biggest portion of GDP growth in the late 2000s (NBS 2010). Intermediate goods are mostly obtained domestically. In contrast to one-sided global production network research, the role of 'processing trade', or firms obtaining intermediate goods from abroad, processing locally and exporting them, is not as important for Chinese domestic firms as it is for foreign ones.[13]

Notably, policymakers gradually and selectively allowed imports and investment to enter domestic markets. Yet in line with the idea of "macro-control" (*hongguan tiaokong*) and of "making plans for markets" (Heilmann 2011), efforts at regulating foreign activity are widespread. While the regulation of the domestic investment regime with regard to national priorities has been relaxed somewhat, preferential treatment of national capital is extensive (e.g. the NDRC's and MOFCOM's Catalogue Guiding Foreign Investment in Industry with categories of prohibited, restricted and promoted sectors for foreign investment, or MOFCOM's Measures on the Administration of Foreign Investment in Commercial Sectors). Various state policies such as subsidies, investment and tax policies as well as public procurement favor domestic companies (Gruss and ten Brink 2016; Butollo and ten Brink 2018). Consequently, there are persistent complaints by foreign firms and their business associations of "continued discrimination" and "unfair competition" (see, as an example AmCham 2011a, 60; AmCham 2011b, 30).

All in all, we have shown that the size and structure of Chinese domestic markets is of major significance for understanding economic growth dynamics. However, this is not necessarily likely to continue. Portents for the challenges ahead are a rising indebtedness of private households as well as of local institutions and non-financial corporations such as property developers (McKinsey Global Institute 2015).

2.4 Comparative advantages, institutional complementarities and contradictions of Chinese capitalism

The Chinese economy enjoyed comparative advantages regarding the processing of labor-intensive goods for a long time. In the 2000s, progress in capital-intensive production also made China a major player in technologically advanced products, although mostly in medium-range segments. Earlier comparative advantages such as low labor costs were complemented by productivity gains, advances in product quality, and the ability of Chinese firms to effectively adapt products for domestic demand. Notably, by filling a gap from deindustrialization trends in the West, several Chinese producers are able to serve regional and world markets for mass consumption. However, China's thriving domestic market is of greater importance for economic growth. While for the most part Chinese firms do not compete with Western TNCs for global market shares in high-end sectors, due to a proactive party-state and a familiarity with national consumption patterns, Chinese firms have comparative advantages on 'their' domestic markets vis-à-vis foreign firms.

A diversified industrial economy, created partially via development planning and anticipatory public policy coordination for the long term, has fostered the rise of competitive national firms in several sectors such as IT, automobiles, machinery, textiles, white goods, heavy industry and resources. Moreover, comprehensive development planning for and with markets created an institutional architecture supportive of medium- to long-term strategies. Also, the Chinese economy in the 2000s was relatively protected from the volatilities of global financial markets, and policymakers were capable of protecting the economy from other short-term fluctuations such as the withdrawal of portfolio capital.

Not unsurprisingly, inequality is embedded in the very fabric of capitalism in China. However, on the one hand, a rise in absolute wealth levels for hundreds of millions has overshadowed this as long as consumption grew rapidly. On the other hand, unequally rising incomes have triggered huge "advancement motivations" accompanied by a surge of entrepreneurial spirit and faith in progress reminiscent of the heydays of modernity. This is an amalgam of elements analyzed as decisive for capitalist dynamics by economic sociologists (Deutschmann 2009).

Regarding the economic growth success of Chinese capitalism, several institutional complementarities can be identified. *First*, we can observe *domestic complementarities* in two institutional clusters. With regard to (a) the *cluster of corporate governance and finance for investment*, Chinese firms can count on both preferential national networks of finance for investment and an enduring national control of enterprises through insiders, making long-term strategies practicable. At the same time, close relations with state managers and a pronounced entrepreneurial stance at virtually all state levels have led firms to count on numerous types of proactive party-state support and a careful, selective opening to the world economy, thereby enabling technology transfer but preventing 'sell out'. Prevalent firm strategies to succeed by forming close, 'crony' relationships with state managers, which also permit the bending of formal rules, if necessary, to gain exclusive access to resources, fit with informality in corporate governance and corporate finance.

With respect to (b) the *industrial relations/education/innovation-cluster*, further compatibilities can be observed. Comparative advantages in the 2000s were based on an institutional match between large low-wage sectors with low and medium skill requirements and an education and vocational training system in which the vast majority of the working population receives a secondary education. Moreover, the (even in the early 2010s, still comparably) cheap, disciplined and adequately skilled mass labor force was complemented by a segment of higher-skilled laborers such as engineers and technicians. This was supported by rising public expenditure on education as a percentage of total government expenditure. In conjunction with some progress in innovation capacity building, this helped Chinese producers to effectively focus on medium-tech production, in which skill and innovation requirements are not overly sophisticated. At the same time, supply mostly matched demand. As exemplified earlier in this chapter, rising medium-range demand in mass consumer products and intermediate goods incentivized domestic firms to specialize here. Moreover, as the segmentation of labor remained vital, wage increases were prevented from spiraling out of control.

An overarching role for stability has been provided by the reciprocal informal local growth alliances between state and business actors. This largely efficient economic coordination mechanism mobilized resources and helped make institutions 'fit' over time. Finally, on the central level, the party-state provided further stability despite vast regional heterogeneity and incessant institutional change. In comparison to other emerging economies, the central government and the CCP were able to weather cyclical economic instabilities well, with macroeconomic policies such as the large domestic stimulus in the wake of the global crisis. Moreover, through the formulation of comprehensive multi-year plans, the party-state was able to achieve administrative integration. It not only demonstrated its authority by setting the agenda and defining (new) priorities; it also compelled state managers at lower levels to pick up national programs and to formulate and justify (if also adapted) local development policies "that must not contradict nationally defined priorities" (Heilmann 2011, 39).[14]

Second, some *transnational complementarities* can be identified. While China was able to prosper because its economy was in a favorable internal starting position, its economy was also able to grow at the expense of other countries. Most importantly, it benefited from growth dynamics in East Asia and from other 'lucky' coincidences related to an increasing over-accumulation of capital in the North. China became the most attractive production location in the world at precisely the moment when real accumulation in the old centers was slowing down. This has been underestimated in liberal marketization success stories (Huang 2008) as well as in a state-centered scenario with the Chinese Leviathan (Yang 2004) as a clever, forward-looking force that shapes the economy at will: namely, the role of unintended but beneficial developments in the global economic system through transnational complementarities.

Overall, then, China's political economy seems to demonstrate advantages over other economies, even if partially driven by fortunate contingencies. Nonetheless, the continued prolongation of the Chinese "miracle" cannot be taken for granted. Rather than being constantly and necessarily stabilized and controlled, the persistence of this growth model is not guaranteed. In fact, socio-economic problems of the 2010s represent institutional dysfunctions and drawbacks of China's distinct institutional architecture.

Among those problems, the literature focuses on a continued dependence on exports in an unstable world economy, i.e. China's vulnerability to global developments. However, internal problems also loom large, if not larger. With regard to *economic coordination*, there is increasing evidence that tensions and conflicts between political and capital fractions are erupting with increasing frequency, as illustrated by serious recentralization efforts in the Xi administration since 2013. Whether Xi's anti-corruption measures only limit harmful types of corruption or also negatively affect 'productive' corruption in local growth alliances, as they might restrict intra-elite economic coordination in this authoritarian form of capitalism, is still an open question (for a pessimistic outlook, see Pei 2016; for a more optimistic view, see Zhu 2018).

Regarding the corporate governance/investment finance cluster, the weakness of this system is its tendency to produce excessive investment that cannot be easily confined. The central government is only partially coping with heavy competition between local growth alliances and the associated high-risk growth and financial policies from subnational actors (including banks), leading to over-investment, bad loans and rising local indebtedness (see Naughton 2016 for recent policies addressing local debt and the somewhat inconsistent introduction of the "Supply-side Structural Reform"; see also Lardy 2016; Song and Wei 2018). Doubts exist as to whether recent SOE mega-mergers in railways, energy and steel intended to create world-class competitive firms are viable.

Regarding the aforementioned complementarities in industrial relations, education/training and innovation, an unresolved problem is about whether the rising demand for higher-skilled labor can be satisfied soon, via serious reforms in vocational training, for instance. This holds as well for the question of whether or not China can manage to move from imitation to real innovation on a broader scale. While upgrading in skills and innovation capacities might also contain detrimental effects on the low-wage regime, underachievement here might backfire on the competitiveness vis-à-vis foreign firms. Foreign competitors have already modified their strategies for medium-range segments on Chinese markets and thus have become more successful. Additionally, efforts by state institutions to foster indigenous industries might fail because of different competition patterns and technology preconditions within various industries (Brandt and Thun 2016). Last but not least, trapped between public promises of social justice and the enduring belief in low wages as a competitive advantage, governmental crisis management oscillates between social appeasement and business-oriented restructuring. Proposed improvements in work conditions are increasingly seen as too sluggish, nurturing the likelihood of an increase in social conflicts and a decrease in individual advancement motivations.

Notes

1. A much broader analysis of the trajectory and current evolution of China's economy as well as on conceptual tools to analyze Chinese capitalism can be found in ten Brink (2019).
2. A much shorter version of the following sections is to be found in ten Brink (2018).
3. This runs counter to conventional wisdom that sees a radical rupture in the late 1970s. Important continuities of the Chinese economy over the course of the second half of the 20th century continued to exist, such as a planning anarchy resulting from a multitude of competing plans mostly at the subnational level. Heterogeneous state and party institutions and a decentralized economic structure already existed, if to a minor degree, under Mao (cf. Lyons 1990; ten Brink 2013a, 90–101).
4. Note the favorable external opportunity structures here. For example, greater fiscal revenues also led to taxes paid by foreign firms as their origin.
5. In terms of currency, SOEs opted for a more drastic appreciation of the Renminbi, while China's coastal exporters were key vested interests in deterring the government from letting it rise faster.
6. While often non-transparent, this can sometimes be gleaned from official regulations as in Shanxi Province. In provincial SOEs, the chairman of the board of directors should be the same person as the chairman of its party organization (www.shaanxi.gov.cn/0/104/5718.htm, accessed December 20, 2012).
7. Differences in industries aside, national SOEs mainly act in oligopolistic sectors, compared to local SOEs that predominantly act in more competitive sectors. SASAC is a special commission directly under the State Council. It is responsible for deciding some members of the board of directors (who choose the CEO), examining annual plans and reports, approving mergers or sales of stock or assets and drafting laws related to SOEs. As an example of a city-level SASAC, Guangzhou SASAC has about 60 officials overseeing over 30 big companies. In its daily practices, Guangzhou SASAC is in fact relatively independent; only decisions that have a national impact are examined by national SASAC.
8. At the center of China's financial system is the People's Bank of China that has determined monetary policy since the mid-1980s, controlled exchange rates and supplied commercial banks with credit. Into the 2000s, the banking system in the PRC has not been strongly profit-oriented. It financed loss-making state enterprises, for instance, together with their social security systems. The granting of loans was also rationed for a long period. Ultimately, the loan plan was replaced by a 'loan recommendation' that gives the commercial banks more room to maneuver without substantially limiting the political power of the central bank.
9. Note that smaller firms on the fringe strongly rely on informal sources as they are disadvantaged by prevailing lending policies. A large sector of alternative finance (non-bank, non-market finance) has emerged, including capital raised from local governments beyond the state budget (Allen et al. 2011).
10. The *hukou*, or household registration system, ties an individual's social benefits to a particular place. Although this system is a complex and increasingly decentralized instrument of administration with important local differences, all in all it institutionalized a spatial and social severing between migrant work life and home and family life. Since they cannot to a large degree enjoy access to public services for urban residents (e.g. healthcare, housing, education) as social insurance is organized at the local level, migrant workers are not able to sustain a decent life in most cities.
11. Note that large Chinese companies, for instance Huawei, led employer opposition to the 2008 Labor Contract Law and openly declared non-compliance with basic rules on employment security for some time.

12 Another reason for China's gap in the innovative frontier has been malfunctions within the Chinese science system, as well as underdeveloped selection processes of applicants for innovation subsidies.
13 China is a global hub for processing trade, yet almost 60% of processing imports are attributable to foreign-invested firms. Another 17% of processing imports are attributable to Sino-foreign joint ventures; see Yu and Tian (2012, 130–1).
14 The main post-2013 reforms of the Xi Jinping government, especially the recentralization of power and efforts to strengthen the party vis-à-vis the state administration, are not covered in this chapter. Their analysis is critical for future China studies, of course.

3 India

Enduring state-permeation in spite of economic liberalization

India often serves as a liberal counterpart to the kind of capitalism prevailing in China (Becker 2013d, 49). Indian capitalism has been a state-command economy since the late 1940s, which shared some features of Chinese capitalism. However, 1991 is commonly considered as the turning point in Indian capitalism, when comprehensive liberal reforms started. Many changes in post-1991 India indeed speak in favor of a genuinely liberalizing economy, similar to many Latin American countries. A strong privatization program, corporate governance reforms, trade liberalization and a strengthening of the stock market (to name just a few elements) seemed to indicate a thorough transformation of the Indian economy. The growth figures of the 1990s and 2000s provided good reason to believe that these reforms actually "uncaged the tiger" (Kohli 2011, 56). Indian GDP growth accelerated during the 1990s to an average rate of 5.8%, even rising to 7.1% between 2000 and 2007 (World Bank 2015d).

At closer look, however, much of the liberalizing verve had already stopped with the mid-1990s. Reforms have often been started in the early 1990s, but not finished. As a result, some liberalization took place, but on the whole, India is a very non-liberal economy that still shares many aspects with China. Beyond these very limited reforms, Indian capitalism remained extremely closed off to foreign control, and the power of established domestic business groups actually increased. Because state and business established a 'relationship of equals' based on interpersonal relations between business, bureaucracies and ministries, they were able to create and sustain an inward-looking growth model that provided a high degree of stability. It therefore shares many operational characteristics with Chinese capitalism, yet India was less able to exploit external opportunities of foreign investment like China. It was also less able to productively manage those capitalist dynamics that can lead to crisis and instability, but also to high growth. India instead opted for a more conservative but less growth-intensive strategy.

3.1 Contemporary Indian capitalism between liberalism and protectionism

Post-independence India is one of the most obvious examples for the import-substituting model of development that seeks not only economic, but also political autonomy from colonial forces (see section 2.2). Furthermore, India's economy in the 1950s and 1960s was characterized by an absolute dominance of the central state in every aspect of economic life. Until the 1970s, it relied on strict state control of the economy, which at times made it hard to distinguish Indian capitalism from socialist command economies, especially in the degree to which producers could freely decide the means of production. The state not only determined who was allowed to produce a particular product, but it also set limits on the size of producing firms in special sectors and kept close control over the inflow and distribution of resources. The 'socialist' character of the Indian economy became even stronger when social equity was prioritized over growth in the 1970s. The Indian economy managed to grow at an average rate of 3%, albeit with substantial ups and downs. Gradually, however, it became ever more insulated from the global economy. Export ratios went down constantly, reaching an all-time low in 1980 (Bhagwati 2007, 40). Apart from problems of low efficiency and limited growth, the more dramatic problems were of a fiscal nature, similar to those of other developing countries. The Indian state became increasingly less able to finance its external debts, not least because sluggish growth led to low tax incomes. The budget was further strained during the 1970s by a wave of bank and factory nationalizations that were often unprofitable and therefore put further pressure on the state's balance sheet (Frankel 2005, 468–9).

The year 1991 is often marked as a turning point or even a "revolution" in Indian capitalism (Kantha 2013, xxii; see also Mukherji 2007a, amongst many others). Increased expenses in the 1980s and declining tax revenues strained Indian accounts. The Gulf War in 1991 effected a sudden fiscal crisis that forced the Indian government to turn to the International Monetary Fund (IMF) for liquidity. There were two reasons for this. First, oil prices went up and put higher burdens on public expenses. Second, remittances by migrant workers in the Gulf region went down. In exchange for liquidity loans worth US$1.8 billion by the IMF (Bhagwati 2007, 47), the Indian government agreed to undertake a thorough structural adjustment program which mainly targeted barriers to private economic activity. Hence, tariffs and import quotas went down, the rupee was devaluated, barriers to foreign investment were lowered, and the infamous licensing scheme was abolished almost completely, as was much of the Monopoly and Restrictive Trade Practice Act (MRTP) designed to prevent big business from monopolizing the economy and to support small-scale enterprises. From the wide array of state-reserved sectors, only three remained in state ownership: atomic energy, railways and defense. Apart from those, private business was now allowed to invest in any economic sector.

At first sight, this seemed like a straightforward neoliberal reform package in which the pendulum swung from the state to the market in almost every dimension of the political economy. Given the static character of the Indian economy during previous decades, these measures are understandably labeled as a "fundamental transformation of the Indian economy" by some and "blitzkrieg reforms" by others (Varshney, cited in. McCartney 2009, 215; Chandra 2012, 101). It was generally perceived that 1991 was the start of a dynamic reform process that would continue to dismantle the old Indian economy.

Understanding what constitutes contemporary Indian capitalism requires an investigation of what happened before and after 1991, in particular the dynamics in a comparative perspective that go beyond an "Indian exceptionalism [that] sees 1991 as a radical break from the past" (Sinha 2004, 26). More importantly, the simple correlation between liberalization and growth encounters empirical problems, because growth did actually take off in the early 1980s, a full decade before these market-oriented reforms were implemented (Kohli 2007; McCartney 2010; Panagariya 2011). Average growth between 1951 and 1974 was 3.6% (the famous "Hindu growth rate") while it topped out at 5.7% during the 1980s and not much higher during the 1990s (Panagariya 2011, 107). This has two implications. First, the liberalization of 1991 had a limited effect on overall growth, thereby questioning the effectiveness of externally induced market-oriented reform programs. Apparently, the Indian economy was able to change from within at the end of the 1970s, even within the confines of Indian capitalism with all its licensing, state ownership and giant bureaucracy. Second, something must have happened at the end of the 1970s that culminated in a relatively coherent model of capitalism which was able to generate growth for at least three decades.

Rodrik and Subramanian (2004) tested a number of popular explanations for accelerating growth in the 1980s, such as a favorable external environment, the impact of fiscal stimuli and increased public investment. Yet, since none of them provides a clear causal connection to the growth phenomenon, they argue that it was not liberalization as such, but rather the particular pro-business approach adopted by the Indian government, notably the Indira and Rajiv Gandhi administrations, which was responsible for accelerating growth (Rodrik and Subramanian 2004; Frankel 2005; Kohli 2007; Mukherji 2007b, 10). In contrast to the 1960s and 1970s, during which government was largely suspicious about the role of big business for the achievement of social equity and redistribution, an 'attitudinal shift' towards private business took place. "This shift and the limited policy changes were pro-business rather than pro-competition, aimed primarily at benefiting incumbents in the formal industrial and commercial sectors" (Rodrik and Subramanian 2004, 14).

Yet, as long as such attitudes do not translate into actual policies and regulations, its benefits for Indian business remain unclear. In fact, many of the crucial pro-business reforms of the pre-liberalization period came only during the second half of the 1980s. These include the facilitated import of capital goods for manufacturing firms, which were later completely exempted from duties, as well as a steady delicensing of economic sectors (Panagariya 2011, 111–12). The state also provided direct cash incentives for private business by allowing firms to make export profits income tax deductible and lowering the interest rates on export credit. Although this shift clearly "had more to do with currying favor with existing business interests (essentially large, politically influential firms in the formal manufacturing sector) than with liberalizing the system as a whole", it is still not clear why these measures became more than just good intentions (Rodrik and Subramanian 2004, 15).

Kohli (2011) provides a political explanation for the pro-business movement of the Indian government. Facing a threat to INC rule by the rising Janata Party (which eventually won the 1977 Lok Sabha elections), Indira Gandhi sought support from the Indian business community. By then, the objective of distributional justice had lost its appeal to unify the Indian people, and the Indian National Congress (INC) in turn lost power in many Indian states during the 1970s. Simply boosting economic activity through market liberalization would have been ineffective in the Indian context. First, there is hardly any corporate competition among long-standing business groups that could have forged new entrepreneurial activity. Second, external liberalization would have led to an even more dramatic account deficit due to an increase in imports. India already had an agreement with the IMF for over US$5 billion, indicating that it had no sufficient resources to compensate for such a cash outflow (Kohli 2011, 68). Hence, there was only the option to encourage private investment by actively pushing particular businesses to do so.

However, when market incentives are absent, businesses want other credible forms of security before risking new investments. This required some form of state-business coordination that would not only ensure the right policies and actions, but that would also ensure that both parties, business and bureaucracy, fulfill their reciprocal commitments. For these reasons, a number of highly ranked committees were established in the 1980s, staffed with eminent persons enjoying the highest reputation in the Indian business community (Ghosh 1998, 319–20; Kohli 2011, 66). The pro-business drift of the 1980s provided the initial move towards a new form of state-business coordination that would continue into the 2000s and that would create an institutional framework through which state agencies and businesses could rely on the commitments of the others. Once the state made commitments in favor of private business, firms would instantly be motivated to invest again.

Another explanation for the growth of the 1980s focuses on the problem of productivity in private capital (McCartney 2010; Sen 2011). While a constantly decreasing rate of productivity had been a huge problem (Bhagwati 2007, 28–9), it started to increase in the mid-1970s and even more in the mid-1980s (Sen 2011). One important reason for this was the fall in the relative price of equipment, which is a direct effect of lowering (or scrapping) import duties for capital imports (Sen 2011, 153). Thus, this has not been a general effect of "integration of Indian firms with the world economy" (Sen 2011, 153), but rather of a particular economic constellation. The import of capital at preferred terms was managed by the state, while the import of goods and financial capital remained restricted. As we will see in the course of this chapter, this reflects the preference of Indian business for a slow or 'engineered' form of integration into the global economy.

So what is left of the "myth of 1991"? First, it is important to remind ourselves about the different type of crisis to which the reforms of 1991 related. Internal (public spending and tax benefits for business) and external (Gulf War) circumstances brought about a sudden liquidity crisis, but not a crisis of the Indian economy. "Unlike previous crises, that in 1991 wasn't preceded by a real shock.

The real economy was in a very healthy condition" (McCartney 2009, 216). The Gulf War lasted only for half a year, and remittances increased continuously after 1991 (Mani 2012, 199). Thus, the reforms of 1991 were a reaction to a short-term fiscal crisis, whereas the 'organic' crisis of the Indian economy had already been addressed in the 1980s. It could be argued that both government and business acknowledged the "secular exhaustion" (Streeck 1997) of the Indian development model during the 1980s and the pro-business drift was the easiest reform option because it "created virtually no losers" (Rodrik and Subramanian 2004, 20).

Second, the "gradualist" approach (Ahluwalia 2007) to reform was rather hesitant and allowed numerous loopholes, limits and exceptions for particular sectors and businesses. The state was able to notice the demands of domestic firms, but it failed to commit them to a particular industrial or economic policy. The limited capacity of Indian capitalism to achieve 'embedded autonomy', i.e. a state that is able to provide crucial resources for domestic business while maintaining clear developmental policy objectives, has been identified in the past (Evans 1995; Kohli 2004). Yet India seemed to be able to establish a mode of state-business relations that enabled a transition to higher growth rates. The change in favor of a more reciprocal and informal mode of coordination was not part of the macroeconomic reform package. It was initialized in the pro-business tilt of the late 1970s and early 1980s. Thus, 1991 added to the tide of reforms, but some earlier turns in economic policy were more important than the liberalization program.

Third, it is helpful to distinguish between internal and external reforms; for example, reforms that affected the Indian economic order and those that were relevant for India's external position. Broadly speaking, reforms that were mainly internally oriented, such as the abolition of the "license-permit-quota-raj" (through terminating the MRTP and licensing requirements) and the privatization of state enterprises, were undertaken with great verve. Externally oriented liberalization, however, happened at a much lower intensity. Tariffs and quotas were lowered, but India still has some of the highest tariffs in the world, effectively protecting domestic producers. Similarly, capital accounts were opened, but the inflow of funds, in particular portfolio capital, is very restricted; the same applies to the acquisition of shares by foreign investors.

Many of the reforms initiated in 1991 have not been continued (financial regulation). Some took years and decades to be drafted and implemented (corporate governance reform), and some have been reversed. While at the beginning of the liberalization process dispersed shareholding amounted to at least 60% of corporate assets, this threshold was brought down to 25% in 1993 and even further down to 10% in 1999 (Chalapati Rao 2009, 263). In other words, there was no serious attempt to change the corporate structure dominated by large business houses that characterized the Indian political economy in previous decades.

The liberalization of *some* aspects of an economy does not automatically turn the latter into a liberal economy. Textbook liberalism assumes that market principles fill the voids created by privatization and deregulation reforms. In the Indian case, it fails to recognize that even after removing, say, 20% of India's statism, there is still 80% remaining. It also fails to see that markets barely exist underneath the formerly regulated economic structures. In an economy where long-standing business houses rule the sphere of production, there is neither a market for corporate control nor a sufficient number of firms that would warrant an efficient form of competition. Similarly, where large (formerly state-owned) banks usually lend to the state rather than to firms, there is hardly a market for capital. Thus, the 1980s and 1990s undoubtedly brought reforms but not liberalization, if conceptualized as an increasing role for markets in the political economy. Ironically, the gradualist approach to reforms, where changes happen slowly and haphazardly, has repeatedly been considered as a success (Williamson and Zagha 2002; Ahluwalia 2007).

We argue that there was indeed an attitudinal shift in the early 1980s, not only among policymakers, but especially in Indian business. At that time, the idea of economic nationalism became a powerful program on which state and business could agree. The idea not only made sense for many changes in Indian capitalism, but it also provided a historical link to the ideas of Indian independence. Economic nationalism provided enough appeal to many protagonists of Indian capitalism to win their support for change without having to fear that 'India Inc.' would have to be sold to foreign capital.

When Indira Gandhi started to approach Indian big business for a joint economic recovery program in the late 1970s, it was clear that the latter would cooperate if macroeconomic growth also came with corporate profits. Gandhi could immediately prove her commitment for a pro-business agenda by dealing critically with the IMF loan agreed in 1981. This loan came with the usual liberalization policy package, in particular for opening the Indian economy to global markets. It met harsh opposition among economists, bureaucrats and the public, most notably because it would put an end to national autonomy in economic policy (Ghosh 1998, 317–18). FICCI, the main business association at that time, opposed trade liberalization as much as the Tatas and Birlas (Kohli 2011, 74). This massive business-driven opposition led the Indian government to terminate the IMF agreement after the first installment and to re-introduce import restrictions (Kohli 2011, 68). By the end of the 1980s, both government and business agreed that domestic liberalization would continue, but "external liberalization was not really an objective of the policy" (Kohli 2011, 70).

Indian firms were therefore against external opening from the outset. Even the more modern parts of Indian business that organized in the Confederation of Indian Industry (CII) joined the traditional capitals in their call for protection from external competition (Kochanek 2007, 425). The broad coalition of Indian industry against an external liberalization of the economy (and, correspondingly, for an Indian government that would protect them from the reforms demanded by the IMF) found its main figure in Rahul Bajaj (head of the Bajaj industrial conglomerate). Bajal acted as the unofficial spokesman of the "Bombay Club" which was comprised of many of India's economic heavyweights (Singh 2011; Piramal 1996, 125–8). The Club "waged a public campaign to slow down the pace of liberalization, precisely in order to bring the particulars of the new regime closer to their interests" (Chibber and Usmani 2013, 209). It aimed to limit the influence of foreign capital, not least in order to take over the capacities that became available through privatization:[1]

> its campaign did have the intended effect. [. . .] the modalities of reform corresponded fairly closely to the business agenda. By the 1990s, the bigger business houses had come to support one kind of liberalizing reform – the dismantling of controls and regulations on domestic investment. What they were more skeptical of, and lobbied against, was a drastic and sudden lowering of protective tariffs, and the unrestricted entry of foreign direct investment.
>
> (Chibber and Usmani 2013, 209)

Although the Bombay Club itself did not last beyond 1994, it had a crucial impact on the way in which the Indian government would approach economic reforms. It acknowledged the need to sell state-owned enterprises in order to level the fiscal deficit. But unlike in the 1960s and 1970s, when suspicion against private business was widespread, policymakers agreed that the national interest would be better met by selling state enterprises to Indian rather than foreign business (Mazumdar 2010). The government adopted a rather lukewarm approach to privatization, which was born out of fiscal necessity rather than economic conviction. While it was happy to get rid of the unprofitable firms it took over in the 1970s, it was reluctant to part with the profitable enterprises in key strategic sectors. Indian business groups were satisfied with acquiring shares in government firms without aiming at full corporate control. So even when privatization became more serious (e.g. through the establishment of the Ministry of Disinvestment), the state sold parts of its most precious enterprises to the Tatas, Ambanis and Agarwals; in other words, to Indian big business, not foreigners (Ahluwalia 2002, 19). Bajaj would later represent the CII in a business-led initiative for an overhaul of India's position vis-à-vis the WTO after Seattle (Sinha 2011, 468). By then, the CII fully subscribed to the protectionist and anti-foreign-capital stance that emerged during the 1980s. In 1996, it vocally spoke out against joint ventures that would only serve the interests of foreign capital. Multinationals, it said,

> brought in obsolescent technology and products; [. . .] they initially accepted 40 to 50 percent equity agreements but quickly moved to acquire majority control, [they] set up wholly owned subsidiaries for the manufacture and distribution of high quality products to avoid technology transfer and profit sharing.
>
> (Frankel 2005, 594)

Essentially, the CII portrayed foreign companies as imperialists[2] in the most classic sense.

The ascending Hindu-nationalist Bharatiya Janata Party (BJP) absorbed the current of economic protectionism and reinvigorated the term *Swadeshi* ("self-reliance"). It connected to the *Swadeshi* movement during the independence struggle, turning economic inward-looking into a political agenda. "It believes that economic development in India has been and should continue to be financed primarily by local capital, with foreign capital playing only a supplementary role" (Nayar 2007, 210; Frankel 2005, 592). Correspondingly, the BJP has been highly critical of most FDI flows, the WTO process and the international patent regime, although it turned the *Swadeshi* concept from the classic idea of protectionism into a vision of Indian greatness (Nayar 2007). Despite the ideological volatilities of the BJP, it managed to turn the ideas of the Bombay Club, which were narrowly economic, into a political program. In merging the economic and the political, the BJP was able to occupy the role of the leader for national development from the Congress Party (leading up to its victory in the Lok Sabha elections in 2014 and the Modi regime afterwards), which helped to consolidate the new style of Indian capitalism.

In sum, liberalization in India did not result in more markets, more competition and an open economy. Rather, it was quite the opposite. It has been limited to a piecemeal of singular policy measures which never amounted to a serious economic program that would be widely supported by the political leadership, big business and the bureaucracy. Macroeconomic policies in trade, production and finance continued to limit the entry of foreign capital. The state not only actively promoted a financial infrastructure that would favor long-term credit, but it also "continued to restrict commercial borrowing in foreign currencies and maintained annual ceilings on the size of, and interest rates on, loans sought by domestic firms" (McCartney 2010, 54). True, there has been a modest decline in state ownership, but this should be put into perspective: many Indian industrial giants are still in governmental hands, and many crucial economic sectors are completely dominated by state firms (e.g. banking). Private business was allowed to take a share in a number of state enterprises, but corporate control remained with the state. Even where private business gained access to sectors that were under full state control, the state made sure that it applied to Indian business only. Bharti, for instance, became the leader in Indian telecommunication (the government even sacrificed the Indian state telephone company ITI), and global telecom giants like Vodafone entered the Indian market only recently.

The reforms in the Indian economy cannot be put on a continuum between statist and liberal types of capitalism. There was privatization and deregulation, but if liberalization entails spreading the rule of markets and competition, Indian capitalism is far from liberalized. In that sense, "as much there was change in Indian capitalism, there was also much continuity" (Mazumdar 2013, 94). What did change was the relation between state and business. Around 1994, when the Bombay Club underscored that all Indian big business supported protectionist preferences, India became a state-permeated economy in which the state serves as a guardian of indigenous capital. This was possible only because Indian business could and would support the "domestic first" program. Unlike in Latin American economies, only a very few firms would seriously attack this limited reform program and push for a stronger opening of the Indian economy. In exchange, the state dispensed with the entry of foreign capital to ease fiscal stress. Such a joint strategy by state and business requires much more communication between the two than had previously occurred. The state has to know the needs of Indian business. Ministries and bureaucracies need to know the specific strategies and preferences of big business in order to effectively control the 'valve' that regulates openness and closure towards the global economy in particular sectors. In contrast to the Chinese case, the preference was more on closure, i.e. on protection from external competition rather than opening for external innovative incentives or 'going out' initiatives by Indian multinationals. By chance, India adopted a Listian development strategy that treated Indian business as 'infant industries' which needed to be safeguarded, while a large and protected domestic market provided ample space to grow and mature. This particular strength of the domestic market is partially responsible for the fact that India was able to grow without switching to an export strategy (which would be part and parcel of a Listian approach). Nevertheless, it proved positive compared to the liberalization programs in Latin America and Central and Eastern Europe (CEE). From our perspective, it would be equally reasonable to account for Indian growth during the last two decades not *because of*, but *despite* liberalization.

3.2 Coordination in the Indian political economy

We argued that the main impact of the 1980s and 1990s reforms were less a liberalization of the Indian economy and more a change in the ways in which it was coordinated. State-business relations in particular are relevant here, as are established forms of coordination within and among Indian businesses. Observers regularly stress the non-liberal and non-transparent character of the Indian political economy. Yet, despite all economic reasoning about the less efficient nature of "crony capitalism" (e.g. Goswami 2002), India was able to reach stable growth without becoming liberalized. Apparently, some aspects of cronyism or clientelism in the Indian political economy allow for a coherent and predictable coordination of economic activities. Anti-corruption measures, therefore, can have detrimental effects on the effectiveness of this form of coordination.

A crucial but often overlooked aspect of the Indian political economy is the prominence of non-market modes of coordination, in particular family ties. As section 3.2.3 shows, the Indian corporate sector is entirely in family hands. Hardly any firms in the higher business ranks are not family-controlled. Although this is sometimes a source of instability in the form of family feuds (the split of the Reliance conglomerate after the break-up of the two Ambani brothers being the most prominent), it is generally associated with a long-term perspective. While shareholders in liberal capitalism sell their shares on average after 20 months (Windolf 2005), families seek to sustain the enterprise for the next generation. But there is a more fundamental feature of family capitalism: managers and owners behave as family members, not as "principal" and "agents", as management theory suggests. Unlike in some Western management models, there is no reason for mistrust between management, owners and stakeholders. Instead, loyalty (and intergenerational hierarchy) prevails between fathers and sons, uncles and nephews, brothers and fathers-in-law. As family members, they have full information about the preferences of the other(s). Furthermore, as loyalty among family members is generally high, it is economically rational for family members to appoint each other to higher levels of management, regardless of their managerial capabilities (Sarkar and Sarkar 2012, 135). The common argument that "[e]merging markets like India have poorly functioning institutions, leading to severe agency and information problems" (Khanna and Palepu 2000, 867) counts only if we limit our perspective to formal institutions such as corporate boards or the judiciary.

In India, as in many other emerging economies "where explicit marked-based contracting is hazardous in view of cumbersome legal systems and weak enforcement mechanisms" (Sarkar and Sarkar 2012, 97), credible informal institutions (such as families) rectify such agency and information problems. However, family ties are there to stay, and hence the perspectives for the establishment of thorough market mechanisms are low. It is unrealistic to assume economic players will betray their historically established and socially grounded dynastic loyalty in favor of largely artificial principles. If families act as gatekeepers, they prevent outsiders (i.e. foreign capital) from entering the Indian economy. This is perhaps the reason why the OECD considers "related party transactions" (RPT), or transfers of funds from one family member to another, to be an illegitimate feature of Indian capitalism (OECD 2009). Of the 1000 largest Indian firms, more than 70% engage in RPTs, with a correlation between business group size and scope of RPTs (Sarkar and Sarkar 2012, 97). Thus, what is sometimes referred to as "crony capitalism" (James 2008; Nagaraj and Motiram 2017) is actually an efficient and rational way to overcome the coordination problems at the heart of the initial formulation of the Varieties of Capitalism argument (Hall and Soskice 2001, 6–7).

Families not only play an important role for the corporate sector (albeit largely unrecognized by the CC literature), but are also very present in the political arena. The INC that dominated Indian politics since independence has been led by the Nehru-Gandhi clan, up until the recent Lok Sabha elections in which the Congress Party 'naturally' nominated Rahul Gandhi to run against Narendra Modi. This is not limited to the Gandhis. Particularly at the level of Indian states, dynastic relations in politics are strongly present.[3] In recent times, business families have tried to become more active in politics, such as Anil Ambani, who became a member of the Upper House in 2004.

To sum it up: families are not just a private affair in India but also a strong feature of public life, both in business and politics. Kinship ties provide an underlying structure of loyalty that is non-negotiable. Critically, they can (and often do) serve as gatekeepers to resources, whether economic or political. They contribute to the institutional stability of the political economy, which would otherwise be much more battered by deep social and political conflicts.

3.2.1 State-business relations

If we follow the initial premise of VoC that the success of a firm "depends substantially on its ability to coordinate effectively with a wide range of actors" (Hall and Soskice 2001, 6), these actors include not only other firms but also bureaucracies and ministries in the Indian case. This means that state-business relations are as important for the overall coordination of the Indian political economy as inter-firm relations in Western forms of capitalism.

Accounts vary about the relationship between the state and business after independence. Generally, it is acknowledged that Indian politics has been rather hostile to private business, manifested in an ever-increasing array of regulations and limitations that inhibited the entrepreneurial freedom of Indian capitalists, which reached its height in the quasi-socialist turn of Indira Gandhi in the 1970s. From this background, the thesis of a pro-business drift starting in the late 1970s makes perfect sense. However, other research points out that the Indian state was in no way strong enough to impose effective limits on private business. In fact, business groups were able to creatively use the license-permit-raj to increase monopolistic profits (see Chibber 2003; Mazumdar 2013; Das Gupta 2016). The fact that the state had crucial resources under its control required firms to stay proximate to decision makers in the administration. All large businesses maintain "embassies" in New Delhi, "designed to act as a listening post, liaison office, and lobbying agency" (Kochanek 2007, 414; Subramanian 2009, 179). Thus, post-independence India has also been characterized by a symbiotic relation between state and corporations, not least due to a close alliance of big business and the INC (Kochanek 1974; Mukherji 2007b, 3; Sekhar 2011, 437). One consequence is a relative weakness of business organizations, most importantly the Federation of Indian Chambers of Commerce and Industry (FICCI) and the Associated Chambers of Commerce and Industry of India (ASSOCHAM). Although the former has been much more influential than the latter, both were unable to coherently represent business interests on the whole (Kochanek 2007; Sinha 2011), mainly for two reasons. First, in an economy in which the bulk of firms are embedded in kinship networks, there is less need for formal collective organizations than in an economy with predominantly atomized firms. Second, there was no possibility to engage in economic policymaking through strategic lobbying within the state-dirigiste regime of the INC. As an effect, coordination between state and business does not happen through sectoral or regional associations but through direct channels on personal levels: "the role of individual influence, connections, and particularistic demands by business houses [was] the dominant factor in business-government relations" (Kochanek 2007, 416). This was possible because "government control and regulation of the private sector placed vast discretionary powers in the hands of political and bureaucratic regulators, affecting every detail of private sector operations" (Kochanek 2007, 415). These relations became even more close when the Congress split in 1969 and politicians became increasingly dependent on private funds for campaigning (see also Majumdar 2018, 58–65).

However, in the 1980s, the specific cooperation between Congress and business eroded, only to be replaced by a general thrust of informal business relations that relies even more on personal connections. The case of Dhirubhai Ambani, founder of India's biggest business conglomerate Reliance Industries, is a telling one. His rise to the commanding heights of the Indian economy depended crucially on his ability to lobby and cajole policymakers at a time when they were looking for dynamic businesses to stimulate the Indian economy. The "politically well connected" Ambanis were outspoken on the need to establish and maintain good connections with figures from politics (Piramal 1996, 9–10; Kohli 2011, 71; see also McDonald 2010). They were instrumental in the establishment of the CII as a counter-association to FICCI and ASSOCHAM. However, it quickly became a lobby organization of Indian business rather than a traditional business association that would help to minimize coordination problems between firms and to maintain institutions beyond the individual firm (such as German associations). Unlike FICCI in previous decades (see Chenoy 2015), CII took a different, more 'modern' stance towards business representation. As firms did not have to grapple with licenses and permissions anymore, it opened up the possibility of influencing macroeconomic policies (Kochanek 2007, 424; Sinha 2011). For this, it needed a kind of lobbying that would respond to the established principles of interpersonal loyalty combined with professional consultancy. This helped the CII to rise to the most important business association of contemporary India (Chibber and Usmani 2013, 209; Sinha 2011, 467–9). The rise of the CII and the Ambanis as "new faces" of Indian capitalism thus actually followed the established principles of interpersonal state-business-relations:

> Over the years the CII has systematically established deep roots in each of the major economic ministries, the Ministry of External Affairs, and the Prime Minister's Office [. . .] The key to the CII's lobbying success is the development of a close working relationship with the bureaucracy [. . .]. CII leaders and staff select key bureaucrats in critical economic ministries and attempt to build a trusting relationship with them. The process involves frequent informal personal contacts, providing up-to-date information, voidance of public criticism, and working to help bureaucrats achieve their policy objectives without asking for a quid pro quo. Having established a close working relationship, demands are submitted in the form of carefully prepared briefs based on reliable data and well-reasoned arguments. Discussions are held in private and are based on a non-confrontational, constructive, cooperative, problem solving and bargaining style of negotiation.
>
> (Kochanek 2007, 424–5)

Thus, the pro-business tilt of the 1980s has not merely been a set of business-friendly policies but entailed a reconfiguration of Indian state-business relations. The state, first and foremost the Planning Commission, enhanced the status of big business, from beneficiaries that received licenses and quotas in exchange for party funding to partners in macroeconomic policy. In Frankel's words, "a *de facto* partnership between the government and large private corporations to coordinate financial and other plans for the modernization of India's industry" (Frankel 2005, 587).

When politics and business get close, observers often refer to concepts like corruption or patronage to describe such relations (e.g. Kang 2002; Yadav 2011). They all play a role in India's economy, albeit at different times and to different degrees. From the 1960s on, "[c]lientelism, cronyism and corruption [. . .] came extensively to characterize the actual working of the control regime" (Mazumdar 2013, 84). When the Congress split in 1969, open corruption and bribery took the stage. At an extraordinarily high level, this has evolved into an institutionalized system of corruption (so-called "briefcase politics"; see Kochanek 1987; Kochanek 2007, 418; Subramanian 2009). It is important to distinguish precisely these different forms of exchange. Through reiterated acts of corruption and bribery, businesses and bureaucrats established a 'working relationship' with a mutual exchange of resources. Although single acts of bribery might be the nucleus of the close connections between the state and business, these interactions evolved with a regularized and routinized character. From this emerged a social system of state-business relations in which reciprocal acts of favor constitute an environment of mutual patronage (Corbridge 2013, 226; Kohli 2004, 261).

However, this system did not perpetuate into state capture, because no "fixed and exclusive set of favored business firms remained the beneficiaries of state patronage throughout" (Mazumdar 2013, 84). Moreover, once business increased its power vis-à-vis the state, these forms of access became less and less efficient. Once politics and business became partners, there was no need for regular bribes anymore. True, beyond these new state-business alliances, there have been (and still are) numerous incidents of corruption, in particular related to the privatization of state-owned enterprises and the distribution of subsidies (Jenkins 1999; McCartney 2009, 217; Sen 2014). Within this process, the large major business groups have been able to exploit their good relations with the government to increase their overall share of the Indian corporate sector (Mazumdar 2008c; Chalapati Rao 2009). When Pranab Bardhan asserts that "the corrupt grip of the corporate oligarchy [. . .] in state allocation of access to land, monopoly rights on natural resources, or telecommunications spectrum, is much too evident", he refers to exactly such kinds of auction markets in which the winner takes all (Bardhan 2011, 422; see also Debroy and Bhandari 2012). However, such procedures are prone to foul play and are by no means particular to India. They exist anywhere the state retreats from economic activity itself and resorts to competitive biddings for public procurement, broadband frequencies, infrastructure or football tournaments.

3.2.2 Cronyism and reciprocity

This indicates that cronyism is in fact much more important for the continuity of Indian capitalism than corruption. Facing a constant fiscal deficit (more than 7% of GDP annually), both state and central governments are much more dependent on the goodwill of large business groups than vice versa (Shome 2014, 383).[4] Recently increased attention on corruption is rather a reaction to the troubled state of Indian politics and the everyday presence of corruption than a popular movement for a transparent economy. The times of perpetual INC rule in India are over, giving way to a multi-party democracy on all government levels. Campaigning became more expensive, party donations increased and more and more billionaires are entering the political stage (Bardhan 2011, 422). The anti-corruption movement grew out of the estrangement of "ordinary people"[5] with high politics as well as recent corruption scams and the fact that a considerable number of MPs have a criminal record.[6]

In short, the anti-corruption movement called for greater transparency and accountability of the elected, not for the dismantling of cronyism. It is believed that increased accountability at the top would trickle down to the everyday level, where citizens would no longer have to be prepared to pay bribes for any kind of public service including getting a driver's license and speeding up tax processes. It is important to distinguish petty corruption from grand corruption (Corbridge 2013, 222). Most people are aware of petty corruption or "harassment bribery" (Basu 2011). However, state-business relations at the "commanding heights" of the political economy is a different thing. A watered-down definition of "political corruption" that includes bribes, favors and other kinds of secret influence (see e.g. Yadav 2011) is not helpful because it not only obfuscates important differences but also ignores the long-term effects of particular relations. Bribery is usually an anonymous relationship: givers and takers have no established loyalties, and the money ensures that the promised services are actually rendered. It involves no social relationship but is in fact a 'market of favors' in which the highest bid wins. 'Grand corruption', in contrast, might establish networks of reciprocal obligations over time. Such social and interpersonal relations arguably have a stronger effect on the continuity of Indian capitalism because they carry with them "a traditional obligation of reciprocal favours" (Bose 2012, 560).

"Cronyism" refers to exactly this social dimension of state-business coordination (Mazumdar 2008a, 2008b). However, the reciprocal exchange of favors within a network of friends is only problematic for those who are excluded. On the whole, interpersonal relations provide a large amount of stability in Indian capitalism where other coordination mechanisms do not work. In that sense, cronyism is indeed a "second-best solution in the absence of limited government" (Mazumdar 2008b, 12). Technically, cronyism attempts to reproduce the coordinating qualities of family ties. In the Indian context, ties between family members and among friends provide the highest degree of anticipatory reliability and, therefore, reduce costs and uncertainty (Allen et al. 2012, 412–13; see also Witt and Redding 2013). These are not an indicator of weak institutions, but rather the exact opposite, especially once the idea of institutions as tools for coordination is taken seriously.

The expectation that liberalization would bring about greater transparency and put a halt to cronyism proved erroneous (Mazumdar 2008b; Dhume 2011; Nagaraj and Motiram 2017). This new form of close coordination between state and business emerged not in spite of, but rather because of liberalization within the Indian economy: "even in a liberalized economy, the importance of having State authorities as allies remains extremely critical to business success" (Mazumdar 2008b, 16; Sinha 2011, 466). This is even more relevant as the state continues to play a huge role in Indian capitalism. Increased contracting of public projects, ongoing privatization and its ability to shape the conditions on which external competition is allowed yields enormous resources for state authorities to distribute. The reforms eliminated the license raj (for production), but many large-scale operations by big business still require (as in most countries) permission by public authorities for landed property, the use of infrastructure (e.g. harbors), the use of telecommunication frequencies and the right to establish banks. Consequently, "the real action has shifted to the infrastructure ministries" (Kochanek 2007, 421). Most corruption scams that become public are in the power, telecommunications, aviation and petroleum sectors, where government contracting follows the discretion of the bureaucracy rather than competitive bidding. At the same time, Indian governments are increasingly dependent on the well-being of private business; therefore, Indian state leaders want to provide attractive business environments. As corporate income tax of Central Government revenues rose from 10% in 1990 to 30% in 2006, 30% of the central budget is tied to the profits made by private capital. Any serious liberal reform that would allow foreign capital or foreign countries to become involved would undermine mutual gains. Thus, political and economic reasons consolidated a politico-economic bloc of bureaucrats, ministers and business families. Liberalization changed "the modalities of the state-capital alliance, not in its very fact" (Chibber and Usmani 2013, 210).

Crony capitalism became an often-referred-to concept in the Indian political economy. It is a common word in the (economic) press, the former head of the Reserve Bank of India (RBI) speaks about it openly (Rajan 2017) and Narendra Modi built his Lok Sabha campaign of 2013–2014 around the promise of eradicating cronyism in India (Crabtree 2015). However, parties and candidates are more than ever in need of party funding, and political elites are increasingly using successful Indian businesses as poster children for the rise of "New India". Obviously, there are also still many forms of bribery that should be minimized, especially for the lower ranks of the Indian economy which suffer most from it, but conflating cronyism with petty corruption obscures Indian realities. Too often, it is part of a populist strategy promising an end to corruption for the lay people while leaving it untouched within the commanding heights of the Indian political economy. A serious attempt to end cronyism in India would actually amount to an end of the state-business partnership established in the 1980s and 1990s. However, this would also undermine the stability of economic coordination which has been crucial to India's growth over the last decades because it provided coherence across the main institutions of Indian capitalism.

3.3 The institutional foundations of Indian capitalism

3.3.1 Corporate governance

The realm of corporate governance constitutes a major pillar of CC because it determines how firms and their relations are organized. A central issue is the ability of different groups to exert control over the activities of companies. And while ownership often entails substantial control over firm strategies, there is often no straightforward correspondence between ownership and control, and the ways in which firms are controlled are often shady. This is also the case for emerging economies. The liberal ideal type, where ownership and control are separated between owners and managers, is usually not the dominant form of corporate organization. Instead, corporate sectors such as in India are characterized by both state ownership and family control of companies.

Crucial for the understanding of the Indian corporate order is the concept of "promoters":

> In companies with concentrated ownership and control such as family-owned corporations, insiders are typically the shareholders who have controlling equity stakes as well as exert management control. Such shareholders are referred to under Indian regulations as promoters [. . .]. Outsider blockholders in the Indian context are essentially non-promoters.
>
> (Sarkar and Sarkar 2012, 93)

Promoters are usually the founders of companies and are always associated with family groups. As they have controlling stakes *and* exert management control, there is no division between ownership and control, as in the joint-stock company in the Anglo-Saxon tradition. Managers therefore recruit from the same family group that owns the majority of shares.

The promoter model, or a company owned and controlled by majority shareholding families, constitutes the most common form of Indian enterprise. Firm size, in turn, is not associated with dispersed ownership; promoter ownership is the highest for the top 20 firms in India (Sarkar and Sarkar 2012, 95). Table 3.1 gives a snapshot view of the ownership structure of India's 20 biggest companies. Two aspects stand out. First, big business is either in the hands of families or the state. Second, they usually hold very large shares (so-called blockholders) that effectively limit the ability of other shareholders to exert influence on the corporation. Even where large non-promoter shares exist, these are officially independent but often belong to other companies of the business. Taking the definition by La Porta et al. (a company is considered as "widely held" if no shareholder owns more than 20% of voting rights), only 7% of Indian business is widely held – the remaining 93% being characterized by concentrated ownership and insider control (La Porta et al. 1999, 477; Sarkar and Sarkar 2012, 93, 143; Allen et al. 2012, 426). The Indian corporate sector is very closed, even if compared to other countries with a high concentration of ownership.

As 96–99% of companies have insiders as sole blockholders, "the potential for institutional activism across Indian companies when measured by the extent to which institutional investors can, through their blockholdings, act as a countervailing force against promoters, is at best weak" (Sarkar and Sarkar 2012, 179). A common practice of pyramidal ownership in India is the establishment of companies formally independent from blockholding promoters, but which are part of the same business group. By this means, own shares can be purchased indirectly, and profits and losses can be transferred between group companies at the expense of minority shareholders ("tunneling"; see e.g. Bertrand et al. 2002).

Table 3.1 The 20 biggest companies of India, by turnover

Company	*Origins of owners*	*Activity*	*Family control*	*Banks*	*Social Security funds*	*Private*	*Limited state control*	*High state control*	*Majority state-owned*	*Strong family ownership*
Reliance Industries	IND	Petroleum	Ambani		x		x			x
Indian Oil Corp.	IND	Petroleum			x				x	
Oil & Natural Gas Corp.	IND	Petroleum			x				x	
Tata Motors	IND	Vehicles	Tata		x	x				x
Bharat Petroleum Corp.	IND	Petroleum			x				x	
Hindustan Petroleum	IND	Petroleum							x	
Tata Steel	IND	Steel & Iron	Tata		x		x			x
NTPC	IND	Electricity			x				x	
Bharti Airtel	IND	Telecommunications	Mittal		x	x				x
Larsen & Toubro	IND	Construction, shipbuilding, machinery			x		x			
Coal India	IND	Mining, finance			x				x	
Hindalco Industries	IND	Copper	Birla		x		x			x
Adani Enterprises	IND	Trading	Adani			x				x
Mahindra & Mahindra	IND	Vehicles, diversified	Mahindra		x		x			x
Essar Oil	IND	Petroleum				x				
Steel Authority Of India	IND	Steel			x				x	
Power Grid Corp.	IND	Electricity			x				x	
Bharat Heavy Electricals	IND	Generators, turbines			x				x	
Tata Consultancy Services	IND	Computer software	Tata		x	x				x
GAIL (India)	IND	LPG			x				x	

Source: CMIE Database, January 2014. Origin of owners = foreign investors do not exceed 25%; The category of “social security funds” is regularly constituted by the Life Insurance Corporation of India.

This structure raises potential conflicts of interest between controlling and minority shareholders. From a liberal perspective, it hampers the efficient governance of corporate affairs because pyramidal ownership separates control from cash flow rights (Sarkar and Sarkar 2012, 134; Chalapati Rao and Guha 2006, 2). However, the question of efficiency is different if the controlling majority is held by families, as is universally the case in India. In this case, principal-agent problems are minimized: first, because kinship trust compensates for the uncertainty at the heart of these problems, and second, because owners who usually have a strong interest in preserving the company for the next generation also have a strong motivation to control managers. In other words, pyramidal ownership and closed company control can have positive effects for corporate governance if governed by family ties.

Although shares are traded rather actively, it follows that the Indian stock market is by no means a "market for corporate control". The trade of shares is rather motivated by the desire to reorganize shareholding within the controlling group as well as to consolidate control of companies and firm groups, to avoid taxation and to raise new capital. As firms attempt to raise funds on the stock market, the concentration of control has important effects. As the Indian Ministry of Finance acknowledged in the early 1990s,

> too high a level of public float discourages closely held well-run profit making companies from going public. While the promoters want the benefits of listing, they are generally averse to giving a larger share in the capital/control to the public.
>
> (cited in Chalapati Rao 2009, 262)

In effect, the structure of corporate control has not changed substantially since the 1950s and 1960s (Bardhan 2011, 422).

Minority investors in Indian companies can hope for a profitable return on investment, but they cannot aim to exercise control over firms. Hence, a crucial aspect of the shareholder value model is corrupted: investors cannot urge the management to pursue investor-friendly strategies that will be reflected in share prices (Lazonick and Sullivan 2000). The structure of corporate control in India ensures that blockholders decide the direction of the firm that reflects their long-term interests in continuing profitability. It means that non-blockholding owners have no means at their disposal to push for more shareholder value profit.

The role of business groups in Indian capitalism cannot be overstated. Indian business groups usually consist of families who control a large part of the equity without necessarily owning it. Instead, they often control a number of entities that actually own companies. Such cross-holdings are remnants of the early years of business group formation, in particular how companies were financed through the (still colonial) management agency system (Sarkar and Sarkar 2012, 134; Mazumdar 2013, 82). As a result, a complex network of trusts, investment and finance companies with different forms of indirect holdings emerged. This corporate structure remains intact today. The Tata Group, which includes Tata Motors, Tata

Steel and Tata Consultancy Services, is ultimately owned by Tata Sons, an investment foundation which itself is unlisted. It is comprised of more than 250 companies through numerous cross-holdings and interlocking directorates, which allows for creative possibilities to transfer profits and losses (CMIE 2014). Interestingly, even India's new capitalists follow established corporate governance traditions, most prominently the Ambani brothers who lead the Reliance conglomerates. The two Reliance companies[7] contain a web of 68 and 102 firms, respectively. The main difference to the Tata Group (and other long-standing business conglomerates) is that many of them are unlisted holdings, making the Reliance Groups even less transparent than other groups.

In the economics literature, the existence of business groups is often attributed to non-existing formal institutions for corporate governance (e.g. Johnson et al. 2000; Bertrand et al. 2002; Chakrabarti et al. 2008; Estrin and Prevezer 2011, 53; Sarkar and Sarkar 2012, 156–9). But given the fact that most business groups already existed in the colonial period and often are more than 100 years old, their existence cannot be explained exclusively by economic motives. Business groups in India are an expression of the embeddedness of the economy in social structures which must not be excluded from the analysis. As large business families are apparently here to stay, there is no realistic possibility that corporate governance will become liberal in India in the near future.

In contrast to the assumption that the Indian government actively promoted liberalization in the 1990s, it is actually lukewarm about liberalizing corporate governance regulation, which would allow foreign capital to take a bigger chunk of the Indian corporate sector. The economic policy of the 1960s and 1970s, which treated business with skepticism, posed many restrictions against any expansion of the private corporate sector (for instance, the Companies Act of 1956 explicitly prohibits firms with fewer than 50 shareholders to sell shares on the stock market). Apparently, this should have changed with the liberalization policies of the 1990s. However, attempts to liberalize ownership by making a minimal ownership quota mandatory have been followed half-heartedly. In a similar fashion, a reform of the relatively restrictive Companies Act, which was already envisaged as part of the 1990s liberalization package, has been postponed multiple times (Chalapati Rao and Guha 2006). Eventually, the new Act came into force in 2013, which indicates the limited interest of the Indian government in actually reforming or liberalizing corporate governance regulation. However, it satisfies the interests of Indian big business in focusing on advantages for their officials and minimizing foreign competition. For a long time, the largest foreign company in India has been Siemens, ranking at 86 out of the 500 biggest firms (Businessworld 2013, 73). Although foreign firms continue to access the Indian corporate sector, it is still a far cry from the foreign penetration that could have been witnessed in Latin America or Eastern Europe.

As Table 3.1 shows, half of the biggest companies in India are directly state controlled, in particular those involved in mining, energy and heavy industry. State-owned enterprises tend to be relatively large given their strategic function in these sectors. Apart from single firms in the telephone and construction sectors, all major state-owned enterprises are in the business of primary goods, energy, infrastructure and chemicals (Businessworld 2013, 90). This means that the state focuses its own business operations in strategic sectors and leaves other sectors such as consumer goods, machinery and chemicals to private enterprises. Since privatization of public enterprises was part of the liberalization package suggested by the IMF, the government was able to take the opportunity to sell unprofitable and non-strategic enterprises. However, this did not result in a more liberalized or open corporate sector. When plans for liberalization became public, promoters immediately raised their shares in companies to prevent foreign owners from getting a hold on Indian companies (Chalapati Rao and Guha 2006, 11). As the first step toward liberalization was the issuance of the government-owned shares, this actually led to an increase of promoter control over Indian companies (Chalapati Rao 2009, 262). The privatization process effectively halted in 2004, but until then, no more than 42 larger SOEs had been partly privatized (Chakrabarti et al. 2008, 68). Large state-owned enterprises in strategic industrial sectors in which private owners have only minority rights will therefore remain a characteristic feature of the Indian economy (Kaushik and Dutta 2012, 90). Together with the almost unchanged structure of the private corporate sector, there is much more continuity than change at the corporate governance level.

3.3.2 Finance for investment

In the liberal model of capitalism, issuing shares on the stock market is motivated by stockholder interest in changing their portfolios. Stock exchanges must be liquid in order to make shareholder value principle work (Aglietta and Réberioux 2005, 4–5). Given that this principle is absent from the Indian corporate sector, stock exchanges in India are actually potential sources of fresh capital (Chalapati Rao 2010). Where founders regularly own more than half of all shares, stock markets cannot serve as markets for corporate control. However, although the Indian stock market is very active, its importance for corporate finance and control has actually decreased. The extent to which Indian businesses access external finance through the equity market is low, not least to prevent external capital from gaining control over the firm. Additionally, returns on equity are relatively low. A high turnover might therefore be reflected in Indian capital markets, but there is not much gain to go along with it. While funds raised from the capital market represented 13% of domestic savings in the 1950s, this rate dropped to 0.4% in the 1980s (Sarkar and Sarkar 2012, 89). By the 2010s, only 5.47% of large Indian firm financing has been based on equity markets (Allen et al. 2012, 421).

So where does the money for new investments come from? First, Indian firms increasingly draw on *internal* funds, such as retained earnings. Between 1990 and 2005, the enterprise saving rate increased by almost 300% because corporate taxes decreased and debt servicing became cheaper (Bardhan 2010, 66, 68; Snowden and Munoz 2012, 1111). Large firms are able to cover over 46% of their total annual financing through internal sources (Allen et al. 2012, 421). The second most important source of financing is equity and debt raised from group companies, promoters and founders, which account for another 30% of financing. Looking at the equity activities of large Indian companies over the last decade, we see that significant shares are traded within the respective business group. Although it appears that Indian companies draw heavily on market-based sources of equity finance, the stock exchange actually serves as a transmission belt for the transfer of capital from one group affiliate to another.

In the literature, these funds are classified as "external" funds because they are actually not on the firm's capital account, but belong to other external sources. Yet the notion of an "external" source is misleading: these funds are indeed external to the individual firm, but internal to the associated business group. It is therefore better understood as an internal source of finance because "[g]enerally operating outside formal institutions, this form of finance is backed by alternative mechanisms such as reputation, relationships and trust" (Allen et al. 2012, 410; Kaushik and Dutta 2012, 36–52). The allocation of funds for investment is ultimately determined by mechanisms of insider control. The use of such financing channels, unlike market and bank channels, usually comes without external control or influence on business operations. With this, we can safely assume that large Indian companies are able to draw approximately 75% of their financing needs from sources within the business group. Similar to the issue of closed corporate governance, such alternative sources of finance backed by a communitarian mode of coordination can actually have beneficial effects for the performance of Indian companies (Allen et al. 2012, 410).

Another 19% of financing needs in large Indian companies (25% for smaller firms) are met by the Indian banking sector (Allen et al. 2012, 421). The relatively modest role of domestic banks is also a result of the historically developed structure of the Indian banking landscape. Until the 1990s, domestic banks (often government-owned development banks) were able to provide long-term credit at subsidized rates, which made it rational for firms to focus on debt rather than equity. This was a means to keep the closed corporate structure in India intact.

> Cheap long-term debt capital meant that most companies could meet their funding needs from bank loans without requiring promoters to access the equity market to raise funds for investment. This way the equity base of promoters remained undiluted and promoters could maintain control of their companies without sinking in much capital.
>
> (Sarkar and Sarkar 2012, 89)

Such a developmentalist lending policy created path dependencies, most notably an organizational predisposition towards big business. Banking was previously conducted on a large scale, involving large state banks and large business conglomerates. Furthermore, as developmentalist banking was based on bureaucratic rationalities partially determined by the prescriptions of the Planning Commission, the banking sector 'inherited' a conservative stance. The average capital adequacy rate of Indian banks is 13–14%, far exceeding Basel II safety benchmarks (Chakrabarti 2014, 858). A large part of bank assets are held in mandatory government debt, which is relatively risk-free but obviously diverts resources from the private sector. As banks in India finance the government rather than the private sector, it is no wonder that the Indian banking sector appears very efficient, for example, with an extraordinary low share of non-performing loans (Allen et al. 2010, 148; Allen et al. 2012, 416).

The strict state control of bank lending has eased over the last decades, but this has not led to dramatic changes in the overall picture. Although major Indian development banks have been privatized, public banks still account for two-thirds of the Indian credit market (OECD 2011b, 121).[8] Since the early 1990s, borrowing from banks and other financial institutions has generally exceeded financing through the equity market (Sarkar and Sarkar 2012, 90). The financial sector reforms of the 1990s and 2000s were intended to remove bottlenecks in external finance and to introduce more market mechanisms. But between 1991 and 1999, the importance of external funds actually declined. Until 2008, external sources of finance never went beyond the level of the early 1990s (Sarkar and Sarkar 2012, 89–90). This happened at a time when equity finance became increasingly available at relatively cheap rates around the globe. But at the same time, Indian businesses were able to increase their corporate savings, which made them independent from external finance and associated pressures to share corporate control. In the end, the promise of finance and equity market liberalization did not lead to higher investments (Rajakumar 2005). Instead, Indian business largely ignored the newly emerging capital market, not least because reforms never really encouraged to switch over to a market-based capitalization model.

A new market-based financing alternative must be at least as reliable as intra-group loans. Within the logic of finance, independent supervisors (such as the SEC in the United States) guarantee the reliability of lenders. India established such a supervisory institution, but it does not provide credibility. In 1992, India empowered the Securities and Exchanges Board of India (SEBI), taking the American counterpart, the SEC, as its main example. Along with extensive disclosure laws, it appears that investors enjoy a high level of protection. However, SEBI barely enforces these laws, especially in areas like price manipulation and insider trading, which are arguably at the heart of the closed corporate governance mechanisms as outlined earlier (Chakrabarti et al. 2008). As Chakrabarti et al. note, "SEBI took action against only 9% of the companies under its jurisdiction, while SEC's corresponding figure was 52%", although the latter supervises much more advanced equity and securities markets (Chakrabarti et al. 2008, 62). Thus, investor protection is indeed quite weak despite limited efforts of the Indian government to change this. In addition to its autonomous function as objective supervisor, SEBI is also equipped with judicial capacities. But as the stock exchange is neither a market for corporate control nor a market for corporate finance, but rather a kind of clearing house for the transfer of intra-group cash flows and liabilities, standard regulatory practices do not apply. It is therefore difficult to understand why a regulatory body is better equipped to settle potential irregularities than the family within which a transaction actually takes place.

Under these circumstances, market finance becomes more insecure and risky, thereby raising the cost for capital. Because irregularities are only loosely monitored by SEBI, affected parties would have to resort to legal litigation. However, these may take years if not decades to settle, a lengthy process which only large firms could survive. Lacking sufficient judges, contract enforcement through courts takes almost four years on average (Chakrabarti et al. 2008, 63). Consequentially, reciprocal and inter-personal linkages are the most efficient mechanisms of coordination: "non-legal sanctions in various forms, such as loss of reputation or future business opportunities or even fear of personal safety, are far more effective deterrents against contract violations and non-payment of dues than legal recourses" (Allen et al. 2010, 128). Indian firms do not suffer as much as Western companies from the precarious legal system because they can rely on coordination through reciprocal obligations. Hence, domestic firms have a structural advantage compared to outsiders.

3.3.3 Industrial relations

We argue that emerging economies are characterized by a particular form of labor relations that not only differs from most OECD countries, but that also complements other institutional pillars of state-permeated capitalism. Specifically, we can explain much of the current form of industrial relations from the prevalent existence of labor informality.

No discussion of Indian labor relations can deny the importance of informal labor. Barbara Harriss-White estimates the size of the informal sector as 83% to 91% of total labor (Harriss-White 2003, 5). This form of labor is often referred to as "non-registered" or "non-organized", as it is usually not accounted for and falls below the threshold for taxation. But another meaning of 'informal' refers particularly to forms of labor in the formal economy, such as contract and casual labor (Harriss-White 2003, 5–6). Most work in the agricultural sector is clearly of an informal nature, but even in the non-agrarian sector, 83.6% or workers are employed informally (ILO 2012, 4) and three out of four workers in the organized sector have no written work contract (Sood et al. 2014, 62). In other words, only a very small fraction of the Indian workforce falls within the organized sector. The organized sector is, of course, covered by official statistics and gives workers access to social security systems and labor protection.

The developments in the 1990s and 2000s only made the situation worse. During the liberalization period, overall employment went up slightly, but its quality did not. Formal employment has remained virtually stable for over 20 years (Jha 2018). The expansion of the private sector was not able to generate enough jobs to compensate for the loss of public employment (Mazumdar 2013, 88–9, Nagaraj 2017). As an effect, India saw a relative increase of the informal sector (Harriss-White 2003, 18; Anant 2009). According to the World Bank (2006, 1), "[m]ost jobs were created in the unorganized sector where the level of productivity tends to be low. Employment in the unorganized sector grew by 1.1 percent annually". As Sood et al. demonstrate, direct employment in the organized sector fell during the 1990s with a corresponding rise in contract labor. Since the mid-1990s, contractual work arrangements have also expanded at the expense of the directly employed (Sood et al. 2014, 60). They also show that the highest increase in contractual workers can be found in large enterprises with 100 or more employees. Thus, big business actually took advantage of the "movement towards increasingly flexible labour markets, erosion of collective bargaining and the greater role of capital in setting the terms of work" (Mazumdar 2013, 89).

The rise in informal labor indicates that growth in the post-liberalization period has been mainly based on extensive production with high input of low-productivity labor. The continuing orientation towards labor-intensive production has crucial implications for the institutional structure of Indian capitalism. First, even the increased productivity in manufacturing was relatively low overall (Mazumdar and Sarkar 2009, 45). But even the services sector, which has often been heralded as the main driver of Indian growth since the 1980s, was not characterized by high levels of productivity. As Mazumdar and Sarkar point out, "the sub-sector 'transport, storage and communication', which includes these IT-related activities, accounted for no more than one-sixth of the total employment in the tertiary sector, though its incremental share was quite high". But rather than IT, " 'trade, hotel and restaurants' continued to play the dominant role in employment in this sector" (Mazumdar and Sarkar 2009, 44). One has to understand that although business process outsourcing (BPO) is related to the IT industry, it is relatively labor intensive and requires only basic English and organization skills, which many of the annual two million graduates and 300,000 post-graduates from universities and colleges can amply provide (Kaushik and Dutta 2012, 217). Second, a persisting strategy of labor-intensive production hampers the transition to higher productivity. This is because manufacturing firms shy away from investments as long as extensive production remains a profitable option and workers remain too disorganized to push for higher wages, which would bring with it a gradual transformation of industrial relations. Third, low productivity growth has direct effects on average salaries and therefore on domestic demand. If Indian business continues to follow a labor-restrictive stance while keeping their focus on domestic demand and growth through an expansion of production, a profit squeeze is a possible outcome.

A characteristic feature of the regulation of labor relations in India is the overwhelming presence of the state. This is probably a recurring feature of late-developing countries in which capital and labor were historically insufficiently organized to establish a stable regime of industrial relations, and which gave rise to different forms of state corporatism (see Cox 1987, 63–82). With independence, an elaborate bureaucratic apparatus has been constructed to implement and enforce labor laws. Following earlier socialist principles, Indian labor regulations are very tight and relatively worker-friendly. The Industrial Disputes Act of 1947 and the Factories Act of 1948 provide a set of strong regulations with regard to working times, healthcare, unionization and worker security (Chibber 2005; Pal and Saha 2014). They particularly control labor relations in large firms: for instance, enterprises with more than 100 workers need permission from the state to fire an employee (Sood et al. 2014, 59). As liberals argue, this labor market inflexibility is responsible for the reluctance of employers to create jobs and to expand the organized sector. According to Jagdish Bhagwati, India would have needed "laws that permit workers to be laid off as necessary" (cited in Corbridge and Harriss 2003, 158). However, liberalization of existing labor regulations would not necessarily lead to a growing organized sector because the most rigid legal provisions apply predominantly to large firms. In fact, only 4.5 million Indian workers enjoy such high levels of job security (Sood et al. 2014, 59).

It is therefore a mystery how big business could actually expand the share of informal work while subject to (allegedly) rigid labor laws. Though labor regulations remain visible on paper, the "loopholes are big enough for the proverbial bus to be driven through them" (Harriss-White 2003, 37). From the outset, incentives to evade these laws were high, and "the state has tended to act in the interests of capital whenever organized labour tried to get the law enforced" (Harriss-White 2003, 37). And similar to developments in Western countries, outsourcing and flexibilization became an important feature of Indian labor relations in the 1990s. But as a consequence of growing informalization, the bargaining power of labor shrank dramatically. Strike activities have gradually decreased since the 1980s. But while strikes exceeded lockouts until the early 1990s, the number of strikes and lockouts has aligned since the mid-1990s (Pal and Saha 2014, 838–9; Sood et al. 2014, 65). In 1992, immediately after liberalization set in, the number of lockouts actually doubled, making it clear that business is willing to take hard measures to defend its new freedoms. Since 1991, more man-hours have been lost due to lockouts than due to strikes, indicating "a dramatic increase in employer militancy" (McCartney 2009, 190; Pal and Saha 2014, 841–2). This refers to a corporate rollback in Indian industrial relations, in which firms seek not only protection by the state to curb labor power, but are also able to defend themselves against labor contention. The pro-business tilt of the 1980s observed by Kohli (and others) manifested in an ever growing departure from the initially labor-accommodating orientation of the Indian state (see Jha 2010). Neither business nor the Indian state has devoted meaningful activities to reducing the size of the informal sector; instead, both sides supported a drift of industrial relations in a more liberal direction, i.e. more market- and competition-based.

These developments have to be interpreted within the general fragmentation of Indian labor relations. Industrial relations are increasingly divided across federal lines, which in turn raises competitive pressures among states. This applies in particular to the unionization of Indian workers, which actually went down in recent years (Sood et al. 2014, 63). This is even more dramatic, as in the absence of a broad industrial class, large-scale unionization is difficult to achieve. Organized labor itself does not engage with the problem of the largely unorganized workforce as an impediment to the pursuit of its own interests. Additionally, the union movement is also fragmented. Apart from sectoral unions, there are corporate and public sector unions as well as unions organized around charismatic leaders (Harriss-White 2003, 40, 191). Sectoral unions at times resemble trade associations, consisting of both employers and workers in the same organization. In the end, it is not unions but the state that tries to enforce labor standards, while treating its own employees preferentially (Harriss-White 2003, 35). To complicate the situation even further, caste is an additional source of loyalty that cuts across the employer-worker line. Facing a set of labor relations with many overlapping social cleavages, it becomes clear that the organization of the labor force is extremely difficult and worker representation in industrial relations will most likely remain weak. Lacking effective institutions at the economic level, capital-labor relations become ever more politicized. At the state level, unions become enmeshed in party mobilization and parties, in turn, tap the organizational qualities of labor unions for the attainment of voters. The weakness of labor, the unwillingness of the state to act as an equalizer between capital and labor and, as a corollary, the delegation of class conflict into the democratic realm reinforces the close connection and co-dependency of politics and the economy in India.

But business associations are relatively weak as well when it comes to their organizational capacities to govern their own affairs. Both labor and business associations are currently not strong enough to institutionalize industrial relations on their own. In a giant country such as India, considerable capacities are required to achieve a state of organizational strength which would allow for some kind of bipartisan coordination. The organizational weakness of capital and labor makes them dependent on the organizational capacities of the state. Yet, the state is not omnipotent, and there are a number of pitfalls and blind spots which the state seems currently unable to overcome. In the 1990s and 2000s, the flexible labor regime in India fit well with the high demands and limited possibilities of Indian business, as long as the state could compensate for these structural deficiencies in Indian industrial relations. But it constitutes a very delicate institutional equilibrium because, unlike the success stories of LMEs and CMEs, it is not grounded in (tacit) support by both labor and capital but rather on the repression of labor demands on the whole.

The strong legal protection of workers in India after 1947 was a reaction to the weak position of labor vis-à-vis giant corporate business houses. As labor has been exposed to the pressures of big business from the 1980s on, it could not adequately defend itself. The inevitable result was a wage level that remained low even as growth took off. For business, this meant concentrating on a labor-intensive strategy and trying to exploit wage levels as the most obvious options. However, a low-wage strategy is relatively vulnerable and must be safeguarded to remain stable over time. Not only does it require keeping wages low, i.e. to keep labor disciplined, but it also requires ensuring that labor-intensive production remains competitive. Here, the greatest danger comes from external competitors that would be able to compete with even lower prices for similar products. To prevent this, the state establishes substantial import barriers, thereby raising the costs for the entry of foreign competitors into the domestic market.

3.3.4 Education and training

The structure of the labor market based on a division into small-organized and large-unorganized is also manifested in the area of education and training. Most work in the informal sector is unskilled, and there are no credible incentives to invest in training that takes place within flexible employment practices (Harriss-White 2003, 20). Just as employment and industrial relations are characteristically different between the organized and the informal sector, so are the various paths related to education and training. Historically, the government could institutionalize education only in the formal segment, including elementary and secondary schools, colleges and universities. India has a diversified system for the organization of academic and technical education, with universities and colleges under public supervision. However, efficient structures for vocational training and education (VET) are lacking. This is partly due to the largely informal structure of private business in India, where skill development happens informally as well. But this is also an outcome of the historically skeptical attitude of Indian political leaders towards business. Just as licensing requirements and widespread nationalization of firms were against the interests of Indian business, it was also difficult for business to demand appropriate vocational training schemes. As an effect, Indian higher education is heavily tilted towards the academic tier. According to the World Bank, only approximately 10% of young Indians aged 15 to 29 have received vocational training, whether formal or informal (World Bank 2008). Only 1.1% of those enrolled in secondary education choose vocational education, which is the same percentage in Pakistan and only slightly higher than in Bangladesh (Tilak 2003, 678). In China and Japan, the rate is around 15%. As a consequence, the business-oriented non-academic segment of the education system is heavily underdeveloped and the skill shortage has been identified as one of the biggest problems in the Indian economy, especially if India eventually aims to reach higher value chains (Kaushik and Dutta 2012, 94).

This has a number of implications. First, there are developmental side effects. The Indian educational system largely provides skills for urban, fully capitalist settings but neglects the agricultural sector. Its bias towards academic tertiary education adds to the dramatic social stratification in Indian society. Additionally, people aiming at educational upgrading can usually follow only the academic pathway, as the possibilities to invest into one's own skill development in the private sector are very limited. The majority who go into academia do not finish by obtaining master's or doctoral degrees, and thus transition into the private sector is difficult because curricula are usually not set to provide students with necessary skills (Singh 1999). As vocational training in India starts relatively late (at the age of 16), most students have already made their choice for college by this point. Broadly speaking, there are few options for upward mobility through education other than the formal college/university path.

Higher education has long been part of the Indian developmentalist program. Rapid catch-up through import substitution required the creation of a technical elite (managers and engineers educated by the Indian Institutes of Technology) well equipped to lead production and development to fulfill the benchmarks set by the Planning Commission (Dahlman 2009, 312). The current situation of the educational system reflects the two main developmental strategies after independence: the establishment of a domestic industrial base run by Indian specialists, and the promise to provide basic development for the rural masses. Business-oriented VET systems would fall into the gap between these two.

This has a dualizing effect. The formal education system is able to supply only low-skilled or highly skilled labor. Workers either enter the job market without specific skills after primary school, or with highly developed technical skills after university or college. Entering the labor market at a halfway point is not a viable option. This hampers upskilling processes, especially if firms demand generally skilled labor rather than specialized workers. Furthermore, since all vocational education is under public guidance, there is no mechanism to ensure the 'fitness' of the vocationally skilled to meet private sector requirements. "Craftsmen" (*Meister*) are trained through a specified scheme devised by the Ministry of Labour and Employment (Agrawal 2008, 57–8). This publicly administered scheme might make sense for the previously dominant sector of state-owned enterprises but hardly ensures that skill demands of the private sector are actually met. Without firm-oriented skill transmission mechanisms through an organized VET system, workers face a high risk of remaining stuck in the low-wage labor market, especially if they are unable to enter the academic career path. Additionally, there is no coherent framework that allows workers to upskill in order to adapt to new technologies and techniques (Dahlman 2009, 312).

As a consequence, we can observe an institutional equilibrium that actually hampers any upward dynamics. Under current circumstances, workers have a low incentive to invest in skill development unless they are able to enroll at tertiary schools, which usually guarantees an increase in wages. Investing in secondary/VET is related to a less probable chance of being rewarded with higher wages. Instead, chances are high that even after investment in vocational training, people will remain employed in the informal sector with low labor security.

Firms also have little incentive to invest in VET systems for various reasons. First, as large firms they are able to direct their educational demands vis-à-vis the state. Medium-sized firms (such as the famous *Mittelstand*) would need to develop skills in order to remain competitive, but they lack the power to address the polity directly (Mazumdar and Sarkar 2012). Why large firm conglomerates in emerging economies are able to develop and sustain complex corporate structures, but are unable to develop a VET system based on collective obligations remains an open question. The most plausible answer is that they simply do not perceive the need to do so.

Second, skill upgrading would be necessary if firms aimed to increase productivity or to move up the value chain. However, profitability can be achieved alternatively by expanding extensive production, i.e. maintaining labor-intensive production. For this, it is crucial that average wage levels remain low. Only if wage pressure rises will higher salaries have to compensate for higher productivity. Total factor productivity and investments in capital rose steadily during the 1990s (World Bank 2006). However, capital intensification (as witnessed in India) does not collide with extensive production if fresh investments are merely expansions of existing production facilities rather than 'upgrading' production processes without increasing the value of the labor force. The Indian government follows a flexibility-oriented approach to disciplining labor that took off with the liberalization reforms of the 1990s. The structural weakening of labor helps to keep wage pressures at bay and allows firms to pursue labor-intensive production strategies which do not require the upskilling of the labor force.

Third, most firms lack the organizational requirements to set up VET schemes. As mentioned earlier, most firms are small-sized entities in which skills are transferred informally and inter-generationally. As large firms in the organized sector often provide in-house trainings and therefore do not depend on extensive VET frameworks, sector-wide education and training arrangements would be most relevant for medium-sized enterprises. However, these are relatively few and are still too small to carry the burden of setting up a sectoral training system.

The state (on all levels) remains virtually ignorant with regard to these issues. Only recently has the central government started to worry about how to get the growing number of young people into work once they reach the appropriate age in order to prevent social and political instability. This issue is being addressed by a "National Skill Development Council" under the chairmanship of the Prime Minister, which aims to upskill 150 million people by 2022. However, such initiatives (such as the "Skill India" program) are of a very top-down nature: the central government might be aware of a skills glut, but as long as skills are not brought into the production process (i.e. absorbed by firms on the ground), they are not going to yield growth or development.

Under current circumstances, the labor market cannot provide all new entrants with jobs. State initiatives for a reform of the VET system are motivated by an interest in combating youth unemployment in the future. But clearly, such a move would have to be complemented by firm demand for such skills. Firms have so far demanded only basic education at the secondary level, which is sufficient for labor-intensive operations in manufacturing and BPO. Firms will have little interest in employing workers through vocational trainings and apprenticeships if their skills are associated with aspirations for higher salaries. In order to exploit the potential for higher worker profitability, investments in production facilities or service processes would be needed. Such investments (i.e. capital upgrading) are largely un-enforceable unless in connection with state enterprises. In other words, unless firms collectively recognize the need to upgrade labor power in order to raise profitability, the institutional configuration will remain at a stalemate. Neither capital (firms) nor labor (employees) wants to bear the high costs of skill upgrading if the outcome is risky. The costs for technical education are at least twice as high as for general secondary education, and often even more expensive (Tilak 2003, 682). However, as mentioned earlier, it is the relatively small medium-sized enterprises for which the state would have to invest in VET capacities, but their lobbying capacities are relatively low. The large, well-connected businesses with in-house training centers which dominate the main business associations see no need to press governments to direct public investment into education and training.

3.3.5 Innovation

The idea of *Swadeshi* has also found expression in the Indian approach to innovation and technology. Indian self-reliance would, in this view, become realized only if genuinely Indian technologies are created. That feature has already been part of the Bombay Plan for the economic development of India in 1945 (Pillai 1979, 122). Accordingly, a technological paradigm of self-reliance had been established by the mid-1960s under strong government control. Foreign investments associated with technology import were heavily restricted and "allowed only in core industries where no alternative local technologies were available" (Joseph and Kakarlapudi 2014, 801). The state supervised the import of technology mainly by granting collaborations and later through licensing agreements, albeit in very few cases and in a limited number of sectors (e.g. automobiles; Pillai 1979; Altenburg et al. 2008). Joint ventures played virtually no role until the mid-1980s.[9]

The success of the Green Revolution supported the idea of science-led development, but it became clear that technological autarky would come at the cost of development. Compared to Western countries, innovation was much slower, but as India was struggling with famines and malnutrition, technology was an urgent matter. The developmental need for new technologies fueled the Indian Patent Act of 1970, which in fact allows the copying of foreign technologies. It ensured "that the final product itself could not be patented, but rather only the process undertaken to produce [it]" (Taylor 2013, 119). Foreign products were no longer protected by patent law, which allowed domestic firms to use reverse engineering in order to learn how a specific product could be produced (see Mani 2009, 44; Joseph and Kakarlapudi 2014, 801). This means that from the 1970s on, the main mode of technology transfer in the Indian industry, particularly in pharmaceuticals and chemicals, has been copying, mimicking and re-inventing.

This is understandable from a development point of view. Countries such as the United States, Japan, Korea and others have all used copying and reverse engineering as an instrument of economic catch-up (Dahlman 2009, 320). However, it had severe effects on the innovative capacity of the Indian industry. First and foremost, technology transfer through reverse engineering is cheap; consequentially, other forms of technology transfer are comparably costly. The state created fiscal incentives to develop in-house R&D units in industrial firms in the mid-1970s. This did not spur a boost in innovative activity in the corporate sector, but actually reduced the cost of copying even further (Joseph and Kakarlapudi 2014, 801). In addition, large business conglomerates profited most from this state-assisted technology transfer, in contrast to the small-scale sector in rural India (Hansen 2009). However, the combined effect of cost incentives and a lack of competition is that big business did not develop sustainable capacities for technological innovation. Historically, both spurred the creation of path dependencies that contributed to a low degree of overall technological development. Established forms of technology transfer like FDI, licensing and joint ventures were less efficient and had no effect on growth or profitability in domestic firms, also in the post-liberalization period (Mani 2009; Kathuria 2010; Joseph and Kakarlapudi 2014, 806). Thus, from an Indian firm perspective, it makes no sense to invest in R&D.

Another problem is the science-driven idea of innovation which views technology as predominantly developed in isolated labs, but neglects the importance of transforming technology into suitable products. Whereas the former is relatively easy to import, it still requires local knowledge to transfer external technologies into appropriate products for domestic markets. Because Indian policymakers have neglected this 'applied' part of technological innovation, adaptation of foreign technology to local requirements remained weak (Pillai 1979; Krishnan and Prabu 1999, 114). This sheds light on some common perceptions about innovation that seem to be less valid in emerging economies such as India. Two of those deserve special attention: the idea that innovation is crucial for growth and that innovation is related to R&D. Conventionally, innovation is deemed necessary to enhance firm productivity or to outperform competitors with better products. For firms, an increase in productivity as well as a leading position in relevant markets must yield sufficient profits that would warrant investments in innovation. We would argue that in emerging economies such as India, firms can circumvent investments in productivity by simply extending existing production lines. Similarly, the oligopolistic position of large business conglomerates reduces competition. External competitors that often have stronger market power are excluded from the Indian market. The situation would be different if Indian companies (similar to Japanese, Korean or Taiwanese firms) aimed for global export markets, thereby increasing incentives to move up the value chain. These assumptions about (global) market competition are by and large not valid for Indian capitalism. As long as these conditions are met (in other words, as long as the institutional structure of Indian capitalism remains intact), there is no need for firms to invest significantly in innovation, nor are there sufficient incentives to withdraw from the path of imitating and adapting existing products. The incentives to continue imitating are relatively high.

This makes clear that measuring innovation through established means such as the amount of money spent on R&D and the output in patents or scientific publications (as, e.g., in OECD 2013c) paints a distorted picture of the state of innovation in India and other emerging economies. This is because they can measure only cutting-edge invention and high-tech investments. From the perspective of the Indian firm, this R&D paradigm is probably less relevant in daily operations because they usually neither produce high-tech goods nor employ sophisticated techniques in the production process. It is much more important for firms to transform innovations into products that sell. In this regard, there has been a vivid debate about "frugal" products and processes and "Jugaad" innovation (Krishnan 2010; Kumar and Puranam 2012; Radjou et al. 2012). Unlike the established concepts of innovation taking place in R&D labs, Jugaad refers to "indigenous grassroot innovation" (Majumdar 2012, 280). The core idea implies that relevant innovation for Indian businesses consists of turning the adversaries of Indian capitalism into entrepreneurial strengths. In other words, the shortages, deficiencies and uncertainties of the Indian corporate economy give rise to "creative improvisation as a tool for evolving business-model solutions" that starts from the needs of the consumer (Majumdar 2012, 175). Following principles such as "do more with less" and "keep it simple" actually provides an alternative to the resource-consuming and sophisticated innovation models of the West (Radjou et al. 2012, 18).

Whether Jugaad is actually a coherent pattern of innovation in India or not, the many examples in the literature point to some important aspects. First, innovation from a firm's perspective is apparently something different from that of governments and researchers. Firms are in need of new products to earn profits, although these do not necessarily have to meet the highest technological standards, especially in a country where purchase power is comparably low. Second, there is a great deal of innovation happening, albeit not captured by established measures for innovation. The R&D content of Jugaad innovations is close to nil. However, what seems to be at work is a smart adaptation of simple solutions and existing technologies to local demands, something which was lacking in the earlier lab-based form of Indian innovation. Jugaad goes beyond the narrow focus on technological innovation and highlights the importance of contextualizing innovation within social and socio-economic parameters. This way, Jugaad is a model of innovation that is particularly targeted at the Indian market, while global (especially Western) markets play a negligible role for businesses.

While Jugaad provides a viable blueprint for Indian businesses to remain profitable, it entails an implicitly pessimistic outlook for the innovative capability of the Indian economy. Rather than hoping for a great leap of innovation, Indian business seems to be better off learning to cope with the status quo. Investment in innovation does not automatically guarantee profits, and since innovation is costly, firms tend to remain shy and conservative. In his analysis of East Asian development, Zysman identified three factors that inhibit investments in innovation and provide incentives for reverse engineering instead: market power of incumbent firms, the possibility for profitable technological reinvention and adaption, and patient capital (Zysman 1994, 250). All three apply to Indian capitalism. Only 13 business groups allocate more that 5% of their sales to R&D – usually pharmaceutical firms. The largest businesses, however, spend almost nothing on R&D. Tata and Mahindra spend approximately 1% and 2%, respectively; Bajaj & Larsen and Toubro, only 0.5% to 1%; Ambani and Birla, less than 0.5% and 40% of all business groups do not invest in R&D at all (Mazumdar 2008b, 22). Liberalization had no effect on domestic innovative capability and only positively affected R&D activities for foreign firms (Vishwasrao and Bosshardt 2001; Mani 2009; Joseph and Kakarlapudi 2014, 805). The innovative laziness of Indian firms is economically very rational: "there is a *weak correlation* between how much money your firm spends in R&D and how well it performs in terms of developing and marketing products that generate a significant financial return" (Radjou et al. 2012, 10; Altenburg et al. 2008). As long as Indian capitalists and politicians focus on the domestic market as they have done in the last decades, this is less problematic than following an export-oriented strategy for which India currently lacks the technological comparative capabilities.

However, firms are understandably reluctant to take on the costs of technological upgrading. All major business associations were, until recently, lukewarm about innovation and usually called for stronger engagement by the state in the form of public innovation initiatives (which materialized in numerous promotion programs). So here again, state activity in this central element of capitalism is crucial. Despite all incentives and privatization, the state still is responsible for 63% of India's R&D, while in China 71% of the national R&D activity is undertaken by business enterprises (Mani 2009, 43). As much as 30% of India's R&D goes to the pharma sector, but expenses have risen since 2005, when the Indian patent law was changed in order to make it compliant with WTO rules (Mani 2009, 44; Mehta 2011, 63). The success of the Indian pharma sector is actually a vivid example of the efficiency of state-permeated capitalism: Indian pharma firms could perform well because they enjoyed long-standing protection against external competition, mostly through the business-friendly Patent Act. In fact, pre-reform growth trend rates were much higher than after 1991 (Mehta 2011, 63). The new patent law of 2005 is made to suit WTO legislation, but exemptions have been made for food, chemicals, and drugs. It also grants patent durations of only five years (Joseph and Kakarlapudi 2014, 801). But even these exemptions do not prevent the Indian state from protecting the Indian drug industry from external competitors. The Supreme Court of India decided against the claim for patent infringement by Novartis in 2013, arguing that incremental innovations are not covered by Indian patent protection. This decision not only has important effects for a range of similar cases before Indian courts, but also expands the possibility for Indian pharma firms to extensively copy foreign drugs.

Thus, there are no credible signs that the Indian state will engage in an innovation program effort similar to the Green Revolution in the 1960s. The new Science, Technology and Innovation policy of 2013 promotes the idea of Jugaad and frugality as an "Indian Model of Innovation" (as the Chairman of the National Innovation Council proudly writes in the Introduction to Radjou et al. 2012, xvi). Essentially, the government has passed the ball back to the business sector by proposing the status quo of a low-level and spontaneous form of innovation as a coherent strategy. Although it acknowledges that innovation is more than labs and has to account for inclusivity and the poor, it denies a commitment to increase R&D and related spending (Abrol 2013; Mani 2013). Thus, neither business nor the state is seriously interested in a concerted effort to upgrade India's innovative capabilities. In the short term, this is not problematic for Indian businesses, as the status quo provides the easiest and most cost-efficient way to achieve profitability. Yet it depends on the stability of flanking institutions, most notably the willingness and ability to protect Indian business from external competitors.

3.3.6 Domestic markets

Technology transfer and the structure of the Indian domestic market are linked together. In most cases of catch-up development, infant industries were protected from external competition and matured by serving the home market long before they were profitable enough to enter global markets. The Indian economy, however, is different in two respects. First, although import substitution was abandoned as an official development strategy in the 1970s, the mechanisms of domestic market protection remain present today. In a way, India is still following an ISI strategy, albeit an 'unintentional' one. Second, the home market for domestic firms has never been exhausted, as with the Latin American examples of the 1970s. This, however, was the main reason why countries turned to an export-led development strategy in the first place, as the domestic market could not generate growth sufficiently. Additionally, building an industrial base at home required imports of capital or credit, both of which strained the current account. In India, in contrast, domestic demand is by far not exhausted and therefore an abundant growth potential exists. Growth of domestic demand takes place at a low level of purchase power and is most dynamic in income ranges just above the poverty line (see section 4.2.3).

Due to the protective measures of the Indian state, export orientation is very costly for Indian firms. It would require investments in product innovation and marketing as well as the establishment of a service infrastructure for customer relations abroad (Kumar 2015). Serving the domestic middle classes, however, implies an orientation towards completely different products, not in cutting-edge technology and premium segments but in "good enough" products (Bijapurkar 2007; Radjou et al. 2012, 24, 90). As we saw, there is no connection between innovation and growth for Indian firms, and liberalization did not change this. In fact, the opposite is true: the medium- and low-technology industry is the "only industrial subgroup which witnessed an overall rise in the trend growth rate in the post reform period" (Mehta 2011, 63). The market for sophisticated motor vehicles and machinery in India is meager, not just because of their high prices but also for practical reasons (lack of suitable roads and buildings, lack of skilled maintenance personnel). The low-end structure of the Indian home market explains the persistent attractiveness of copying and re-invention. Reverse-engineered products might not be as good as the original ones, but they are sufficient for the demands of Indian consumers. Generics, in this respect, are a prominent example of "good enough" products. All in all, the large domestic market in India has served as an obstacle to R&D and FDI activities in Indian firms (Altenburg et al. 2008, 330). As a consequence, the list of the biggest companies in India is not only of completely Indian origin, but most of the firms on it have a very low presence in the global market.

The size and the exclusive access of domestic firms to home markets made the domestic framework the ultimate reference frame for Indian businesses.[10] Indian business did not care about exports at all:

> business persons and business associations [. . .] did not know or care about the ongoing WTO negotiations till as late as 1999–2000 [. . .] the CII, the so-called professional association, thought that the WTO was not at all important in the mid and late 1990s.
>
> (Sinha 2011, 467)

As previously discussed, India made its Patent Act only haphazardly compatible with WTO regulations. The Indian state is nevertheless committed to taking a hard stance against trade liberalization or any intrusion into the domestic economic order, simply because the large (and increasing) domestic demand allows for a high degree of independence from external market pressures.

The importance of a large domestic market is a particularity of Indian capitalism that it shares with a small number of other large emerging economies. It is a crucial precondition for the kind of development that India has been undergoing since the 1980s. Protection of this sheltered market for indigenous business by the state is a necessary but insufficient condition for its salience. Another necessary factor for the stable growth over the last two decades is the fact that the particular structure of the domestic market complements other crucial institutions in Indian capitalism.

3.4 Comparative advantages, institutional complementarities and contradictions of Indian capitalism

During the 1990s and 2000s, India was able to grow with previously unknown speed and relative stability. Although the reforms of the early 1990s are often held responsible, it is clear that the institutional structure of Indian capitalism actually has not changed much. It seems that the elements of a relatively successful form of capitalism were present but required some kind of re-arranging in order to create a somewhat efficient form of capitalism. Above all, Indian industry has been able to specialize in particular segments and develop them continuously without being jostled around by external shocks, erratic policy changes and macroeconomic turbulences. The state has been responsible for keeping the conditions stable by defending Indian business against these disturbances by any means. Although the state dominated the Indian economy in the decade after independence, it finally chose a strategy that would accommodate private business. India took a different trajectory from that of most other developing countries when it comes to industrial policy, debt management and integration into the global economy. For this reason, India has not been shaken by dramatic crises 'from the outside' as with other developing countries; the budget crisis of late 1990 has perhaps been the only significant episode in which India had to react to sudden external changes (triggered by the Gulf Crisis in 1990–1991).[11] Other than that, Indian capitalism developed a remarkable immunity to external distortions, whether attempts by foreign liberal capitalists to penetrate the Indian market or external markets that quickly change the terms for foreign credit, or the exchange rate of the rupee. As India has amassed huge currency reserves, it was able not only to pay back all external debt immediately, but also to defend the value of the rupee against foreign speculators.

India's growth did not stem from a turn to export-led strategies. Exports played a minor role in the growth story of the 1990s and 2000s. Also, growth cannot be attributed to a thriving services and IT sector alone because, as discussed previously, its impact on the development of Indian growth has been relatively modest. Instead, Indian businesses developed a specialization in the medium- and low-tech sector, for which the capacities were already available. Yet it required the proactive engagement of the state to create demand for these goods and services.

This combination, with a particular class of products and corresponding demand, proved to be India's comparative advantage in the 1990s and 2000s. Thus, the Indian case casts some doubts on the general hypothesis that growth requires increasing technological innovation. Apparently, emerging economies are able to grow without subscribing to the (Western) R&D paradigm. Theoretically, India can thrive on the comparative advantage of large domestic markets for products of low and medium sophistication indefinitely. As India is still rather poor on average but has a very young population, there is ample room for rising incomes and, thereby, domestic demand.

There is no single factor that has determined Indian growth since the 1980s. It is the combination of the different but compatible effects of the institutions of Indian capitalism that made a relatively stable growth path possible. By slightly changing the crucial institutions of Indian capitalism and re-arranging their mutual relations, these institutions acquired a high degree of complementarity that gave the Indian economy a boost. Some of these complementarities deserve to be explicated. Clearly, the highly concentrated corporate ownership structure complements the negligible role of financial markets in financing investments. If firms depended on (foreign) venture capital or company debt, shareholders would not accept the dominance of insider control in Indian businesses. Indian firms can draw on financial sources from within the business group, and as such, they do not have to negotiate (and to compromise) with external creditors or investors. As a consequence, the Indian government does not have to provide conditions to attract foreign capital, thereby keeping the institutional structure of Indian capitalism intact.

The strong position of business groups in Indian corporate governance limits the degree of inter-firm competition, which allows firms to remain patient and to refrain from investing in productivity through upskilling labor and/or obtaining higher technology. The fact that labor is fragmented and informal and that skill levels and technological sophistication are low not only drives down costs for Indian business, but it also ensures that they can avoid future costs by inhibiting upgrading processes. Any upward movement in industrial relations (through higher wages), education and training (through upskilling) and innovation (through R&D) would increase the costs for Indian enterprises. If one of these three factors were to rise, the other two would eventually follow – potentially threatening the stability of the current growth regime. As high technology products currently provide less profits than medium- and low-tech goods, an increase in technological intensity comes with the danger of decreasing returns. Thus, in the realms of industrial relations and education and innovation, we identify mutual complementarities among institutions that provide clear objectives to Indian firms on how to behave in order to be most profitable. Yet this complementarity is a rather delicate equilibrium of the relevant institutions and as such, has to be protected. This means that foreign technology and foreign products, which are more sophisticated, have to be kept away from the Indian economy where workers are not too ambitious. All this works only when supply and demand is administered and limited – a necessary condition to maintain control over a market that is large enough to absorb sufficient volumes in order to make enterprise profitable, but at the same time exclusive enough to enjoy monopolistic advantages. The combination of large and monopolistic domestic markets, along with static corporate structures in the form of family-led business groups, provides strong incentives to refrain from investing in upgrading strategies.

Overall, the economic structure of India is characterized by mutually supporting institutions which in combination produce a very stable but less dynamic type of capitalism compared to China. For stakeholders, its stable and static character has important advantages. There is minimal competition, minimal upward pressure for wages, education and innovation, and there are no significant rivalries among competing capital fractions. These dynamics that are a regular part of capitalist economies, and that could easily inhibit disruptive qualities, are strictly harnessed and rendered relatively harmless. True, this led to a growing but overall low degree of productivity in the Indian economy (Rani 2009); but ironically, Indian business learned to turn low productivity into a comparative advantage because it allowed a transition to a strategy of extensive production based on cheap labor. Being unwilling (due to monopolistic profits) and unable (to establish an efficient VET system) to turn to a productivity-led growth model, Indian firms had a strong interest in shaping the institutions of the economy in a conservative way. What followed was a case of path dependency. As institutions became more and more part of this low-productivity growth regime, the potential costs for leaving this model continued to rise and provided more incentives to remain on the trodden path and seek to perfect it. In this way, institutional complementarities amplify themselves and reinforce the effectiveness of Indian capitalism as a whole.

Business alone would never have been able to maintain such a growth regime. Without the active contribution of the state in restructuring Indian capitalism, this model could not have produced growth rates for more than three decades. But it is important to recognize the specific ways in which the state contributes to the Indian growth regime – in other words, the particular kind of statehood that was crucial for the effective activity of the state in India. Here, we have to go conceptually beyond the established discourse about the state in the economy. The Indian state clearly plays a role as 'owner', as it holds the majority in half of the biggest companies on the subcontinent. It also clearly played a large role as a traditional maker and implementer of policies (McCartney 2009, 217). These accounts, however, often take state capacity for granted in terms of the capacity of the state to effectively guide and regulate the economy. In India, the state took on a more direct role in the economy, without acting in a top-down commanding manner. Instead, it positioned itself as a partner of business within the Indian political economy. By establishing a partnership mode based on close connections at the administrative level, it turned to a new form of coordination that is itself a result of the simultaneous strength and weakness of the state (Rudolph and Rudolph 1987). By relying on a fine web of interpersonal relations, the state gets closer to the 'operational business', which allows for a more nuanced and targeted kind of regulation. This smooth permeation of the economy through interpersonal webs proved to be a very efficient method of coordination in Indian capitalism.

In a comparative perspective, the Indian state might not be as strong as the Korean state in the pursuit of economic development; yet it is not as weak as the average satellite state in peripheral economies. Rather than looking at actual policies or reform packages, we might learn more by investigating the state's "non-decisions" (Strange 1986). It is striking how little the Indian economy is actually liberalized, despite the initial verve the reform movement took in the early 1990s and the enthusiasm it created on the side of liberal observers. If liberalization had truly happened, we would observe a stronger role of market-based mechanisms and a greater intrusion by foreign capital. It can be said that the state is not putting much energy into driving liberalization and at times tries to drag the process out. Compared to China, the Indian state is less proactive but often compensates for the organizational deficiencies of private business.

The future success of Indian capitalism depends on how India is able to deal with a number of problems that are looming or exist as potential challenges. For one, India's economy would have to grow further in order to achieve a more thorough integration of the lower classes into the economy. At the same time, industrial growth has to remain limited to some extent. If India experienced a rural exodus similar to China, it would not only have dramatic effects on land and food security, but the state and central governments would also not be equipped to deal with such massive social transformations. This touches upon the perhaps most severe challenge to Indian capitalism, which stems from the political arena. On the one hand, corruption and bribery can turn into a truly malignant element that absorbs much of India's economic capacities. At the same time, full liberal transparency, as often advocated by Western commentators, cannot be the alternative because this would contradict the social foundations of the Indian economy. On the other hand, there is a high probability of the politicization of economic affairs in Indian democracy, especially as the Indian society is torn along a number of fundamental cleavages between urban and rural, poor and rich as well as religious and caste-related lines. If political leaders mobilize on the distributional aspect of Indian wealth, they can put social groups against each other and leave the economy in deep-seated societal conflicts. In China, these developments are somewhat limited due to the absence of liberal democracy. In Brazil, the very success of capitalism has indirectly fueled political and social upheaval. There is no guarantee that India will be preserved from such developments.

Notes

1 An early case of privatization led to the joint venture of the Japanese motor company Suzuki with the local Maruti brand. Alhough Suzuki held only a minority share, it served as an example of selling out to foreign capital. Bajaj himself would have been keen on acquiring the shares in Maruti that Suzuki eventually got (Piramal 1996, 126), but his conviction was that such sales to foreign investors should be the absolute exception.

2 Compare to, e.g., Galtung (1971).

3 For example, the Deora family (which is close to the Gandhis) is perhaps the most influential family in Mumbai's Congress. Murli Deora used to dominate Mumbai politics

in the 1970s, for a time as president of the Regional Congress Committee, trusted and respected by all large businesses alike (The Hindu 2014). His son, Milind Deora, became Lok Sabha member and minister as well.

4 Effective tax exemptions and reductions can thus be seen as 'negative' corruption, by which funds that flow from politics to business to persuade the latter to invest in the state or municipality of the former.

5 The Aam Aadmi Party literally calls itself the "party of the common people". It first won the municipal elections in New Delhi but failed to scored in the Lok Sabha elections so far.

6 See the data compiled by the Association for Democratic Reforms on www.myneta.info.

7 The Reliance Group split when the two brothers, Anil and Mukesh Ambani, decided to separate their operations.

8 Allen et al. (2010, 149) even estimate that state banks account for 80% of all assets and deposits.

9 And then the joint venture between the state-owned Maruti Udyog with the Japanese car manufacturer Suzuki would still be the exception rather than the rule.

10 As an illustration, for Rahul Bajaj the main goal of doing business was to be the biggest car manufacturer in India. If he could not overtake Maruti, he said in the mid-1980s, "I don't want to be in cars" (cited in Piramal 1996, 120).

11 India went through a number of heavy crises, most notably recurrent famines in particular states throuout the 1960s and 1980s.

4 Brazil

On the way to becoming a state-led economy (again)?[1]

In contrast to China and India, Brazil was a more mixed case of state-led capitalism during the first decade of the 21st century.[2] On the one side, the Brazilian state played an important role in economic decision-making, for example through its famous development bank BNDES (Banco Nacional de Desenvolvimento Econômico e Social). The stable and nationally dominated corporate governance system permitted long-term strategies, supported by large currency reserves and low foreign indebtedness. A sustained investment into education and technological upgrading has led to a number of highly competitive enterprises within a diversified industry. On the other side, many sectors of the Brazilian economy continue to be dominated by foreign multinationals. Brazil still has a fairly open financial account and suffers from fluctuations in international currency and financial markets. A fragmented political system inhibits smooth economic policy coordination.

Brazilian capitalism is also a moving target, showing several reversals of course over the last decades as well as shifting balances between domestic class fractions. From a historic perspective Brazil was more open to economic conditions of the world market than China and India, and was thus fully affected by the 1980s debt crisis and subsequent structural adjustments, including substantial privatization and denationalization. However, Brazil not only has an important history of state-capitalist industrialization between 1930 and 1980, but it also has returned to a more state-driven model during the 2000s, before reversing course again after 2012. Slowly, starting in the second half of Dilma Rousseff's first administration (2011–2014) and continuing during her second, but much amplified by her impeachment and the subsequent Temer presidency (2016–2018) as well as his successor Bolsonaro (from 2019), Brazil moved back to a more liberal model.

Even during the recent state-driven phase – which will be the topic of this chapter – Brazil suffered from adverse macroeconomic conditions. These conditions are in part a remainder from the measures chosen to combat the 'lost decade' of the 1980s, in particular extreme inflation, but also reflect the dividing weights and preferences between capital fractions in Brazil, with commodity exporters and the financial sector as main beneficiaries of recent macro conditions, and manufacturers as losers. Whereas high interest rates and a highly valued exchange rate have helped to combat inflation, they have at the same time reduced the inclination of Brazilian industrialists to invest for regaining global or domestic market shares.

4.1 Contemporary Brazilian capitalism in global context and historical evolution

Brazil has the longest and most consistent history of a developmental state in Latin America (Cervo 2012, 28). Since the 1930s, the original dominance of primary goods export has been relegated to a certain degree in favor of a state-led industrialization strategy. Until about 1980, both civil and military governments followed a fairly successful strategy of import-substitution industrialization combined with corporatism. The global debt crisis and the related fiscal crisis of the state brought this model to an end, and after the lost decade of the 1980s Brazil turned toward a more liberal model during the 1990s, characterized by a much higher openness to global capital flows. During the 2000s, however, Brazil has again favored a more state-led capitalism, now based on a fiscally somewhat sounder model with substantial commodity exports and a growing number of Brazilian multinationals. Brazil thus shows a "cyclical pattern of development" (Abu-el-Haj 2007, 111), moving from state-led to liberal and back to state-led capitalism.[3]

The state was at the origin of Brazilian industrialization, dating back at least to the government of Getúlio Vargas and his slogan of the *estado novo* in the late 1930s (Kingstone 1999, 29). More important for the key political decisions favoring the developmental state project in Brazil (such as the promotion of the auto industry and the setup of BNDES and Petrobras) were the democratic governments between 1945 and 1964 (Schneider 2015a, 119). Both civil and military governments subsequently pursued a strategy of speeding up economic growth based on rapid industrialization, with a selective role for foreign multinationals (Baer and Figueroa 1981, 60). During the 1970s, for example, the exchange rate was kept artificially low with an average taxation of 50% on the import of industrial goods and a subsidy of 50% on the export of industrial goods (Diniz and Bresser-Pereira 2012, 202). This import-substitution industrialization strategy was temporarily very successful in terms of GDP, particularly during the *milagre econômico* with average growth rates of 11.5% per year from 1969 to 1973 under military rule (Schmalz 2012, 266).

At the center of the developmentalist model stood large-scale state interventions in the economy towards a broadly diversified industrial structure. This included a special focus on sectors that were deemed of strategic significance, such as ethanol production, steel production, civilian aircraft, petroleum exploration and agricultural research (Schneider 2013, 169). These interventions were combined with the appeasement of capital and labor via corporatist institutions and patronage resources, with an asymmetric construction favoring capital (Kingstone 1999, 30; Boschi 2013, 127). The shadow side of the model included not only the exclusion of large groups of the population and the weakening or destruction of democratic institutions, but also its negative long-term fiscal resource balance. Both imports of industrial input and the need to buy political support led to large fiscal deficits and foreign borrowing (Kingstone 1999, 32). The exhaustion of the model became obvious in the late 1970s, particularly when rising oil prices and the related availability of (then) cheap foreign credit led to the explosion of foreign debt, from US$5.7 billion in 1970 to US$71.5 billion in 1980 (Schmalz 2012, 266), or from 17.7% of GDP in 1973 to 27% in 1980 (Leubolt 2015, 170).

After the interest rate hike of the US Fed ("Volcker Shock") around 1980, the debt situation became completely unsustainable, and Brazil had to accept strict conditionalities in exchange for a loan from the IMF. The 1980s was a period of very low growth and high inflation as well as political instability: the so-called lost decade which was not limited to Brazil alone. Several heterodox attempts to stabilize the situation failed, including the Plano Cruzado in 1986 and the Plano Collor in 1991. In order to overcome the deep crisis of the 1980s, the Cardoso era (1992–1994 as Minister under President Collor de Mello, 1995–2002 as President) saw a very thorough change towards liberal (and dependent) capitalism, with an important role for global capital markets. The Cardoso governments opened the Brazilian markets by drastically reducing tariffs, privatizing state companies and encouraging foreign multinationals to acquire Brazilian firms. The period saw more than 1200 acquisitions by foreign multinationals and a reduction of state enterprises among the top 100 Brazilian companies from 44% in 1989 to 21% in 1999 (Schmalz 2012, 269). Given that ISI had created a particularly rich field of manufacturing companies in Brazil, the Brazilian manufacturing sector became a particularly attractive target for foreign multinationals, leading to a rapid process of denationalization, for example, in the auto parts industry (Schneider 2013, 76–7). Denationalization moved hand-in-hand with deindustrialization, and the share of industry in GDP declined from 40% in 1994 to 27.1% in 2002 (Dierckx 2015, 133). Funding for infrastructure became extremely limited, leading to shortcomings in ports, airports, public mass transit and roads that are still hampering Brazilian growth dynamics (Casanova and Kassum 2014, 100).

Although leading to a certain denationalization and deindustrialization of the Brazilian economy (Cervo 2012, 30; Diniz and Bresser-Pereira 2012, 193), the neoliberal reforms pursued in the Cardoso era crucially succeeded in reducing inflation, in particular by creating a new currency that was (temporarily) linked to the US dollar, even if this required overvaluation and high interest rates (Leubolt 2015, 195, 197–202). Moreover, the liberalization of the Brazilian economy did not lead to a complete destruction of domestic industrial capital and its dominance by foreign investors, as occurred in the dependent market economies of East Central Europe (Nölke and Vliegenthart 2009) and in other Latin American countries (Bizberg 2014). Important development institutions such as BNDES were preserved (Boschi 2013, 131). The surviving private or (partially) privatized companies (e.g. Embraer or Vale) became more competitive than before (Abu-El-Haj 2007, 110; Fleury and Fleury 2011). The very comprehensive Brazilian ISI strategy of the previous decades in effect led to a liberal form of capitalism that was less deindustrialized than in other Latin American economies undergoing neoliberal reforms during the 1990s (Phillips 2004, 70). During the last years of the Cardoso administration, however, national industrialists and associated developmentalists increasingly became dissatisfied with the liberal model. Several issues were at stake (Abu-El-Haj 2007, 109; Schmalz 2012, 269–70). These included the increasing denationalization of the Brazilian economy mentioned earlier, but also fairly low growth and the volatility that went hand-in-hand with greater exposure to world market conditions, international financial agencies and global financial markets. Of particular concern were developments in the strongly growing financial sector, where very high real interest rates were successful in combating inflation, but also led to massive capital inflow and an overvaluation of the Real. This led to further discouragement of industrial investments, leading to suboptimal growth rates and high budget deficits (Barbosa-Filho 2006, 5–6). Brazil experienced the problems of a "growth cum foreign savings strategy" (Bresser-Pereira and Nakano 2002) in a very forceful manner.

The (re)turn to state-led capitalism had already started in the late phase of the second Cardoso administration and was carefully continued when the first Lula administration took office in 2002. The neo-mercantilist program involved measures such as non-institutional restrictions on imports using exchange rates, regulation of financial flows, and active promotion of exports (Abu-El-Haj 2007, 109; see also later in this section). Although the program was not fully implemented, exports strongly increased and were considered important in order to accumulate currency reserves and decrease vulnerability in global financial markets and institutions. At the same time, export promotion policies favored parts of domestic capital, particularly in the (agricultural) commodity sector, thereby securing their support for the new state-driven economic strategy (Abu-El-Haj 2007, 111).

Given widespread concerns about the leftist character of the administration (as demonstrated by strong capital flight) and the limited support in Congress, the newly elected Lula government made sure to broadly continue the macroeconomic course of the late Cardoso administration, as promised in the famous "Letter to the Brazilian People" during the 2002 electoral campaign. Thus, the macroeconomic "tripod" of fiscal prudence, exchange rate flexibility and inflation targeting was upheld (Canuto and Schellekens 2014, 2; Dierckx 2015, 136–41). However, a major strategy change reduced vulnerability to external financial investors. Foreign public debt was reduced from about 14.3% of GDP in 2002 to nearly zero during the first Lula term, by paying back these debts and rescheduling the remaining debt with domestic debtors, which was supported by a favorable trade balance, particularly driven by agricultural exports (Schmalz 2012, 271). At the same time, short-term debts that were vulnerable to fluctuations were replaced by more medium- to long-term debts (López and Garralda 2014, 11–14). Brazil also multiplied its foreign currency reserves, an important buffer against externally induced fluctuations, from US$54 billion in 2005 to US$239 billion in 2009 (World Bank total reserves databank, accessed 26 August 2015). These deliberalization changes proved to be very important during the 2008–2009 financial crisis, which impacted Brazil much less than otherwise would have been the case (López and Garralda 2014, 14–17). Still, the global financial crisis highlighted the openness of the Brazilian economy to capital mobility, when massive portfolio outflows first took place in spite of sound economic fundamentals, to be followed by equally massive portfolio inflows after January 2009. In response to these massive speculative flows, the government introduced very moderate temporary capital controls in the form of a series of taxes on foreign financial investments (Dierckx 2015, 149–50).

In addition, the recessionary effects of the financial crisis were successfully combatted by a public investment program, a massive increase in "earmarked" (subsidized) lending and regulatory changes that led to a boom in housing, also for low-income individuals (López and Garralda 2014, 18–21). Moreover, the Lula governments, succeeded by the first Dilma administration, strongly expanded some social policies started in the late Cardoso administration. These policies, most notably a strongly increasing minimum wage and the "Bolsa Família" cash transfer program, led to an expansion of domestic demand, another boon for domestic industrial capital (see section 4.3.6. The latter was also supported by more public funding for firms, substantial growth in financial resources for industrial and technological policies, and national content policies (see section 4.3.5. As mentioned earlier, these policies were very successful in stimulating economic development, at least until the early 2010s.

Still, the Brazilian economy in the first decade of the new millennium should be characterized as in a transition phase towards a fully state-driven economy (Diniz and Bresser-Pereira 2012, 207; Schmalz 2012, 265), as a "hybrid of neo-developmentalist neoliberalism" (Dierckx 2015, 145) or as "liberal neo-developmentalism" (Ban 2013). Not only were the push for technological upgrading (see section 4.3.5 and the redistribution of income in favor of domestic demand (see section 4.3.6 limited, but also the neo-mercantilist macroeconomic program remained haphazard, e.g. by shying away from the introduction of more comprehensive capital controls, or through a reinstatement of the mechanism combatting the Dutch disease before 1990.[4] The large trade surplus in the agricultural sectors has proved to be a mixed blessing under conditions of a still fairly open financial account, contributing to overvaluation of the currency and even deindustrialization (Diniz and Bresser-Pereira 2012, 207). Between 2003 and 2010, the Real appreciated by 74% against the US dollar (Thompson 2011). There is now a fairly broad consensus of economists from different theoretical perspectives that long-term overvaluation of the domestic currency was one of the major causes of the mixed Brazilian economic record in manufacturing during the previous two decades (Nassif et al. 2015, 1314–15).[5] However, compared to other major emerging markets, Brazil still had the lowest share of US-dollar-denominated bonds, with most bonds issued in Real. Moreover, the central bank had ample reserves and could step in to support currency hedges to companies in times of stress (IIF 2015, 3–4).

By the mid-2010s, Brazil had halted or even reversed its movement towards state-led capitalism, arguably because of exhaustion of the moderately social-democratic Lula-Dilma model. Domestic demand still was stifled by a very unequal distributive situation, in spite of the improvements of the previous decade, as witnessed by the reduction in absolute poverty and an improving Gini coefficient (see section 4.3.6. The liberalization of credit to lower- and middle-class households that was temporarily able to support domestic demand had also run its course, due to strongly increasing private indebtedness (see section 4.2). The state was no longer able to compensate for decreasing private demand, due to an increasing budget deficit (and the renouncement of more radical redistribution measures). External demand for Brazilian commodities, although not central to Brazil's rather closed economy (see section 4.3.6, had suffered from lower growth rates in China. Because of the weakness of both international and domestic demand, growth rates had already been meager since 2011. A crisis of confidence, also supported by rising political turbulence (see section 4.2), lead to a full-blown recession in 2015–2016.

However, the stagnation of the semi-state-led model in the mid-2010s also had supply-side causes. These can be linked to a haphazard turn towards the establishment of the institutions necessary for a successful state-driven economy. Most notably, labor productivity was stagnating based on increased wages combined with slow capital accumulation, as well as low investments and lagging improvements in education (Canuto and Schellekens 2014, 3–4; see also section 4.3.4). Correspondingly, the domestic manufacturing industry was continuously losing ground vis-à-vis large-scale agricultural exporters as well as services (e.g. finance), thereby weakening the political case for a massive state-led industrialization strategy (Bresser-Pereira 2015, 6–7).

Due to increasing domestic political opposition and decreasing fiscal room to maneuver, the Dilma Rousseff government returned to a more liberal path, as, e.g., indicated by the appointment of Chicago-trained Joaquim Levy as Minister of Finance in January 2015. All in all, the volatility of political majorities and the remaining reliance on global economic developments such as short-term currency flows have inhibited the long-term stability necessary for a fundamental change of capitalist institutions to a coherent state-led model in Brazil.

4.2 Coordination in the Brazilian political economy[6]

Though economic coordination in Brazil shares important commonalities with China and India, it has become heavily contested over the last two decades. Compared to the other two countries, coordination in Brazil during its state-led decade was more inclusive, but also more controversial. Not only a more prominent role of foreign capital, but also a government with a prominent role for a labor party clearly were among the most important factors inhibiting smooth (and exclusive) coordination between representatives of state and domestic industry.

However, a state following only the traditional preferences of Brazilian capital would not have led to the dynamic state-led growth witnessed during the first decade of the 21st century, or the upgrading of Brazilian capitalism in terms of skills and innovation. For example, during the 1990s, Brazil's economic policymaking still was famous for its "stumbling ad hoc pragmatism" (Kingstone 1999, 257) that was unable to create a coherent policy program. Thus, it is not without irony (or tragedy) that large parts of the Brazilian bourgeoisie continue to oppose governments led by a labor party for principled reasons (opposition to a 'leftist' government). This is especially noteworthy given that the latter pursued a "social democratic" economic long-term-development strategy that was primarily intended to benefit domestic industry (Diniz and Bresser Pereira 2012, 207). Although some industry associations have temporarily supported the labor party governments, this has proven to be an unstable alliance, particularly under more difficult economic conditions. The issues pursued by the labor party included rising wages, higher taxation for increased public expenditures, an increased role of public banks and political guidance on investment, all issues that were not too popular with most representatives of industry. Also socially, the labor party was not part of the densely knit network of domestic family capitalists and the state, traditionally dominating economic decision-making, based on a similar social and educational background. The rise of the labor party thus somewhat complicated the established coordination processes in the Brazilian political economy, even if parts of the party became part of the establishment during the Lula and Dilma administrations. When still a minister, Dilma "favored generally 'an intimate relationship, in the good sense' between government and business" (Schneider 2013, 171). Still, the democratization of political decision-making together with the end of the military dictatorship and the later rise of the Worker's Party "broke up many cozy backroom relations between business groups and authoritarian governments" (Schneider 2013, 140).

However, Brazil broadly shares an economic coordination model with China and India, based on strong informal ties between individual state agency representatives and legislators on the one side, and domestic capitalists on the other. Similar to India, business associations are rather weak, which is a marked contrast to the informally powerful role of individual Brazilian capitalists (Phillips 2004, 195; Schneider 2013, 147). Business is rather fragmented, focused on the solution of specific company problems and not on exercising broad political power (Kingstone 1999, 244–6). At the same time, we do not find a powerful, centralized state with an overarching planning body as in the classical East Asia model. In contrast, the Brazilian state is strongly fragmented between competing ministries and agencies internally (Phillips 2004, 237–9). State-business cooperation is strongly personalized (Bazuchi et al. 2013). Given the power of individual politicians (e.g. legislators) and the weakness of most collective organizations such as parties or bureaucracies, organizing a powerful business association is of limited usefulness. Still, in contrast to many other countries in Latin America as well as to the Brazil of previous ages (Evans 1995), the Brazilian state during the first decade of PT rule had developed a fairly high degree of autonomy and was able to interfere in the economy, sometimes even against powerful opposition (Gaitán and Boschi 2015, 179).

The importance of informal relations between the Brazilian state agencies and domestic capitalists has become famous based on the social network analyses conducted by Brazilian scholar Sergio Lazzarini (2011). His book *Capitalism of Ties* (*Capitalismo de Lacos*) includes a formal analysis of the ties among private capitalists, and between private capitalists and the state. The network analysis of over 800 enterprises in 1996, 2003 and 2009 demonstrates that these informal networks not only are a product of the established ties between the old oligarchy and the state, but also intensified during the privatizations of the 1990s. The privatization auctions usually favored investor consortia active in several companies and linked to several investment sources, including the state bank BNDES and the pension funds of state-controlled enterprises. Correspondingly, the privatizations intensified the dense connections between state representatives and domestic capitalists. The PT governments have built upon these close linkages in order to combine the long-term stability of Brazilian capitalism with a high degree of consensus and piecemeal changes (see May et al. 2019b, 100 for a more detailed discussion).

Cooperation between business and state, as well as other social forces, is supported by the prominent articulation of a national developmentalist ideology that is supported by prestige projects such as the 2014 World Cup and the 2016 Olympics (Ozturk and Farhan 2015, 13). Moreover, the establishment of two dominant programmatic centrist parties (PSDB and PT) during the Cardoso, Lula and Dilma presidencies has contributed to the ability of the Brazilian government to formulate coherent policies (Schneider 2013, 177–8). Particularly in comparison to other Latin American countries, this coherence seems to be an important precondition for the successful implementation of long-term development strategies.

While Brazil thus shares some important state-business coordination features with China and India, it also shows some special features that make this economic coordination comparatively more contested. These features include (1) the incorporation of foreign capital as a third party, (2) the deep divisions between domestic capitalist class fractions in Brazil as well as between these fractions and the new/lower middle class, (3) the functioning of Congress based on individualism and local constituencies and (4) the additional institutional fragmentation brought about by the rise of the labor party and its allies (for a more detailed debate, see May and Nölke 2018, 12–15). In addition, the large sections of the population working in the informal sector have proven to be an unstable supporter of the PT governments, sometimes defecting to neoliberal alternatives (Leubolt 2015, 194; Saad Filho 2015), even if they have a number of common interests with the working class and lower middle class (e.g. expansion of the formal labor markets, redistribution of resources, provision of public services). Their motivations for the support of neoliberal parties vary, from a preference for strong leadership and order or an aversion to 'insiders' (including workers in formal contracts) to short-term economic benefits, including higher purchasing power regarding imported goods stemming from an overvalued exchange rate (Anderson 2011; Saad Filho 2015). Given that the very poor are most sensitive to reduced economic growth due to the absence of safeguards such as formal contracts and social security nets, they tend to shift political allegiances very quickly in times of economic crisis (Leubolt 2015, 194).

4.3 The institutional foundations of Brazilian capitalism

4.3.1 Corporate governance

Similar to the cases of China and India, ownership of Brazilian companies is usually concentrated, and control rests with insiders. The state plays a prominent role, for example, through important pockets of state control via pyramid schemes and the utilization of pension funds from major state-controlled companies for strategic investments. These features are meant to make sure that long-term development strategies are possible in principle, under firm national control. In contrast to China and India, however, foreign companies dominate important parts of industry, thereby bringing a certain measure of volatility and external dependency into play.

Most large Brazilian companies are exchange-listed, but usually dominated by family shareholdings or other major holders such as the state (see the data in Table 4.1). In 16 of the 25 biggest private Brazilian firms, families play a decisive role in corporate control. The majority of exchange-listed firms are controlled by pyramid schemes, usually with families as ultimately the largest shareholders (Aguilera et al. 2012, 326). In 93% of Brazilian companies, one single shareholder controls a share of more than 20%. In 88%, the largest shareholder is of Brazilian origin. Even the liberal economic reforms of the 1990s by the Cardozo administrations were unable to break the grip of domestic capital on Brazilian companies, although the dominant role of family capitalism has been modernized, moving from majority to minority control (Abu-El-Haj 2007, 106). Later, families were complemented by domestic banks and institutional investors such as pension funds (Aguilera et al. 2012, 322–6), as well as the state, mainly via BNDES and its holding branch BNDESPAR (for a more detailed discussion of the latter, see May et al. 2019b, 101–3). Though only 6 of the 30 non-foreign firms in Table 4.1 are owned by the state, 9 have substantial positions by BNDES and 10 by social security pension funds, most prominently the employee pension fund of the Banco do Brasil, PREVI. Moreover, the state does not necessarily remain a passive shareholder. BNDES and pension funds sometimes use their shareholdings to prevent major company decisions that are not in line with state preferences (Schneider 2013, 172).

In both cases (family and state control), the management of major Brazilian companies is fairly independent from short-term fluctuations on the stock markets. Controlling holders take a long-term perspective on the survival of companies, not on the maximization of short-term returns. There is no open market for the control of companies, as is characteristic for LMEs, but rather an 'insider'-dominated mode of corporate governance more in line with traditional CME-structures. Completely dispersed shareholding is very rare, and minority shareholders tend to be disadvantaged by dominant shareholders (Aguilera et al. 2012, 323). Stock markets are not markets for corporate control, but rather a means of raising capital or organizing the control of companies via pyramid schemes and non-voting shares (Schneider 2013, 151–2; Sibal 2014, 188–90). Correspondingly, the

Table 4.1 The 20 biggest companies of Brazil, by turnover, 2013[1]

Company	*Origin of owners*	*Activity*	*Family control*	*Public holdings*		*Private*	*Limited state control*	*High state control*	*Majority state-owned*	*Strong family ownership*
				BNDES	*Social security funds*					
Petrobras	BRA	Petroleum & Gas							x	
Vale	BRA	Mining		x	X				x	
JBS	BRA	Foods	x	x	X			x		
Ultra	BRA	Retail, Petroleum & Gas, Logistics	x		X	x				
Pao de Acucar	BRA, FR	Retail, Finance	x			x				x
Bunge Alimentos	NED	Foods				x				
Gerdau	BRA	Metals, Steel	x	x		x				x
Braskem	BRA	(Petro-)Chemicals	x					x		
Eletrobras	BRA	Electricity							x	
Telefonica Brasil	ES	Telecom								
AmBev	BRA, BEL	Beverages and tobacco								
Cosan	BRA	Sugar and alcohol, Ethanol	x							x
Odebrecht	BRA	Construction and engineering	x							x
BRF (Brazil Foods)	BRA	Foods			X		x			

Carrefour	FRA	Retail				x	
Volkswagen	GER	Vehicles & Parts				x	
Oi	BRA	Telecom		x	X		x
Cargill	US	Foods				x	
Fiat Automoveis	ITA	Vehicles & Parts				x	
Marfrig	BRA	Foods	X	x			x

Source: Valor (2013a, 2013b); company websites.

1 This is a further refined version of Table 1 in May et al. 2019b.

LME-inspired "Corporate Governance" movement of the 2000s met with considerable resistance in Brazil, and initiatives for the improved protection of minority shareholders were not very successful (Grün 2010; Schneider 2013, 152). Generally, formal LME-type liberalization has been subverted by traditional private and public elites, similar to the fate of the liberalization reforms in India.

A Brazilian 'specialty' is the incorporation of parts of the labor movement into company decision-making via pension funds.[7] The Lula administration gave the democratization of pension fund governance high political priority, thereby giving union representatives a greater voice on pension fund boards (Habbard 2010, 37). The strongly growing role of union-dominated pension funds was intended to lead to a learning process whereby unions should understand the perspectives of industry and the financial sector, while some of the more destabilizing forces of the financial markets were tempered by the presence of union representatives (Boschi 2012, 188; Datz 2013, 119–20). The PT government promoted the idea that pension funds should not follow the usual financial sector prerogatives of speculation for profit maximization, but should instead further national economic development by using domestic savings for the support of the national economy via long-term investments (Datz 2013, 119–20). Still, corporate law favors the dominance of Brazilian capital on company boards. Furthermore, most pension fund assets are in government bonds and infrastructure, not equities (Habbard 2010, 38; Datz 2013, 117).

Alongside the Brazilian companies portrayed earlier, there is a substantial role on the part of foreign multinationals, particularly since the privatizations of the 1990s. Twenty of the 50 biggest companies in Brazil are foreign-owned. Still, these companies are less relevant than in more liberal Latin American countries such as Chile, or even the dependent market economies of East Central Europe (Nölke and Vliegenthart 2009). Moreover, they are exposed to fairly strong competition and thus cannot play out their powerful position to the same extent as in other Latin American economies, as indicated by a fairly low financial transfer to their company headquarters (Abu-el-Haj 2007, 108).

In comparison to China and India, however, Brazil is far more open to foreign ownership and the contestation of economic policy-making is thereby increased (see section 4.2) and the effectiveness of demand stimulation for the support of Brazilian industry is decreased (see section 4.3.6). Since the 1990s, TNCS have drastically increased their prominence in the Brazilian economy, as measured in terms of sales and share of manufacturing and revenues (Schneider 2013, 76). The effect was "to box domestic firms out of most dynamic manufacturing sectors like electronics and automobiles" (Schneider 2013, 82), leading to a suboptimal sharing of tasks between national and foreign capital in manufacturing.

4.3.2 *Finance for investment*

During the last decades, capital markets have gained increasing relevance for the financing of Brazilian companies. However, companies are still protected by families and other stockholders, as well as through investment financing through retained earnings and domestic banks, thereby strongly limiting the short-term pressure emanating from internationalized equity or bond markets. In 2009, only 4% of all investments in Brazil were met by financial markets (compared to 13% in the United States and 10% in Germany; World Bank 2014). Most important in the Brazilian context was the role of the state in the provision of long-term investment finance. Direct and indirect state support for investment financing can take many shapes, including tax rebates, guarantees and subsidized credit, all contributing to financing conditions that are more favorable than the usually very high interest rates in Brazil.[8] A far more important factor for the long-term expansion of large Brazilian companies, however, is the public development bank BNDES that was strengthened after Lula took office in 2003. The same applies to the pension funds of state-controlled enterprises that are another source of state-controlled long-term finance. Small companies, in contrast, are disadvantaged by these lending and investment policies. Given very high interest rates, investments by these companies are extremely limited. Still, the Brazilian system of company finance is able to provide a high degree of long-term stability, as witnessed during the global financial crisis.

In contrast to other Latin American countries, large conglomerates are less frequent in Brazil (Schneider 2013, 48), with some notable exceptions such as Votorantim, Camargo Correa and Andrade Gutierrez. This has repercussions for the financing of investments, since conglomerates often finance new investments through retained earnings in other fields of business. Diversification has assisted Latin American conglomerates in surviving the massive crises and adjustment programs of the 1990s, as well as the turbulence of the global financial crisis (Schneider 2013, 49–50). On the negative side, conglomerates are somewhat less inclined to focus on dynamic investments in one economic sector. Brazilian companies, in contrast, frequently focus their activities on a small number of sectors, with higher investments in innovative activities and increasing use of financial markets to raise funds. Still, even exchange-listed companies in Brazil financed about 75% of their investments via retained earnings in 2000 (Schneider 2013, 43–4). Although the importance of financial markets in terms of corporate bonds (see section 4.3.1) has increased since then, investors on these markets still do not get a say in company decisions (see the previous section on corporate governance). Strong and growing stock market capitalization, as indicated by the quantitative expansion of the Brazilian stock exchange BOVESPA, should not be confused with powerful equity markets, in particular given that corporate investment financing via equity capital markets is 10% or less of overall financing (Sibal 2014, 188).

Aside from retained earnings, the most important source of finance for Brazilian companies is domestic bank loans (32.3%, according to the World Bank Enterprise Survey in 2009; see World Bank 2014). In contrast to dependent market economies, however, so far there is no "sell-out" of domestic banks towards foreign investors, with more than 70% percent of total financial endowments in Brazil controlled by domestic public and private banks in 2000 (Abu-El-Haj 2007, 104). Finally, most 'private' banks are listed on local stock markets, but de facto controlled by public bodies. Approximately half of the national banking assets in Brazil are held by state-controlled banks. In addition to BNDES, Banco do Brasil and Caixa Economica Federal are important funders for domestic companies, including the very big businesses in Table 4.1. Firms that use bank loans therefore effectively receive credit from the state, at usually favorable rates, if compared to global credit markets (Masiero and Caseiro 2012).

Generally, public influence on credit provision in Brazil during the PT rule was massive, not only because of public bank ownership of BNDES and other public banks or state influence on pension funds. Even private commercial banks provided a substantial share of their credit as "earmarked", i.e. subsidized and focused for certain purposes such as long-term investments for private companies or specific credit for rural areas and housing (López and Garralda 2014, 18–24). This has led to a segmentation of the credit market, with a large gap between highly subsidized earmarked credit for public purposes and rather penalized non-earmarked and fully private credit. Combined with a low domestic savings rate (IMF 2013, 17–19), this segmentation has had considerable implications for investments by Brazilian companies. While it supported the investments of large companies with access to BNDES and other subsidized funding, it is a major constraint for small companies without access to this funding. High interest rates, frequently more than 30%, are thus a major investment hurdle for small- and medium-scale enterprises in Brazil (Arnold 2011, 12).[9]

Another state lever for long-term investments in Brazil are large pension funds, particularly those linked to the Bank of Brazil (Banco do Brasil), Petrobras and the National Savings Bank (Caixa Economica Federal), with funds such as Previ, Petros and Funcep. The role of these private funds, with domestic assets under management of nearly 20% of GDP, has become so massive that observers often refer to "pension fund developmentalism" in Brazil (Datz 2013). After the election victory of the Worker's Party in 2002, the pension funds developed close linkages to the state based on the integration of trade union members into the leadership of these funds (Datz 2013, 115). The PT government urged pension funds to invest in infrastructure projects, including energy, transportation, oil and gas, and modified the regulatory framework accordingly. In fact, the most important investment in Brazil's recent history, the exploration of the pre-salt oil fields off the coast of Sao Paulo, would have been impossible to finance domestically without the support of these funds, most notably Petros (Datz 2013, 121–4).

In the heyday of labor party rule, BNDES, the most famous institution of Brazilian state capitalism, lent approximately 7.5% of Brazilian GDP and disbursed four times as many loans than the World Bank (Lazzarini et al. 2011, 32). The development bank has been particularly instrumental in supporting the recent global expansion of Brazilian companies, in particular by opening a credit line with favorable conditions for investments abroad and supporting mergers between formerly mid-sized Brazilian corporations (for a more detailed discussion of BNDES funding, see May et al. 2019b, 103–7). This has, inter alia, led to the creation of Brasil Foods, Fibria and Banco Itaú Unibanco (Casanova and Kassum 2013, 17). The objective behind BNDES lending is therefore not to provide credit for small firms facing constraints on the private credit market, but rather to boost the investments of already profitable firms (interview with an economist, Sao Paulo, 4 March 2013; Lazzarini et al. 2011).[10] This is part of a 'national champions' strategy aimed at creating Brazilian multinationals with substantial world market positions. Given the structure of the Brazilian economy, this has mostly supported multinationals with low technological intensity, such as meat-packing (Masiero et al. 2014, 136–41). The provision of credit is one arm of this strategy, and the acquisition (or retaining) of minority stakes in these companies by its subsidiary BNDESPAR is another. The latter has become so prominent that BNDES was instrumental in developing the "Leviathan as a minority investor" model, arguably at the heart of the recent "reinvention of state capitalism" particular to Brazil (Musacchio and Lazzarini 2014).

The national champions strategy as symbolized by BNDES supports the concentration of businesses (Schneider 2013, 172). State support for business follows a vision for national economic rise but does not necessarily support a more equitable distribution of economic resources on the national level. While this observation was already made ages ago (Baer and Figueroa 1981, 79), these concerns have been confirmed by recent studies highlighting the extraordinarily high degree of concentration of revenues (and power) in the largest Brazilian companies (Casanova and Kassum 2013, 6). This unequal outcome is the price to be paid for a national champions strategy. The main distributive advantage of state banks and state-supported companies is that they prevent the transfer of profits abroad, as would be the case if the relevant economic transactions were conducted by foreign multinationals. An important element of this strategy was to create highly productive companies able to obtain market shares abroad, a strategy that was at least partially successful. A famous example is the company JBS, which became a world leader in beef production in a fairly short period with massive support from BNDES (Schneider 2013, 64). Linking BNDES credit to successful establishment on world markets is an important instrument to prevent these companies from becoming less productive because of ready state support (Schneider 2013, 180). Without this provision, the negative aspects of this strategy may have become more prominent, for example advantages for incumbents and disadvantages for new entrants, leading to rigidities in product markets and slow aggregate productivity growth (Arnold 2011, 23).

4.3.3 Industrial relations

The importance of pension funds and the prominent representation of labor unions on their boards, together with the long rule of the PT, could give the impression that Brazil has developed some kind of corporatist or social-democratic system of industrial relations. However, this would be misleading. Although some sections of Brazilian industry have developed worker participation institutions based on state support, the largest share of Brazilian employment is characterized by low wages and no representation. This segmentation of industrial relations in Brazil also relates to the geographical dimension, with quite different labor conditions in the north and south of the country. Generally, the labor-led government has led to a slow but steady process of working-condition improvement that still has not affected broad groups of the workforce. However, unemployment during the PT rule was very low and the growth of the labor force has been reduced, with increasing labor costs contributing to inflation.

The importance of labor cost advantages, as discussed in the cases of China and India, is also important with regard to Brazilian industrial relations. Although there is fairly sophisticated labor law, this pertains only to a part of the Brazilian workforce in the dynamic sectors, compared to a large but slowly decreasing share of workers in the informal sector that is not protected at all. This is not an unusual situation in the Latin American context. To put it very simply, labor markets are dualized between a well-paid, organized and protected segment of core workers in the public sector as well as in major private companies. Then there is a (semi-) informal economy that can be further subdivided into an informal sector (mainly self-employed in micro enterprises) and precarious work in the formal sector, with very short job contracts affected by the minimum wage.

Again, state support for this fragmentation is important, as far as the "labor elite" is protected by law and fairly well integrated into the collusion between national capital and the state (Phillips 2004, 161–4). In contrast, the state (including the PT-led administrations) puts much less emphasis on the protection of precarious workers in the formal sector, and it even deployed the military to prevent mass strikes in the construction sector (Nowak 2015, 89–91). Various forms of company-specific worker committees do exist for the labor elite, as do board-level employee representatives (Habbard 2010, 38). Workers in state-controlled companies are especially privileged in this regard, although a 2010 law intended to further improve board-level employee representation (with 40% female representation on company boards) did not pass the Brazilian Senate (Orsagh 2014).

Workers in large companies in the dynamic sectors as well as those working in the public sector thus enjoy privileged conditions. Small- and medium-scale enterprises that operate in fairly close relationships with or within the informal sector, however, are much more critical of stringent labor protection due to cost considerations. The same is true for corporate social responsibility (CSR). Whereas small enterprises are highly skeptical of these initiatives, the large "multilatinas" are somewhat more open to the campaigns of private CSR drivers such as the Abrinq Foundation and the Instituto Ethos, strongly supported by the Lula administrations (Pena 2014). This openness is also motivated by cross-border campaigns within this field, by multilateral institutions or transnational NGOs. In particular, well-known Brazilian companies with direct exposure to markets in industrialized countries are open to CSR initiatives (Arraya 2006, 33). However, even those companies would be less than keen on introducing powerful unions and better working conditions on a universal basis, because affordable services and other inputs from the informal sector contribute considerably to the cost advantages of the Brazilian economy. Thus, we cannot speak of a functioning corporatist system as in CMEs. Even in parts of the economy where labor unions are important (union density in the formal sector is high by international comparison), they operate not only based on collective action and negotiations with employer associations, but also through direct political ties with the state (Schneider 2013, 95).

Surprisingly, even after some pro-worker reform policies of the Lula and Dilma governments, Brazil's system of labor relations can still be partially considered a low-wage regime. A government affiliated with a broad section of the trade union movement should not be confused with a powerful union organization on the shop floor. Overall, labor representation is strongly fragmented, similar to the fragmentation of the workforce (Sibal 2014, 180–2). Segmentation not only exists between public and private sectors and different company sizes, but also operates strongly along the lines of gender and race (Leubolt 2015, 215–22). There are also huge regional gaps in terms of wages and working conditions. Brazil's own internal 'migrant workers' from the northeast are employed in the industrialized areas such as the southern state of Sao Paulo and are often racially discriminated against, as witnessed during the 2014 electoral campaign (Pitts 2015). At the same time, some mature manufacturing industries such as clothing and shoes have moved from the south to the northeast, thereby creating additional formal jobs in the northeast, even if low-skilled and low-wage. Reducing the large share of informal and precarious work takes time. Although the share of the latter has been reduced since 2007, it is still approximately the same size as the protected labor market. The informal economy in 2010 still had a share of about 18% of GDP, down from 23% in 2003 (Melleiro and Steinhilber 2012, 220).

However, there are several indicators that the growth of the labor force has been stagnating since 2010, highlighted by steadily increasing and historically low figures in various measurements of the GDP share of the informal economy (G20 2014, 4, 8; Forte 2015). One factor limiting labor supply is the strongly decreasing fertility rate after the 1980s (Bresser-Pereira 2015, 6). The percentage of the working population considered economically active increased from 55% in 1970 to about 75% in 2010, with stagnation since then (IMF 2013, 7). The relocation of factories to the northeast, low formal unemployment figures, decreasing informality and high inflation all point to the fact that Brazil has closed the output gap and the economy was working at maximum capacity at the end of the first decade of PT rule (Canuto and Schellekens 2014; G20 2014, 4). Correspondingly, there is a need for stronger increases in productivity (more in line with the high wage increases), based on better education and training among other factors.

4.3.4 Education and training

Traditionally, neither companies nor workers had strong individual incentives to significantly invest in skill upgrading. During the first decade of the 21st century, however, the PT-led Brazilian governments spent considerable resources on training, thereby highlighting the importance of educational upgrading within a state-led development strategy. The majority of the working population now receives a secondary education. Vocational training has also been extended, although still limited to skills of relatively low complexity and to a rather small share of secondary education. This corresponds to the large low-wage sectors in domestic manufacturing with only medium-level skill requirements. The PT administrations have also tried to cover the rising demand for higher-skilled work through investment in technological upgrading via fairly generous funding of universities and/or research centers. Broadly raising the level of skills, however, takes a lot of time as well as fiscal resources, and Brazil has been only partially successful, in part due to social segregation.

Similar to the practice in other Latin American countries, most Brazilian companies traditionally did not invest much in comprehensive education and training for their workforce, but rather relied on the activities of their own government (Dahlmann and Frischtak 1993, 415; Arbix 2010, 19; Schneider 2013, 65). Thus, they not only passively followed the priorities of the given government but also suffered quite considerably during the heavy macroeconomic crises of the 1990s, with extensive resource cutbacks in education, even if less pronounced than in other Latin American economies (Bizberg 2014, 47). A few large companies (e.g. Embraer) have started their own training programs, however limited to a small group of employees (Goldstein 2002, 108).

Limited investment by employers in their workers' skills has various reasons. First, many activities require only a basic skill level. Particularly in the export sector, there is very limited demand for higher skills, either because of capital-intensive production (few highly qualified workers) or because of low-skill labor-intensive production, e.g. in agriculture (Schneider 2013, 118). Second, improving the education system is a very cumbersome and lengthy task that exceeds the time horizon for many companies, in particular for TNCs (Schneider 2013, 130–2). Third, a large share of the labor force has a short job tenure, with annual turnover rates of 30–40% and average job tenures of less than two years (Schneider 2013, 95f). Due to the system of labor regulation, companies basically have two options: either "hire for life" or "hire and fire", because firing costs become very expensive after a few years of employment (Sibal 2014, 186).

Short job tenures reduce not only the employer incentives to invest in worker skills, but also the incentives for worker investments into their own education (World Bank 2006). Similar to the field of industrial relations, there is a fragmentation between small groups of highly qualified labor (education in universities) and a much larger group of poorly qualified labor with a focus on general skills of limited complexity. Only very slowly are we witnessing a process of increased secondary and tertiary education, but again, this is still dominated by students from the middle and upper classes with better social relations, supported by a system of private schools and spatial segmentation. Students from the lower classes may find their way into (public) universities but are still confronted with class barriers in terms of well-paid jobs, for example, based on issues of appearance, manners, cultural capital and social networks (Schneider 2013, 124, 128). Still, in contrast to many other Latin American countries, demand for skilled workers in Brazil is growing strongly. This corresponds to education, as measured by salary increases per additional year of education (Schneider 2013, 122–3).

Traditionally, broad sections of the population have not considered low levels of education as a major challenge with high political priority (Schneider 2013,

132; Leubolt 2015, 259). The PT-led governments, with their focus on long-term national industrial upgrading, have been willing and capable of creating a modern skill formation system, at least for important segments of the workforce. They have been able to overcome some of the fiscal constraints to better education that are typical for Latin America (Schrank 2009). Thus, public expenditure on education as a percentage of total government expenditure has become relatively high when compared to other Latin American countries as well as to the dependent market economies of East Central Europe, in which the dominant multinational companies are not in favor of a generous public education system (see Chapter 6 for a comparison). Although the Cardoso administrations started educational reforms, increases in educational spending took off only with the PT-led administrations (Leubolt 2015, 197). The increasing discontent with the education system, as witnessed during the mass demonstrations in the 2010s, even seems to indicate a growing awareness within the Brazilian population that good education pays. In response, it was decided in 2013 that 75% of all net oil and gas revenues should be spent on education (Casanova and Kassum 2014, 117).

Due to recent investments in education, average years of schooling increased from 2.5 in 1970 to 7.25 in 2010 (IMF 2013, 7). Moreover, the number of people formally employed with 11 or more years of schooling increased from 21.7% in 2001 to 36.1% in 2012, and the completion rate for secondary education jumped from 17.2% in 1996 to 55.2% in 2013 (G20 2014, 9). Generally, the workforce in internationally competitive sectors has an average of nine years of education, with on-the-job training provided by companies. On the other hand, in companies that do not export or innovate, the average is less than seven years (OECD 2011a, 186). PISA scores have also improved across the board during the first decade of the millennium (OECD 2011a, 177). However, both the share of the adult population with a tertiary education and the PISA science scores remain low in comparison to OECD averages (OECD 2012, 252–3; Casanova and Kassum 2014, 116–21).

In contrast to other Latin American countries, Brazil has a long-established and fairly diversified system of vocational training. It consists of public, semi-public and private elements, with the public elements considerably strengthened during the PT administrations. The oldest and most consolidated institution for vocational training in Brazil is the public-private "S-System", created in 1942. It is jointly run by the state and business associations, with separate sections for manufacturing, trade and agriculture. The system is financed by a compulsory tax from worker payroll, paid by firms. Traditionally, private investments in vocational training have been very low, as in other countries in Latin America. Since the early 2000s, however, considerable financial resources have been invested in public vocational training, with moderate but slowly increasing success in the more recent initiatives. The most important initiative is the Pronatec program (national program for access to technical education and employment), which has provided 8 million course places in technical schools and is intended to benefit 12 million students by 2018 (G20 2014, 7, 9). The main focus of all types of vocational training, an important input for small- and medium-scale enterprises, is on skills of limited complexity (e.g. operating machinery), and not on support for incremental innovation as in CMEs. Moreover, the share of students enrolled in vocational training is still quite small, approximately 12% in contrast to 48% of upper secondary enrollments in the EU (Schneider 2013, 126). Thus, there is still room for further extension of vocational training for the purpose of industrial upgrading, particularly in tripartite governance together with labor (Balestro 2014).

The Lula and Dilma administrations have also spent considerable amounts of money on higher education. Among the most well-known initiatives is the Science without Borders Program, with more than 100,000 scholarships for university students to study abroad (G20 2014, 7). Although these programs will take time to reach fruition, the number of undergraduate degrees has more than doubled in the 2000s, with similar tendencies in the postgraduate sector and in the fields of science, technology, engineering and mathematics (Gupta et al. 2013). Due to the massive investment in higher education, particularly the large pool of PhDs with more than 10,000 graduates per year, Brazil has been able to establish itself as an R&D center for TNCs in Latin America, even if this involves only a small number of companies (Schneider 2013, 84). Still, in comparison to China and India, the share of students in science and engineering remains rather low (Schneider 2013, 173) and has proved to be a major restraint for additional high-tech investments, for example by Foxconn (Casanova and Kassum 2014, 118).

During the first decade of the 2000s, the Brazilian governments invested massive resources in education. In comparison to other Latin American countries, Brazil now has a better-educated workforce with regard to schooling, vocational training and, recently, even university education. High enrollment and low unemployment figures, as well as the relocation of some R&D by TNCs to Brazil indicate that both workers and employers accept these measures. During the early 2010s, skill shortages and increasing wages for qualified staff have even become a major growth constraint, contributing to high inflation. If this strong demand for higher skills can be sustained in the long run, Brazil may be able to escape the "low skill equilibrium" so vividly identified by Ben Ross Schneider (2013) for most of Latin America. Still, educational upgrading not only takes a long time and suffers from social segregation, but also requires massive fiscal resources that cannot be spent for other purposes and may generally be cut back in a period of economic crisis. From this perspective, the process of educational upgrading in Brazil has achieved a lot, in particular in comparison to the more limited GDP share of education expenses in Dependent Market Economies, but it is still precarious.

4.3.5 Innovation

Most Brazilian companies focus on technological activities that are not very challenging. Still, Brazil has a much better track record on innovative companies than other Latin American countries. This is due to a series of initiatives from the Brazilian state and considerable expenditures in R&D that far surpass the usual share of GDP in Latin America. Already under ISI, the Brazilian government instituted local content policies that required foreign multinationals to transfer at least some technology to local production. Even more important was the decision of the Brazilian state to reserve strategic sectors for domestic producers, and to support these producers with extraordinary public research assistance. These support measures have led to the emergence of global technology leaders in a small range of sectors. While some of these innovation policies were reversed during the liberal 1980s and 1990s, the PT governments renewed the attempts at creating innovative companies, in particular in sectors where Brazil was favorably endowed with natural resources. Again, this led to the emergence of a number of national champions. The last PT government has attempted to broaden innovation policies to further sectors, but fiscal resources were too limited to attain this goal in a comprehensive way.

Brazilian firms are traditionally hesitant to massively invest in research and development activities and spend much less on these issues than Chinese and Indian firms (Arbix 2010, 19). Only 1.7% of Brazilian companies invest in innovation, while more than 77% situate their competitive advantage in a low-cost but also low-productivity environment (Arbix 2008, 5). Similar to other Latin American economies as well as to the dependent market economies in Central and Eastern Europe, many very innovative sectors of the Brazilian economy, such as IT, electronics and car manufacturing, are dominated by foreign multinationals (Schneider 2013, 82). Given that these companies conduct most of their R&D in their headquarters in the United States, Europe or Japan, this limits the development of an innovative economy in Brazil. Particularly smaller private firms are usually able to evade investments in technological development (Condé and Delgado 2009, 20; Kattel and Primi 2012, 274–5). In their sectors, a high degree of innovation is not necessarily important for the production of 'good enough' products for the domestic market by Brazilian companies. These small and medium companies have traditionally been content with successfully providing goods for the domestic market, sheltered by a protective trade policy. Similar to India, tariffs are relatively high, on average above 30%. Most companies are thus content to adapt foreign innovations for the local and regional markets, without seeing the need to invest huge amounts of resources in cutting-edge innovation (Gupta et al. 2013). Given the increasing demand in the South American economy during the 2000s, this has been a very successful strategy, although its long-term viability depends on a continuous expansion of domestic markets; this is a condition that does not seem guaranteed (see section 4.3.6).

Due to the traditionally very limited role of internal research and development in large parts of Brazilian business, innovations in other sectors are usually imported from abroad, usually via northern multinational enterprises and partnerships with foreign companies. Brazilian companies have a much higher average of patent cooperation treaties than the OECD average (OECD 2010a, 160). However, in contrast to many other Latin American countries, the Brazilian state very actively promoted the industrial upgrading of domestic manufacturers early on through the forced acquisition of foreign technologies. During the ISI era, foreign innovation transfer was enforced by the state, e.g. by national content policies.

> The state favors and wishes to perfect the model of tripartite association (public enterprise, national and multinational private enterprise) by imposing conditions and demanding guarantees. Thus all associations must involve a substantial investment by the foreign partner in the form of risk capital and an actual transfer of technology, and the studies and engineering works must be carried out locally by or in collaboration with Brazilians.
>
> (Faucher 1981, 20)

National content policies have been particularly prominent in the oil and gas industries (and still are today) as well as the automobile supply chain, at least until the liberalization of the 1990s (Schneider 2013, 77). In contrast to other emerging markets, however, Brazil has not used lax intellectual property rights protection as a measure for (involuntary) technology transfer (The Economist 2012). One of the reasons for this stance is the fact that Brazilian companies have become global technology leaders themselves, although only in a small number of sectors (interview with representative of FINEP, Rio de Janeiro, 28 February 2013). A crucial long-term feature of Brazilian innovation policies is massive state support for a number of strategically chosen sectors, such as in the PITCE program (Política Industrial, Tecnológica e de Comércio Exterior; see ABDI 2005).

Based on these massive investments, Brazil by far exceeds other Latin American countries with regard to its science and technology workforce, as well as to public funding for research (Schneider 2013, 65). These sectors include oil and gas (particularly deepwater oil extraction, Petrobras), large-scale agriculture (various activities supported by EMBRAPA, the public Brazilian Agricultural Research Corporation) and small civilian aircrafts, for example those produced by Embraer (Gupta et al. 2013). A particularly striking example is the production of ethanol derived from sugar cane, beginning in the 1970s and paying off with a leading role on world markets in the 2000s (Schneider 2013, 168). These investments demonstrate not only that the state can play a crucial role in industrial upgrading, but also what long periods of time and massive resources these processes of upgrading require. Nearly all of these sectors have received massive state support over many decades, usually initiated by the military governments of the 1960s and 1970s (Schneider 2013, 134, 169; see also section 4.3.1). Particularly in the case of Petrobras, the government made a special effort from the start to create a technologically advanced company in order to reduce the economic imbalances experienced in the oil crisis (Carvalho and Goldstein 2008, 18). After the mid-2000s, the government extended this strategy with a considerable increase in R&D investments (based on receipts from the natural resource boom), particularly in the biofuels and pre-salt oil drilling sectors (Gupta et al. 2013).

In other sectors, the PT governments have supported the emergence of Brazilian companies that play a leading role on regional Latin American markets. These companies work in food processing, mining and basic metals, and construction and engineering services, all of which are sectors where a limited level of innovation is sufficient and mostly required in management and logistics rather than in technology (Schneider 2013, 66). In this case, core state support was not in the field of R&D funding, but rather in the provision of subsidized credit for mergers with large companies able to operate on international markets. The corresponding reduction in competition is often to the disadvantage of Brazilian consumers, but to the advantage of a few major Brazilian companies enabled to mobilize the resources needed for successful cross-border expansion.[11] In contrast to the ISI period, however, these Brazilian national champions are not protected from cross-border competition, but receive state support only if they are willing to submit their operations to competition in regional or even global markets.

Outside of these strategically chosen companies, the low inclination for investments in indigenous innovation is a constant source of frustration for Brazilian state actors (Interview at the Ministry of Industry and Commerce, 26 February 2013). The share of private R&D is only one-third of the OECD average, in spite of heavy subsidies (Schneider 2013, 170–1). Similar to India, the Brazilian state has only recently taken a more active stance in supporting collaboration between universities and enterprises through research and development as well as through direct subsidies, mainly led by the Brazilian innovation agency FINEP. Traditionally, public institutions were involved in the transfer of innovations only to a limited degree, and industry-university linkages were fairly poor (Gupta et al. 2013). Public support for science and technology has existed in particular since the 1970s, but in basic rather than applied sciences, with a focus on the production of conference papers and academic articles (Graf and Stehnken 2014, 168–9).

Cooperation between universities and companies, however, has intensified more recently (Dahlmann and Frischtak 1993, 415; Arbix 2010, 18–20; OECD 2012, 254). During the Lula and Dilma administrations, these linkages became a matter of high political significance, as symbolized by the establishment of numerous new (semi-)public institutions as well as fiscal incentives (Graf and Stehnken 2014, 164–7). Among the most important measures was the multiplication of financial resources as 'sectoral funds', non-reimbursable funds in more than 10 sectors aimed specifically at technological development. The success of these measures is still somewhat muted, even if the share of innovative companies has gradually increased. Resource limitations do not allow for equally massive state intervention into high skills and innovation in a large number of economic sectors, as practiced in China, given that the tax burden at 36% of GDP (PATRI 2015, 1) is already much higher than in other emerging markets, and innovation programs compete with other purposes for scarce fiscal resources.

4.3.6 Domestic markets

A major feature of the Brazilian economy that stands out in comparison to other Latin American countries is the importance of the large and (until recently) very dynamically growing domestic market. This market has been the backbone for the rise of many well-established Brazilian companies. Both during the ISI period and later during the PT-led administrations, the domestic market, in particular mass production for private consumption, has become the core driver of economic growth in Brazil. Very important ingredients of demand stimulation were pro-poor social reforms. Brazil's policies with regard to the protection and utilization of the domestic market as a basis for national economic development, however, have been marred by contradictions and inconsistencies, in particular with regard to the remaining openness towards foreign multinationals. A more dynamic growth process based primarily on domestic markets is also hampered by the still-extreme social inequality in the country, as well as by high taxes and shrinking fiscal resources more recently.[12]

Already during the ISI phase between 1930 and 1980, the domestic market was the backbone of the development of the Brazilian industrial structure. The opening of this market during the Collor de Mello and Cardoso administrations, however, led to considerable denationalization and deindustrialization in many sectors of the Brazilian economy. Although domestic demand was at the core of the rejuvenation of growth during the 2000s, the domestic market was never similarly protected from foreign market entry as in the cases of China and India. Still, the very broad diversification of the Brazilian economy under ISI made sure that domestic demand did not exclusively benefit foreign multinationals. After the macroeconomic stabilization of the 1990s, the domestic market took over from the export sector as the core engine of growth. Between 2003 and 2009, private consumption increased for 24 quarters in a row (Melleiro and Steinhilber 2012, 219; see section 4.1 for a more detailed discussion). According to IMF calculations, "consumption – both public and private – has accounted for almost all the growth in Brazil" (2013, 15).

Similar to China and India, Brazil protected its domestic markets during the PT rule in order to make sure that domestic demand was able to support domestic industry. In contrast to China and India, however, the beneficial effects of a growing domestic market have to be shared with foreign multinationals in a more open manner.[13] Compared to these two countries, Brazil has a low level of FDI restrictions, as measured by the OECD (see section 6.3 for a comparison). Since the 1990s, many foreign multinationals have set up shop in Brazil in order to access the dynamically growing local markets, in contrast to the motivation of natural resource exploitation typical for investments in other countries in the South (Kingstone 1999, 249; Abu-El-Haj 2007, 107–8). Similarly, Brazil has a lower level of protective product market regulation than China and India, as measured by the OECD, but this level is still much higher than in all advanced economies (Arnold 2011, 29).

During the 2010s, however, the process of stimulating demand for the products and services of Brazilian companies seems to have experienced a certain degree of exhaustion, particularly on the side of domestic demand (for a more detailed discussion of the problems, see May and Nölke 2018, 10). While measures for redistribution were politically unpopular, fiscal resources increasingly became scarce. During the early 2010s, the decade-long process of reducing public debt was already revised, thereby limiting the fiscal space to maneuver (IMF 2013, 49–57). Due to high interest rates, about half of the federal budget was directed to paying off public debt (Dierckx 2015, 153), thereby posing limits to additional social or infrastructure programs that could further raise domestic demand.[14]

Unfortunately, this exhaustion of domestic demand-driven growth happened at the same time that export demand-driven growth was weakened, in particular due to decreasing demand from (and increasing competition by) China.

However, it is a very widely shared misconception that Brazil's economic fortunes are primarily dependent on commodity exports in general, and to China in particular. In 2011, Brazil ranked lowest in terms of export share in GDP (12%) among the top 10 global economies, even after the similarly closed economies of Japan (15%) and the United States (14%), and much behind export-led economies such as Mexico (32%) and Germany (50%). "Growth in Brazil is still largely made in Brazil" (Canuto and Schellekens 2014, 3; see also Bizberg 2014, 14). This is a clear contrast to the "extractivist" export-driven models dominating other Latin American economies such as Chile and Venezuela (Jäger et al. 2014); the latter are far more thoroughly affected by decreasing demand from China. And although Brazilian manufacturing exports have suffered from Chinese competition, particularly in Latin America, the small share of manufacturing production for export (about 20%) limits the negative effect of this external factor (Jenkins and Freitas Barbosa 2012, 77). Comprehensive macroeconomic analyses confirm that the slowdown in Brazilian growth between 2011 and 2014 was overwhelmingly triggered by a sharp decline in domestic demand, and not only by a fall in exports or external financial conditions (Serrano and Summa 2015).

4.4 Comparative advantages, institutional complementarities and contradictions of Brazilian capitalism

Compared to its neighbor countries, the Brazilian economy is fairly diversified, a consequence of the decades-old strategy of import substitution as well as the recent return to state-led capitalism. Correspondingly, a number of clusters of Brazilian companies have specific comparative advantages. Most of these clusters can be identified by looking at the sector distribution of Brazilian multinationals (Flynn 2007, 17; see also Abu-El-Haj 2007; Arbix 2010; Casanova and Kassum 2013, 2014; Schneider 2015a). One obvious focus is on the processing of raw goods, e.g. by companies such as Votorantim (conglomerate with cellulose, paper, cement, aluminum), Vale (iron ore), Petrobras (oil) and Gerdau and Usiminas (steel). The Brazilian agricultural industry is also globally renowned (e.g. the food processing companies Brasil Foods and JBS), supported by globally rising prices and the increasing production of organic fuels. The comparative advantages of Brazilian companies are very often based on natural resources combined with low labor costs rather than on high labor productivity or product quality/innovation; the latter is usually not necessary in the commodity sector (Schneider 2013, 67). However, in contrast to many other economies in Latin America, Brazilian exports are not dominated by the export of raw goods, but rather by processed products (Phillips 2004, 74). Furthermore, many Brazilian companies are very successful in adapting products and providing services for the large domestic markets in the country and the region. This includes companies in construction and engineering services as well as food processing, but also many small- and medium-sized manufacturing companies in auto parts and IT services that are globally less well known, as highlighted in section 4.3.4. Finally, in a few cases we can identify companies that are also globally competitive in technology, such as Embraer (small civil aircraft) and Petrobras (deep-sea oil mining) as well as in large-scale agricultural research, supported by the nation agricultural research institution EMBRAPA.

After the domestic demand-led boom in the first decade of the 2000s, growth in Brazil stagnated and even fell into a recession during the mid-2010s. Still, the unemployment rate and public indebtedness were rather low by international comparison. The country has gained some means of protecting itself from short-term fluctuations in the global markets, most notably a high amount of foreign reserves. While Brazil was in a better economic situation than comparable economies in Latin America or South Africa during the first decade of the new millennium, its economic dynamic was still more limited than in the cases of India and China. Whereas some institutional complementarities of state-led capitalism worked well, others worked to a very limited degree or not at all.

On the positive side, the strong role of domestic capitalists and the state as well as the established means of coordination within this dominant social bloc, for example based on institutions such as BNDES, allowed for the ability to pursue a long-term economic development strategy. This is true even if domestic capitalists apparently needed a Worker's Party-led government (and dictatorships in earlier times) to actively formulate and pursue such a strategy. A long-term perspective has been supported by strongly reducing foreign indebtedness and accumulating substantial foreign currency reserves. Stable corporate governance based on family capitalism as well as the state as a minority shareholder combined with BNDES credits has enabled a group of Brazilian multinationals to become global (and, even more often, regional) leaders in their fields. The basis for the diversified structure of Brazilian industry was already in place during the ISI phase, including policies for national content that have supported technology transfer into Brazil. Massive state support for research and development in selected sectors (oil and gas, large-scale agriculture, small aircrafts) over many decades has led to the development of 'pockets of efficiency' and also global leaders in terms of technology.

Comparative advantages for other companies focused more on 'good enough' production for the domestic market are based on complementarities between still fairly cheap labor and an education system (still) providing for a medium-skill level. Expanding domestic demand, for example in construction and in service consumption, has increased the demand for skilled workers. Both the strategy for global technological leadership in selected sectors and the 'good enough' strategy focused on the domestic Brazilian market (and the neighboring region), profit from comprehensive attempts to upgrade the level of skills in Brazilian manufacturing. Compared to the hierarchical, less progressive type of capitalism dominating other South American economies, these policies can even be considered 'incentive incompatible', because they do not fit the low-skill equilibrium typical for this model of capitalism:

> Although some policies, such as the BNDES' promotion of national champions in commodities, are incentive – compatible in hierarchical capitalism, other technology and skills policies (such as training scientists and investing in R&D), and local content restrictions on TNCs push firm hard in incentive-incompatible ways.
>
> (Schneider 2013, 190)

Macroeconomic stabilization as well as the social policies of the Lula governments have bolstered the role of the domestic market as an important demand factor for Brazilian industrialization. During and after the financial crisis, the state compensated for the economic downturn by massively stimulating private credit, e.g. for housing and consumer goods. Given a smaller domestic market in comparison to China and India, demand stimulation in Brazil has mostly worked via redistributive policies, including social programs and the increase of the minimum wage. Here, Brazil demonstrated a complementarity not to be found in the other large emerging markets, between a government with close proximity to labor unions and a domestic demand-driven economy (Bizberg 2014, 38). Generally, the state and its dense coordination with domestic capital have played an overarching role in mobilizing these positive institutional complementarities. It was key to the long-term stability of corporate governance and finance, has massively supported the education and innovation systems and has provided the basis for a demand-led boom through redistributive policies and macroeconomic stabilization.

On the negative side, we need to distinguish between problems that are more or less necessarily caused by a state-directed development model, which are also to be observed in China and India, and problems that stem from the haphazard turn towards state capitalism in Brazil on the other. Among the former, inherent problems of the state-led model are fragmented labor markets and a fragmented education system that limit upward social mobility. In order to exploit cheap labor but also to serve the requirements of technologically demanding economic activities, the labor markets and the education system are segregated between highly qualified labor in long-term employment and low-skill labor with short tenure and limited qualification. While the PT-led governments generally lifted the level of the education system as well as the wage system, they did not overcome this general segregation, in part because of additional fiscal constraints. Growth is still linked to the continuous mobilization of cheap labor.

Among the Brazil-specific deviations from the state-led model, the country shows some problems that are mainly linked to its political system, the remaining openness to foreign financial flows, or the scarcity of savings. Economic coordination is quite cumbersome because of the still-prominent role of foreign capital as well as the deep divisions between domestic capitalist classes in Brazil, the functioning of Congress based on individualism and the additional institutional and political fragmentation brought about by the rise of the labor party and its allies. Given this cumbersome economic coordination, it is very difficult to implement a coherent long-term economic strategy.

Moreover, the 1990s reforms towards a liberal-dependent development strategy have made the country more vulnerable to global economic developments. Many of the most technologically dynamic economic sectors are still dominated by foreign multinationals. Generally, the openness to international financial flows forces a 'prudent' macroeconomic policy that does not allow a strategy of currency devaluation, as for example in China. The continuing need for high interest rates to prevent inflation has led to speculative inflows, which together with the booming commodity export sector have led to an overvaluation of the currency that inhibits a broader industrialization strategy. The heavy mid-2010 devaluation of the Real offered the opportunity to regain competitiveness, but these massive exchange rate fluctuations are also problematic for a long-term industrialization strategy. At the same time, the build-up of foreign currency debt by non-financial corporations also exposes Brazil to the risk of credit withdrawals in the case of rising interest rates in the North. Strong fluctuations in the exchange rate are very detrimental to the formation of stable long-term expectations, an important precondition for the investment process.

Finally, although the size of the internal market is fairly substantial and much larger than any other domestic market in Latin America, it may still be too small and the Brazilian economy too open for the domestic markets to work well as the dominant engine of accumulation. Increased financialization through extending consumer and housing credit could only temporarily increase domestic demand because of increasing private indebtedness. Domestic demand stimulation also only partially benefited Brazilian companies because of the ongoing massive presence of foreign multinationals in important economic sectors. The moderately redistributive Brazilian model was able to stimulate demand, but then domestic savings were lacking for higher-productivity investments. The well-reasoned reluctance to utilize foreign savings led to tensions with regard to the utilization of domestic savings. In contrast to China, Brazil has a low rate of domestic savings. Given the rather small economy as compared to China and India, this high degree of consumption was necessary to assist demand-driven growth. However, low domestic savings are now an important constraint for the mobilization of means for productivity-enhancing investments. There are massive fiscal constraints regarding even more investments in education and technology development, thereby preventing the development of globally competitive manufacturing companies in a larger number of sectors, for example as in China. While strong wage increases and social programs have proved to be very powerful instruments for stimulating a domestic demand-led growth process, they have to be combined with strong increases in productivity to maintain competitiveness. Deindustrialization and high inflation are only two indicators that the increase of productivity in Brazil is not sufficient.

During the mid-2010s, the competitive situation of Brazilian industrial exports in many sectors worsened considerably, mainly due to macroeconomic factors that are difficult to control by the Brazilian government. Brazilian car production, dominated by foreign multinationals, has become too expensive in comparison to other car exporters, not least because of a high exchange rate. The situation in other industries is similar, particularly given heavy competition from China. It remains to be seen whether the mid-2010s devaluation of the Real will be able to reverse this tendency. While the PT administrations have invested heavily in education, training and research, additional massive investments are necessary in order to increase productivity. These initiatives take time to bear fruit, particularly outside of the small number of priority sectors where huge amounts of financial resources were spent. Moreover, the remaining massive inequality and the corresponding limits on internal demand put limits on an alternative development strategy centered even more on production for domestic markets. This is particularly problematic after the consumer credit boom has run out of steam and public indebtedness has soared. Given rising indebtedness, the state is lacking the means for a massive counter-cyclical public investment program in a situation of economic slowdown. Given the dependence on the domestic markets, negative expectations with regard to future economic developments can become a self-fulfilling prophecy, where limited consumption leads to less production and growing unemployment leads to further limited consumption.

By the mid-2010s, the existing, soft state-led growth model had run its course, while a full state-led model would have faced massive political opposition. The 2015–2016 recession exposed the sensitivity of a domestic demand-driven economic model to crises of confidence, as well as the remaining vulnerability to the withdrawal of speculative financial flows. A further move towards state capitalism, including more thorough limitations on capital flows and higher taxes for the rich in order to mobilize fiscal resources for investments in education, technology and further expansion of domestic demand, would have been fiercely opposed by financial capital, foreign multinationals, agribusiness elites and the upper middle classes. At the same time, broad sections of the population, including those that moved out of extreme poverty during the last decade, seem to lack the patience for the long and cumbersome path to the upgrading of skills and technology required for higher value-added production. At the end of the 2010s, Brazil has left its temporal path towards state capitalism, in order to return to a more liberal regime.

Notes

1 Comprehensive and most useful contributions by Moises Balestro (University of Brasilia) are very gratefully acknowledged. This chapter further develops ideas that have first been published by May and Nölke (2018), as well as May et al. (2019a, 2019b).

2 It is therefore not without some irony that Brazil was the country at the origin of our reflections about state-permeated capitalism (Nölke 2010). In contrast to our original assessment, however, our refined perspective also takes the insertion into the international economy, domestic power structures and the macroeconomic context into account, thereby coming to somewhat different conclusions.

3 Some early measures taken by the second Dilma administration in 2015 even indicated a further move back to liberal.

4 The Dutch disease consists of a competitive disadvantage for the non-commodity tradable goods sector, combined with an overly profitable commodity sector operating via currency appreciation. The Brazilian mechanism, an average import tariff of 45% of

GDP and a subsidy to manufacturing exports, also 45%, was dismantled in 1990; only a 12% import tariff remained. A modern mechanism would consist of a tax on the export of these commodities (Bresser-Pereira 2015, 7).

5 For a more detailed discussion of the residual dependency of Brazilian capitalism during the PT presidencies and their macroeconomic effects, see May and Nölke (208: 12).

6 For additional discussions on state-business coordination in Brazil see May and Nölke (2018) as well as May et al. (2019a: 8–10).

7 The role of pension funds for investment financing is discussed in the next section.

8 Direct state subsidies are also possible and have, e.g., financed a substantial share of Embraer development costs, thus leading to a trade dispute with Canada due to competition with Bombardier (Flynn 2007, 19; Goldstein 2002, 111).

9 Another causal relationship between the high amount of directed (earmarked) lending via BNDES and other channels on the one side, and high real interest rates on the other, is more controversial (for an overview of the debate, see Arnold 2011, 14). Earmarked lending is based on a different, long-term interest rate. Thus, large portions of credit in Brazil do not react to the policy rate set by the central bank. If the central bank wants to tighten credit because of inflation, it has to increase interest rates for non-earmarked lending even more, thereby leading to high interest rates.

10 As Marcelo Odebrecht, head of the Odebrecht conglomerate, said, "to be competitive, you have to take those BNDES loans into consideration" (quoted in Leahy 2015).

11 Recently, the disadvantages of economic concentration for Brazilian consumers seem to have received somewhat more attention, e.g., with antitrust investigations started against meat producers by the Brazilian competition agency CADE (Conselho Administrativo de Defesa Economica), one of three current competition agencies (Bazuchi et al. 2013). However, the Brazilian competition policy system, established in 1994, still suffers from fragmentation and lack of staff resources (OECD/IDB 2010).

12 For additional discussions of the role of the domestic market for the support of state-driven capitalism during the PT governments, see May and Nölke (2018: 5–6, 9–11).

13 A good illustration of the limited effects of demand stimulation for domestic manufacturing in an economy with a heavy presence of foreign multinationals is the US$805 million support package for car production in Brazil in August 2015 – it was considered a "present" for German manufacturers in the Sao Paulo region (Rüb 2015).

14 For an alternative view that disputes the need for fiscal tightening and inflation control during the early 2010s and therefore that the Brazilian government pursued a completely misguided policy, see Serrano and Summa (2015).

5 South Africa

Destabilization through fragmentation?

In comparison to the other three countries, the South African economy did not present a very coherent picture in the 2000s. It was characterized by economic turbulence, with uneven growth rates, currency fluctuation and high inflation combined with high rates of unemployment, poverty and inequality. During the Apartheid era the state had a strong impact on economic development; but today, the state finds it difficult to implement successful policies towards economic development due to fragmentation and racial segregation, liberalization of the economy as well as the continued predominance of the 'Minerals-Energy Complex' (MEC).

In China, India and even Brazil, economic growth is largely driven by domestic demand, unlike in South Africa. The economic growth in South Africa peaked between 2004 and 2007, with average growth rates between 4.6% and 5.6%. It rapidly declined to −1.5% in 2009 and recovered to about 3% in 2010–2011, but it stagnated at 2.2% in 2012 and 2013 and declined to 0.56% in 2016 (World Bank 2015d, 2016). The global economic crisis hit the other three countries less because even though their growth rates declined as well, they fell from higher levels. Moreover, their markets proved to be less vulnerable to the ongoing financial and economic crisis compared to the rather open South African economy.

South African society is still characterized by extensive racial segregation and fragmentation. This was a key feature of the Apartheid regime, which had, and still has, substantial repercussions on South African capitalism. These effects are noticeable, on the one hand, in the limited access to finance, education and the labor market for a majority of the black[1] population. On the other hand, they are visible in the fragmentation of capital under the ANC's (African National Congress) leadership, which is inextricably linked to class relations and racial divisions. In addition, state-business relations are also fragmented because the ANC has strong ties with the new capitalists. Moreover, the powerful voice of labor organizations hampers the 'smooth' coordination of economic relations. Thus, the South African elites and their leadership have failed to arrive at a common goal that will steer the country towards national economic development. Besides, a dynamic development of South African capitalism is also constrained by the strong role of the MEC (Fine and Rustomjee 1996), especially as the mining sector is in decline and MEC companies are shifting their focus towards the finance industry and related services (McDonald 2008, 2011). This leads to the dependence of the rest of the economy on the predominantly resource-based accumulation regime. Generally, South Africa was unable to pursue a coherent strategy towards state-permeated capitalism. After the end of Apartheid, the economic system and ownership structures largely remained the same and merely became more liberalized during the 1990s, especially as several liberal economic policies were enacted and several sectors were opened up for foreign capital. Between 2000 and 2010, there was a shift in the dominant discourse as well as in leading policy conceptions towards a more interventionist state (Claar 2018, 46–9).

Nevertheless, liberal policy elements remained present in shaping national economic strategy because of the preferences of the most influential actor in the state apparatus: the National Treasury (Claar 2018, 146–9). In general, efforts to change the liberal economic strategy to a more protectionist one with a stronger role of the state have largely remained on paper.

By highlighting these structures, one can understand how fragmentation, the strong role of the MEC and liberal economic policies together resulted in a destabilization of the economy. As will be shown in this chapter, crucial institutions of South African capitalism do not 'fit' together with regard to a relatively strong developmental strategy, and therefore, the economic development is marred by incoherent policies and strategies. Overall, the economy remains a hybrid in which we can identify a mix of elements of liberal, coordinated and state-permeated market economies.

5.1 Contemporary South African capitalism in global context and historical evolution

The historical evolution of South African capitalism is highly pertinent in understanding both the current economic situation and the contemporary features of capitalism in South Africa.[2] This section will present a brief historical account of the foundations of South African capitalism and will focus specifically on racial fragmentation, the role of the Minerals-Energy Complex and on the various phases of economic liberalization.

First, racial segregation and forms of class fragmentation have existed since the colonialization of the Cape. South African capitalism has its roots in Dutch, Portuguese and British colonialism, where the latter played a significant role in shaping the current institutional setting that evinced several liberal market economy features (see below). The Dutch were based in the Cape because they were using Cape Point as a shipping port. The British, however, were focused on other regions, mainly the current Gauteng area, where British settlers established gold, diamond and uranium mines. After the collapse of the Dutch hegemony, the British became the colonial rulers in South Africa in the 18th century (Lester et al. 2000, 45–55). The British system was based mainly on unfree labor recruited from among the Africans as well as on the dominance of the whites. Before the National Party took power in 1948, the British had already introduced a policy of segregation with several laws in the first half of the 20th century. This formed the legal backbone of racial capitalism, where class position is reinforced through racial categories among the dominated and which reached its zenith over the 50 years of the existence of the Apartheid system (Saul and Gelb 1981, 12).

Central to this form of capitalism was the exploitation of unfree labor and policies that privileged the whites and oppressed the black (south) Africans. The Afrikaaner, i.e. the non-British Europeans that settled in South Africa, and the British found a compromise in the economic sphere, whereby the latter continued their mining activities while the former concentrated on agricultural production. However, South African capitalism was built on, and continued to be dependent on, the oppression of black people as a major source of cheap labor, with lower wages than white workers (Terreblanche 2002; Hart and Padayachee 2013). The ruling National Party used the state to privilege Afrikaaner agriculture, labor and business in the private and public sectors as well as the Afrikaaner urban bourgeoisie. Moreover, the National Party limited competition from black labor (Lipton and Simkins 1993, 5–6). White, English-speaking businesses aligned with the Apartheid state and profited from its support (Terreblanche 2002, 276).

Second, fragmentation in South African capitalism was fostered by a specific accumulation regime focused on mining and energy. Mining expanded in the early 20th century, and the demand for energy to run the mines increased. Originally, mining and energy activities were organized under one institutional entity; however, in 1923 the South African state established the Electricity Supply Commission (Escom; today it is known as Eskom).[3] This led to a close relationship between mining and energy entities and resulted in the formation of the Minerals-Energy Complex (Fine and Rustomjee 1996). This accumulation regime is shaped by one core industry and has existed since the establishment of mining at the end of the 19th century. Energy played a crucial role for the mining industry (Fine 2008, 2; McDonald 2011, 66), which has long been supported by cheap black labor. The success of the mining and energy sectors was predicated on their combination with racial fragmentation (Fine 2008, 2; Gentle 2008, 53; Davies 2011). It is still evident in the current form of South African capitalism, but though the mining sector is declining, the rise of the associated financial and services sectors still fosters the MEC accumulation regime (McDonald 2008, 11). During the Apartheid era, the MEC firms had already invested in the financial markets and had shares in financial institutions (Fine and Rustomjee 1996, 100–4; McDonald 2011, 67). In South Africa's current context these investments are becoming central, for as the finance and service sectors become more relevant, observers speak of an "MEC plus" regime (McDonald 2011). Within this MEC system, the state continues to have an important role in creating legal security for the MEC conglomerates, in addition to being an important shareholder. Furthermore, the state has played an important role in securing access to energy with Eskom as well as with other (partially) state-owned companies like Sasol (petroleum). The MEC accumulation regime not only discriminated against other industries, but it also had crucial social effects due to the racial repression of labor which continued into post-Apartheid South Africa (Gentle 2008, 53–6; McDonald 2008, 13–14, 2011, 67). However, the MEC regime has strong ties to the global economy due to its foreign capital ownership structures and its heavy dependence on exports. These features thus inhibit a coherent state-permeated industrialization strategy.

Third, economic liberalization was a key feature of the short-term policy interventions that created institutional incoherence for South African capitalism. During Apartheid, South Africa followed a strategy of state-led industrialization and import substitution (Bell 1993, 81; Gelb 1991, 15–16; Marais 2001, 106). In contrast to other ISI models like the Brazilian one, the South African model differed because the Apartheid laws restricted specific activities like self-employment (Seekings and Nattrass 2005, 141–2). Moreover, while Brazil followed the ISI strategy rather systematically, the South African trajectory has been much more erratic, with phases of liberalization followed by returns to the ISI model. There were two main liberalization phases during Apartheid: the first between 1972 and 1976, and the second that started in 1983 (Bell 1993, 84–5). One of the main reasons for the liberalization policies was the fact that ISI was not producing growth in several sectors as expected. Furthermore, the main export commodity (gold) was not so lucrative on the world market. As a first step towards liberalization and a more export-oriented strategy, the Export Development Assistance was introduced in 1972. Additionally, quantitative restrictions on imports were reduced to systematically drive down protection of the local producers (Bell 1993, 84–5, Edwards et al. 2009, 153). Nevertheless, the "overall trade policy remained protectionist" (Alves and Edwards 2009, 207) and was not given up in favor of a completely export-oriented approach. During the early 1980s, these economic weaknesses were aggravated by political problems, as the economy was also hit by international economic sanctions as well as local struggles against the Apartheid system (Bell 1993, 90–3). In order to address the economic crisis, a second significant interruption of the ISI model in the form of liberalization took place between 1983 and 1985. South Africa then had a dual exchange rate system including the commercial Rand and the financial Rand, and exchange rate controls for foreigners were abolished (Bell 1993, 87). The reduction of quantitative restrictions continued, but protection subsequently rose again, especially due to the debt crisis in 1986. Consequently, the South African economy was more protected in 1988 than in 1984 (Bell 1993, 89; Alves and Edwards 2009, 207–8). This led to the demand to roll back the state and focus more on a market-driven economy when the Apartheid regime finally collapsed. This indeed fitted well with the international trend of rolling back the state during the late 1980s and early 1990s (Lipton and Simkins 1993, 7–13, 17–21).

As shown in this short historical sketch, racial segregation, the central role of the MEC, as well as the shifts between liberalization and state intervention phases were major features of South African capitalism during the Apartheid era. These features also remained prevalent for capitalism under the new democracy. The African National Congress (ANC) government continued on the liberal pathway between 1996 and 2005. The government implemented the Growth, Empowerment and Redistribution program in collaboration with South African capital, but against the avowed preferences of their two political partners, the South African Communist Party (SACP) and the Congress of South African Trade Unions

(COSATU) (Habib and Padayachee 2000, 252). Central to the Growth, Empowerment and Redistribution program was that redistribution could take place only with growth. In addition, it called for a strict monetary and fiscal policy. It followed the global trend of the 'Washington Consensus' of rolling back the state. Once the South African government joined the World Trade Organization (WTO) in 1995, it liberalized the tariff system, which at the time was marked by a strong degree of protectionism. As a result, many national companies, in particular in the textile and clothing industries, were badly hit by the introduction of international competition. The South African state also followed the United States and the European Union in extending liberalization within the WTO beyond tariffs and quotas in the 1990s and early 2000s (Claar 2018, 65–6). In addition, the South African government started to negotiate several bilateral trade agreements, and thus followed the global liberalization pathway. However, these liberalization policies did not result in either an increased growth rate or in substantial increases in foreign direct investment.

With the Accelerated and Shared Growth Initiative of South Africa in 2005, a new phase of economic policy began that included a demand for more state intervention. In the following years, the South African government, and the Department of Trade and Industry in particular, put forward/advocated more interventionist 'developmental state' policies. Issuing the National Industrial Policy Framework and the Industrial Policy Action Plan (DTI 2007) in 2007 thus reflected a certain renunciation of/movement away from the Washington Consensus. Over the last few years, the Department of Trade and Industry has updated and refocused industrial policy on a regular basis. It highlights transversal interventions in the areas of public procurement, competition policy, trade, industrial finance, innovation and technology, regional integration and special economic zones (DTI 2014, 41). However, devising an Industrial Policy Action Plan alone is not sufficient for industrial development, especially "given the political will required to move from an administrative to a productionist perspective" (Haines 2015, 164). The implementation of policies is slow, and external investments remain weak. Moreover, the South African perspective on the developmental state, as highlighted in the "National Development Plan – Vision 2030", differs from the traditional developmental state approach by highlighting the need for a more democratic approach.

> The National Development Plan highlights the need for a developmental state that is capable of driving the country's development. Building state capacity is the most important step to achieve a developmental state. [. . .] A robust democracy is therefore not just compatible with building a capable and developmental state, it is an essential prerequisite for the sort of developmental state needed to tackle poverty and inequality.
>
> (NPC 2011, 409–10)

The South African strategy, which is marked by a strong commitment to democracy, thus shies away from following the Chinese model (NPC 2011, 408–43).

In practice, however, the implementation of the plan is limited due to a weak state bureaucracy as well as divergent class positions on the matter. The three main economic departments, the National Treasury, the Economic Development Department and the Department of Trade and Industry, have articulated different positions regarding economic and trade policy. The National Treasury has strong links to liberal capital, while the Economic Development Department, as a relatively new department, is seen as more heterodox. While the National Treasury and the Department of Trade and Industry had similar takes on economic development in the first phase of post-Apartheid South Africa (not least due to personal ties to the ministers), the Department of Trade and Industry been characterized by a more developmentalist approach (Pillay 2011, 42; Claar 2018, 149–51). These different positions within the government create insecurity and incoherence in the implementation of industrial policy. The option for state-led capitalism, therefore, remains limited.

Overall, the historical provenance of fragmentation and liberalization are reflected in some recent developments. First, they are evident in that the highly organized trade unions that are able to strike for several days and weeks at a time for wage increases further complicate the picture. An illustration of the peak of the struggle between capital and labor was the Marikana massacre at the Lonmin mine in 2012 (de Waal 2012). Second, the historical trajectories of fragmentation and liberalization are reflected in the severe and brutal xenophobic attacks by South Africans living in the margins on foreigners (in particular those from other African countries) in 2008 and again in 2015 (The Economist 2015a). Third, the service delivery protest (Grant 2014) as well as the student protests (England 2015) show the growing differences between the interests of the state and society. Fourth, the fragile economic status of various state-owned companies like South African Airways, Eskom and others (Daniel 2018) also show the cleavages within the various bodies of the government. Finally, the stable but also somewhat crony political system makes it difficult to attract investment (Isa 2013; Vegter 2015). For more than a decade, the corruption ensuing from the close ties between Zuma and the Indian businessman Gupta (see more, e.g., in Myburgh 2017) shaped the South African state until it was ended with the former president Zuma being thrown out of office and replaced with the vice-president Cyril Ramaphosa in February 2018 and investigations being initiated against investments by the Gupta family (see, e.g., BBC News 2018).

These current developments highlight the problems of state-led capitalism in South Africa. As we have argued earlier, racial segregation and fragmentation are central to South African capitalism. This is combined with the strong power of mining and mining-related capitalist fractions under the umbrella of the MEC as well as an incoherent alternation between liberal and state-led development policies. Moreover, we need to take into account that the social formation in South Africa also changed with the emergence of a black business class that differs from the established white business class. This fragmentation continues within the state and leads to the time-consuming battles between different fractions. The state thus lacks the capacity to find a coherent economic policy approach in order to consolidate the unstable economy.

5.2 Coordination in the South African political economy

South Africa's economic coordination is characterized by a fragmented dominant social bloc. Two fault lines are central here: one between fragmented capitalist class fractions along racial lines, and another between monopoly and non-monopoly capital (for details, see Claar 2018, 91–4). On a superficial level, there is less close cooperation between public authorities and major business in South Africa than in China, India and Brazil. After the democratic transformation in South Africa, state-business coordination became more difficult due to the high fragmentation of the capitalist class fractions. Formerly personalized state-business relations were interrupted by the establishment of a formal tripartite dialogue on economic and labor issues in the National Economic and Labour Council (Nedlac). In addition, the relationship between the state and business experienced changes due to more interaction between black capital and public authorities. At the same time, foreign capital remains strongly entangled in South Africa's economy. Generally speaking, three major structures can be identified that shape coordination in South African capitalism: (1) fragmentation of the capitalist classes, (2) the tripartite dialogue between state, business and trade unions and (3) the relation between black capital and public authorities.

(1) Looking back to the Apartheid context, we can see that state-business cooperation was based on very close personal relationships and family ties, especially in the mining sector, as exemplified by Anglo-American owner Harry Oppenheimer. The capitalist classes were divided between Afrikaaner and English capital that had different relationships with the state. This means that Afrikaaner capital profited from close ties to the National Party government and English capital organized a compromise with the state as it owned most of the South African mines (Clarke 1978; Nattrass and Seekings 2010, 31, 38; Hart and Padayachee 2013, 69). These personal relations between the state and business, however, changed with the end of Apartheid. The early 1990s saw a total interruption of the earlier state-business relations. During the negotiation phase, the political transition to democracy was more present in the public eye than the restructuring of the economy (Terreblanche 2002, 95). Both white-owned business as well as the rising black-owned business had to (re-)establish their relationships with the state. In this context, there were several options for a change of the coordination mechanism between state and business. After merging white- and black-owned business associations, business had one umbrella association, called the Business Unity South Africa. However, this was riddled with fragmentation between foreign-national-white capital and national-black capital and thus led to the emergence of a second umbrella business association, the Black Business Council, which represented the interests of companies associated with the new Black Business Empowerment (BEE) policy (Mail and Guardian 2011a). Although business is thus superficially fragmented between white and black businesses, the

fundamental division is based on different capital interests of capitalist class fractions (Claar 2018, 91–4). Looking into this in more detail, different class fractions notably have a variety of linkages to the state. The mining capitalist class fraction, for instance, consists mainly of foreign/English capital and has close linkages to the state because of its central role in the MEC regime.

This also is true for MEC-related manufacturing as well as other foreign capital-related capitalist class fractions like the automobile sector. Within these fractions, white capitalists still own companies, and new black capitalists own only some divisions in the mining sector. Furthermore, finance and banking capital also has strong interests in the MEC-related system. In contrast, protectionist manufacturing capitalist class fractions in labor-intensive sectors are interwoven with the working class and had less influence on the state, at least during the first post-Apartheid liberalization phase. However, this changed with the more developmentalist approach of the state in the mid-2000s. The differences between English and Afrikaaner capital remain visible today, as the latter mainly appears in the form of large commercial farming and the former in the form of mining capital. Besides, racial affiliation becomes evident as a category of business separation (Claar 2018, 94–5).

Against this background, South African economic policy orientation is caught between two major class interests, more liberalization versus more protectionism. During Mbeki's leadership, all parts of the economic state apparatus (National Treasury, Department of Trade and Industry) had one common goal: to foster liberalization. Under Zuma's leadership, the pro-liberalization fraction was challenged in terms of its institutional foundation. For instance, the National Treasury was restricted in its power (The Presidency 2009). Moreover, changes in personnel within the state apparatus had a significant impact on policy. Alec Erwin, for instance, who had personal ties with Finance Minister Trevor Manuel and Mbeki himself, had led the Department of Trade and Industry, and these three shared a strong liberal economic policy orientation. Within the Zuma administration, Rob Davies represented the more protectionist wing, and as a result, a more state-led industrial policy focused on protectionism was observable during this time. A further example to illustrate this is the National Industrial Policy Framework and Action Policy that were established in 2007. This development was strongly supported by the trade unions while business was rather reserved on the matter. In addition, a new economic state apparatus was also introduced, called the Economic Development Department (Pillay 2011, 42). Thus, under the Zuma administration, more national protectionist fractions gained political ground while the liberalization fractions in the state apparatus became more marginalized (Claar 2018, 146–9).

(2) The introduction of a formal tripartite dialogue in the National Economic and Labour Council (Nedlac) disturbed the mechanism of personal relations between the state and business. Prior to 1994, white politicians and white business collaborated and shaped the political economy, though white business was already divided into English and Afrikaaner fractions (Clarke 1978, 34–5; Padayachee 2008, 60). In post-Apartheid South Africa, state-business relations changed,

although personalized relations remained important. Labor became a central player in the official South African political economy. Nedlac provides space for a tripartite dialogue that includes the labor movement as well as civil society alongside the government and business. In general, representatives of the major business associations, currently Business Unity South Africa and the Black Business Council, and trade unions, mainly from COSATU, sit together with government to discuss all state initiatives that are related to labor (Sadie 2006, 219). The government is obliged to consult with the other Nedlac participants. As a result, the state does not have as much flexibility in implementing certain policies without having business and labor on board. In this body, state and business as well as state and labor maintain a cooperative relationship. These relations are a result of specific conditions in South Africa such as the alliance that was formed by the ruling party, African National Congress, and the labor movement, COSATU. They also have an alliance together with the SACP in order to have a joint election list (McKinley 2003, 46). Therefore, some trade union leaders are also part of the government, and this has meant that the trade unions are closely associated with parts of the state. At the same time, trade unions see business as their enemy in the fight for higher wages, but also have to collaborate with business in Nedlac. The formalization of state-business relationships within Nedlac has also reduced access via informal personal relations, but at the same time business uses informal negotiations along Nedlac (Claar 2018, 153). This complex setting substantially differs from that in China and India, as compared to South Africa, labor is not as strongly present in the state-business relations of these two countries.

(3) Turning to the third issue, policies of affirmative action and Black Economic Empowerment have been used to shape a new dominant social bloc based on a similar coordination mechanism as in the relationship between the state and white business. Informal relationships between white capital and public authorities have been complemented by close links between black capital and public authorities. In practice, the state introduced BEE policies in order to establish a new relationship between the state and business on the basis of (positive) racial discrimination and redistribution of ownership from whites to blacks. This fits well into the overall policy orientation because the ANC-led state is not interested in changing the overall structure of South African capitalism. BEE thus allowed for the possibility to include blacks in economic ownership structures, despite the fact that only a small section of black elites were actually included rather than aiming for a wider, more equitable distribution among the population (Hirsch 2005, 7; Padayachee 2008, 67). In most circumstances "the beneficiaries of BEE are a small elite, closely linked to the ruling ANC and the trade unions" (Padayachee 2008, 60). BEE has also created a culture of crony capitalism and has made black entrepreneurs dependent on the state (Jeffery 2014, 359–60). Again, this supports further capital fragmentation. Nevertheless, the state, in the form of the ANC, has also reproduced this dependency with their own Progressive Business Forum that links black business with the party (Gumede 2007, 165).

Similar observations can be made with regard to the separation of black business, mainly medium-sized firms, from Business Unit South Africa, which represents large companies and business associations. In the debate over the split, the Black Business Council was in fact strongly supported by the state (Claar 2018, 92). This points to the fact that the state's strategy is to have a close relationship with black capital. With the rise of a new black business elite, coordination appears to have become even more difficult within the various fractions of national capital, especially with respect to the split in the black business association. Against this backdrop, a further important point needs to be considered: black capitalists, for the most part, have a double function in business and in the state apparatus (Nölke and Claar 2013, 44–5). We find several examples such as Cyril Ramaphosa, who was a trade unionist in the National Union of Mineworkers and also involved with the ANC. He left politics after Mbeki won the ANC presidential election at the end of 1997 and went into business. In 2007 he came back into the national executive committee of the ANC, in 2014 he began serving as their vice-president and he took office in February 2018 as the new South African president. In 2012, when the Marikana strike at Lonmin mine led to the death of several workers due to police violence, Ramaphosa was not only an important ANC politician but also a board member of Lonmin. Most likely due to these personal state-business ties/nexus, the state acted in the interests of the capitalist owners of the mine in Lonmin by intervening with the use of brutal police force against the striking workers (Hlongwane 2012; Munusamy 2012). This illustrates how the state acts in support of not only one particular company, but it secures the interests of all mining companies in the country and that of the entire MEC. The example illustrates the general structure of the South African economy, where state power/machinery is used to protect particularistic economic interests.

In sum, the South African state apparatus has developed a diverse set of policy strategies but is unable to implement them due to weak state capacity (Interview with an economist, Pretoria, 4 April 2013). South African capitalism is further influenced by foreign capital that pushes for ever more economic liberalization. At the same time, the state apparatus is fragmented by different points of view/differences of opinion on the shaping of economic policies. Thus, while the National Treasury fraction is in favor of continuing on a liberal path, the Department of Trade and Industry fraction follows a more state-led development path (Claar 2018, 145–52). Such state fragmentation also has an impact on the relationship between state and capital. The relationship has been marked by increased divisions, mainly between internationalized mineral-related capitalist class fractions on one side, and national capitalist class fractions like protectionist manufacturing and the agricultural sector on the other. In addition, the rise of black capitalists and new forms of interaction between the state and black capital are creating even greater fragmentation among the capitalist class fractions. Within South African capitalism, various foreign and national capital fractions thus coexist uneasily. However, while in China and India, national capital plays a dominant role in economic coordination, in South Africa historically, there has always been a stronger role played by foreign capital that is an obstacle to national-level economic coordination. While the dominant social bloc in the form of state-business relations undergirds effective economic coordination in China and India, and somewhat less so in Brazil, it appears to be far less coherent in the case of South Africa (Nölke and Claar 2013, 45).

5.3 The institutional foundations of South African capitalism

5.3.1 Corporate governance

Although like China, India and Brazil, state and family control also exists in South Africa's corporate governance, it is much less because family control declined after 1994 once a privatization of state-owned companies took place. Corporate governance is shaped through specific national governance concepts in order to address the former disadvantages of the black population. Therefore, black shareholding in the context of BEE and a consideration of the whole society represent specifics of South African corporate governance. At the same time, due to the historical linkages to British institutional development, corporate governance structures include liberal components as well.

Under the Apartheid system, family control was predominant in large mining companies. For instance, the Oppenheimer dynasty was one of the most important families in the South African economy (Habbard 2010, 38). The South African business elite during Apartheid was composed of families controlling large companies, but family businesses experienced a decline since 1994 (Habbard 2010; interview with a corporate governance expert, Johannesburg, 4 April 2013; Padayachee 2013b; Padayachee 2008, 69–71). Yet, South African corporate governance continues to include an important role for family control, even though the concentration of corporate ownership has been considerably diluted since 1994 (Habbard 2010). Mohamed argues that "[m]ost of the pyramid structures, which were at the centre of the MEC as a system of accumulation and were used by the powerful families to control most of the South African economy, were restructured and disentangled" (Mohamed 2010, 45–6). This took place primarily due to mergers and acquisitions in the 1990s that also were used to transfer shareholdings to black businesspeople. At the same time, this also changed the predominant "one big man" representation to a more democratic structure in the view of the executives within the companies (Mohamed 2010, 45–6; Padayachee 2013b, 267).

The transformation in company ownership structures began in the 1980s and continued into the 1990s. The state control of firms also changed with the democratization of the country because of (partial) privatization of former state-owned enterprises. Privatization had already started under the Apartheid government. However, the state-owned enterprises that were of crucial importance for South African infrastructure, like electricity, telecommunication, rail and air transport, as well as airports and seaports, remained in state hands (Black and Roberts 2009, 231). For instance, while Eskom remained a state-owned enterprise that was crucial for the provision of electricity, Telkom is currently a hybrid company after the state sold 30% of the shares to a USA/Malaysia consortium. South African Airways was first privatized and sold to Swiss Air, but was taken back by the state upon encountering problems (Black and Roberts 2009, 233–4), though it

Table 5.1 The 20 biggest companies of South Africa, by turnover, 2013

Company	*Origin of owners*	*Activity*	*Family control*	*Government*	*Industrial Development Corporation (IDC)*	*Government Employee Pension Fund (GEPF)*	*Private*	*Limited state control*	*High state control*	*Majority state-owned*	*Strong family ownership*
Glencore Xstrata	CHE, UK	Commodities, Metals & Mining					x				
BHP Billiton	AUS, GB	Metals & Mining			x	x	x				
Anglo American	ZAF, GB	Mining				x	x				
British American Tobacco	GB	Tobacco				x	x				
Sanlam	ZAF	Insurance				x		x			
SABMiller	ZAF, US, COL	Beverages				x	x				
Sasol	ZAF	Chemicals				x	x				
The Bidvest Group	ZAF	Diversified				x		x			
MTN Group	ZAF	Telecommunications				x		x			
Steinhoff International Holdings	ZAF	Furniture & Retail	Steinhoff			x		x			
Compagnie Financière Richemont	CHE	Luxury goods	Rupert				x				
Standard Bank Group	ZAF	Finance				x		x			

Shoprite Holdings	ZAF	Retail		x		x
Imperial Holdings	ZAF	Diversified		x		x
Vodacom Group	GB, ZAF	Telecommunications	x	x		x
Barclays Africa Group	GB	Finance			x	
FirstRand	ZAF	Finance		x	x	
Barloworld	ZAF	Diversified		x	x	
Massmart Holdings	ZAF	Retail		x	x	
Mondi	ZAF	Packaging & Paper		x		x

Source: Financial Mail 2014, 27.

continues to perform rather poorly. In addition, several other state-owned companies were sold, including railway stations, airports, resorts (Pitcher 2012, 245) and South African Broadcasting. As Table 5.1 illustrates, the ownership of the top 20 companies in terms of turnover is predominantly private, though in a few cases the state has some shares via state-owned companies or banks. In contrast to China, India and to a lesser extent Brazil, the South African economy is not under the firm control of national capital and thus shows patterns similar to the United Kingdom and the United States. However, South African firms are not formally allowed to serve shareholder value as they have to consider the interests of the society as a whole (interview with a corporate governance expert, Johannesburg, 4 April 2013). Foreign ownership of South African companies strongly increased after 1994 due to the movement of major companies to the London Stock Exchange (Terreblanche 2002, 122–4; Armstrong et al. 2005, 23). In the last decade, institutional investors like the government pension fund have played an increasing role in corporate governance (interview with a corporate governance expert, Johannesburg, 4 April 2013). Moreover, major private equity holders are foreign institutions (Habbard 2010, 18–19).

In general, due to its historical ties to Britain, South Africa's corporate governance system, with its links to British traditions, is based on British corporate law and practices (Andreasson 2011, 654; Diamond and Price 2012, 62). Therefore, corporate governance in South Africa has many linkages to the LME/shareholder-oriented model of corporate governance (Padayachee 2008, 69–71; Nölke and Claar 2013, 47). However, this Anglo-American model does not fit into the South African system, and there are signs of a more European stakeholder model being visible (Mthani and Olaj 2016, 136).

After democratization, the shape of corporate governance in South Africa was formally based on the King reports in 1994, 2002 and 2009 (IODASA n.d.). Central to the King reports is the 'Code of Conduct' for South African companies that since 2010 has required listing on the Johannesburg Stock Exchange as well as for public entities (Habbard 2010, 13; Padayachee 2013b, 264). The current corporate governance system is thus built on a shareholder system that formally has to address financial as well as social aspects (interview with a corporate governance expert, Johannesburg, 4 April 2013). The Anglo-American model remains predominant, though the second King report shifted to a stakeholder focus (Mthani and Olaj 2016, 125). State-owned enterprises have more experience in the combination of financial and social aspects than their private counterparts, but they lack the ability to recruit their boards of directors based on expertise and knowledge rather than on personal political relations (interview with a corporate governance expert, Johannesburg, 4 April 2013). The King reports were flanked by several laws in the last decade. Central among them were affirmative action programs, Black Economic Empowerment as well as the replacement of the 1973 Companies Act. Since the end of Apartheid, companies have been influenced by Black Economic Empowerment to promote black capital. State rhetoric often supported a change in ownership structures, but in reality BEE regulations and black ownership demands often remained on paper. Legal reforms of the corporate governance and shareholder system did not change the de facto corporate governance system (ibid.). A new Companies Act replaced the 1973 Company Act in 2011 after 10 long years of consultation. The Act regulates the formal composition of the board and the duties of directors. The previous Act had contained a high degree of personal liability for companies, and the new Act extended these into civil liabilities. Many observers were afraid that given this additional burden, qualified directors would leave (Habbard 2010, 13–14; Padayachee 2013b, 268–9).

To conclude, the South African corporate structure continues in part to consist of state- and family-owned companies, though foreign ownership has increased over the last two decades. Despite privatization, the South African state still owns several companies that play a crucial role in the country's economic development, but these companies, which are facing major crises, are not economically successful (Daniel 2018). Large parts of the corporate governance structure are based on an Anglo-American model, but this is complemented with the South African emphasis on addressing local demands like BEE and the need to benefit the society as a whole (Andreasson 2011, 665). In this regard, BEE also shapes the ownership structures of all state- and private-owned enterprises, which have to give shares to black business. All in all, corporate governance in South Africa is thus shaped by a divergent and incoherent mix of ownership imperatives.

5.3.2 Finance for investment

Within the investment regime, the MEC dominates as it experiences a transformation towards financialization. This limits the possibilities of the South African state to steer investment finance. Access to finance differs depending on the ownership and size of South African firms. Large foreign-owned companies are supported by their parent companies or have access to the capital markets. In addition, financial resources are mainly provided through private banks, although also a few public institutions do provide some funds for investment.

The South African financial market works according to global liberal standards. This is the result of the close relationship between foreign capital (mainly British) and domestic Afrikaaner capital, including the emergence of finance houses within the MEC system. With the growth of financialization, these financial institutions have become more important, and we now find a 'Financialized MEC', as Ashman and Fine demonstrate (Ashman and Fine 2013, 146). In reality, the South African financial sector largely developed through the MEC, and both are thus highly interrelated (Ashman and Fine 2013, 162). The presence of the MEC in the field of finance and a strong connection to the liberal British model have shaped the current financial sector. Due to the increasing financialization of the South African economy, domestic capital was able to sell off its holdings to global financial investors via private equity companies or via listings (Padayachee 2008, 64–6, 69–70; Fine 2009; Ashman and Fine 2013; Nölke and Claar 2013). This restructuring of the corporate landscape intensified the financialization of the South African economy (Mohamed 2016, 142). At the same time, short-term capital is increasing while medium- and long-term strategies become more difficult (Nölke and Claar 2013, 47). Financial capital, with its focus on speculative rather than committed investments, increases profit expectations on a short-term basis (Mohamed 2010, 43; see also Mohamed 2016, 141). This short-term capital, however, is indispensable for economic growth, as growth is largely based on capital-intensive production. Thus, the demand for short-term profits in the context of financialization, besides the appropriation by the BEE black elite, result in the decrease of long-term investments and close coordination for domestic development strategies (Nölke and Claar 2013).

The South African economy is also experiencing substantial capital flight as former South African companies reduce their investments in the country. They could

> move a large amount of capital out of South Africa legally because it would not be bound to exchange control restrictions on residents, and thus large amount of capital could leave the country in the form of dividends or other payments.
>
> (Mohamed 2010, 46)

The state allowed big companies like Billiton, South African Breweries, Anglo American Cooperation, Old Mutual and Liberty to leave the country, but they continue to dominate the economy. The state did not intervene for fear that other investors could be frightened off. Foreign investment in smaller volumes came from the return of Toyota and increased foreign shareholdings in parastatals such as Telkom and South African Airways (Mohamed 2010, 46; Mohamed 2016, 141). This has limited the state's options for holding the latter accountable with regard to national development strategies and has led to even greater fragmentation among business.

In contrast to China, India and Brazil, the South African state provides credits for South African firms only on a very small scale through the Development Bank of Southern Africa (DBSA), the Industrial Development Corporation (IDC) and the Ithala Development Finance Corporation Limited ('Ithala'). These are all state-owned development banks with roots in the Apartheid state. The DBSA was established in 1983, and its goal is to promote growth and economic development, working closely with the World Bank (Marois 2013, 12). In 1940, the IDC was established with the role of supporting domestic industrial capacity, mainly in manufacturing goods. The key industries were petro-chemicals and minerals. Generally, IDC funding was highly MEC-related (Maia et al. 2005, 8). IDC finances its projects through different mechanisms like loans, equity investment and borrowing from other banks (IDC 2014, 4). In early 2014, the IDC had only a small number of loans (15%), while equity investment was 67% of all assets (Matsilele 2015). In addition to DBSA and IDC, Ithala also has roots in the Apartheid setting. Its goal is to support development in the Kwa-Zulu-Natal province and to increase the number of black people in the supported sectors through job creation and skills development (Ithala n.d.). Ithala thus focuses on a small geographical region, while IDC and DBSA operate not only in South Africa, but also beyond in the region. They are both seen as "principal agencies of South Africa's economic diplomacy in Africa" (Games 2012, 3).

Early in 2015, the rating agency Moody's downgraded the two development banks on the basis of a perceived weakness in the South African government's capacity to provide financial resources for these banks. This was due to the fact that the South African state needs its state-owned companies to be profitable without financial support by the state (Matsilele 2015). Over the last years, the rating oscillated between negative and stable for the two development banks and the country's banking sector in general (Khumalo 2018; Moody's Investors Service 2018). On the whole, however, the financial resources of the state-owned banks are relatively small in comparison to the Brazil's BNDES (Mohamed 2010, 48; Interview with an independent consultant, Johannesburg, 17 April 2013). The state-owned development banks neither engage in long-term lending nor provide finance for small- and medium scale companies (Olawale and Garwe 2010, 731; Padayachee 2008, 61–3). The strong position of the MEC and its increasing financialization result in limited access to finance for non-MEC industries.

Private banks provide only short-term credits to the private sector in addition to their support for credit-based consumption, e.g. by issuing credit cards and vehicle leases (Mohamed 2010, 48). It is important to acknowledge that all major South African Banks are private banks. The South African state has no shares in the top four banks ABSA, Nedbank, First National Bank and Standard Bank. According to the Banking Association (2014, 1) "[t]he SA banking industry is currently made up of 17 registered banks, 2 mutual banks, 14 local branches of foreign banks, 2 cooperative banks and 43 foreign banks with approved local representative offices" in 2013.

Remarkably, the Industrial and Commercial Bank of China, a state-owned bank, bought 20% of Standard Bank shares (Orr 2007, 4). South African domestic private banks continued lending during the global financial crisis, which they handled fairly well (South African Reserve Bank 2010, 368).

South African firms are financed by domestic or foreign-owned commercial banks, trade credit and ordinary shareholder equity (Clarke et al. 2007, 275–6; Erasmus 2009, 145). Access to finance and loans depends on the size and ownership of the firms. Large and foreign firms find access to finance more easily than medium/small domestically owned firms. Similar patterns can be observed with regard to white- and black-owned firms as the former have easier access to finance. Foreign-owned firms can mainly rely on their parent company for finance and are less dependent on bank loans (Clarke et al. 2007, 78–82). Although small- and medium-scale enterprises are important job creators, as in Brazil, they "are not large enough to access the stock exchange to raise capital [and] they have little resources to institutional sources of finance others than banks, they tend to rely heavily on the personal savings of properties, family and friends" (Goodspeed 2012, 498).

Overall, financial resources for investments are mainly provided by private South African and global banks, while the financial capacity of public development banks is relatively small. Correspondingly, their capacity for promoting growth remains limited. In addition, the focus of the South African financial sector is mainly on large companies, as access for small and medium-sized enterprises is also limited. The implementation of a coherent state-driven national development strategy is thus not only inadequate but also contradictory in terms of allowing large South Africa-created companies to leave the country.

5.3.3 Industrial relations

Industrial relations in South African today are still influenced by the Apartheid era, during which these were strongly shaped by the MEC as the economy was dependent on (black) cheap migrant labor for the mining companies. With democratization, however, some degree of change took place in the structure of industrial relations. Current industrial relations are shaped through a highly protective legal framework that relates back to strong trade union involvement. Moreover, South Africa's industrial relations are formed through a largely dysfunctional trilateral cooperation, strong unionization and a high degree of fragmentation among the workers.

To understand industrial relations and the labor force today, it is useful to look at the central mechanisms of the industrial relations that shaped Apartheid. Industrial relations were based on a low-wage regime that was constructed along racial lines and used cheap black migrant labor reserves to work for white capital (Wolpe 1972, 433) This was crucial for creating and sustaining a labor surplus value for the capital sector because subsistence production allowed wages lower than the cost of reproduction (Wolpe 1972, 434). However, this profitable system started to disintegrate as the pre-capitalist reserve economy began to decline while the labor force remained in the urban areas (Wolpe 1972, 447–8). Racial segregation that privileged white workers continued to be central to industrial relations. Interestingly, a rise in unionization among the black population in the 1970s to challenge this led to the emergence of a black working class. These new black unions also supported the liberalization struggle in order to achieve political change (Webster 2013, 208–12). In the early 1990s, they also supported the restructuring of industrial relations, which involved the implementation of (1) new laws on bargaining councils and (2) the trilateral cooperation body Nedlac.

(1) Central legislation included the new Labor Act and government regulation of the collective bargaining councils as well as of the Commission for Conciliation, Mediation and Arbitration. This was meant to increase the coordination of industrial relations and supplement other regulation, such as the Law on Basic Conditions of Employment, Employment Equity and Skill Development (Webster 2013, 213–15). In general, this form of labor regulation requires "high levels of collaboration between capital and labour" (Pons-Vignon and Di Paola 2014, 30). Industrial relations in South Africa are mainly regulated at the sectorial level (Pons-Vignon and Di Paola 2014, 30), which is very different from the Chinese firm-level model. Formally, the central mechanism for collective bargaining is

the institution of the bargaining councils, though their numbers have declined in recent years. The councils are the space for negotiating collective agreements that are valid for all employers and employees falling within the scope of the council, independent of the geographical location of the companies. However, some unions have been more successful in wage negotiations without the involvement of bargaining councils, for example, Numsa in the automobile assembly sector (Pons-Vignon and Di Paola 2014, 30–1). Overall, only one-third of all workers are covered by bargaining councils. Thus only a limited number of workers actually profit from the councils, let alone from the extensive labor regulations (Webster 2013, 222). Hence, although South Africa has strong labor laws and labor rights, as well as a comprehensive sector-based collective bargaining system, its fruits are enjoyed by only a small part of the workforce.

(2) Another institution has been also established in order to represent the state, organized business and organized labor in industrial relations, namely the tripartite body Nedlac. On a symbolic level, it has been the most significant change with regards to the restructuring of South African industrial relations since the end of Apartheid. Nedlac includes government, business and labor as well as a fourth chamber: civil society. Its main task is to find a common position on economic and social policy issues before the government and parliament pass new laws. However, the government does not need to follow the advice of Nedlac. Through the implementation and incorporation of Nedlac, trade unions have, however, succeeded in bringing in coordinated elements of industrial relations (Nattrass 2013, 7; Webster 2013, 213; Claar 2018, 154). In addition to Nedlac, coordination takes place in an informal manner between the state and business, mostly behind closed doors (Webster 2013, 222). Within Nedlac, COSATU represents two million workers (COSATU n.d.), and its member organizations have been the strongest union in most large companies and in the public sector for a number of decades.[4] Trade union officials, therefore, have been very close to the state because of the tripartite alliance with the leading party, African National Congress, and the South African Communist Party (Webster 2013, 224–5).

Considering Nedlac and collective bargaining councils as spheres for the articulation of workers, it becomes clear that only a small number of workers are represented by these bodies. There is still a high level of fragmentation within the South African workforce, as workers are divided according to their work contract and social origin. First, there are the core workers with contracts, regular wages and organization or access to a union as well as to the legislative system. This segment of workers is fairly well protected. Second, there are the non-core workers who belong to the working poor with job insecurity, low wages, and limited access to trade unions or further education in the firms. Some are employed via labor brokers in the segment of core workers, which puts pressure on the labor conditions of the core workers. Moreover, skill development in this segment barely takes place and most remain semi/low-skilled. Third, a much larger segment of the workforce is unemployed, involved in subsistence activities or informal work (Seekings and Nattrass 2015, 115, Webster 2013, 219). These low-skilled workers provide labor in the informal economy. Like their legal status, their wages too are highly unequal and much lower than those of core workers (Leibbrandt et al. 2010, 24). These distinctions highlight the interrelation of wages and unionization in the South African workforce.

According to Statistic South Africa, the monthly median earnings of an employee were R 3300 in 2016, up from R 2900 in 2010 and R 3033 in 2014. But these median monthly earnings still reflect a high fragmentation of the labor force in favor of the white population, followed by the Indian communities. In 2016, a white person earned an average of R 12,500 and an Indian R 7200, while a black person earned R 3000 and a "Coloured" person R 3250 (Statistic South Africa 2015b, 4, 18–20; Statistic South Africa 2018, 8, 61). Despite the interrelation of wages and unionization, it appears that wages are strongly correlated with race. Wages among the black population are still lower than among other racial groups. This is due to the fact that most blacks are working in the informal sector, but it is also attributed to a lack of skills (Leibbrandt et al. 2010, 10–11, 17; ILO 2013a, 32; see also Claar 2018, 131).

In terms of skilled, semi-skilled and low-skilled labor, the median monthly earnings also indicate relatively stark differences. In 2016, skilled workers such as managers and professionals earned R 18,500 per month. The gap between them and semi-skilled workers like clerks is more than R 14,900 per month, as they earned only R 3600 monthly. Low-skilled workers like domestic workers only earned R 1500 per month (Statistic South Africa 2018, 8, 61, see also Claar 2018, 131). Thus, in the South African case we have a very low-paid segment with median monthly earnings showing a large gap compared to the earnings of skilled and semi-skilled workers. Generally speaking, union members earn higher monthly wages irrespective of occupation. While on the level of skilled workers the wage gap is rather small, the gap between union members and non-union members increases at the level of semi-skilled and low-skilled workers (COSATU 2012, 4; Claar 2018, 131). But wages for skilled/semi-skilled or low/unskilled workers also depend on firm size. In general, in smaller firms, the wages are lower than in larger firms (Clarke et al. 2007, 48). In this context, the high formal unemployment rate is another indication of the strong segmentation of the workforce. The official unemployment rate averaged 24.04% between 2003 and 2012 (World Bank 2015d). The expanded unemployment rate, which also includes discouraged jobseekers, ranged between 30% and 40% during the same period. In reality, 70% of these jobseekers have been waiting for years to find a job (Pons-Vignon and Di Paola 2014, 23–4).

Given the political power of the unions and the shortage of highly skilled labor, the core workers in the formal economy have a powerful position to negotiate and increase their wages, while semi/low-skilled non-union members are unable to profit from their bargaining potential. The strike potential in South Africa also remains high and has been crucial for advancing unions and workers' struggles. In 2007, 754 days were not worked due to strikes and lockouts, while in 2008 it was only 36 days. The main sectors in which the strikes and lockouts occurred were in the mining and related sub-sectors, for instance, in the community, social and personal service activities sector (ILO 2015).

To conclude, industrial relations in South African are largely shaped by the heritage of Apartheid inequalities. They are characterized by a strong legal structure of labor regulation for the formal sector including sector-level bargaining councils, a semi-functional tripartite coordination body (Nedlac), a substantial informal economy, strong fragmentation of earnings along racial lines and skill levels, high unemployment and inequality. Due to their political connections and high unionization rates in strategic sectors such as mining, trade unions are very strong and have a powerful potential to increase core worker wages and influence relevant public policies together with business while also engaging in crucial workers' struggles. Additionally, the interrelation between education, earnings and unionization has been crucial for industrial relations and the education system in South Africa, which continues to be highly fragmented. Overall, we find in this context "a hybrid [. . .] defined historically in racial terms" (Webster 2013, 210; cf. Nattrass 2013 for a similar argument) that includes not only liberal and coordinated elements, but also state-led and hierarchical elements. Such a high degree of fragmentation and a mix of various kinds of elements results in a dysfunctional and incoherent industrial relations system, in particular in connection with the education system, as unequal wage earnings also result from the highly differential quality of schools (van der Berg 2009, 337).

5.3.4 Education and training

The incoherence of the industrial relations system also affects the education and training system and vice versa. Like the industrial relations system, the education and training system too is highly fragmented. While the education system itself is established in a way similar to that of liberal market economies, the basic education base is too narrow for the demands of firms. Despite the state spending a large amount of the GDP on education, skills development continues to be limited in degree.

Here, too, the Apartheid system has left a specific legacy that also has an impact on the education system and development of human capital in contemporary South Africa. During Apartheid, the black, Indian, Coloured and white populations had separate schools, all based on the Bantu Education Act of 1953. Over the years, the black schools had a typical developing-country status, while the white schools were comparable with those in developed countries (Collins and Gillespie 1998, 34–5). Until 1994, the official school languages were English and Afrikaans, and the third languages were mostly native tongues. At the same time, the teacher-student ratio was much better in white schools than in black schools (Sedibe 1998, 270–1). Whites were consistently privileged in receiving a good education in contrast to blacks. This segregation and fragmentation, as well as the bad reputation of black schools (Collins and Gillespie 1998, 34), remain key indicators for the differentiation of the contemporary education system along racial lines.

In 1996, the old education system was dismantled on the basis of several new laws and the merger of several educational departments on all levels. The new constitution gives the national Department of Education the right to provide the general framework for education (Sedibe 1998, 272; Vally 2007, 45–6). Everyone has a right to basic education, and school is compulsory for students between 7 and 15 years of age, but parents have to pay school and tuition fees (Vally 2007, 45–6). Despite government spending of more than 5% of the annual budget on education between 2000 and 2010 and around 6% since then, there is a continued lack of skills development (UIS Data Centre 2015). However, this increased public spending does not translate into actual school resources but is used primarily towards salary increases for teachers (van der Berg 2009, 346).

Students attend grades 0 to 9 for general education and up to grade 12 to receive the matric school completion (comparable with the A-level) that gives them access to higher education at universities (SA info reporter 2015). Politically, the state tries to increase the graduation rates in order to increase higher education possibilities. With a matric, the chances of finding employment are substantially higher than without (Statistic South Africa 2015a). This shows the high correlation between the labor market and the education system. According to the OECD, "the education system is not producing the skills needed in the labor market" (OECD 2013b, 2). This is reflected in the high drop-out numbers (AfricaCheck 2015) as well as changes in matric pass rates (see Table 5.2). It is important to note that particularly in mathematics and physics, the pass rates are even lower in international comparison (van der Berg 2009, 331–2; OECD 2010b, 98), though in the last years the mathematic matric pass rate has shown an increase (van der Berg and Hofmeyr 2018). This also has an impact on the lack of skills for labor markets. Here, too, racial fragmentation is still visible as black students are less likely to pass the matric exams than their white classmates due to unskilled parents and poor quality of schools (van der Berg 2009, 333–7). These pass rates have their roots already in previous grades. For instance, in Grade 9, only 19% of no-school-fees-paying pupils pass the mathematics exam (van der Berg and Hofmeyr 2018). Therefore, the limited pass rate can explain the high unemployment rate among the black workforce and the low monthly earnings in the same group, as shown in the previous section.

Higher education is a national competence as stipulated by the constitution (Jansen 2003, 300). Since 1990, the university system has undergone institutional

Table 5.2 Matric pass rate, 2009–2014

Year	Pass Rate
2009	60.60%
2010	67.80%
2011	70.20%
2012	73.90%
2013	78.20%
2014	75.80%

Source: Motshekga (2015).

changes that have included mergers between white and black universities as well as the relocation of specific programs to other universities. Through measures like these, "21 universities became 11 institutions; 15 technikons became five 'stand-alone' technikons and six comprehensive institutions (combinations of universities and technikons); 150 technical colleges became 50 merged technical colleges" (Jansen 2003, 296). The South African government followed the global trend by renaming the technikons to universities of technology in 2005, which now focus more on applied research (Mtshali and Sooryamoorthy 2018, 6, 10). The government was under pressure to restructure universities as a means to increase capacity as well as global competitiveness (Jansen 2003, 305). In the South African higher education system, students have to pay tuition fees. Access for blacks is, therefore, not only restricted due to their grades in previous examinations, but also due to their financial background. The perception that the higher education system is exclusive and not conducive for black students thus has a base in reality, a fact also highlighted by the student protests in 2015 and following years (Bawa 2014, 229). The protests have been successful, as from 2018 onwards the state has "fund(ed) free education for students who come from poor or working-class families with a combined income of R350 000" (Tshwane 2018). This is a first step towards overcoming the limitation of the effectiveness of higher education as a key pillar for socio-economic development (Makhanya and Botha 2015).

In the area of vocational education and training, the Further Education and Training (FET) colleges provide access to higher education on a non-traditional basis. The purpose of the FET colleges is to meet the skill demands of the South African economy. However, only half a million students are participating in public FETs. In these FET colleges, young people and adults are the target group for upgrading skills and retraining (Powell 2012, 645). In South Africa, there is a public and private FET system. In practice, the public FET system looks fragile and less valuable for firms than the private FET system (McGrath and Akoojee 2009, 153). Mainly, private FETs are multi-institutes that can offer more industry-relevant skills (McGrath and Akoojee 2009, 153). As their purpose is skill development and employability, the Department of Labor supports private FETs. Overall, South Africa focuses on the development of intermediate skills in the public and private FETs (McGrath and Akoojee 2009, 150; Powell and McGrath 2014, 143).

Despite being challenged by various social movements, the South African education system has undergone an increasing liberalization following the norm that good education should be costly. On the one hand, higher education restrictions related to tuition fees show similarities to liberal market economies like the United States or the United Kingdom. On the other hand, the state spends a large amount of the GDP on education, but without these expenses leading to a qualitatively good education system (Modisaotsile 2012, 1). With the transformation of the education system, the structural segregation during the Apartheid regime continues to shape the education system. Racial fragmentation remains a relevant feature, though new problems with regard to class and regional settings, in particular between urban and rural institutions, have also arisen (Jansen 2003, 301).

This results in black students having less access to education because their parents already belong to a disadvantaged group. Despite high government spending on education and the variety of higher education institutions in the country, the quality of skills developed is insufficient for a competitive labor market. In addition, a balance between public strategy and the demands of private firms is missing. Overall, it can be concluded that there is a strong interrelation between industrial relations, monthly earnings and the degree of education, particularly with regard to the disadvantages suffered by black students.

5.3.5 Innovation

The South African innovation system, similar to the spheres discussed earlier, is equally marked by incoherence. The innovation system was established around ideas from developed economies. In general, the focus is more on incremental/product-oriented innovations like in CMEs, rather than on radical innovation as is common in LMEs. The South African state plays an important role in shaping the innovation system. At the same time, the state regulates the protection of intellectual property rights, which in turn has impacted public and private collaboration on innovation (Kruss and Lorentzen 2009, 175; interview with innovation expert, Stellenbosch, 12 April 2013).

South Africa's innovation system evinced a radical break in the early 1990s. Previously, the Apartheid government's focus was on innovation and technology in the defense industry, in the mining industry (with finance by the Industrial Development Corporation) and technological support for large-scale agriculture. In the area of private enterprise, innovation and technology was similar to the whole economy and concentrated in only six corporations. Moreover, there was fairly close interaction between the state, business (as well as state-owned enterprises) and regulatory and financing organizations (OECD 2007b, 87–8). Despite the reasonably well-functioning innovation and technology system, it was still a fragmented system that favored the white population. Therefore, the radical break with the transition from Apartheid provided a window for innovation policies that could also address fragmentation and inequalities (Kruss and Lorentzen 2009, 163). South Africa applied a 'National Innovation System' framework that at the time existed only in developed economies. The main focus of this framework was on the public rather than the private sector (Kruss and Lorentzen 2009, 166–7; also more on the development of the National Innovation System). In 2007, the South African Department of Science and Technology started to focus on developing a 'knowledge based economy' with a 10-year plan.

Concerning R&D, there are four categories of funding: government, business, foreign (e.g., parent firms, global foundations and research programs like the EU) and other South African sources. In 2004 and 2005, for example, business spent the largest proportionate amount on R&D. Besides, business also conducted the most R&D activity, followed by government and higher education. The areas with the largest spending and increase in R&D have consistently been natural science, engineering, life science and communication (OECD 2007b, 92–4). As a percentage of GDP, government spending on R&D was 0.79% in 2006, 0.93% in 2009 and 0.76% in 2010 (UNESCO Institute of Statistic/UN Data 2015). While these are remarkable numbers in comparison to other developing countries, the South African state nevertheless cannot compete with, for example, Chinese investments in R&D. In addition, the absolute numbers of researchers, particularly in the fields of natural science and engineering, are far below the OECD average (OECD 2007b, 95). Driven by the higher education sector, South Africa's R&D personnel in full-time-equivalent employment increased from 30,978 in 2011–2012 to 35,050 in 2012–2013 (HSRC/CeSTII 2014a, 2014b). This low number has its roots in the lack of human capital and low skill development in the South African basic education system. The number of completed PhD degrees is also too low in order to increase the number of researchers. In 2012, 1249 South African graduates received a PhD, while in China, 50,000 PhDs were completed in 2009 (Cloete et al. 2015, 76, 83, 85, 91). Despite the low number of PhDs, the government nevertheless sees the PhD degree as the key vehicle for innovation (Kruss and Lorentzen 2009, 173). Given this priority, innovation policy has focused on higher education as well as on public research and science institutions rather than on private firm innovations (Kruss and Lorentzen 2009, 181). Thus, in South Africa, as in the case of Brazil, innovation rarely takes place in private firms, but rather in public research institutions.

Despite the focus on public research institutions, the state also provides some financial support for private sector innovation, for instance, through the "Innovation Fund" and the Department of Trade and Industry "Human Resources for Industry Program". Moreover, it also appears that the government focuses on incremental innovation rather than radical innovations (Kruss and Lorentzen 2009, 175, 181; The Innovation Hub n.d.). Thereby, the limited financial resources for innovation, only 1.7% of turnover in 2005–2007 (Moses et al. 2012, 2), provide further evidence of incremental innovation (OECD 2007b, 100). Innovative enterprises (65.4%) are more export-oriented, in particular for the African market and less for the global market. At the same time, non-innovative enterprises (34.6%) predominantly produce for the domestic market (Moses et al. 2012, 3–4).

Large corporations such as South African Breweries, a global giant in the beverage industry, often profit from foreign knowledge via acquisitions, similar to some Chinese companies. Moreover, most large companies like Eskom and de Beers focus only on applied research (interview with innovation expert 2, Johannesburg, 17 April 2013). It can thus be assumed that these MEC companies have limited interest in extending research beyond their operations, as they do not see themselves as innovation hubs for the whole industry. Generally, the linkages between private firms and state-funded entities are extremely weak, and the state is not aware of business needs (interview with innovation expert 2, Johannesburg, 17 April 2013).

In the innovation process, patent rights and intellectual property rights play an important role. While in China and India intellectual property rights have been weakly applied, in South Africa the new Intellectual Property Rights regulations, which have been influenced by European policies, might be considered an example of over-regulation (Kruss and Lorentzen 2009, 175). For instance, the new Intellectual Property Rights from Publicly Financed Research and Development Act is very challenging, because it stipulates that if the state funds research and technology, it has the copyright of the respective outcomes. In some cases, research agreements cannot be concluded due to ownership of the results (interview with innovation expert, Johannesburg, 17 April 2013). Thus, the transfer of innovation has become legally more complicated, which demonstrates the difference in the (non-)adaptation of these regulations in South Africa as compared to China and India.

Furthermore, the Intellectual Property Rights regulations are more in favor of foreign investors (Kaplan 2009, 5). Regarding Intellectual Property Rights, the South African state has adopted liberal norms, while in the field of patents it regulates more strictly. The TRIPS regime stipulates a minimum of 20 years for a patent. The South African Patent Act allows 20 years, but not more. This law has thus not found favor with pharmaceutical firms (Gregory 2008, 14). The constitution also allows the patent to be ignored if it is in the larger public interest; however, the South African state has so far not utilized this option often (Kaplan 2009, 5; Interview with innovation expert, Johannesburg, 17 April 2013).

Although the South African state supports the innovation system through policies and by providing it with financial resources, the transfer of innovation continues to remain low, especially in comparison to China and India. Given the lack of human capital in combination with liberal 'over-regulation' of Intellectual Property Rights, a focus on small and medium enterprises and a lack of innovation policy implementation, South Africa does not have a 'state-permeated' transfer of innovation. Instead, there are liberalization elements, and the MEC system acts as a blocking mechanism.

5.3.6 Domestic markets

South Africa is the most open of the four economies in our sample as far as IFDI is considered, and far more dependent on foreign capital than any of the other three. These conditions also have an impact on the domestic market. Consequently, there is a high dependence on foreign capital results in limited niches for own products on the local consumer market because foreign investments are usually aimed at the more technologically sophisticated and export-oriented firms. Therefore, in South Africa, less innovative firms develop for the domestic market while innovative firms produce for the regional and global markets (Moses et al. 2012, 3–4). In a way, the regional market is the sphere of economic development and growth for several firms. In comparison to China, India and Brazil, South Africa's domestic market is rather small. Due to unemployment, poverty and inequality, the number of consumers remains low, despite the growing middle class (Jerschefske 2011; Kew 2013). Generally, the potential to strengthen domestic markets through rising incomes has been ignored during the last decade (see Chapter 6).

While the other three emerging economies protect the domestic market, or at least certain sectors, from foreign investors, the South African economy has generally not done so. This is partly due to the fact that after exclusion at the end of Apartheid, openness was the South African strategy to become once again integrated into the global economy. The openness of the market and the historical linkages to the British economy have led to strong interlinkages with foreign capital and global markets, thereby leaving the local market behind. This development affects the domestic market as local production is struggling. While China and India can count on a large number of domestic consumers, South Africa has too small a domestic market to boost economic growth. Furthermore, consumer markets are fragmented because black and white consumers have different demands, and the potential of black consumers has only recently and slowly been discovered as a growing market (Chase et al. 2010). Hence, the regional (rather than global) market provides an important opportunity for investments, production and distribution. South African firms such as the telecommunication company MTN, the financial provider Standard Bank and the retail chains Shoprite and Pick'n Pay are expanding regionally rather than nationally (Hattingh et al. 2012, 4; Holmes 2013; The Economist 2013a). South African domestic sales at Shoprite, for instance, grew by only 9.8% from June 2012 to 2013, while during the same time frame they achieved 28% growth on the rest of the African continent (The Economist 2013a).[5] These eye-catching numbers are just an indicator that the regional market compensates for, and substitutes for, the domestic market, which provides an insufficient potential for profit. If South African firms increasingly 'exit' the domestic circuit, it will become more difficult for the South African state to commit local firms to a state-led development strategy.

In addition to the African market, formerly South African listed companies like the mining company AngloAmerican and the insurance company Old Mutual changed their listings from the Johannesburg Stock Exchange to the London Stock Exchange in order to be more competitive on global markets. These companies are still operating in the domestic market, but they refrain from investing in South Africa (Mohamed 2010, 46). With no investment in the domestic market, the South African economy remains highly dependent on foreign investments and imports from Western economies as well as from emerging economies like China. It is, therefore, vulnerable concerning short-term FDI outflows as well as currency depreciation, with negative impact on the domestic market; for example, through increasing inflation rates (Mohamed 2010, 42) that directly hit consumers. As shown previously, racial fragmentation remains a crucial element in several institutions and with regards to local consumers; in an economy with millions earning a small income, the prospects for capital accumulation are also limited (see section 6.2).

To counter these trends, the South African state, through the Department of Trade and Industry, has aimed to boost industrial development and provide more room for state intervention. It followed the idea of building a developmental state as an institutional driver of national economic growth within the National Industrial Policy Framework as well as the National Development Plan. The National Industrial Policy Framework was therefore launched in 2007, and five sectors were identified to receive increased support: (1) natural-resource based sectors, (2) medium technology sector, (3) advanced manufacturing sector, (4) labor intensive sectors and (5) tradable sector (DTI 2007, 40–3; EDD 2010, 54). These policies should have translated into better market performance, but the implementation capacity of the state apparatus has been limited (Interview with an economist, Pretoria, 4 April 2013; Claar 2014, 203). The state has so far not intervened in a forceful manner, though there are discussions about whether the state should intervene, for example, in the currency exchange rate (Draper 2010, 5–10). From our perspective, there is no active state intervention concerning reshaping a specific economic development path. The state rather intervenes with its security forces to undermine protests and strikes, as it sees these as an obstacle not only to the party's reputation but also as a possibility of losing power. In a way, South Africa reflects the situation of the 1970s and 1980s in India, during which the state was able to exercise its power to curb industrial unrest and social struggles, but unable to proactively improve the living standards of its population (Rudolph and Rudolph 1987).

5.4 Comparative advantages, institutional complementarities and contradictions of South African capitalism

Synthesizing our analysis so far, we arrive at a model of South African capitalism that differs from that of China, India or Brazil. Institutional cohesion and its complementarities are not strong enough for a thriving economy in South Africa, not to speak of a positive impact on reducing poverty and inequality. Since the end of Apartheid, South African capitalism has been hit several times by high inflation, currency crises or capital flights, resulting in limited growth. Also, the largest South African multinational companies have changed their major listing from the Johannesburg to the London Stock Exchange (Mohamed 2010, 42). Furthermore, although access to the South African corporate sector is more open, foreign direct investment has been limited. These developments are the major reasons for lower economic growth and development.

If there is one comparative advantage that South African capitalism has, it lies in mining backed by the MEC regime. South Africa's advantage is its large resource base and the cheap electricity that it guarantees. According to a Citygroup report, South Africa is the world's richest country in mineral resources, though production could be higher (Sake 24 2010).

However, this boosts capital intensive industries that accumulate capital but do not increase employment. Further limits to coherence in South African capitalism are fragmentation/racial segregation, the MEC and liberalization, all of which affect the institutional spheres as well as the economic coordination in different ways and to varying degrees. These structures also result in a minimal degree of state-led developmentalism.

Fragmentation occurs in every single institutional sphere of South Africa's capitalism, and the dominant social bloc itself is deeply fragmented. Domestic capital is rather weak and still mainly in the hand of the whites, but with a growing share of black capital. At the same time, large corporations are foreign-owned to a large degree, have strong foreign connections and remain mainly in white hands (besides the official BEE shares).

While in China and India, the dominant social bloc contains close state/business alliances, the situation in South Africa is different. Trade unions are institutionally embedded as a partner of the ruling party as well as in Nedlac. Therefore, in South Africa, we have greater fragmentation within the power bloc. The presence of a diversity of actors in state-business-labor relations hamper the state from pushing through because of divergent interests and goals like securing jobs and more business expansion. Various interests in the power elite, as well as fragmentation along racial and class lines, lead thus to a more dysfunctional economic coordination. Fragmentation can also be found in the workforce: a high degree of informality and extreme wage differentials between low-paid organized groups of workers (with some institutional Apartheid features having changed only superficially) coexist with relatively well-protected employees in certain industries (Hirsch 2005; Nölke and Claar 2013, 48).

As a consequence, institutional complementarities are limited. The institutional framework of South African capitalism was interrupted by the end of the Apartheid state, and a new institutional constellation emerged in which different approaches collided. Due to historical ties to Britain, corporate governance and investment of finance complement each other but have little compatibility with the other three spheres of industrial relations, education, and innovation. Fragmentation of the education and labor system results in a lack of participation by black South Africans. These spheres, therefore, show, in contrast to China, India and Brazil, no institutional complementarities. Indeed, the MEC adds to the incoherence in South African capitalism because it favors the principle of liberalization and benefits from fragmentation. All in all, South African capitalism is a hybrid composed of several 'varieties of capitalism', from liberal to state-led and coordinated. The systemic fragmentation that is apparent in all institutional spheres and economic coordination, which are rooted in the country's colonial and Apartheid history, further destabilize South African capitalism.

The following two chapters attempt to systematically address their commonalities and differences, with the purpose of developing and discussing a new ideal type of capitalism to complement the established CME, LME and DME types. We call this ideal type of capitalism in large emerging economies 'state-permeated market economy' (SME). To prove our point that this constitutes in fact a distinguishable model of capitalism, we compare it to countries that are characteristic cases of liberal, coordinated and dependent forms of capitalism.

Our explication of state-permeated capitalism proceeds in two distinct steps. Chapter 6 is strictly synchronic and attempts to yield as much explanatory power from the analytical repertoire of institutionalist CC as possible. Based on an analysis of the growth performance of the four large emerging economies as well as their comparative advantages, we compare their mode of insertion into the global economy and their domestic economic institutions. This leads us to the establishment of an ideal type of state-permeated capitalism that is suited for the analysis of large emerging economies.

However, the identification of an ideal type of state-permeated capitalism is insufficient for a comprehensive explanation of capitalism and growth in large emerging economies. Real economies do not usually reflect theoretical ideal types. Therefore, in a second step (Chapter 7), we adopt a diachronic perspective in which the inherent historical dynamics, tensions and contradictions of really existing SMEs come to the fore. In addition to clarifying the relationship between the four economies and the theoretical model as well as reflecting on the historical context of the evolution of this type of capitalism, we discuss the question of whether this type of capitalism will be economically and politically viable in the foreseeable future.

Notes

1 The terms Whites, Blacks, Indians and Coloreds are regularly used in South African politics. However, they still reproduce structural inequalities and simplify the complexity of social relations.
2 This section is partially based on Claar (2018, 39–73).
3 It is a mixture between the English (Electricity Supply Commission) and the Afrikaans (Elektrisiteitsvoorsieningskommissie) spelling.
4 Currently, we can observe changes. For instance, National Union of Mineworkers lost his bargaining right to Association of Mineworkers and Construction Union (Faku 2013) and National Union of Metalworkers of South Africa was forced to leave COSATU due to political differences regarding the support of the ANC (Marrian 2014).
5 The South African government supports expansion in the region through training and trade agreements (Games 2011, 11).

6 The contours of state-permeated capitalism

The previous chapters not only dissected the institutional configurations of capitalism in China, India, Brazil and South Africa, but also documented their economic achievements from the 1990s to the 2010s. All four countries have grown quite strongly. The purpose of this chapter is thus to identify the 'pillars' of an economically successful kind of state-led capitalism in large emerging markets. By identifying such a type of what can be labeled state-permeated capitalism, the diverse histories and particularities of these four economies are rendered more comparable.

This chapter starts with the balance sheet of BICS growth trajectories over roughly the first decade of the 2000s. Rather than comparing these countries for the sake of comparison, we stress that it is the outcome which matters, measured grossly by GDP growth (section 6.1). In the next step, we identify the main reason why large emerging economies have been able to grow substantially, which is their specific 'comparative advantage'. This advantage consists of a situation in which domestic mass markets for middle-range products allow for stable growth (section 6.2). A crucial factor for the stability of this growth regime is selective integration into global capitalist structures which are actively managed by the state (section 6.3). Moreover, this form of capitalist production is supported and stabilized by a set of institutions that fit together (section 6.4). The institutions for corporate governance, investment finance, industrial relations, and education and training as well as innovation form a coherent assemblage that supports specialization in the 'niche' of middle-range products. Altogether, these institutional factors form a model of state-permeated capitalism that is different from other types of capitalism and, at the same time, is successful in the pursuit of GDP growth because its institutions effectively complement each other (section 6.5). This especially holds true in two institutional clusters, namely the realms of corporate governance/investment finance and the realms of industrial relations/education and training/innovation. We highlight the differences of state-permeated capitalism vis-à-vis other models by comparing our country sample with countries that stand for one of the distinct varieties: the United States and Great Britain for LMEs; Germany and Japan for CMEs; and the Czech Republic and Slovakia for the DME variety.

6.1 The outcome: growth in global perspective

The rise of Brazil, India, China and South Africa (BICS) fundamentally changed the global political economy over the last decades. The share of the BICS of world GDP has more than doubled since 1990, with the share of established economies (United States, Great Britain, Germany and Japan) decreasing simultaneously. Large emerging economies continued to boost their economic performance since the 2000s, while many developed parts of the world economy have stagnated (see Figure 6.1).

Emerging market growth is a real macroeconomic tendency. Growth rates represent real economic development and not just price inflation, inflow of funds or an effect stemming from an increased recording of economic activities in national statistics. It is true that accounting for these activities is often difficult, and aggregated GDP is probably a rather weak indicator. Nevertheless, there is a core of capitalist accumulation that has grown over the last decade(s). This is in marked contrast to many established economies in the West, in particular LMEs, where growth has mainly been driven by financial sector activities (Krippner 2011).

Capital formation serves as an indicator of real investments, which in turn is the essence of capitalist accumulation. In that sense, we observe increasing BICS 'capitalization' in the 2000s (Figure 6.2). Their growth is less attributable to agrarian production or merely the sale of primary commodities and financial investments but to increased industrialization. It is also less a product of 'good' economic policy but a structural phenomenon which is partly independent from economic policy changes (although these definitely impinge on the 'performance' of these structures, as we will see later). Therefore, China, India, Brazil and South Africa grew by following a rather classic model of capitalist development – a model which has been declared obsolete since the proclamation

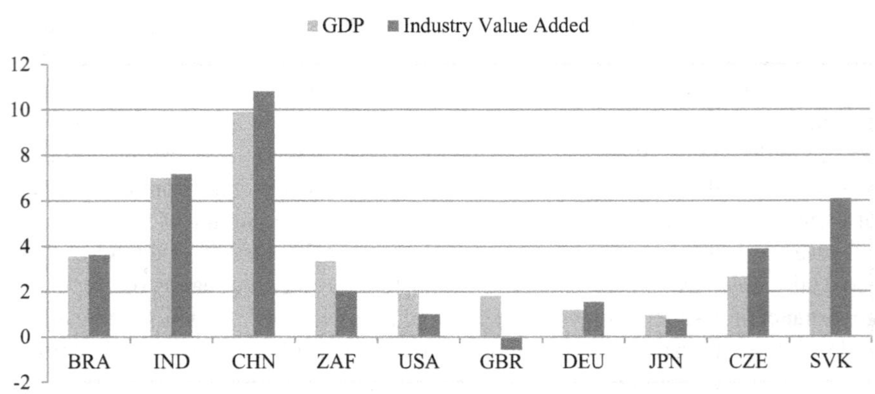

Figure 6.1 Industrial growth compared, average growth of GDP and industry value added, 2000–2013

Source: World Development Indicators.

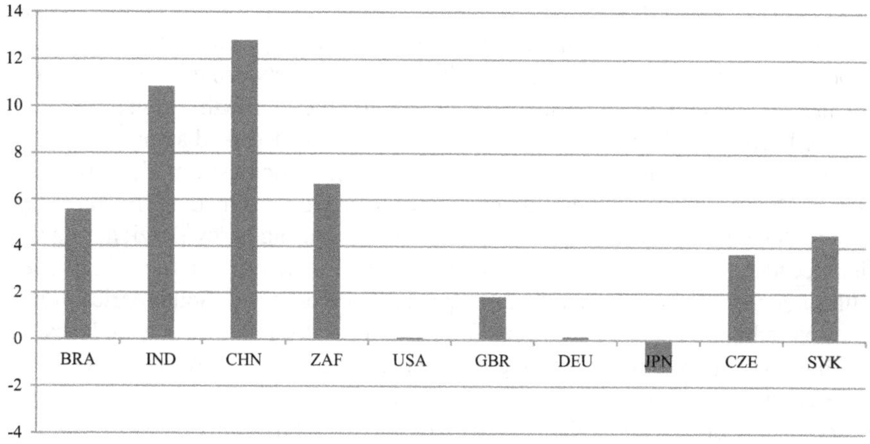

Figure 6.2 Average capital formation rate, average annual growth rate in percent, 2000–2010

Source: World Bank.

of the post-industrial society (Bell 1973). The subsequent sections shed more light on the particular properties of capitalism in large emerging economies, arguing that there is actually a 'growth model' which provides sufficient stability in order to bring about sustained economic growth.

6.2 Identifying the 'niche': products for domestic consumption

But what exactly are the sources of economic growth in the BICS? Conventionally, this is attributed to the competitive advantages of emerging economies on the world market, such as the export of Brazilian commodities, Indian IT services or Chinese manufacturing (see Lardy 1998; Srinivasan and Tendulkar 2003; OECD 2007a; Brainard and Martinez-Diaz 2009; Elliott and Zhou 2013). The domestic markets of emerging economies, however, do not play a significant role in these accounts. Historically, inward-looking development strategies such as import substitution failed to generate sufficient growth in order to propel large-scale increases in productivity (see Chapter 1). This is partly because capital goods could not be substituted so easily as technological capacities were often lacking. Furthermore, with low export volumes, import-substituting countries chronically lacked funds to purchase foreign machinery. As a consequence, those countries faced two kinds of external dependency: on foreign multinationals that would provide capital and knowledge, or on foreign credit. Either way, both were detrimental to the main goal of import substitution, which is national autonomy over the course of development (Baer 1972).

Yet the widely shared assessment of the futility of import-substitution industrialization (ISI) has distracted contemporary observers from the crucial importance of domestic market expansion for high growth rates in *large* emerging economies. From our perspective, there is no exclusive causal link between growth and export orientation. As we will demonstrate, countries can achieve growth within an inward-oriented economy if conditions permit. In contrast to widespread assumptions that the rise of emerging economies is based on exports, large domestic markets, particularly in Brazil, China and India, are crucial for their growth dynamics. As Table 6.1 shows, the bulk of industrial production in China, India and partly Brazil during the first decade of the 2000s has been sold within the respective countries. Only one-fifth to one-quarter of all manufactured products are exported. South Africa, however, has a higher export share which furthermore shows an increasing tendency.

Thus, strong growth in emerging economies is not necessarily associated with increasing exports. Actually, Chinese export shares have decreased in recent years, raising doubts about the one-sided thesis of China mainly being the 'workbench of the world'. Conversely, developed countries such as Germany and Great Britain increased their export shares between 2000 and 2010 while generating lower single-digit growth rates. CEE countries which opened widely for foreign investments during the 1990s and 2000s show a strong dependency on exports for their respective industrial sectors, but mostly grew slowly.

Table 6.1 Export share of total industrial production, in percent[1]

	2000	2001	2002	2003	2004	2005	2006	2007	2008	2009	2010
Brazil	18.6	21.7	24.35	25	26.2	25.5	24.9	23.2	23.4	21.4	21.1
India	21.2	21.9	21.7	22.1	21.4	23.8	23.9	23.3	27.1	22.4	23.4
China	27.8	26.4	27.7	26.9	26.5	27.1	26.6	26.7	23	17.4	17.6
South Africa	32.8	34.9	36.3	30.6	30.8	31.9	35.4	39.5	46.5	37.4	47.3
Czech Republic	61	n/a	59.9	61.1	n/a	68.8	n/a	70.9	73.6	76	79.6
Germany	47	48.7	50.6	50.1	52	53.8	56	56.8	58.7	58.5	60.5
Japan	n/a	17.1	19.4	20	21.6	22.2	23.8	26.3	25.5	22	24.9
Russia	117	96.4	85.3	66.2	64.2	65	62.9	54.8	58.1	57.5	57.8
Slovak Republic	117	119	117.4	117.4	115.8	113.5	114.7	104.2	98	100.1	95.9
United Kingdom	42.9	44.6	45	45.6	44.4	49.3	54	46.98	51.7	55.2	59.5
United States	18.6	18.4	17.7	18.2	18.9	19	20.4	21.6	23.5	n/a	n/a

Source: UNIDO Industrial Statistics Database, WTO SDB Statistics Database.

1 This indicator uses the statistics for industrial exports as provided by the WTO and statistics on industrial production by UNIDO at gross levels. Due to intermediate exports, transfer pricing and not least statistical accounting values above 100% are technically possible as these are yearly aggregate data.

Clearly, growth has to be generated internally if exports do not play the main role and products have to find markets domestically. Surprisingly, the most dynamic emerging economies have similarly large domestic markets at their disposal, as, for example Japan and the United States, albeit of a different kind. On the one hand, the domestic markets of China, India, Brazil and (only to a limited degree) South Africa are large enough to absorb indigenous industrial production. On the other hand, they serve different demands from those in developed countries. This has important consequences for indigenous firms. Their entrepreneurial strategies will be mainly oriented towards the requirements of the domestic rather than the global market in trying to design and manufacture products that public or private Indian, Chinese and Brazilian customers ask for. As Table 6.1 shows, the tendency for strong domestic markets has remained rather constant over the 2000–2010 period (and earlier). Under these stable conditions, firms in large emerging economies were able to bring their domestically oriented business strategies to maturity, thereby creating competitive advantages vis-à-vis foreign firms which lacked access to these markets as well as to supplier networks and knowledge about appropriate market behavior.

As a consequence of their privileged access to home markets, firms have not faced the same pressure to massively invest in upgrading products and processes technologically as they would with a focus on global markets. This is because, first, efficient competitors were rare, and second, because domestic demand for simple products was rising. If we, as a first step, adopt the classification of industrial production by the OECD into sectors of high-, medium-high, medium-low and low technological intensity (see OECD 2011c) and apply it to the countries in focus, we see another surprising phenomenon. Comparing the value added of these four classes (to see which product segments yield the highest productivity), we find that the segments of medium-level technological intensity produce the highest value added, while low-tech manufacturing has produced less value over the last decade (Figure 6.3). Arguably, technological upgrading plays a minor role here than widely assumed. Thus, although there are undoubtedly particular firms that engage in the manufacturing of high-tech products such as computers, optical instruments and pharmaceuticals, the returns from increasing technological intensity across the whole of these economies are actually slightly decreasing.

As the country chapters have shown, three factors have fostered the rise of medium-range domestic markets. First is the rise of new consumer classes with a propensity for medium-range goods. Second, high levels of investment led to a rise in medium-range capital goods, especially with respect to intermediate products. This is particularly true in India and China, where exceptionally high investment rates in infrastructure and production facilities has led to a surge in demand for capital goods and intermediate materials such as buildings, vehicles, office equipment, plant and machinery.

Third, the proactive role of state institutions for the enduring relevance of domestic firms has to be emphasized. The sheer potential of large domestic markets does

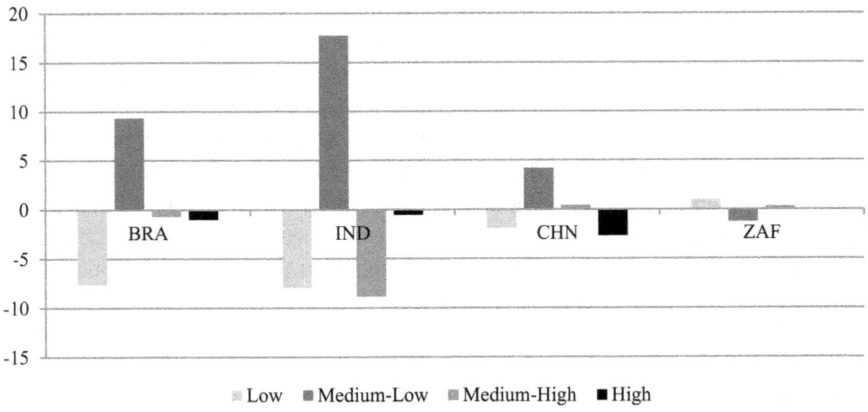

Figure 6.3 Value added of different segments of technological intensity, growth rate in percent (over a 10-year period)

Source: UNIDO Industrial Statistics Database (Industrial Statistics Database, 3- and 4-digit level of ISIC (Rev. 3, US$), data for Brazil 1996–2007, India 1998–2008, China 2003–2007 (only four years, growth rate therefore understated), South Africa 1999–2010 (values, especially for high-tech sector, are incomplete).

not automatically mean that this is actually realized by indigenous firms. Usually, countries that specialize in low- and medium-tech sectors are prone to outperformance by competitors with even lower production costs. However, this risk is minimized for the countries in question because production costs are still very low, and more importantly, foreign low-cost competitors have difficulty accessing these markets because the state actively manages the entry of foreign firms and goods.

6.3 Selective insertion into global capitalism

The previous section documented that large emerging markets rely much less on exports than dependent market economies, such as in East Central Europe. A way of highlighting protective insertion into the global economy is to look at the level of openness in large emerging economies. In order to make sure that expanding domestic markets in large emerging economies stimulate industrialization, these markets have to be protected against foreign competition. This protection is indicated, for instance, by the OECD product market regulation score (Figure 6.4). The regulation of product markets is considerably more restrictive in Brazil, India, China and South Africa than in all other compared cases.

As long as the state has continued to proactively support domestic firms and to foster markets via public procurement, for instance, firms from large emerging economies have been able to enjoy the comparative advantage of cost-effective, medium-tech production for domestic mass markets.

As shown in Table 6.2, tariffs are higher in the BICS than for developed countries, but they arguably constitute only a fraction of a country's trade restrictiveness.

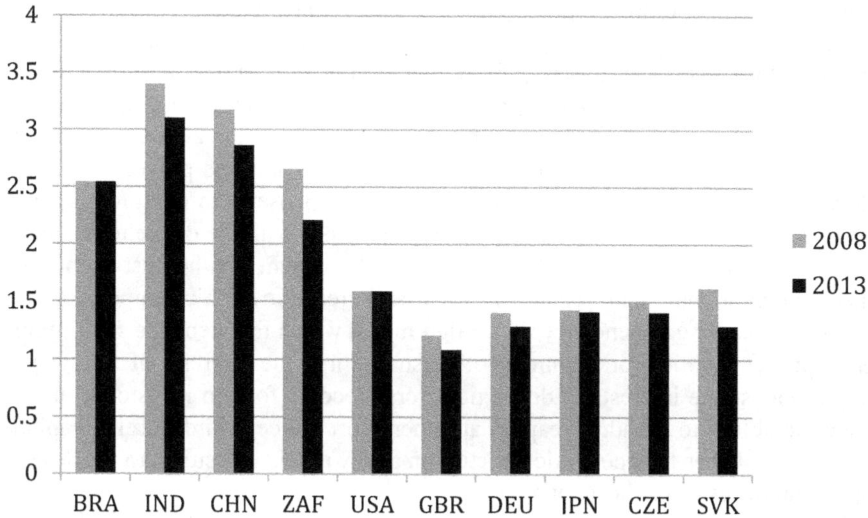

Figure 6.4 Regulation levels of national product markets, Product Market Regulation Scores

Source: OECD, Product Market Regulation Index.

Table 6.2 Tariffs and non-tariff barriers to trade, 2001–2013

	Average tariff rate (in %)	*Non-tariff measures and Specific Trade Concerns*
China	10.7	2567
India	18.1	1244
Brazil	13.3	2337
South Africa	7	340
United States	3.6	5070
United Kingdom*	4.3	33
Germany*	4.3	46
Japan	3.1	1063
Czech Republic*	4.4	201
Slovakia*	4.4	23

Source: WTO i-Tip Database.

* Common external EU tariffs.

Equally important for the domestic economy are non-tariff trade restrictions as an indicator of the selectivity with which countries regulate the inflow of goods.

As Table 6.2 illustrates, China, India and Brazil are considerably protectionist (similar to the United States). South Africa imposes much fewer trade barriers, indicating a much higher trade openness. Yet the latter still is less open when compared to DMEs such as Slovakia, which adopted a neoliberal trade policy during the 1990s before integrating in the EU free trade regime.

This leads us to another important dimension of production-related insertion into the global economy: the role of foreign investments. For our question, inward foreign direct investments (IFDI) are more important, although outward foreign direct investments by the BICS have been on the rise since the 2010s. IFDI flows exert pressures on domestic structures. If commodity imports provoke the outflow of currency needed internally, these can be compensated through funds from abroad. However, the inflow of capital usually comes with the desire to exercise control over what happens with that money.[1] The benefit for the host economy, then, is conditional. With regard to capital and credit flows, high imports result in a corresponding dependency on foreign funds, which threatens the stability of emerging economies for a number of reasons. First, the interests of foreigners might oppose the interests of domestic actors. Second, foreign investors usually have the ability to withdraw capital at rather short notice. Third, foreign capital potentially shapes the economic structure in a way that is less suited to the developmental needs of the host country.

However, exposure to external investment is relatively low (Figure 6.5). For all of the BICS, we can safely say that their contemporary dependency on foreign capital is in no way similar to the economies of the Czech Republic or Slovakia, where the stock of inward FDI has represented more than half of each country's respective GDP since 2000. FDI exposure developed differently for the BICS, but compared to dependent CEE economies, foreign capital never gained dominance.

If we look closer to the IFDI share of gross fixed investments, the picture is again striking. China has been able to control the influence of foreign capital over the last 20 years. Growing IFDI in absolute terms has even been surpassed

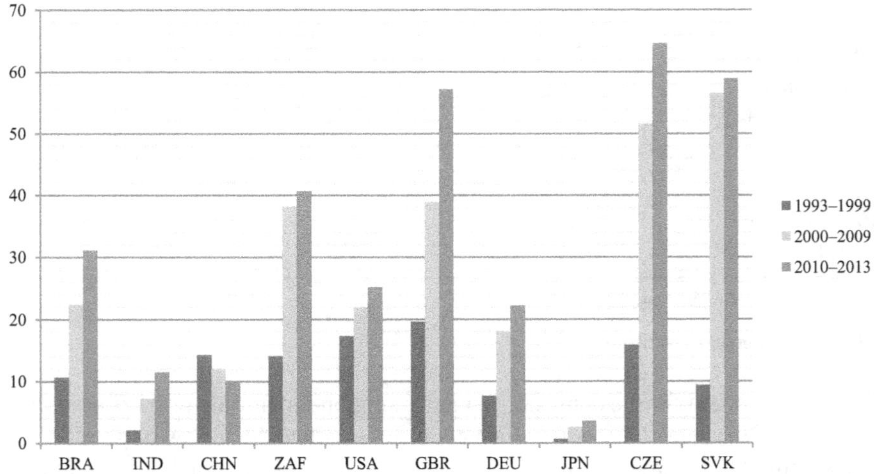

Figure 6.5 Stock of inward FDI (in % of GDP)

Source: UNCTAD.

by higher domestic investments, resulting in a decline of the relative ratio of FDI to overall investment (UNCTAD 2015). While the IFDI share of gross fixed investments in the 1990s was at nearly 14%, it declined to 7.7% in the 2000s. China therefore benefited from the external IFDI stimulus by way of increased competition and with respect to foreign technology and know-how, but it did not develop a growing dependency on foreign capital that would diminish control of its development trajectory. In other countries, the share of foreign capital in overall fixed investment rose, at times dramatically (UNCTAD 2015): from 13.6% to 23% in Great Britain, from 3.3% to 10.2% in Germany and from 12.6% to 33.6% in Slovakia. India kept its IFDI ratio low, at about 5.47% in the 2000s, while Brazil (14.86%) and South Africa (10.53%) were able to keep the internationalization of their investment structure at bay.

Regulation of inward FDI, though, must not be understood as a bold restriction of foreign capital. In particular, the *time* at which foreign capital may enter the domestic economy matters, depending on *when* and *how long* foreign capital will play an essential role. Only China effectively managed to regulate both of them. Therefore, a low rate of foreign ownership in emerging economies is not primarily an indicator for a business environment hostile to investors, but rather for the barriers that the state erects against foreign capital.

The OECD has identified China and India as the countries with the highest FDI restrictions (Koyama and Golub 2006), far above the degree to which OECD countries regulate incoming FDI. This comes as no surprise given the data source, but it nevertheless reveals some insights about how the state actively regulates incoming FDI in large emerging economies. Particularly restrictions on the holding of equity are responsible for the high levels of FDI restriction (OECD 2015). Of the various means by which countries can hamper the flow of IFDI, large emerging countries predominantly prohibit foreign firms from acquiring shares in domestic firms. The state regularly inhibits the free flow of capital into the economy through different forms of capital controls. It also prohibits (or at least does not encourage) the development of full markets for corporate control. Thus, even if foreign capital could flow freely into the country, it would still be difficult to actually acquire shares in domestic companies, not least due to their corporate structure. Crucially, the BICS were able to erect barriers to the inflow of portfolio and speculative capital (albeit to varying degrees). These barriers are an element of national economic strategies to support domestic firms against foreign takeover and subordination to global production networks led by Western firms. However, selective imports of foreign technology for industrial modernization are enabled but without losing control over the national business structure (Brandt and Thun 2010).

The BICS were able to increase their currency reserves to levels that effectively protect them from the destructive effects of foreign debt. This is not surprising in the case of China, which not only covered its (limited) own external debts with foreign reserves but also the debt of other countries, most notably the United States. More remarkable is the way in which countries such as Brazil and India, as erstwhile major recipients of external credit both from the IMF and private lenders, were able to decrease their vulnerability. As Figure 6.6 shows, since the

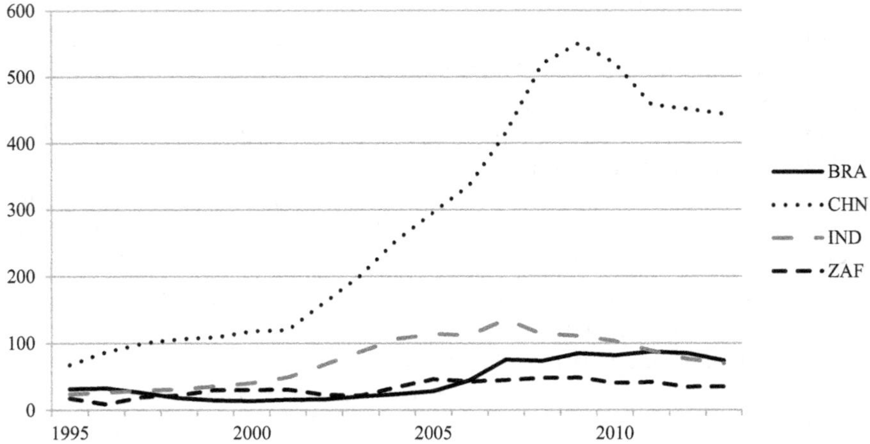

Figure 6.6 Total reserves (in % of total external debt)

Source: World Development Indicators.

2000s, both have been able to cover about 80–85% of their external debt with currency reserves. This means that they could in principle pay back 85% of their external debt from one day to another. In 1995, they could have only done so for 25–30%. The state actively follows a stability-oriented strategy, which supports long-term macroeconomic development by connecting central bank policies with regulatory instruments to inhibit a free flow of foreign capital into the country.

High currency reserves make speculative attacks on single currencies, which were responsible for both the UK pound exodus from the ECM as well as for the Asian Crisis of 1997–1998, less likely. They also serve as an instrument to stabilize the exchange rate of the national currency. With high reserves, countries are able to support their currencies against appreciation and current balance deficits if the currency is quasi-pegged to the US dollar, such as the Renminbi.

6.4 Institutional features of capitalism in large emerging economies

The previous two sections have established that large emerging markets were able to grow on the basis of a 'niche' in production for domestic markets, based on protective insertion into global capitalism. Firms in large emerging markets can tap this 'niche', but other institutional conditions have to be met to establish a relatively stable growth regime. In order to achieve the benefits of such comparative advantage, firms require stability. Therefore, institutions are crucial for the strategic calculations of companies and other economic actors because they reduce complexity by providing blueprints for regularized and patterned behavior. The previous two sections have highlighted important parallels (and some differences) between China, India, Brazil and South Africa with regard to economic growth and the type of specialization on which this growth rests. To what extent do similar domestic institutions foster this development?

6.4.1 Corporate governance

Large companies in the SME ideal type are dominated by indigenous capital. In reality, BICS ownership structures differ but the effects are similar, as they all produce high levels of capital concentration in a few national hands, in particular state actors, national actors close to the state and well-connected families. This allows for a high degree of stability and exclusive control over the national corporate sector. The countries deviate heavily from the liberal standards of corporate governance that promote the control of firms by a large number of unrelated shareholders (Aguilera et al. 2012). In large emerging economies, the state, state agencies, business groups and families own the vast majority of domestic business. China perhaps comes closest to the 'old' mode of state capitalism, as the state actually owns a large part of Chinese corporations, especially when we look at the largest firms. However, as the state gradually drove down direct ownership, a move towards forms of state-permeation through indirect funding and minority shareholding has been observed. In fact, this can also be observed in India and even in Brazil (Musacchio and Lazzarini 2014). As ownership is very concentrated, insider control dominates, with the effect that owners tend to use 'voice' and 'loyalty' much more often than 'exit', as is the case for non-related external owners who readily sell their shares when unsatisfied with the management. Commonly, high posts in management are recruited from within circles of ownership, i.e. state officials, business groups and (particularly) families. We can assume that intra-corporate communication and coordination is higher than in firms that follow a liberal idea of dispersed ownership and arm's-length control, thereby reducing uncertainty with regard to strategic decisions. This not only allows for a high degree of corporate stability, but also of durability, especially when firms are inherited.

Following the discussion of country openness to inward FDI (Figure 6.5), foreign ownership of companies is much less relevant. The contrast is most obvious when comparing SMEs to DMEs, but it is also noticeable with regard to LMEs. However, empirical data show a division between China and India on one side (more restrictive), and Brazil and South Africa (more open) on the other. Yet, as we have seen, Brazilian companies share commonalities with Chinese and Indian firms following from state minority shareholding and various forms of blockholder control such as pyramid schemes (see section 4.3).

6.4.2 Finance for investment

Unlike in LMEs, CMEs and DMEs, global capital markets are rather insignificant for funding investments in SMEs (Figure 6.7). Firms in large emerging economies rarely turn to private equity or other forms of marketized credit, domestically or

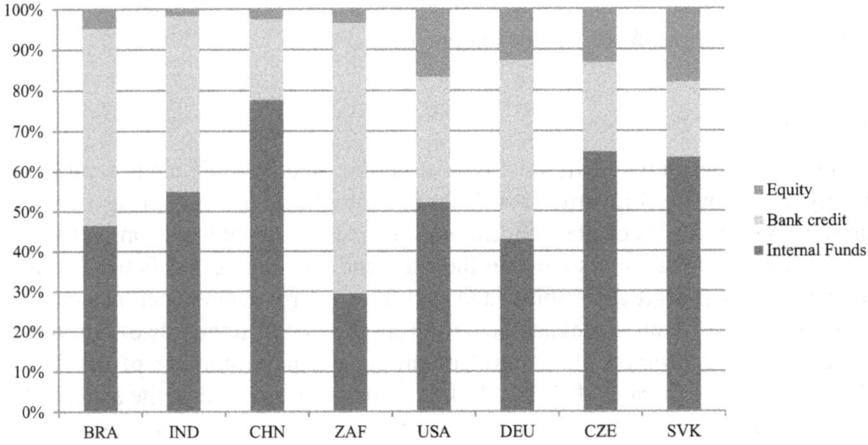

Figure 6.7 Sources for financing investments in manufacturing in percent, 2007–2011

Source: World Bank 2014, China National Bureau of Statistics, US Census (no comprehensive data for Great Britain and Japan available).[1]

1 As outlined in Chapter 3 (section 3.2), the definition of internal and external depends on perspective. While we account for a much higher share of internal funds understood as funds that are internal to a business group (and hence, under internal control), the World Bank and other institutions treat related parties and group affiliates as external to the firm entity. From our perspective emphasizing the nature of control over firm strategies, the World Bank figures underestimate the degree of closed control over investment capital.

(more importantly) internationally. Instead, they primarily invest through internal funds and bank credit. Due to the prevailing corporate governance structures, the use of internal funds is directly controlled by owning families, state-business networks or state institutions. This enables firms to pursue autonomous business strategies which would be less possible if they were to rely on (foreign) shareholders or creditors, as is the case in liberal economies like the United States, but also in dependent economies such as Slovakia which follow a market-led approach to investment.

Major lending banks are not private, as in bank-based financial systems such as Germany, but state-owned: Around 50% of the national banking assets (and up to 75% in India) are held by the state. While foreign banks represent more than 75% of the banking sector in DMEs, but also in countries like Mexico, they hardly play a role in the BICS economies (Verhoef 2009; Deutsche Bank Research 2011). And although most 'private' banks are listed on stock markets, their shares are mostly held by the state or state agencies. This means that bank loans are, especially in Brazil, India and China, in fact credit lines by the state. This allows the state to have a certain 'grip' on national companies, but more importantly, it gives companies a strategic advantage: they enjoy lower interest rates, longer credit maturities and require less strict conditions of creditworthiness than e.g. global credit markets. Development banks and state-related commercial banks play a crucial role, too. Through favorable and huge credit lines, they create incentives for investments in alignment with development policies. Furthermore, the state restricts the free flow of portfolio capital through capital controls (Brazil, China) and limits on the trade of financial products or firm shares (Brazil, India, China). Thus, in contrast to LMEs, CMEs and DMEs, state regulation of the credit sector in SMEs effectively limits the influence of foreign capital and thereby maintains the concentration of capital within domestic capital fractions.

6.4.3 Industrial relations

With regard to the relations between capital and labor, our sample does not fit well into established categories of corporatism. The fact that the BICS depart from "coordinated" versions of capitalism has led some observers to the interpretation that we are dealing with a liberal mode of capital-labor coordination (Witt 2010). Although there is a grain of truth in it, the BICS significantly differ from conventional liberal models as well.

A well-known feature of large emerging economies is the low level of average wages, which has been crucial for their competitiveness in the 2000s. In comparison to other types of capitalism, the average salaries for workers in SMEs remain much lower. While average real monthly wages are roughly US$3000 in the United States, Great Britain, Germany and Japan, they amount only to approximately US$300 in China and even less in India (ILOSTAT 2016). Moreover, although the share of wages in gross national income decreased on a global scale, this trend is somewhat less dramatic in large emerging economies (ILO 2013a). Average wages have rather risen more strongly in China, Brazil and South Africa than in developed countries, which has had a positive effect on domestic demand for indigenous products.

In contrast to many other labor regimes in the Global South, the SME model is characterized not only by low-cost labor but also by increases in labor productivity, which can compensate for wage rises. Particularly in China and India, this has led to a significant increase in labor productivity per person employed resulting from a mix of heavy capital investment, positive infrastructure and transportation network externalities as well as investment in human capital (see the next section).

Alongside labor productivity increases, the working population in SMEs is highly fragmented and struggles with considerable levels of informality. Fragmentation refers to the segmentation of the workforce into relatively contained segments of a small number of high-skilled, well-paid and generally protected workers, and a vast amount of low-skilled, low-waged and precarious workers, who are further divided among themselves. The size and heterogeneity of the BICS further allows employers to exploit the inequalities of diverging regional conditions of accumulation, regional working systems and various industry sectors. A key factor for this is the segmentation and segregation of the labor force. Due to this segmentation, labor costs only reflect worker qualification because there are no concerted wage systems across qualification levels that could be

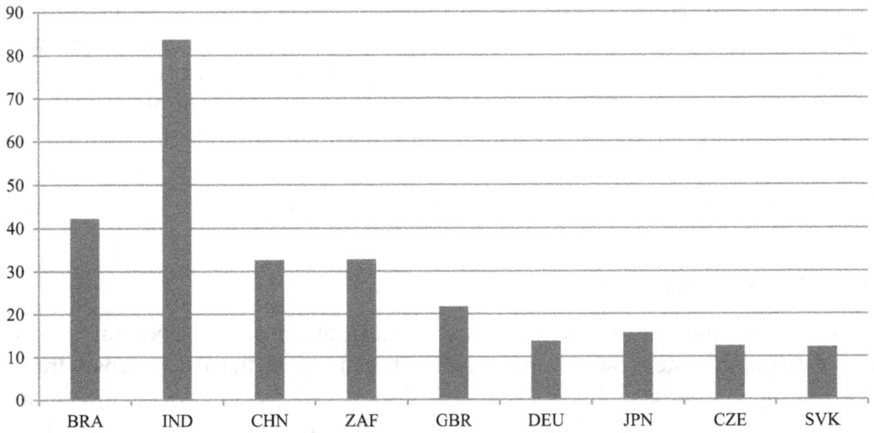

Figure 6.8 Informal employment as % of non-agricultural employment, 2010

Source: Benson 2011, 40; Hazans 2011, 33; Haigner et al. 2013, 512; ILO 2013b. No data for USA available.[1]

1 Concepts of informality differ across countries as does measurement, which is naturally hard to undertake. Chapter 2 stated that only half of Chinese employees had an employment contract in the mid-2000s, which, in our view, indicates a high degree of precarity for Chinese workers. However, employment contracts are more central to some systems of industrial relations than others. From this perspective, these figures can give only a rough approximation of the problem.

enforced by unions. The effect is limited upward mobility and consolidated social inequality.

This is partly a consequence of another characteristic, which is the high rate of informal labor (Figure 6.8). The degree of informality varies across the country sample, but is non-negligible in all of them. Particularly in India, informal labor is the rule rather than the exception, with more than 80% of the workforce having almost no job security at all. Developing-country scholars would rightly object that informality is a common feature in many emerging countries, yet this aspect has only partially entered analyses of southern or peripheral capitalism, although it has severe repercussions on inner logic as well as stability. It also stands in contrast to established LME/CME categories and indicators (see Chapter 1). Applying standard measures for industrial relations such as unionization rate are at best only partially able to account for labor realities in emerging economies. Officially, China has a union density rate of over 40% (ILOSTAT 2015), but, as highlighted in Chapter 2, the national union ACTFU does not act as a union in the common sense. Conversely, the rates in India and Germany are very similar to each other (at around 12.5%), but this tells us little about the collective bargaining capacity of Indian unions.

What explains more of SME industrial relations is the state's role in the persistence of low wages, segmentation and informality. On one hand, the state often regulates labor relations in a top-down fashion by establishing labor laws where bipartist coordination is absent or inhibited. On the other hand, driven by its pro-business stance, the state is at the same time unwilling to seriously enforce these laws, enabling firms to undermine these provisions by way of loopholes and exceptions. Due to this lack of implementation of labor laws and standards, informality rates will probably remain high. In addition, government attempts to individuate industrial disputes and to channel conflicts into the judicial apparatus help to keep labor unrest at bay.

Yet, the key role of the state in industrial relations should not be confused with a common understanding of tripartism, in which employers, employees and the state collectively manage labor relations. Specifically in China, India and Brazil, effective trilateral collective bargaining bodies are missing. Attempts to establish these have largely failed to create a corporatist system of industrial relations in which labor has a say. This is due to actor unwillingness and inability. In China and India, local state-business alliances are crucial for high levels of growth, and both the state and firms are reluctant to incorporate labor. Since both local governments and firms benefit from their individual alliances, there is no urgent need to establish peak business organizations for the coordination of industrial relations. Business associations do exist, but they do not play an 'organic' role as in CMEs. What is more, informalization precludes efficient unionization. As wages are regulated mainly at the firm level, effective collective and cross-sector regulation of labor and social standards is lacking, and the organizational and bargaining power of workers is low.

6.4.4 Education and training

The BICS have developed an education and vocational training system in which the vast majority of the industrial working population now receives a secondary education, although mostly of a lower quality than in CMEs and LMEs. Still, this corresponds to the large low-wage sectors with low- and medium-skill requirements. At the same time, public expenditure on education as a percentage of total government expenditure is relatively high (Figure 6.9). This is in opposition to DMEs, in which dominant multinational companies neither invest substantially in the labor force nor favor a generous public education system.

Thus, large emerging economies put more effort into education than dependent market economies. Yet, segmentation in all fields of education is striking, as in the domain of industrial relations. Both state and business engage only selectively in skill upgrading initiatives. As labor markets are very flexible, there is a high turnover rate, with the consequence that firms do not invest much in training due to poaching risks. Likewise, workers are usually not motivated to invest in skill formation. In principle, the state is willing to compensate for this institutional flaw, and it seems that SMEs are better able than DMEs to make comparably effective investment in skill upgrading, with the ultimate goal of industrial upgrading. However, the state does not play an exclusively compensatory role but acts as a proactive supporter of education and skill development. The closely interwoven

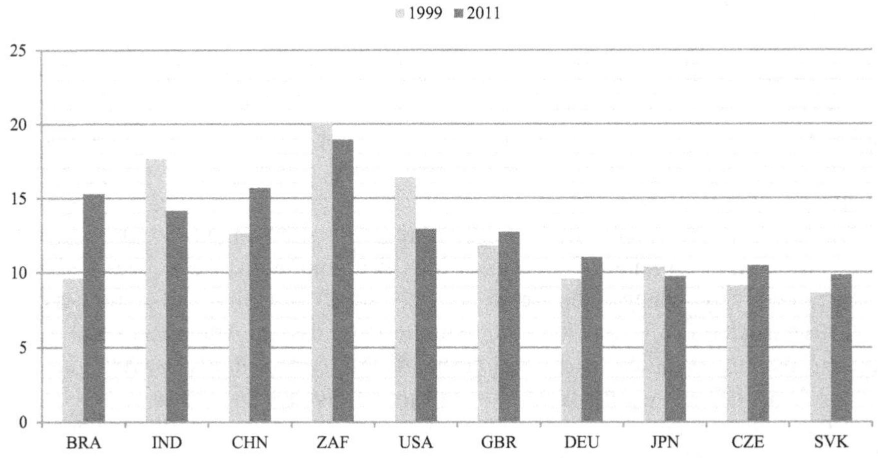

Figure 6.9 Public expenditure on education, in % of total government expenditure

Source: World Development Indicators, National Bureau of Statistics of China.

networks of (local) indigenous capital and state actors show comparably more concern about long-term national development in education than do most managers of foreign multinational corporations. They have thus been more willing and capable of creating a modern skill formation system, at least for important segments of the workforce. Public support measures are often directed selectively to vocational training in areas in which allied companies operate. Generally, this works better where local state-business alliances are strong. Bureaucrats and entrepreneurs are able to organize local employment and to attune training schemes that are sometimes outside of national VET systems and strategies. There are also attempts to cover the rising demand for higher-skilled work through investment in technological upgrading via fairly generous funding of universities. Although large domestic firms are able to provide in-house training, companies generally depend on the ability of the (local) state to maintain levels of educational quality.

6.4.5 Innovation

Research and development expenditures are lower for SMEs when compared to CMEs and LMEs, but higher than in DMEs (Figure 6.10), with China scoring the highest.

In DMEs, new products and technologies are usually imported by foreign MNCs, whereas SMEs have become competitive through the creative adaptation of imported products, which they can reproduce at cheaper terms for the local market. Due to the size of their home markets, these countries can thrive on a mode of innovation through imitation, reverse engineering and re-invention longer than previous examples of catch-up development.

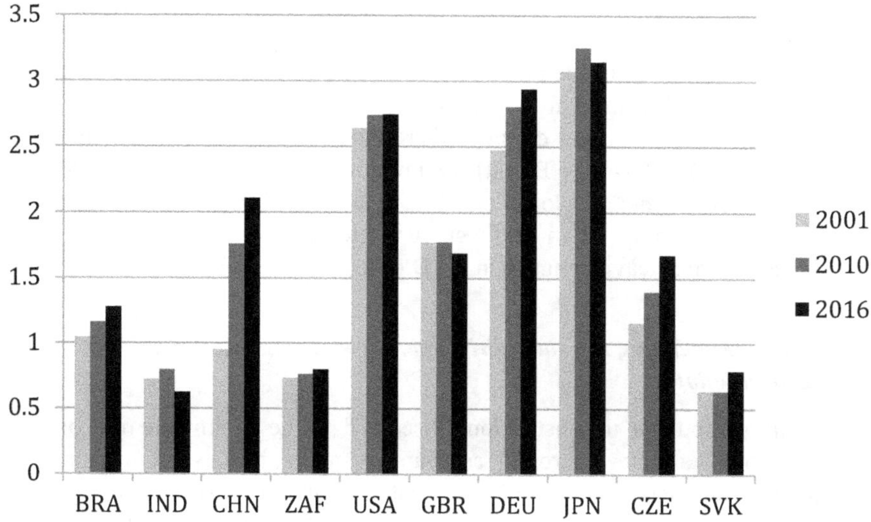

Figure 6.10 R&D expenditures, in % of GDP

Source: World Development Indicators.

As mentioned, large emerging economies can be competitive without being highly innovative if they focus on their home markets and a supply of medium-tech goods. Still, firms in emerging economies might engage in high-tech sectors, but usually not at the cutting-edge level. They would, for instance, not produce the most technologically advanced computers and smartphones, but rather low-tier models for which no ground-breaking innovative effort is necessary. Hence, the underlying assumption of a correlation between technological intensity and competitiveness (as championed by the OECD, for example) seems not to be universally valid. As domestic firms are most profitable at home by producing medium-tech goods, a limited level of innovation and technological intensity is sufficient. This not only prevents firms from spending huge resources on R&D, but it also enables them to exploit labor-intensive production (although this is in dramatic flux; see Chapter 7). As long as domestic markets are sheltered and domestic products are not competitive on the world market, most firms can be satisfied with the status quo of limited investments in innovation.

In this realm, firms again depend on the effective protection of the state, which is best ensured within close state-business alliances. The state affects the nature of innovation in a number of crucial ways. First, external technology has to enter the economy but without exerting too much competitive pressure on domestic firms. SME companies rely on various forms of interaction with Western companies (such as joint ventures or as contractors in global production networks), often accompanied by local content policies. Additionally, patent rights systems are often rather weak and courts regularly prioritize domestic firms in disputes with TNCs regarding the ownership of technology. Finally, the state is actively involved in fostering innovative activities of various kinds. Mostly incremental technological innovations are fostered through public support in selected sectors, spin-offs and thickly embedded national firms. Similar to its role in the realm of education and training, the state acts as a compensating agent and as a supporter of local firms. It compensates directly where indigenous businesses (as in India and South Africa) or TNCs (in Brazil) are unwilling to invest in substantial R&D, which also includes the development of tools to adapt foreign technologies for domestic use. It is more of an 'indirect' supporter in China, where private and state-invested firms heavily engage in R&D (ERAWATCH 2007; UIS database).

6.4.6 State-permeation, not state-dirigisme: the state and economic coordination

Central throughout all the institutions discussed is the prominent role of the state, whether via state control of companies, state subsidies for investment, state-assisted maintenance of a segmented labor regime or state support for education and limited technological upgrading. However, our research on economic coordination in the country chapters has highlighted that the state is not an all-powerful, centralized steering bureaucracy as in the classical developmental state or 'dirigisme' model (Wade 1990; Boschi 2011). In large emerging economies, the state is territorially fragmented, albeit to different degrees. Although the Chinese party-state is the strongest among our cases and the central government regularly sets benchmarks which provinces are set to fulfill, limits on central state steering capacity have been identified (ten Brink 2013a, 2013b). The economic rise of China is inherently related to the transfer of authority to subnational levels and to subnational competition. Also in India, subnational state actors compete with each other for productive investments. Unlike in China and India, where big business finds allies in state/provincial and municipal governments that are potentially more open for (and more dependent on) business demands, this kind of competitive state-permeated 'federalism' to stimulate investment and growth is less visible in Brazil and South Africa.

However, state devolution and limited central state capacity applies not only to the BICS, but to many other emerging countries. How have these countries apparently found a way to get around this problem? We argue that state-permeated economies provide for a higher coherence because they can compensate for fragmented central state power through a public-private mode of economic coordination that is highly economically effective. Economic activity rests on close cooperation between various state and domestic business actors leading to growth alliances at the national and subnational levels, which gives rise to the notion of a fragmented yet dynamic economy. More specifically, these large economies are coordinated through reciprocal mechanisms of loyalty between members of (competition-driven) state-business alliances based on informal and non-transparent personal relations, family ties and shared social or political backgrounds. At the same time, the role of business associations is weaker than in Western types of capitalism.

State authorities and their cooperating companies are largely kept in balance, thereby preventing the comprehensive capture of public policies by private interests as witnessed in patrimonial regimes (or vice versa). In a way, this type of state capitalism requires a pluralist element that ensures stability by providing checks and balances between bureaucracies and firms. Thus, limited central state power is indeed compensated by strong, multilayered and reliable interpersonal public-private relations at different levels. The country chapters highlighted the ways in which these close cronyist connections between (big) business and the state apparatus manifest themselves. Notably, often what appears as an anomaly or a deficit according to a textbook definition of 'corruption' actually represents a pattern of politico-economic coordination that is characteristic of contemporary state capitalism of the more successful kind, i.e. in China or India.

What results from this setup? In the conventional economist view, limited central state capacity combined with a comparably weak role of unfettered, liberalized markets and associations for economic coordination should actually lead to poor economic performance because actors face a high degree of uncertainty. However, we argue that behind multiple forms of 'corruption' in SMEs hides an effective mechanism for overall economic coordination. A 'productive cronyism', based on the reciprocity of interpersonal relations, largely outweighs harmful types of corruption, e.g. rent seeking and bribery for individual luxury consumption.

6.5 An ideal type of state-permeated capitalism

6.5.1 A distinct form of capitalism

To conclude the discussion in this chapter so far, there are remarkable commonalities between China and India and partially Brazil, but fewer in the case of South Africa. State-permeation and a pro-business policy supporting national development and large domestic markets are its main characteristics. Other crucial aspects are a strong protection against foreign capital and market instability, segmented systems of labor and limited skill formation and innovation efforts. Other economies following a catch-up industrialization strategy share some of these features, too, but only in single institutional spheres (e.g. a low-wage regime). It is the concurrence of all of these institutional features that gives rise to a dynamic form of state capitalism different from other emerging and dependent market economies. This new form of state-permeated capitalism generates dynamic economic development in important parts of the economy rather than patrimonial structures.

In order to make this statement more lucid, we have established an ideal type of state capitalism in large emerging economies called a 'state-permeated market economy' (SME). Obviously, ideal types and empirical features of a given country should not be conflated (Becker 2013a). In fact, we consider China the typical case of an SME, while the elements of the ideal type are slightly less present in India and even less so in Brazil (not to mention South Africa).

Our SME model starts from the observation that state actors, driven by strong pro-business support for national development, are more vital than in established varieties of capitalism. We argue that the state in this model rests on close cooperation between various state and domestic business coalitions at the national and subnational levels. This is the reason why we speak of a fragmented yet dynamic state-*permeated* market economy. At the heart of this model is a mode of coordination through reciprocal mechanisms of loyalty and trust between members of competition-driven state-business coalitions. SMEs therefore are distinct not only from 'traditional' state capitalisms, but also from other capitalist models in which coordination takes place through the market and formal contracts (LMEs), formalized networks and associations (CMEs) or hierarchies within multinational enterprises (DMEs). SMEs also differ from hierarchical market economies (HMEs) as they are able to unfold the dynamics of productivity-enhancing education and training, although only for specific segments of the workforce. For this reason, SMEs are not doomed to fall into the low-skill trap that precludes a stable path of enduring development. Yet, ideal types and individual cases must be distinguished. South Africa, from our perspective, exhibits fewer characteristics of the SME model and more incompatible sets of institutions with a hybrid mix of SME, LME, CME and HME traits.

The SME model is typical only for *large* emerging economies. Undoubtedly, state-permeated economies are part of international trade and production networks. Yet, the size and dynamics of their domestic markets allows governments to remain cautious vis-à-vis foreign investors and to open their economies only selectively. Therefore, SMEs are characterized by the dominance of national capital rather than by dependence on foreign capital as in dependent market economies in East Central Europe and other emerging economies like Mexico (Nölke and Vliegenthart 2009; Schneider 2013).

Table 6.3 summarizes the SME model in contrast to other varieties of capitalism. It contains the 'dependent variable' of comparative advantage as well as a dominant mode of coordination that achieves institutional compatibility across institutions. The model refers to the assets that emerge from a particular institutional configuration and maintains that actors embedded in it can make productive use of them. It moreover comprises the central institutional spheres of the institutionalist CC research program, including corporate governance, investment finance, industrial relations, education and training, and innovation. We have expanded this program by including the realm of international economic integration.

Comparative advantage: SMEs do not achieve the highest growth by aiming at constant qualitative upgrading through radical or incremental innovation (LMEs and CMEs, respectively), nor do they grow by following a strong export orientation (like DMEs). Instead, they have the strongest growth potential if they specialize in the production of medium-tech goods for the domestic market.

Dominant mode of coordination: Firm relations in SMEs are governed by strong interpersonal ties based on reciprocity, in contrast to: LMEs, which ideal typically are coordinated by market mechanisms; CMEs, which are coordinated by reconciliation and bargaining; and DMEs, where inter-firm hierarchies are dominant. Crucially, these ties reach beyond the firm and into the realm of the

Table 6.3 The main varieties of capitalism

Institutions / *Type of capitalism*	*Liberal Market Economy (LME)*	*Coordinated Market Economy (CME)*	*Dependent Market Economy (DME)*	*State-permeated Capitalism (SME)*
Comparative advantage	Global product and capital markets, radical innovation	Global product markets, incremental innovation	Weak domestic product markets, export orientation	Strong domestic markets for medium-tech products
Dominant mode of coordination	Competitive markets and formal contracts	Interfirm networks and associations	Hierarchies in multinational corporations	Reciprocity within local private-public alliances
Corporate governance	Outsider control: minority shareholders	Insider control: concentrated shareholders	Control by headquarters of multinational corporations	Insider control by families, national owners and the state
Investment finance	Domestic and international capital markets	Domestic bank lending and internally generated funds	Foreign direct investments and foreign-owned banks	Internal funds and state-owned banks, limited foreign finance
Industrial relations	Pluralist, market based, few collective agreements	Corporatist, rather consensual, sectoral or national-wide agreements	Appeasement of skilled labor, company-based agreements	Informality, fragmented low-cost labor
Education and training	Promotion of transferable skills	Highly sophisticated VET schemes for specialized education	No provisions beyond basic education	Basic education plus segments of specialized skills
Innovation	Market and formal contracts	Inter-company co-operations and business associations	Intra-firm transfer within multinational corporations	Reverse engineering and creative adaptation
International integration	Linked to liberalized global economy, expansion via financial markets	Highly integrated in global production and trade, limited into financial markets	Full orientation towards global product markets	Selective integration, cautious against global capital markets

state at various spatial and organizational levels. This dominant mode of coordination becomes manifest in (local) public-private growth alliances which are able to reconcile the developmental interests of state managers with the profit interests of private business.

Corporate governance: Major companies in SMEs are dominated by national capital rather than by transnational financial investors. They are usually controlled by well-connected families, the state and actors close to the state. This stands in contrast to liberal market economies, where minority shareholders and transnational financial investors dominate most large firms. It is also different from both coordinated market economies, where large companies are dominated by block-holders such as families, other companies or banks, and dependent market economies, where large firms are usually part of MNCs.

Investment finance: Enterprises in SMEs are relatively independent from volatilities on global capital markets as well as from international investors and shareholders. They raise investments mainly through internal savings and loans by national banks, often enjoying preferential support from the state – for example, through cheap credit. Although banks are important creditors in both SMEs and CMEs, SME banks and capital markets largely controlled by the state, which also controls the inflow of foreign capital. The institutional characteristics of firms and financial systems in SMEs create a business system with a small role for the market for corporate control. In LMEs, major corporations tend to be oriented to global capital markets. This also applies to DMEs, where investment funds are primarily allocated from the parent branches of multinational enterprises.

Industrial relations: In the SME model, state institutions assist the preservation of a low-wage regime so that labor productivity gains compensate for wage increases. The labor force is segmented and segregated into a comparatively highly paid and well-protected segment, and large low-cost, unprotected and informal segments, often in addition to segmentation between regions and industrial sectors. While there is a continuous supply of low-wage (rural) labor, labor regulations, which appear relatively comprehensive, are hardly enforced by the state. As a consequence, industrial relations are regulated at the firm level, which makes them different from sector-corporatist arrangements in the CME model. SMEs therefore feature some similarities to LMEs and DMEs, where labor relations are also predominantly organized at the firm level but are still characterized by lower wages, limited worker protection and, most notably, a large informal sector.

Education and training: SMEs have developed an education system in which the vast majority of the population receives a secondary education. While this system functionally benefits the demand for relatively low and medium skills, state actors and state-business alliances also address rising demand for higher-skilled labor by increasing education expenditures, at least in some segments, and through local attuning of training schemes. Overall, expenditures are still lower than in LMEs and CMEs. However, SMEs devote higher public education investments than DMEs, which cannot afford expensive education systems due to the all-out competition for FDI and dominant multinational corporations not in favor of a generous public education system.

Innovation: SMEs usually have relatively weak patent provisions. It facilitates reverse engineering and technological catch-up, which is supported by, for example, preferential tax treatments for in-house labs designed to investigate and adapt the technologies of imported products. Innovation capacity building in SMEs takes place through state support in selected sectors for technological upgrading. Most innovation falls under the category of creative adaptation of foreign technology into products that sell on domestic markets. This is in juxtaposition to: LMEs, where innovations are intended to spread via markets; CMEs, where innovation is frequently based on inter-company cooperation and associations; and DMEs, where innovation is based on intra-firm transfer in multinational corporations. In contrast to SMEs, the other three types also place importance on a stronger regime for the protection of intellectual property rights.

International integration: In comparison to higher degrees of openness in LMEs, CMEs and DMEs, SMEs employ a policy of selective integration into the global economy. This means that integration into global capital markets is considerably lower than integration into global trade and production networks. The size of their domestic economies and attractiveness for multinational corporations allows SMEs to become more tenacious negotiating partners in bi- and multilateral decision-making processes than other emerging countries (van Tulder 2010). Therefore, state managers do not necessarily have to cater to the demands of foreign multinationals, but instead strive for selective or conditional opening to also allow technological modernization. Large domestic markets allow for a high degree of independence from external economic pressures and provide a stable framework for the growth of industries, as well as for a national strategy to protect this beneficial internal structure. In contrast, other forms of capitalism are oriented towards global product markets, and therefore home markets are secondary for the formulation of industrial or macroeconomic policies.

6.5.2 Cohesion, complementarities and institutional clusters

However, it is not only the quality of these institutions that matters but also the quality of their mutual connections. One decisive factor which affects this quality is the degree to which institutions are mutually compatible. Following our discussion in section 1.5, we are able to identify strong and weak complementarities across the set of institutions analyzed (Table 6.4). Our comparative assessment of the institutions of state-permeated capitalism indeed shows that some institutions are more closely connected than others. Strong complementarity refers to the mutual amplification of each institution's performance, while weak complementarity indicates that institutions at least do not immediately hamper the functionality of the other(s). The predominant notion of institutional complementarity refers to the first notion. However, we assert that a minimal condition of weak complementarity assures that each institution is able to exercise its functions (see Chapter 1).

The institutions of *corporate governance* and *investment finance* are mutually complementary in a strong sense, not only because they ideally reinforce

Table 6.4 Institutional complementarities in SMEs

	Corporate governance	*Investment finance*	*Industrial relations*	*Education and training*	*Innovation*
Corporate governance		Strong	Weak	Weak	Weak
Investment finance	Strong		Weak	Weak	Weak
Industrial relations	Weak	Weak		Strong	Strong
Education and training	Weak	Weak	Strong		Strong
Innovation	Weak	Weak	Strong	Strong	

each other, but also because changes in one institution directly affect the other. A change to a liberal system of investment finance would, for example, have direct effects on the nature of corporate governance. In SMEs, the closed control of companies by domestic capital complements the relative independence from foreign financial capital. A closed and restrictive financial system limits the sources of external investment finance and thereby enhances the insider control of capital flows in general. As long as both spheres remain under domestic control, it can be ensured that the long-term returns of the national elite are higher than under liberal conditions, not least because it is more difficult for many foreign capitalists to fully appropriate the fruits of economic growth in SMEs. Additionally, as families (and friends) play a dominant role in the corporate landscape of SMEs, their rationale is not only short-term profit maximization but also the preservation of the company for the next generation. Thus, firms enjoy some leeway when it comes to growth imperatives.

In contrast, the institutions of corporate governance and investment finance have only an indirect effect on, e.g., education systems at best. Even if SMEs turned to LME- or CME-style corporate governance, education systems and industrial relations would likely tend to remain as they are. A liberalization of investment finance in China would probably directly affect the structure of the Chinese corporate sector, but it would have only limited effects on the institutions of labor, education, innovation and the structure of the domestic market.

At the same time, we saw in the country chapters that firms have rather feeble incentives to change the institutions of *industrial relations*, *education and training* and *innovation* because radical reform in one would undermine the efficiency of the other two institutions in yielding SME-specific comparative advantages. We therefore assume strong complementarities in this institutional cluster as well. First, a low-wage regime combined with limited but non-negligible efforts at state-assisted upskilling ensures that workers become more productive without raising the costs for firms too high, which would have to be compensated with huge investments in order to remain competitive. Second, the SME labor regime strongly complements a system of innovation transfer that builds on emulating or adapting imported technology and generally avoids large-scale investments in cutting-edge radical innovation. If firms were to invest too heavily in cutting-edge innovation, they would have to target global markets where they were to face fierce competition from foreign multinationals. Developing high-tech products would also require considerably greater investment in education and training, which would overburden the education system. In turn, it would also require the establishment of more sophisticated corporatist labor relations going beyond high levels of informality. Substantial upgrading in any of the three institutions is very cost-intensive and must therefore be compatible in a way that avoids 'too-high' upgrading pressures in any of the three. Although comparably low wages are constitutive for state-permeated capitalism, they can come to full fruition only if these are complemented by appropriate institutions for education and innovation.

Overall, we are now able to make more specific propositions about SMEs than simply stating that 'everything hangs together' or simply excluding those institutions which seem to have a lower effect on economic growth. *First*, the institutional properties of corporate governance, investment finance, industrial relations, education and innovation alone cannot determine the shape of this form of capitalism. However, combinations of particular institutional clusters are crucial for the establishment of state-permeated capitalism. Hence, we assume strong *complementarities* in the *corporate governance/investment finance* cluster and in the *labor/education/innovation* cluster as necessary factors in explaining the success of state-permeated capitalism.

Second, even a refined analysis of 'cluster' complementarities cannot be understood as the sole source of institutional cohesion and robust growth. Equally important is the dominant mode of *coordination* that structures institutions in largely similar ways. While such isomorphism (see Chapter 1) is indeed different from complementarity, it is in our view impossible to neglect overarching economic coordination as a factor in explaining the viability of state-permeated capitalism. The common mode of coordination through public-private alliances is hence a further key to explaining why state-permeated capitalism works.

Third, and finally, we have to take into account the *inter/national and historical context* under which state-permeated capitalism can prosper. As depicted in both this chapter and the country studies, specific historical conjunctures have aided the success of effective integration into the global economy, while large and protected domestic markets supported this general orientation because they guard national firms against too much foreign competition. As a consequence, firms were not forced to undertake colossal, i.e. unrealistic, investments in order to compete globally. These investments would otherwise have required additional funds from global financial markets that probably would have threatened the stability of the domestic institutional setup.

Taken together, we identify three factors for the relative economic success of state-permeated capitalism: *complementarities* within two institutional clusters; *coordination* through interpersonal public-private networks; and a specific inter/national and historical *context* which served the needs of SMEs.

To conclude, the SME model is a clear juxtaposition to other capitalist models. It is an appropriate conception of state capitalism that exists alongside other varieties (see Whitley 1999; Amable 2003; Boyer 2005; Schmidt 2009). SMEs are less dependent than DMEs, less liberal than LMEs and less coordinated than CMEs. Yet, there is no guarantee that countries which once came close to this model will forever be on a high-growth trajectory. Strongly growing political economies are very dynamic entities. We therefore assume that large emerging economies can deviate from the model or that the model contains the seeds of its own destruction; in other words, that it will eventually exhaust itself or erode from within. In order to tackle these issues, we now have to deal with country divergences from the SME model and current developments in the BICS that may undermine growth and solidity.

Note

1 In fact, this is how UNCTAD defines FDI: "The most important characteristic of FDI, which distinguishes it from foreign portfolio investment, is that it is undertaken with the intention of exercising control over an enterprise" (https://web.archive.org/web/20150415030955/http://unctad.org/en/Pages/DIAE/Foreign-Direct-Investment-(FDI).aspx).

7 Perspectives and problems of state-permeated capitalism

State-permeated capitalism, as discussed in the preceding chapter, can be conceived as a coherent type of capitalism. Specific countries, however, will never be a perfect match with a theoretical model and will always deviate in some respects. Having outlined the contours of an efficient model of state-permeated capitalism, we are now able to offer explanations for why China and India were able to grow more strongly and consistently than Brazil, not to mention South Africa. Based on our findings, the proximity of existing economies to this model is critical for explaining the varied growth across the four countries. If countries close to the SME model perform well, countries whose institutions are partially or even completely different from the model should perform worse. This is not to say that differences in growth are due only to their endogenous institutional endowments. Of course, other factors that further help to explain why China and India have grown most substantially play a role, and we will deal with some of them later. Though we address non-institutional factors for different growth performance, we primarily want to exploit the value of our extended institutional CC approach for explaining variance across our country set as much as possible, thereby focusing more strongly on endogenous factors. Section 7.1 compares the country cases of our empirical study with our theoretical model. It establishes that China is closest to the model, followed by India, Brazil and South Africa, the latter differing significantly. Moreover, real countries may differ over time and may move towards or away from the model. As will be seen, this is most obvious in Brazil, which moved towards state-permeated capitalism in the 2000s but moved away in the early-to-mid-2010s. India, in contrast, has been moving towards the model.

Some observers have recently assumed that the rise of emerging economies is only a temporary phenomenon that will eventually find an end as they face a number of obstacles to further growth. We discuss these obstacles in section 7.2, among them the notions that state-permeated capitalism increasingly provokes overinvestment and rising debt, that catch-up potential has been exhausted thereby creating a 'middle-income trap', and that 'capital flight' and related issues of further opening and financial liberalization foster instability. From our perspective, while some weaknesses of SMEs can indeed be detected, we also argue against overly pessimistic outlooks in that a thorough pursuit of the state-permeated model is able to overcome these challenges.

We, however, assume in section 7.3 that the true challenge of state-permeated capitalism in large emerging economies is not in the field of economics, but rather in the social and political realm. As state-permeated capitalism leads to increasing income inequalities, social discontent within the new 'middle classes' may increase as well. The mobilization of the new classes might, under adverse economic conditions, amount to political pressures for improved representation. This, however, may potentially undermine the stability of the growth model based as it is on cronyist private-public growth alliances.

7.1 From China to South Africa: country divergences

In Chapter 6, we showed that a particular form of capitalism lies at the heart of the development of large emerging economies. The structure of 'state-permeated capitalism' forms the internal grammar of the Chinese, Indian and Brazilian economies, if to different degrees. South Africa, in contrast, rather represents a hybrid. An 'inner core' of 'state-permeated capitalism' has been, as we argue, responsible for the relatively strong growth performance since the 2000s. We proposed an alternative to arguments that either conceive the most successful of our cases (the Chinese variety of capitalism) as unique and thus incomparable, or explain strong growth performance based on historical, locational or political specificities without denying their role altogether.

As country experts know, and as our country studies demonstrated, the BICS are not all the same. In addition to an intrinsically analytical interest in understanding and explaining economic development, our motivation in depicting commonalities and differences between the four economies was to identify potential lessons that can be drawn for the pursuit of stable and sustainable economic growth. If, as we argued in Chapter 6, an extended CC perspective sheds light on the relation between growth rates and particular institutional configurations in the BICS, we aim at equally hypothesizing whether economic achievements should decrease the more the countries deviate from the state-permeated model.

Alert readers will have already identified how and where China, India, Brazil and South Africa are different from each other. Essentially, we argue that it is the more or less appropriate design of institutions identified in the preceding analysis on the one hand, and their better or worse mutual 'fitness' on the other. This follows from our theoretical premise that institutions have to be efficient in stabilizing particular economic practices and that institutional complementarities form institutional clusters that are larger than the sum of their parts. Consequently, deficiencies in any of these may result in a less dynamic, more unstable and conflicting economic regime. We hence explain much of the differentiated trajectories of these four countries by looking closely at their endogenous properties. However, this does not mean that we have ruled out other factors, in particular those stemming from their external economic and political environment. In this book, we try to account for those external factors that we can credibly address. As Vivien Schmidt put it, "stuff happens" (Schmidt 2010, 12); in other words, actions foster unintended consequences, events beyond control occur constantly, and researchers can only do so much in order to understand these occurrences and consequences. Still, our analysis enables us to promote mostly endogenous arguments that account for the institutional differences and historical change in emerging economies.

The differences between existing economies and the SME ideal type can, in principle, be thought of as a continuum on which country cases deviate from the model (see Becker 2013d and Chapter 1). While we see the heuristic value of this image, we are critical of the linear image it suggests, as if we could credibly assign values on a scale that indicates 'state-permeated-ness'. Instead, we simply refer to a central hypothesis formulated in the CC literature: that hybrids usually perform worse than pure types. We thereby show that China actually comes closest to the ideal type of state-permeated capitalism, which corresponds to its growth performance and comparative advantages. South Africa is furthest away from it, indeed making it a hybrid.

Let us turn to our institutions and realms in order to compare the BICS and identify main differences.

Comparative advantage: The fact that China is growing strongest and most persistently of all four countries confirms our argument that 'pure' SMEs perform better than economies which only partially share the features of the model. With an average growth rate of around 10% in the 2000s, China is not only the most dynamic economy but also the most constant. Although GDP growth fell below two-digit values in the 2010s, it is still robust, especially when compared to Brazil and South Africa which experienced GDP slumps. In contrast, India, which is the second closest example when compared to the model, experienced stronger growth rates and could at times even outpace China. A similar picture emerges if we look at real investments. Growth of gross capital formation during the emerging economies' 'golden decade' between 2000 and 2010 was at around 5% for Brazil and South Africa, but 10% for India and even higher for China. As industrialization is a crucial feature of economic development, China and India were galloping ahead of Brazil and South Africa.

One of our main arguments for lower growth in Brazil and South Africa is their lower ability to effectively exploit the competitive advantages of SMEs: the production and sale of medium-tech commodities for domestic markets. Remarkably, the countries that increased their export shares, Brazil and South Africa, fared worse in terms of GDP growth. Certainly, Brazil came closer to resembling the trajectory of China and India with respect to its medium-range technological specialization. Apart from South Africa, where no significant changes in overall technological composition took place, value added from low- and high-technologically intensive production fell in all countries while the medium-low segment was able to yield the highest growth of value added (see Figure 6.3). Brazil has thus been on its way to tapping the 'niche' of good-enough production, but it nonetheless failed to reap the benefits in the same way as China and India. Three reasons stand out. First, with a population of around 200 million, Brazil's domestic market is smaller than those of China and India, although Brazil's GDP in absolute terms is slightly higher than that of India (but still only one-fifth of

China's). Second, investment rates in Brazil are much lower than in China and India. This especially refers to the segment of intermediate goods required for production and construction, rather than production for end consumption. Despite a number of domestic stimulus programs and massive investments, infrastructure development and government procurement in Brazil lags far behind China (FGV 2014). Moreover, the state was not able to significantly boost domestic investment by compensating for a lack of private investment.

Third, Brazil (and even more so, South Africa) has focused more on the world market than Chinese or Indian domestic actors and opened earlier and more extensively. While an export-led strategy seems promising when domestic demand is wanting, it requires not only that firms orient their production towards global consumption, but also that they become competitive with global TNCs. Yet, SMEs are most productive in the medium-tech segment. By manufacturing goods that consumers in the North typically buy, Brazilian firms usually cannot exploit the genuine competitive advantage of SMEs – firms such as Embraer are exceptions that prove the rule. Moreover, Western TNCs have become dominant players in Brazil and South Africa on the basis of their long-standing presence and thus are better able to adapt to the specificities of demand in these countries.

International insertion: As the country chapters illustrated, BICS historically developed along different lines to reach a state in which stable growth became realistic. They all adopted a rather liberal and open stance towards the global economy in the 1990s, albeit under different preconditions. This enabled some to actively yet selectively participate in the expansionary world economy. For the more successful ones, globalization is what they made of it. China was particularly able to selectively engage with some dynamics of the global economy while rejecting others. India chose not to significantly integrate into the global economy, and Brazil and South Africa followed, to various degrees and depending on their institutional endowment, a more comprehensive liberalization path. This also increased the intrusion of global finance, leading to detrimental economic effects, as exemplified earlier.

It is helpful here to distinguish between trade openness and openness towards foreign (financial) capital. Both realms have been examined in Chapter 6, with the overall verdict that China, India, Brazil and South Africa are less integrated into the global economy than expected. However, the main indicator is not so much the broad level of global integration but rather the selectivity with which countries engage with these two realms. Specifically, inward flows are more important than outward flows because they influence the shape of the domestic economy in the medium to long run.

As shown in Chapter 6, China, India and Brazil have adopted a protective stance towards the import of manufactured goods. Their average tariff and non-tariff 'hurdles' are much higher than in other countries. South Africa, in contrast, imposed only a fraction of trade-restricting measures by comparison. This indicates that South Africa adopted a more liberal stance to international trade, which allows almost universal access to home markets on the basis of global free trade principles. In this regard, South Africa deviated heavily from the SME model which emphasizes selectivity vis-à-vis foreign trade inflows, and regulates strictly according to national rather than universal preferences.

The picture comes into sharper focus when we look at the role of inward capital flows. Chapter 6 demonstrated that the stock of foreign investments is higher in Brazil and South Africa compared to China and India. This comes as no surprise. South Africa inherited a liberal corporate governance and finance system with Anglo-Saxon characteristics, and Brazil was forced to open up to foreign capital in times of stress, particularly in the late 1980s and 1990s. However, once FDI is inside the domestic corporate sector and becomes a key element, it is hard to get it out again, because TNCs are legally entitled to own property in the host countries. Not least due to these historical conditions, Brazil and South Africa in particular are far less restrictive to incoming FDI than China and India (OECD 2015).

In addition, different investment types produce different effects on the host economy. In general, investments in 'bricks and mortar' have positive effects due to the creation of jobs and an increase of knowledge and technology, even if it is foreign-owned. Portfolio capital imports instead can be said to have little positive effect on a country's industrial structure, but rather represent a gradual financialization of an economy which is often not well equipped to deal with the side effects of finance-led accumulation. Thus, even if foreign capital formation is low, this does not tell anything about the role of foreign financial capital, as Figure 7.1 illustrates. While foreign capital accounts for only 6% of all US investments, more than half of all foreign capital consists of portfolio investment.

Notably, for the BICS the picture is divided. Only about 10% of all FDI into China and more than 20% in India is portfolio, the rest predominantly 'bricks and mortar'. More dramatically, Brazil and South Africa attract considerably more portfolio FDI (44% and 42%, respectively). Their higher share of portfolio

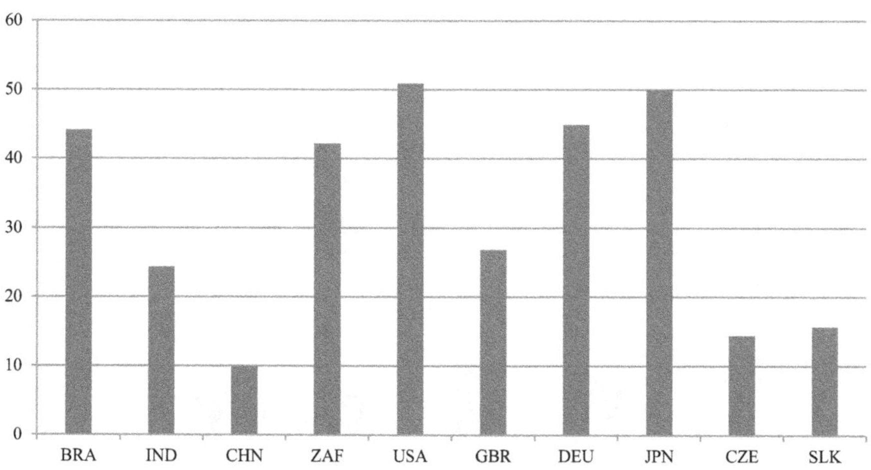

Figure 7.1 Share of portfolio investment of total FDI inflows, average 2000–2013

Source: IMF, Balance of Payments Statistics, International Investment Position.

investment increases macroeconomic vulnerability. Since portfolio capital is much more mobile than greenfield FDI, foreign investors are able to withdraw their funds at much shorter notice than investors in productive capacities (given that there is no liquid market for corporate equity, as is the case for all four countries). The exposure to portfolio volatility is almost equally high for Brazil and South Africa. For emerging countries, this is often a reaction to looming current account deficits, which have to be balanced through the import of capital in order to compensate for insufficient export revenues and/or currency reserves. Countries issue debt or equity securities to attract external funds but are at the same time obliged to pay a sufficient rate on investment. Brazil in particular found itself on a foreign capital treadmill in which high interest rates were necessary to attract foreign portfolio capital, but also with the effect that a considerable share of GDP flowed out of the country by way of interest payments (see Chapter 4). Avoiding these market-mediated external dependencies is an essential element in the development of more autonomous SME policies. For these reasons, FDI inflows have to be regulated, while capital account liberalization often has the opposite effect.

Some countries, in particular Brazil, increased the weight of financialized credit (Figure 7.2). Brazil doubled its international debt securities between 2000 and 2014, thereby increasing its reliance on foreign market-based credit. This creates a particular dependency on foreign volatile financial capital because Brazil, in contrast to China, is less able to compensate for any sudden flight from foreign creditors by way of its giant currency reserves.

To be sure, there is still a difference with South Africa. By the end of the first decade of the 2000s, Brazil has been better equipped to cope with external shocks than in earlier periods because it devoted the revenues from oil exports, for example, to arm itself against speculative attacks and capital flight, while South

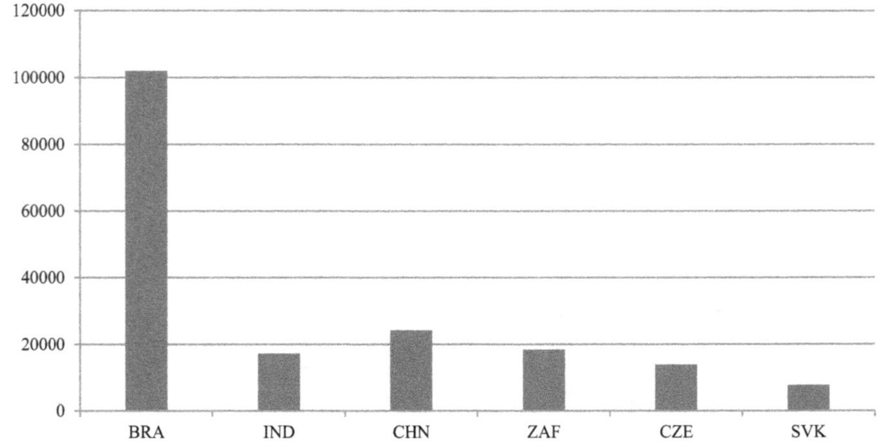

Figure 7.2 International debt securities, average 2000–2014 (in billion US$)

Source: BIS.

Africa did not. Somewhat alarmingly, South Africa is still only able to cover about 35% of its external debt with foreign reserves. This is perhaps surprising because in the 2000s, the surge in primary commodity prices could have actually resulted in a strong inflow of foreign currency.

Thus, we can safely say that by managing to selectively integrate into global flows, China has been most successful in growing on autonomous terms. It avoided large crowding-out effects on indigenous production and investment. Furthermore, it prevented high levels of dependency on foreign capital. On the other hand, India could probably have benefited from a more open stance towards global product markets. All in all, however, a higher degree of integration into global financial markets was more detrimental to stable economic growth, as indicated by the trajectories of Brazil and South Africa.

Corporate governance: As a consequence of the more open stance of Brazil and South Africa to foreign capital, the share of foreign-controlled firms is higher than in China and India. Although below the levels of foreign permeation in DMEs, foreign ownership plays a much stronger role. In contrast, IFDI barely amounted to 11.5% of GDP in India, and it actually decreased in China from 14.2% in the 1990s to about 10% in recent years, indicating that domestic investment has increasingly surpassed IFDI (see Figure 6.5). Both countries were able to keep foreign control at bay. Brazil and, even more so, South Africa were more open to foreign capital in their corporate and financial sectors. In Brazil, foreign capital now accounts for more than 30% of GDP. In South Africa, foreign capital even constitutes more than 40% of GDP, which means that large parts of the economy are controlled by foreign firms.

As argued, SMEs aim for insider control of operational and strategic activities which is achieved through high levels of ownership concentration, whether through high levels of state ownership or other forms of relational or pyramidal ownership structures. Liberal mechanisms such as dispersed ownership, minority shareholder rights and markets for corporate control are detrimental to the success of SMEs. Clearly, many Western TNCs have diversified holdings and headquarters abroad. As a consequence, the state is less able to influence their strategic preferences and include them in development strategy. In that way, Brazil and South Africa (again) deviate from the SME ideal type. Another deviation rests in the increasing role of liberalizing stock markets in both countries. Liberalization of capital markets gives rise to an orientation by owners towards shareholder value principles, which are often incompatible with owners and managers in SME firms that seek long-term stability. This, however, differs from the Chinese stock market, which is more state-controlled and with a limited market for corporate control in the 2000s.

Investment finance: We demonstrated how China strategically allowed productive inward FDI to boost competition and technological innovation. At the same time, from the 2000s onwards, the foreign investment share of Chinese GDP has been shrinking. India, Brazil and South Africa have, in contrast, increased their share of foreign capital in domestic investments. Again, a well-known pattern has emerged lately: while the share of foreign capital in Indian investments is not significant (although rising), the increased openness of Brazil and South Africa indicates a diversion from the more inward-looking trajectory followed in the 2000s.

Compared to liberal, coordinated or dependent capitalisms, stock and bond markets are of less importance in SMEs. High levels of operational autonomy matter for the ways and means by which firms raise the funds for their investments. The SME 'gold standard' is large firms that do not require large amounts of external capital but are able to cover investments mostly by internal means, supported by long-term credit via de facto state credit lines. While this indeed occurs in India and China, high levels of bank finance in Brazil (and low levels of internal funds) are compensated by the strong position of state actors in the very banks that lend funds for investments. As shown before, South African firms rely much more on private bank credit by contrast. While this might comprise less volatility than relying on marketized credit, it still means that firms are subject to external private control that does not necessarily follow a national developmentalist outlook.

Industrial relations: We identified high degrees of informality and fragmentation of the labor force as characteristic of industrial relations in SMEs. Additionally, business and labor associations are comparably weak in organizing and effectively asserting themselves. Rather, state actors actually assist businesses in keeping (low) wages from increasing substantially, and help to foster labor productivity increases. All these features were present in China and India, which sheds light on their respective growth spurts in the 2000s.

Brazil and South Africa, however, deviated much more from the SME model, as they have a smaller degree of informality, lower increases in labor productivity, and a stronger representation of workers. Moreover, although efforts at establishing trilateral frameworks for the organization of industrial relations on a broader scale have been made, these were primarily motivated by political objectives and not very efficient. They have been predominantly designed to overcome social and/or racial segmentation rather than to organize capital-labor relations in a "pro-indigenous business" way (Kohli 2007).

Education and training: According to our model, a segmented education system may functionally benefit the demand for low- and medium-skilled workers, and state actors may partially address rising demand for higher-skilled labor. In reality, the BICS vary with respect to the functionality of their skill formation system as well as educational quality. Chinese workers in general better fit the needs of firms than their Brazilian or South African counterparts. The same holds for the higher education segment, although excessive higher education expenditures have recently generated an overcapacity of Chinese 'white-collar' academics vis-à-vis skilled 'blue-collar' workers (see Chapter 6). Yet the Chinese system still comes closer to the SME model when compared to India, where efficient structures for vocational training and education are less available and formal education mostly supplies low-skilled or highly skilled labor segments.

While the quantitative output of Chinese higher education is enormous, with quality improvements of Chinese graduates underway, the situation in India, Brazil and South Africa is worse (OECD 2013c). As these countries do not have or provide sufficient resources and capabilities to produce sophisticated graduates, they require the import of educated human capital from abroad, for example by importing foreign professionals and technicians. This complicates skill supply for indigenous business, resulting in friction losses because the skills acquired abroad are likely not the ones that indigenous firms need.

Innovation: At the time when Goldman Sachs presented their BRICs studies, these countries (excluding Russia) did not spend significantly on R&D activities. This was consistent with a catch-up strategy that largely imports technology from abroad and adapts it to the needs of local consumers. Actually, China spent less on R&D than Brazil. In 2014, it spent more than Great Britain, though not as much as other developed countries (see Figure 6.10). Of all countries in our sample including developing and developed countries, only China showed a significant increase in R&D engagement. Remarkably, this rise is mostly attributable to the activities of firms, although most of these are in turn supported by state actors.

Much of this R&D spending refers to the profitable transformation of technologies into marketable products. The Chinese state heavily promoted the "commercialization of scientific and technological achievements" from the mid-1990s on, while an explicit strategy to support indigenous innovation was formulated only in 2006 (Ping 2013, 201–3). At the end of the 2000s, a rise in (mostly incremental) technological innovations began. This was accomplished through public support in selected sectors, spin-offs and increasingly by thickly embedded national firms. All this fits within our SME model. Although the extent and quality of Chinese innovation capacity is controversial, the basic fact that China invests substantially more in technological upgrading while other large emerging economies largely do not, still holds true. India has not nearly approached the innovation capacities of China. Furthermore, there is evidence for a cross-institutional causal link between technology upgrading, wages, and financialization, whereby countries experience a less dramatic fall in the wage share of GDP if they heavily invest in technological upgrading and avoid financialization (Stockhammer 2013). From this perspective, rising R&D spending might not have direct effects on firm productivity, but might in fact indirectly affect the institutional configuration of capitalisms in a positive way.

The state and economic coordination: Finally, the four countries also differ with respect to the quality in which the state permeates the institutions of capitalism. As China shows, successful local informal growth alliances work best when mutually supportive in a competitive setting. It also helps if state officials thereby cultivate a self-understanding of state *managers* rather than bureaucrats. Chinese state managers take entrepreneurial risks, and their (often creative) economic activity is in a way reminiscent of the Schumpeterian entrepreneur, yet in a novel 'state-capitalist' sense. Because government jurisdictions are subject to competitive pressures, the capacities involved in accumulation activities by (mostly local) government officials have a lot in common with private capitalist managers (ten Brink 2019).

Notably, our findings suggest that subnational competition between reciprocal state-business alliances in India has become more significant over time, indicating the degree to which India has indeed approached the SME model. In contrast, this competitive setup as well as strong domestic state-business alliances are lacking in Brazil and South Africa. State actors are less entrepreneurial and may find themselves more committed (again, to various degrees) to goals of social equity and welfare. This is sometimes tackled through redistributive means, such as conditional cash transfers in Brazil, but often through specific industrial policies that primarily seek to raise the number of industrial jobs.

In China and India, the fragmented political structure helps keep state-business coalitions more local, i.e. closer to the everyday realities of businesses. This not only enables these alliances to respond more quickly and flexibly to changing political and economic situations, but also to establish a system of 'checks and balances' between competing localities which works as an important corrective against state-capturing and economically harmful types of corruption. In Brazil and South Africa, state-business coordination, in turn, takes place mostly at the national level. This may enable the design of national development strategies. At the same time, it lacks the capacities to control their (local) implementation, and state action is often too distant from the needs of local businesses. Furthermore, powerful national businesses are able to monopolize the flow of resources from the state, with a strong role for oligopolistic rents.

Last but not least, further country-specific factors play a role in explaining differences in the quality of state-permeation and the role of private-public coordination. In Brazil, for instance, smooth coordination between state and industry is hampered by a high degree of political contestation. South Africa's political economy is still ridden with racial segregation, where growth in general matters less than its distribution among social groups. Political contestation is thus likely to continue, rather than the unification of the South African political economy behind a common development project.

To summarize, an appropriate design of institutions and their 'fitness' placed China closest to the SME model. India followed suit, even showing signs of a successive approximation of the model recently. In contrast, Brazil has moved away from the SME ideal type, while South Africa failed to ever come close to it.

7.2 Contingent global conjunctures: further factors for SME success

Our comparative explication of BICS differences helps explain their divergent growth trajectories. While it is beyond our means to fully explain their differences in socio-economic development, we want to complete this chapter by highlighting three further factors that contribute to an understanding of why China in particular and India to a lesser extent experienced such exceptional growth paths. They all have to do with beneficial and time-bound global conjunctures.

When time comes into play, it is necessary to remind ourselves that the success of the state-permeated model of capitalism depends on beneficial factors present only in particular historical world economic conjunctures. Economic development can best be understood as uneven and combined, unevenly evolving across the globe but combined as economic locations are functionally related to each other. Even the most complete realization of state-permeated capitalism depends on global economic conditions which the ruling elites themselves can only partially influence. State-permeated capitalism thus may not be a strategy for any time, but rather a specific model of capitalism for the decades around the millennium.

What have been these beneficial factors? *First* and most notably in China, successful SMEs have enjoyed advantages of global economic processes acting favorably upon economic development. An expansionary global economy since the 1980s provided ample resources that TNCs (also of East Asian origin) could and would invest. While the situation has been similar in the 1970s, when developing countries received considerable credit and investment from abroad, based upon positive growth rates, one difference to the 1970s was crucial: the structural stagnation of industrial growth in the Global North, including Japan. In contrast to the 'golden years' of the 1950s and 1960s, old industrial countries were accumulating at a slower rate (Brenner 2006; Streeck 2014a). An over-accumulation of capital occurred, which meant too much capital with too many unprofitable productive investment prospects.

One consequence of this was a slowdown in the level of accumulation and a decline in average industrial growth rates. This investment crisis within the old global production centers eventually facilitated the relocation of capital investment to the Global South. It manifested in the changing investment strategies of TNCs 'going abroad' not only because they were pulled by cheap labor but also because they were pushed to look for new investment locations to realize profit. As a result of the Asian Crisis of 1997–1998 and later with the Dotcom crisis in 2001, Western companies began to shift their orientation towards the Chinese mainland, which offered a promising internal infrastructure for profitable investment (for example, in the electronics industry). Thus, under such a global conjuncture, endowed with an effective endogenous institutional setup, China was in a more favorable position historically to benefit than other developing countries. Notably, the Indian economy did not profit as much as China from this trend. Although it exhibited promising investment opportunities as well, a more comprehensive defense against global real investment and product markets blocked this.

Second, China and India specifically profited from advantages of backwardness. In the classical Gerschenkronian sense, countries can 'skip' stages of development by adapting existing technologies from developed countries, thereby omitting many of the costly errors and dead-ends of technological innovation. Again, China profited most from this as the country which accelerated its catch-up process the latest, thereby enjoying the biggest late-mover advantages. A favorable opportunity structure to skip stages, especially on the Chinese mainland, was created by the global, IT-related technological and organizational revolution since the 1980s, a transnationalization of production and the development of production networks that enabled (and encouraged) industrial outsourcing. Erstwhile subordinate contract manufacturers were able over time to leapfrog technological stages, because the possibilities for a transfer of technology had increased. India was also able to thrive (if to a minor degree) by way of new international divisions of labor, for example with its IT service sector which expanded substantially.

Our analysis eventually leads to the following assumptions regarding backwardness. First, it is hard to achieve the merits of successful state-permeated capitalism without these catch-up advantages (see section 6.2). Second, it is clearly only possible to benefit from these advantages if channels exist through which modern technology can enter the economy. Technologies must be accessible, not only in a technical sense but also in the ways they travel the globe through products and investments. Ironically, illiberal state-permeated capitalisms grew best in a very liberal global environment, as witnessed from the 1990s on. Third, it is important that countries do not skip too many stages in development at once. Adapting foreign technologies that are incompatible with domestic demand (i.e. with the domestic income structure) will not lead to sustainable growth. Simply specializing in export markets will not do so, either, especially if the West spends less. Also, skipping too many stages will result in an imbalanced industrial structure in which state-of-the-art infrastructures, productive facilities and skills are lacking. China and India have been most successful in keeping a balance between enjoying the advantages of backwardness and avoiding the external dependencies that occur with high levels of 'advanced-ness' and export-orientation.

Third, both China and India could benefit from a 'political' advantage of late catching up, which was learning from the experiences of other developing countries. Both countries have been in a more formidable position than other large emerging countries to learn from the fallacies of other developing countries. They have been largely left untouched by the 'lost decade' of the South in the 1980s. In addition, this episode, along with the demise of the Soviet Union, fostered intra-elite discussions that ultimately led to a more autonomous approach to development. It is instructive to be reminded here that the Neo-Listian approach to industrial development, which SMEs basically follow today, has been out of fashion broadly since the 1970s. Instead, developing countries opened up, believing that added investment capacities would boost domestic development and accelerate catch-up. For most developing countries, however, this did not materialize. Foreign indebtedness proved to be a high societal burden. While Brazil in particular had to grapple with these developmental setbacks, China and India remained largely under the radar of debt-based development strategies. Another strong argument for political learning in China was the Asian Crisis of 1997–1998. The ruling elites could witness how Asian countries, including South Korea and Singapore, deteriorated under the weight of foreign private credit. They could also observe how foreign assistance by the IMF mostly made things worse. As a consequence, China amplified the strategy of not becoming indebted to foreign capital but instead developing autonomous sources of investment funding as well as means for financial 'self-defense' (e.g. through the Chiang Mai Initiative, a regional multilateral currency swap arrangement, and by upholding state control of capital movements and exchange rates). China's recent development would have perhaps been more liberal and open if the Asian Crisis had not served as a lesson in financial dependency. Thus, China and India were overall able to learn from such disastrous episodes rather than those countries directly involved.

All in all, on top of their appropriate endogenous institutions, these three beneficial 'external' factors further help explaining the growth trajectories of the most successful SMEs. However, in the very recent past, doubts have been rising about the longevity of non-liberal capitalisms in the Global South, especially in China. In the next sections, we look more closely at factors that may undermine SMEs' capitalist development.

7.3 Economic exhaustion? The resilience of state-permeated capitalism in difficult times

As we have argued, countries which diverge from the SME model have tended to be less institutionally compatible and to produce less economic growth in the 2000s and beyond. By adopting a diachronic historical perspective, we have not only revealed South Africa's institutional incompatibilities, but also Brazil's recent divergence from the model. The idea of a homogenous emerging country or 'BICS-group' has thereby been qualified. Still, India and China largely seem to resemble the SME model and are therefore correspondingly successful.

US monetary policy changed during the mid-2010s, beginning with the end of quantitative easing policies through the acquisition of large amounts of bonds in 2014, followed by an increase in federal benchmark interest rates in 2015. Large amounts of speculative capital have therefore been withdrawn from emerging markets. This led to massive devaluations, in some cases followed by interest rate hikes and growth slowdown or even recession. Many observers in the business world have concluded that this is the end of the rise of emerging markets (e.g. Frankel 2012; Åslund 2013; Fischermann et al. 2013; The Economist 2013b; Business Insider 2015).

Is this a realistic assumption? In the following, we will argue that such turbulences are recurring but affect only some emerging markets, not all. More specifically, these problems typically pertain to large emerging markets that differ from the SME model. Countries that largely fit the SME model, such as China and India, are much less affected by these developments. In order to substantiate this assessment, we will show how institutionally sound SMEs such as China and India (and partially Brazil), are, so far, robust enough to weather many external and internal dynamics that would potentially undermine the effectiveness of state-permeated capitalism. Given the manifold divergence of South Africa from the SME model, it will not be covered in this or the subsequent section.

China in many ways is the 'poster child' for state-permeated capitalism (see Chapter 2 and section 6.1). If China is in trouble, the whole SME model might prove to be troubled. During the mid-2010s, a significant swing occurred in Western public and academic opinion. While up until the early 2010s we could speak of some kind of 'Sinomania', the later debates highlighted a number of potential obstacles to further growth: slower GDP growth rates, industrial overcapacities, increasing problems of debt as well as instabilities in the financial system. Some of these challenges relate to short-term cyclical developments and are part of the regular up- and downswings of capitalist economies. Others, such as growing resistance against corruption or cronyism and repercussions of social inequality, are more political in nature and will be addressed in the next section. This leaves us with three main medium-term challenges for state-permeated capitalism:

- Problems associated with capital flight and further financial liberalization of SMEs.
- The tendency of state-permeated capitalism to provoke overinvestment and excessive debt.
- The assumption that the economic catch-up potential has been used up, resulting in a 'middle-income trap'.

Each of these issues potentially reduces the complementarities and institutional efficiencies of SMEs. The first relates to the internal-external nexus, i.e. the relation between domestic markets and international integration. The second is especially related to the institutions of corporate governance and investment finance, while the third mostly refers to the realms of industrial relations, education and innovation. On the basis of our previous examination of institutional foundations for long-term growth, we will assess these challenges by studying potential weaknesses of their recent and prospective trajectories. Our extended CC perspective argues against overly pessimistic outlooks that tend to neglect the distinct architectures of large emerging economies. The focus of our argument will be on China, because China is the best test for the SME model – similar to Germany for CMEs or the United States for LMEs.

7.3.1 Challenges to the form of international insertion: capital flight and financial liberalization

During the mid-2010s, commentators speculated about a coming recession in China and other emerging countries, triggered by a massive capital flight (Gallagher 2015; Kynge and Blitz 2015; Kynge and Wheatley 2015; Wheatley and Fleming 2015). Some were motivated by the wish to see those countries fail, particularly China, while others actually feared that a crash would harm Western economies such as German machinery exports and Canadian commodities exports to China, not to mention the consequences for global financial markets. Many emerging market worries thus were rather Western market worries. Nevertheless, there is something to it. Instabilities in SME financial systems and demands for further liberalization have grown lately. Indeed, global financial markets may be counted as the most potent long-term economic force of erosion in SME-style capitalism.

Some of these developments such as the alleged role of capital flight have to be put into perspective, while others can be addressed properly within our CC perspective. This also holds true for an increasing domestic financial instability in China. Given the strong institutional complementarities within state-permeated capitalism, though, China should be able to overcome these instabilities. If, however, China chooses to leave this path and to unleash the full power of financial liberalization, this might change. Continuing liberalization and opening of the financial sector may undermine the SME model in the long term because new (domestic and international) financial actors may threat to hollow it out.[1] Thus, against the common notion that a slowdown in liberal economic reforms will harm the Chinese economy, our CC-based assessment argues against one best-practice model of (financial) capitalism, concluding that continuing to liberalize financial markets may rather endanger state-permeated capitalism.

For the moment, however, our account casts doubt on the assumption that all large emerging markets suffer from externally induced instability. There are enormous differences in large emerging economies' vulnerabilities to external shocks. Among those challenges, the end of high prices in oil and commodities (the latter lasting from about 2003 to 2012) is often perceived as a serious problem (IMF 2012a, Ch. 4, 2015; Economist 2015b). Yet while South Africa (and partly, Brazil) indeed suffered from price declines due to its dependence on exporting commodities, China, as a major commodity importer, has rather benefited from decreasing prices. Moreover, India actually experienced considerable positive effects from declining oil and commodity prices, as this positively influenced domestic prices and reduced inflation (World Bank 2015a). In contrast to economies that primarily depend on the export of commodities, of which Russia and the Arab world may be the most prominent examples, state-permeated capitalism is based on domestic industrialization and may rather benefit from lower prices for commodities.

A challenge noted perhaps even more often for large emerging countries has been the role of 'capital flight' or capital outflows. This issue relates to the end, or the 'normalization', of one of the greatest credit booms of all time in the 2000s, prolonged from 2008 until the mid-2010s by quantitative easing in Western economies which resulted in flooding the global markets with cheap finance. Indeed, this has negatively affected the Brazilian economy, as documented in Chapter 4 (and later in this chapter). Yet again, differences exist that lead us to qualify the argument. When it comes to dependency from external finance, Brazil and South Africa are far more vulnerable than China and India (see Chapter 6).

In China, non-FDI capital outflows reached an estimated US$295 billion in 2014, and the numbers indeed increased in 2015 (Dubrovsky 2015) before being effectively limited by the Xi Jinping administration. Analysts estimated the devaluation of China's foreign reserves at a range between US$220 billion and US$300 billion from June 2014 to June 2015. Yet China's foreign exchange reserves are still tremendous at over US$3000 billion. Moreover, a reduction of these huge foreign reserves may be counted as a rather healthy development towards a more balanced world economy, given the corresponding vulnerability to fluctuations of the US dollar in which most of these reserves are denominated. As portfolio investment is still rather low (although their absolute size is relevant), capital controls remain in place, the RMB is still only partially freely tradeable and the effects of these outflows were less severe than often argued. On top of this, while money was indeed flowing out of the country, this was also due to outflows directed by Chinese actors. Capital for international activities affect the Chinese capital balance, for example the US$40 billion Silk Road Fund, the US$30 billion to the Asian Infrastructure Investment Bank and the US$10 billion for the BRICS Development Bank.

Capital outflows are no major concern for the stability of state-permeated capitalism in India, either. Although there has been an increase in volatile portfolio capital (out)flows, India has deliberately "rebuilt its reserve buffer" to cushion the domestic financial system (World Bank 2015a, 22). These buffers are also supported by somewhat idiosyncratic factors not necessarily related to the core model of state-permeated capitalism, such as steadily growing remittances that have made India the largest recipient of remittances in the world (World Bank 2015a, 28). These remittances are steady long-term inflows of capital which are relatively independent of shocks and conjunctures.

While all of this does not necessarily imply a comfortable development, other problems in the financial sphere are of potentially greater significance for the stability of state-permeated capitalism. This especially relates to instabilities in China's financial system. Since 2014, the Chinese equity market has been gripped by speculative frenzies, in part fanned by the party-state media (Naughton 2015b). After the Chinese stock market crash, a sharp correction took place and the state stepped in several times, introducing drastic measures to stop the market decline. Accordingly, liberal authors sent warning signals:

> For foreign investors, the implications are quite stark. If the Chinese government can freeze trillions in assets of its wealthiest citizens, it certainly will not hesitate to freeze or seize the assets of foreign investors. This logic pertains to both the equities market and the fixed income market.
>
> (Shih 2015)

What does this tell us about contemporary China? On the one hand, Chinese stock markets are a weak indicator for the health of the real economy. Stock prices fell between 2010 and 2013 when the real economy was growing strongly, and rose in the first half of 2015 when the real economy was slowing down. As has been shown in our study of Chinese state-permeated capitalism, this is due to distinctive features of China's capital markets and its comparatively small role in the overall economy. However, some concerns about China's financial system can be raised. *First*, the stock market crash and surrounding debates within China possibly signify a stronger role for capital markets in general. This includes new pilot zones that permit yuan convertibility, foreign currency exchange, a more liberal climate for investors, a rise of bond markets and shadow banking. These processes go along with the easing of controls on capital movements, a relaxation in the use of the RMB by foreigners and by Chinese abroad – the major channel for foreign investment (and a role model for mainland financial actors) being the liberal Hong Kong stock market. All in all, new financial players have gained significance lately, and their activities are increasingly threatening the coherence of the overall economy. Yet, the Chinese administration seems to notice the implications for their model of capitalism very well, as financial markets have not been opened for foreign capital as much as observers forecasted. *Second*, domestic and international investors have lost some faith in China's once-renowned ability to manage the economy (Naughton 2015b), not least due to contradictory signals from the Chinese leadership. They promote market forces yet turn instantaneously to massive state intervention when capital markets do not deliver intended results. As these conflicting signals can also be interpreted as contradictions within the power elite itself, they expose limits on the state's ability to control ever more liberalizing financial markets. *Lastly*, the growth slowdown in the real economy has led the central state to further enhance the role of capital markets in directing financial resources to real investment. All of this denotes that rising capital markets and new actors are increasing domestic financial instability. Even in China, the largely unquestioned belief in the CCP's capacity to command the key actors in the financial system may finally come into doubt. The aura of economic solidity that was sustained through the 1990s in terms of SOE reform, Asian Crisis, WTO accession, and especially the global slump has been questioned. Chinese policymakers face a delicate balancing act in the coming years in order to reduce the systemic risks arising from capital markets and increased financial opening while also maintaining high levels of GDP growth to ensure overall political stability.

The recent trajectory of Brazil also demonstrates the dangers of a too-open stance towards global financial markets in a vivid manner. Chapter 4 has shown how the Real suffered from a mid-term trend towards overvaluation. During their fight against the global financial crisis, Western central banks made matters much worse by flooding global financial markets with liquidity, much of which found its way to Brazil, thereby further supporting a currency overvaluation and a deterioration of export competitiveness. According to UNCTAD calculations, the Real was overvalued by 80% in relation to its long-term optimal value in April 2011 (Nassif et al. 2011). At the same time, these short-term financial flows, in the absence of wide-ranging currency controls, make Brazil vulnerable to the devastating effects of a 'sudden stop', as witnessed during the speculations about US interest rate increases from 2013 onwards. Although the devaluation hand-in-hand with financial outflows may prove to be helpful in the medium to long term, businesses require stability for their investment decisions, and sudden currency swings are thus problematic (Casanova and Kassum 2014, 48; Kaltenbrunner and Painceira 2015, 1301). And while Brazil has successfully combatted traditional forms of vulnerability to global financial markets based on high public foreign currency debts, it has also created new ones based on very short-term domestic currency assets. To an extent, this is part of a strategy to stimulate domestic demand by (temporarily) increasing private indebtedness. Not least because of rising interest rates, a process of modest financialization as exemplified by easier access to credit for poor households based on various reforms such as the *crédito consignado* program[2] also seems to have been exhausted in Brazil by the mid-2010s (Serrano and Summa 2015, 14–16). Easier access to consumer credit for lower- and medium-income groups temporarily boosted demand for medium-tech industrial goods (such as refrigerators and television sets) that can be manufactured domestically.

Yet strongly increasing private indebtedness terminated this boost of domestic demand. In 2011, the consumer debt service ratio in Brazil reached 23%, a significantly larger value than in other Latin American countries or even the US (IMF 2012b, 5b; see also Lavinas 2018).

Similar problems exist for mortgage credit, which strongly expanded in the wake of a series of subsidized mortgage schemes during the early 2010s, although it has been kept within certain limits in order to prevent a subprime crisis (López Vicente and Serena Garralda 2014, 21). Additionally, company indebtedness has increased, leading to an increase in combined household and company indebtedness from 107% of GDP in 2007 to 139% in 2014 (FAZ 2015b). Subsequently, a loss of confidence in the repayment of debt on the side of transnational capital has led to a rating downgrade and capital outflows, triggering a strong devaluation of the Real.[3] In order to combat rising inflation, the central bank increased the benchmark interest rate (Lewis and Jelmayer 2015). This has led to a decrease of consumer, mortgage and industry lending and to a subsequent implosion of domestic demand. The recession that followed demonstrated the vulnerability of a growth strategy based on domestic private demand, fueled by increasing private indebtedness. Domestic demand reduction led to increasing unemployment and, as a consequence, further demand contraction and fewer investments. At the same time, deceasing tax revenues and increasing social security expenses resulted in higher public indebtedness and interest payments, thereby making any major program for public demand stimulation to combat the enfolding recession impossible.

Brazilian firms are, as we have seen, traditionally better protected against short-term financial turbulences (Ocampo 2009, 19). Domestic banks did not have to undertake high-risk speculation because they enjoyed good returns on high domestic interest rates, although this element of the "Custo Brasil" also happens to be a major cost disadvantage for Brazilian companies and consumers (Dowbor 2009, 125). Brazil also suffered a relatively small degree of capital flight and its international currency reserves are substantial (about US$380 billion in 2014; G20 2014, 6). Not least, the 2008 crisis has been mitigated through short-term public measures. BNDES and other public institutions increased their loan volume massively (by 50% between September 2008 and January 2010) in order to compensate for the decrease in private credit supply (Arnold 2011, 20–1). Capital controls have been introduced in 2009–2011 but had only limited impact (Dierckx 2015, 154). Due to a rising current account deficit and decreasing capital inflows, these capital controls have gradually been lifted from December 2011 onwards. In line with the semi-closed nature of the Brazilian economy, many non-financial companies are increasingly making use of marketized credit such as corporate bonds, including foreign currency bonds, in order to escape the limitations within the state-controlled Brazilian credit system. By 2014, nearly 20% of total corporate debt financing was issued in bonds, indicating a strong increase over the last years (IIF 2015, 2). In addition, many companies turned to a multitude of short-term alternative assets. This adds a degree of vulnerability because sudden capital outflows, in particular when interest rates in the North rise again, are a permanent option.

7.3.2 Challenges to corporate governance and investment finance: overinvestment and debt

According to some observers, emerging economies are suffering from high levels of corporate investment and related problems of debt (see e.g. Lee et al. 2012; Schnabl and Hoffmann 2008). This is especially relevant for China, which recurrently failed to reach the official target GDP growth rate of 7%. Although even at 5–6%, the PRC would generate substantial growth the slowdown might become a problem if proactive measures, such as credit incentives for higher investments, nurture unsustainable levels of debt (Chen 2015).

Since large firms in state-permeated capitalism can draw on preferential national networks of finance for investment and numerous types of proactive state support, they usually enjoy a more-than-sufficient supply of capital. Ample support of capital and heavy competition between local growth alliances leads to high-growth policies that carry a risk of wasteful investments. In China, a slowdown of economic growth is typically addressed through enormous state-led domestic stimulus programs, i.e. monetary and fiscal policies, industrial policies and regional strategies to boost promoted areas (Cai 2015). Such large programs can result in industrial overcapacities and rising debt, while keeping the economy on a solid growth path with low unemployment. Because cheap credit from state banks and financial institutions close to the state has been made available for local partners in industry, the partner investments have become less 'risky'. For instance, supported firms did not have to generate profits on a short-term basis in order to finance investments through retained earnings. Indeed, optimistic economic forecasts and an exceedingly loose credit policy caused a surge in bank and other forms of lending after 2008. In this way, China outperformed other large emerging countries in investment. While Brazil and South Africa had low investment ratios of 18% to 21% of GDP between 2010 and 2014, resulting in very slow growth, China's investment ratio permanently stood at about 47%. This is exceptionally high, also compared to India with 31% to 39% between 2010 and 2014 (World Bank 2015d).

To some extent, high volumes of investment are characteristic for developing countries. However, this growth may become unsustainable if demand development does not match its pace. Exclusive access to resources, also with respect to the prominent role of large firms in the huge stimulus plans, may lead to misplaced investment and nurture (mostly local) indebtedness. Local growth alliances in China, for instance, made excessive investments in the construction of machinery factories that were in fact unnecessary. While in the case of India there is continuing leeway in fixed investment, especially in infrastructure, the Chinese economy of the mid-2010s is struggling with problems of industrial overcapacities, a fall in producer prices and a subsequent deterioration of the investment climate (Chen 2015). Because much Chinese investment was financed with debt, loans went bad and inefficient use of credit inundated the banks with non-performing loans (Liang 2010). Furthermore, expansive monetary policies enabled creditors to additionally acquire other types of funds, which resulted in speculative bubbles, particularly in the real estate sector. As state-permeated capitalism does not encompass straightforward state-dirigisme or an almighty central state, Chinese economic development is a hardly controlled process with dynamics fueled by the activities of competing local growth alliances. Thus, a major factor for the success of state-permeated capitalism is also a source of potential instability. Although the state has attempted to curb bank lending several times over the last years, it could not prevent risky financial policies and overinvestment, nor could it prevent a strongly growing sector of shadow banking from becoming more significant. As it is more than likely that new stimulus programs will be utilized to keep the economy growing, these might speed up existing overcapacities and produce new debt. Correspondingly, China has undergone several cycles of growth slowdown, fiscal stimulus, overcapacity and, finally, debt restructuring (Nölke 2015). Ultimately, this could increasingly challenge the possibilities of effective state intervention and macroeconomic steering in volatile Chinese markets.

Yet, there is a substantial cushion in terms of public funds as well as large foreign economic reserves. This indicates that in spite of the aforementioned tendencies, the central government was in fact able to keep excessive investment and rising debt at bay. When debt actually reached around 25% of GDP in late 2014 at the local level (Naughton 2015a), the central state-initiated strategies for local debt restructuring, including long repayment periods and lower interest rates for local governments (which, incidentally, meant that banks paid a cost). In a penetrating tug-of-war between central ministries and local governments about debt classification and debt management, local governments "in danger of paralysis due to large debts coming due, were given a pathway to restructure and resume normal activity. Local government financing costs were cut significantly" (Naughton 2015a, 6; cf. World Bank 2015b, 9–12). As the overall level of central government debt remains well within limits of sustainability, it still has leeway to act. Debt restructuring seems to actually be an effective means of tackling the dangers of overinvestment. Most of the debt is denominated in RMB, and almost all debt is owed to institutions ultimately kept or backed by the state. Therefore, much debt can be written off by state agencies; there are no global creditors or international economic institutions able to put serious pressure on the country such as in Latin America in the 1980s.

Moreover, the issue of overinvestment seems to be a Chinese specialty among large emerging markets and thus an idiosyncratic problem rather than a general issue. In India, in contrast, there is still a yawning infrastructure gap. The government plans to increase infrastructure investment to 8.2% of GDP by 2020, but whether these plans can be fully implemented is not guaranteed, as past plans have suffered huge delays and cost overruns (OECD 2014c). Similarly in Brazil, the problem is one of under- rather than overinvestment, as we saw earlier. Taken together, the stimulation of domestic demand has served the growth of Brazilian capitalism very well during the 2000s, even if it was an exhaustion of this process during the 2010s. While the latter could potentially be overcome by a (politically very controversial) higher degree of redistribution towards the poor and improved industrial production based on a more competitive exchange rate and substantial capital controls, several observations indicate that the medium-term growth constraints in Brazil stem mainly from the supply side (Canuto and Schellekens 2014; see also Chapter 4). Demand-side stimuli have to be balanced by the supply side. This is in line with the perspective of the Brazilian government, which has announced a shift from demand stimulation to supply-side policies. "The Brazilian growth strategy so far has focused on the expansion of domestic consumption [. . .]. The focus now will be to make investment grow more than consumption" (G20 2014, 5). An important warning sign is the rising level of inflation, in spite of low growth.

As discussed previously, wages in the formal economy have grown very strongly and unemployment has been very low, with a decreasing 'reserve army' of workers streaming in from the informal sector. Higher growth combined with a fairly closed output gap requires massive investments in capital (including infrastructure) and education to increase worker productivity (IMF 2013, 9; G20 2014, 4). Although Brazil has made some improvements on both accounts, its industry was not able to quickly exploit the surge in competitiveness provided by the massive devaluation of the Real after 2013. Despite the dampening effects on imports and support for exports, the current account deficit did not close as expected, but increased further (FAZ 2015c). Yet, despite tendencies of deindustrialization in the Brazilian economy, it can still draw on a large and diversified manufacturing sector as a basis for further catch-up industrialization (Nassif et al. 2015, 1327).

7.3.3 Challenges to industrial relations, training and innovation: a middle-income trap?

According to some voices in the contemporary economics literature, large emerging economies are confronted with medium- to long-term structural limits on growth (Eichengreen et al. 2011). Fast-growing emerging economies are threatened with being stuck in a low-growth equilibrium or a "middle income trap" (Gill and Kharas 2007; Kharas and Kohli 2011; ADB 2011; World Bank 2012; Aiyar et al. 2013; Doner and Schneider 2015). The middle-income trap consists of a growth slowdown at middle-income levels which persists over time. The slowdown is associated with a loss of competitiveness in labor-intensive low-cost production. This entails rising wages and the end of large productivity gains through a reallocation of labor from agriculture to manufacturing or service. Moreover, looming technology gaps (compared to Western economies), deficient human capital, and the associated inability to upgrade in global value chains are seen as factors that prevent such countries from developing knowledge-based economies (Ohno 2009). What follows from our analysis of SMEs in this debate? We argue, in short, that India and China are better prepared than other emerging economies to cope with problems associated with the middle-income trap. The SME model therefore provides potential antidotes to overcoming these dilemmas of growth and economic upgrading (also see Doner and Schneider 2015).

Frequently, in order to avoid the middle-income trap and to move into high-income status, economists suggest strengthening technology and innovation capacities, increasing the value content of products and processes and spurring investments in education as well as in advanced infrastructure networks (Agénor et al. 2012). As "poor institutional quality" is regularly seen as the cause of remaining stuck in the middle-income trap (measured e.g. by the World Bank Governance Indicators), the case is also made for the establishment of "good" institutions. These would be liberal institutions with the accompanying "social technology" that complements physical technologies and vibrant entrepreneurs keen to take advantage of new opportunities (Paus 2012). Besides the one-sided emphasis on liberal policies, however, the question of which institutions should be prioritized and how policies should be designed also remains contested (see e.g. Mazzucato 2013; Vivarelli 2015; Witt forthcoming).

The most important indicator for identifying the location of a middle-income trap is a country's GDP per capita income. Recent research has identified two ranges of middle-income trap: one in the range of US$10,000–11,000 and another at US$15,000–16,000 (Eichengreen et al. 2013). Notably, the countries in our study are at very different levels (see Table 7.1).

If we consider the lower range of the two, Brazil would have been in danger of falling into the trap. However, the crisis of 2013 and beyond reduced GDP per capita dramatically. China still has some years to reach the threshold, while India seems to be far away from any middle-income level. However, as Chinese per capita income has increased by approximately eight times between 2000 and 2014, it may reach the threshold in the foreseeable future. Moreover, the most developed regions of China are beyond or close to the lower middle-income threshold. Beijing had a GDP per capita of US$16,278 in 2014, and Guangdong of US$10,330. Thus, despite these concerns over whether the concept of the middle-income trap and its measurement is actually applicable to our country cases, we understand the problems of the middle-income trap more broadly as problems in terms of (1) dealing with rising wages, (2) upgrading human capital/education and (3) developing greater innovation capacities. For these issues, we can identify several important points from our analysis.

Table 7.1 GDP per capita, current US$

	2000	*2005*	*2010*	*2014*	*2017*
China	954.6	1,740.1	4,514.9	7,593.9	8827
India	457.3	740.1	1,417.1	1,630.8	1942,1
Brazil	3,766.2	4,792.6	11,318.1	11,612.5	9821,4
South Africa	3,099.1	5,444.1	7,390.0	6,477.9	6151,1

Source: World Bank.

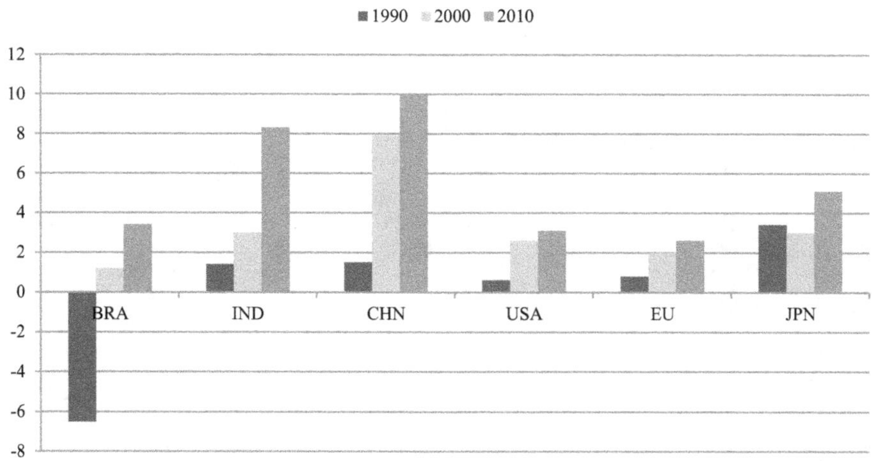

Figure 7.3 Labor productivity per person employed, average annual growth in %

Source: The Conference Board.

(1) *Rising wages* have indeed been a salient phenomenon, weakening former comparative advantages of even the most dynamic SMEs. Wage increases, however, become problematic only if they can no longer be compensated by an increase in labor productivity. As Figure 7.3 shows, labor productivity has been rising, in some cases even to large degrees, as the examples of China and India suggest.

Except for India, however, real wages have risen even more strongly when measured against labor productivity growth (Figure 7.4). Of the four countries analyzed, only India still seems to fit into the well-established picture of emerging economies (again, epitomized by China) as competitive only because of super-low wages.

Do rising wages thus diminish the catch-up potential of even the most dynamic SMEs? We should be cautious here. First, wage increases above labor productivity growth do not necessarily translate into an actual loss of competitiveness. As elaborated in our country chapters, China in particular has been able to build prerequisites for profitable investment such as developed and cost-saving production and logistics infrastructures and large mature supplier networks. "China has more than 140,000 machinery suppliers, 75,000 companies in communications and equipment industries, and 104,000 companies in the transportation equipment sector. This is over five times the size of the supplier base in Japan" (McKinsey & Company 2015, 12). This favorable manufacturing ecosystem prevents domestic and foreign firms from exiting when labor costs increase. Furthermore, this structure allows for an effective implementation of imported technologies. Second, state institutions still attempt to arrange for the preservation of 'sound' wages,

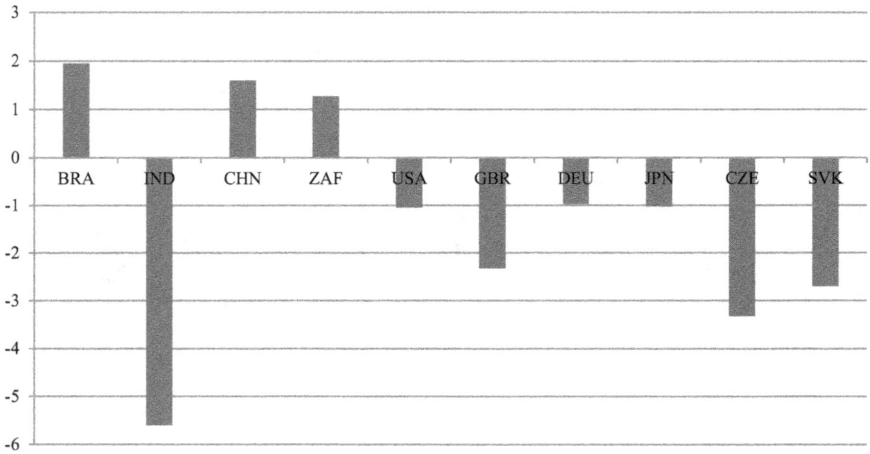

Figure 7.4 Spread between real wage growth and labor productivity growth in %, average 2009–2012

Source: ILOStat: real monthly earnings, average annual growth rate 2009–2012; World Development Indicators: Labor Productivity, measured as GDP per person employed, average annual growth 2009–2012.

for example by non-intervention into business misconduct, urging trade unions to preserve 'harmonious' labor relations, and containing worker protests. This also holds true for India. The Indian economy may be behind China regarding infrastructure and a less developed manufacturing ecosystem, but its manufacturing sector continues to benefit from informal labor and, recently, a rise in low-paid temporary contracts (OECD 2014c).

Finally, the conclusion that labor surplus from the agrarian economy has already come to an end (a "Lewisian turning point") thereby driving wage increases ever faster, seems premature (World Bank 2012, 303). This is clearly not valid for the case of India, though perhaps it is more so for Brazil and South Africa. Herd noted in 2010 that in China, despite labor shortages in coastal provinces,

> [it] may take another decade for the share of labour in agriculture to fall to 25%. In Japan, it was only when farming employment fell to this level that the wages of people moving from farms to cities started to take off rather than remaining at a subsistence level.
>
> (Herd et al. 2010, 14)

(2) Historically, East Asian developmental states were, above all, able to overcome the middle-income trap with heavy investments in *education* and *skills development* (Vivarelli 2015, 7).[4] With regard to large emerging economies, capacity problems loom large, probably larger than in the area of industrial relations (see e.g. Mehrotra et al. 2013). Employers in SMEs are increasingly

identifying shortages of qualified staff as a main business concern (for example, along the lines of the German system of qualified, specialized vocational training; see e.g. FICCI 2006). This holds true not only for Brazil and South Africa, but also for India and China. Two types of problems are typical here: limited fiscal resources for the qualification of large amounts of graduates on one side, and limited motivation on the side of both employers and employees to invest in the qualification of the workforce. Although the state may hold more fiscal resources to address the latter problems, there are doubts about whether the state can substitute for missing business and worker incentives to upgrade the skill level of the workforce. It is laudable that government plans want to ensure 12 years of education for all children in China by 2020 so that both participation in higher education rises and the quality of higher education improves (Koen et al. 2013, 12). However, there is now an oversupply of university-educated academics vis-à-vis qualified personnel from vocational education. The Chinese government has thus introduced more vocational education and training programs since 2009. Similarly, the Indian state, particularly with the Modi administration, has started putting greater emphasis on education and training, for example by establishing the Ministry of Skill Development and Entrepreneurship in 2014, including a massive reorganization of relevant agencies and institutions (Economic Times 2015a, 2015b). In Brazil, the overheating of the economy in terms of capacity utilization before the mid-2010s recession has even led to a situation in which both companies and workers now have stronger incentives to invest in higher (also vocational) skill levels of the workforce (see section 4.3). Both the incentive and the fiscal capacity problems thus need not be unsurmountable challenges for large emerging markets.

(3) In the *realm of innovation and technological upgrading*, a mixed picture emerges. Again, lacking business and worker incentives might raise serious problems. Other problematic issues are weak innovation spots in less advanced regions and the inefficient connection of public research and companies. Nonetheless, as with the other problematic areas, a thorough pursuit of the state-permeated model and following a state-led process of technological upgrading might help to overcome these challenges. In fact, the Indian as well as the Chinese state has begun to increase efforts at structurally improving innovation systems and public innovation activities (Jefferson et al. 2014). On the one hand, both China and India can benefit from their specific domestic market structure which implies no need for radical innovation in the coming years. It rather allows domestic producers to focus on adaptive and incremental forms of product and process innovation to reach new consumers (see Chapter 6). As argued in Chapters 2 and 3, Indian and Chinese firms are already innovative in the production of medium-range products, even without drastic investments in R&D. Tencent's "WeChat", a very successful social media platform in China, creatively adapted Western communication services (from Facebook, WhatsApp, etc.) into a mobile text and voice messaging communication service that combines messaging with services like hospital pre-registration, visa renewal, credit card usage and functions to hail and pay for a taxi. Tencent has thereby become one of the giant new media firms in China

alongside Alibaba or Baidu. Tencent, as well as successful smartphone producers such as Xiaomi, point to another 'Gerschenkronian' advantage of backwardness: enjoying the "benefit of jumping directly on a relatively new technology" such as the "diffusion of mobile telecommunications in countries where the traditional telephone networks are limited to few urban areas" (Vivarelli 2015, 14). Last but not least, consumers in China

> seem to be more willing than other consumers to participate in the innovation process by acting as perpetual beta testers [. . .]. Developers at Xiaomi [. . .] regularly post proposed features for smartphone software on an online forum. Consumers vote for their favorite ideas, and the company adds popular ones to the product development system, sometimes within a week. The result: Xiaomi has more competitive products and more loyal customers.
>
> (McKinsey & Company 2015, 10, 25)

Thus, domestic demand and domestic market growth act as essential factors for boosting innovation activity, driven by increasing returns of scale, for instance. What is more, medium technology-range markets are nowhere near exhaustion, although rising competitiveness with foreign firms in these segments complicates the situation. Domestic markets still have huge growth potential. Large populations in India and China generate a significant 'middle-income stratum' in which consumption will increase in the near future. Consumer spending in both countries still has ample room, although this touches on problems of social inequality and the need for 'social upgrading' (see section 7.4.1).

To sum it up: although we see the potential of the dynamics which underpin the middle-income trap hypothesis, we first identify empirical trends that do not indicate a massive problem of this type in China, which is arguably best suited to measure the validity of the hypothesis. Analyses that seek to extend observations on East Asian developmental states to large emerging economies fail to account for the particular incentive structure that large domestic markets entail. Under these circumstances, there seems to be no straightforward connection between growth, income level and technology upgrading. Second, these analyses underestimate how the state is able to react to such tendencies through counteracting policies and investments. The state regularly acts as an economic player in a counter-cyclical and/or compensatory manner, and there are no indications that this ability is in retreat. Therefore, systematically including the state in its various forms into the various accounts of slowdown and economic exhaustion fundamentally alters the equation of politico-economic analysis.

Again, our extended CC approach emphasizes that there ought to be more than one coherent form of capitalism able to reach high-income status. We thereby not only agree with recent CC literature (e.g. Doner and Schneider 2015) that stresses how different institutional arrangements impede the smooth implementation of liberal policy proposals. We also highlight the different institutional trajectories of state-permeated capitalism that focus on large domestic markets. Moreover, a massive investment of public resources is able to assist processes of technological catch-up, even if this takes somewhat longer. Problems for state-permeated capitalism arise if fiscal resources are too limited for a broad-based push towards technological upgrading, as witnessed in Brazil.

7.4 Political exhaustion? Inequality and the rise of the middle classes

The previous section addressed a number of recent developments and skeptical arguments about the sustainability of state-permeated capitalism, which are broadly of an economic nature. We came to the conclusion that the SME model, in its most 'pure' form, may be able to weather those potential sources of destabilization easier than other, less coherent capitalisms. These debates, as we argued, tend to be rather technical, as they assume macroeconomic regularities at work in all phases of the development of large emerging economies. Essentially, these are about the question of whether or not high growth can be sustained. What is missing, however, is the social and political dimension in which dynamics can both support and undermine the effectiveness of SMEs. Here, the question is more about the distribution of growth. While we think that state-permeated capitalism could in fact be 'social' and therefore able to draw on popular support, we also think that growth in large emerging economies alters the social structure in a way that is potentially destabilizing for this particular type of capitalism. We will first assess the record of state-permeated capitalism with regard to the reduction of poverty and the distribution of wealth within these countries, before spelling out the potentially destabilizing dynamics that go along with a further increase of welfare. The fact that rising incomes produce new forms of socio-economic stratification, and are often associated with a reorganization of the political arena, is potentially destabilizing because it undermines the very mode of coordination on which the whole model rests.

7.4.1 Poverty reduction and inequality in large emerging economies

The rise of China, as is widely accepted by now, has been accompanied by a record reduction of poverty. Economic growth has lifted tens of millions into what is commonly referred to as "middle classes", particularly in China but also in India and Brazil (Ravallion 2009). This phenomenon, albeit usually unaccounted for in the CC literature, deserves a closer look, not least because it has important consequences for the overall thesis of the book. Table 7.2 shows the dramatic decrease in absolute poverty. The number of people moving out of extreme poverty (i.e. less than US$2 per day) in these four countries exceeded more than 500 million by 2011. The share of the population living in poverty decreased between 1999 and 2011 in all four countries: from 44% to 13% in China, from 46% to 25% in India, from 8% to 4% in Brazil and down to 18% from 35% in South Africa (World Bank 2015e). Adopting the World Bank definition of the lower medium-income-level group (with an income up to US$3.10 per day), about 600 million people were able to move up beyond the threshold.

Table 7.2 Poverty reduction between 1999 and 2011 (in millions of people)

	Below US$2	*Below US$3.10*
Brazil	−13.16	−21.66
China	−377.19	−477.2
India	−168.69	−97.36
South Africa	−7.31	−5.69

Source: World Bank (2015e). Data for China 2010, 2000 for South Africa, 2004 for India.

Table 7.3 Income levels and poverty measures for large emerging economies

	Mean income monthly in USD	*Mean daily income in USD*	*Median daily income*	*60% of median income (poverty level)*	*Percentage below 60% median level (2011)*	*In millions $*
China	218.54	7.28	4.89	2.94	25.14	336.3
India	111.73	3.72	1.69	1.01	0.98	12.11
Brazil	492.16	16.41	6.16	3.69	14.2	29.38
South Africa	358.24	11.94	3.33	2.00	18.08	9.32

Source: Gallup (2013); UNU-WIDER (2015); World Bank (2015e).

It is difficult to understate the meaning of these figures for our analysis. As large emerging economies focus their industrial development on serving the domestic market with low- and medium-tech products, they are aiming exactly at those 600 million people that have joined the consumer ranks. However, China, India, Brazil and South Africa have very different income levels, which gives the comparison along global threshold lines limited validity.

Basically, there is a difference between being poor in a very poor country and in an advanced developing country. In China, one-quarter of the population has less than 60% of the median income at their disposal and are thus considered poor. However, the same measurement leaves only a handful of Indians counted as poor (Table 7.3). This means that Indian poverty is due to a generally low national income level, while Chinese poverty is due mainly to intra-Chinese income inequalities. Poverty thus can be alleviated in two ways: either by making the country wealthier in its entirety or by shifting the very poor within a country into higher income ranks, leaving the overall national income to remain constant. As Table 7.4 shows, India is by far the poorest country, indicated by both mean and median income levels. If we apply the standard poverty threshold of 60% of median income,[5] we obtain daily income levels that indicate nationally specific poverty. For South Africa, the national indicator for poverty matches the global indicator (US$2 a day), whereas the Indian poverty line (roughly US$1 a day) is much lower. This means that 200 million Indians living with less than US$2 per

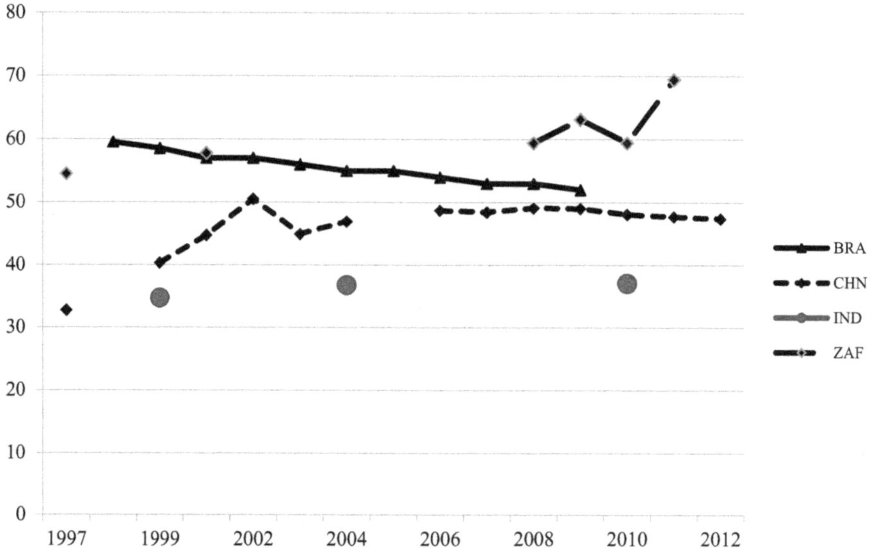

Figure 7.5 Development of GINI

Source: UNU-WIDER (2015).

day still have between 1 and 2 dollars a day at their disposal, and are therefore not extremely poor by Indian standards.

Yet, when it comes to the distribution of relative poverty across the country, emerging economies show vast divergences as manifested in the development of their respective GINI measures (Figure 7.5). India is on average the most equal of the four, while South Africa has become the most unequal country of the four. However, inequality persisted or even increased during the first decade of the 2000s, in particular in China, but also in India. The only country that was able to reduce inequality is Brazil (Ravallion 2009; Barbosa and Moretto 2013; Boschi 2013, 136–8; Leubolt 2015, 237–46). However, this decrease started from very high inequality levels, as some of the poorest and richest people in the world live in Brazil (Milanovic 2008). But even there, inequality is still very high and still much higher than in China and India. To be sure, GINI does tell us how unequal a country is, but not how inequality is distributed within a country. For this, we have to look more closely at the distribution of income classes, in particular the development of lower and middle classes.

We should be careful with qualifying this development as a rise of the 'middle classes', even as we use this term in our subsequent debate, because it strongly depends on the definition of middle classes. In the traditional Western sense, this notion was related not only to a certain level of income, but also to a number of social features such as education, occupation and values (Guarin et al. 2014,

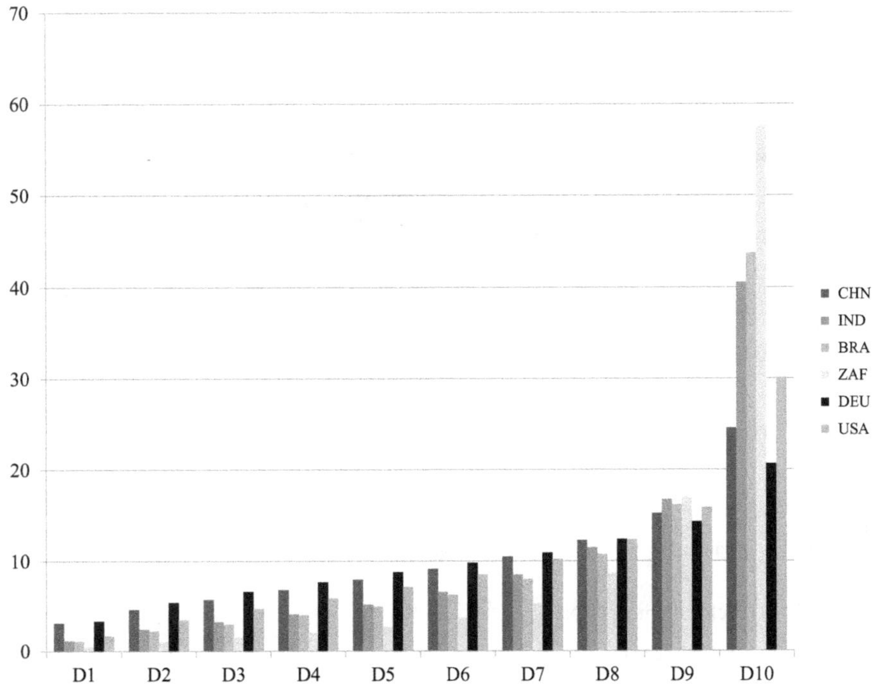

Figure 7.6 Distribution of household income within countries, in deciles

Source: UNU-WIDER (2015); values for 2004, except China (2002) and South Africa (2008).[1]

1 Detailed data on the distribution of household income in deciles is available only for selected years. However, where quintile data is available, the picture looks similar. Even taking more pessimist values (i.e. assuming stronger inequality), China is still much more equal than BIS, if only at the level of the United States.

29–32). As definitions of what constitutes a middle class vary, we take a minimal approach where middle class refers to people not threatened by absolute poverty who are able to increase their standard of living through consumption.

Looking at national income distribution (Figure 7.6), we see that China, India, Brazil and South Africa have had a strongly unequal income structure in the 2000s. On average, the richest decile accumulated more than 40% of each national income, while for developed economies (represented by Germany and the United States), the share of the top decile is only about 25%. Remarkably, China stands among the other large emerging economies in that it is frankly less unequal. In fact, China's income distribution is similar to Germany's: the poorest fifth account for 7.9% of national income in China and 8.8% in Germany, the richest 20% and 35%, respectively.

Clearly, the concentration of wealth in the top range in India, Brazil and, most of all, South Africa, is gross. The upper middle class (deciles 8 and 9) in China have roughly the same share of national income as the other three countries. The main differences are the comparably low wealth of the richest 10% and the higher wealth of the poorer half of Chinese households (D1–5), which have more income at their disposal than the households in the same income class in Brazil or India. In light of our analysis, this again supports our thesis that growth in large emerging economies, most visibly in China (notwithstanding potential miscalculations due to inaccurate reporting by very rich Chinese), is based largely on the domestic consumption of relatively cheap medium-tech products. Usually, the richest 20% to 30% demand Western luxury or high-quality products, and therefore their demand is not very relevant for the growth of the domestic industry. From this perspective, China has been best able to shift income into the classes which complement its industrial output the most.

How has inequality developed over the first decade of the 2000s? The overall increase of inequality as measured by the GINI index is a 'natural' part of economic (capitalist) development, and thus not particular to large emerging economies as such. Yet, these countries show stark differences in the development of inequality if we look at the change across income classes over time (Table 7.4).

Inequality occurs if either (or both) the richest and the poorest income classes shrink; in other words, if the poor become richer or the rich become poorer (relatively speaking). The macroeconomic effect of each phenomenon is very different, though. Table 7.4 illustrates these two movements very clearly. In South Africa, the poorer and middle classes (the lower 60%) shrank by 8.81% in total, while the rich income class increased by almost the same rate, 8.43%. In contrast, both China and Brazil decreased the share of their richest 20% of national income by approximately the same rate: 8.87% for China and 8.10% for Brazil. Only India largely maintained the national income distribution.

Looking at the decade between 1998–1999 and 2009–2010 (data availability for these countries varies), we can get a more nuanced look at shifts in income distribution. If we take the interpretation of the middle class as those people that moved out of poverty but are not as solvent as Western middle classes, we would look at the second and third quintiles and assume that the lowest quintile are relatively poor.[6] As we saw already, the only income class that grew in South Africa was the rich, with the poor and middle classes becoming smaller. The reverse trend can be shown for China, where the lower and middle classes grew from

Table 7.4 Growth of income classes between 1998–1999 and 2009–2010

Country	*Income level of Q1 in US$ (2011)*	*Q1*	*Q2*	*Q3*	*Q4*	*Q5*
China	2.5	2.78	3.38	2.28	0.42	−8.87
India	1.9	−0.46	−0.28	0.06	−0.05	0.73
Brazil	4.5	1.21	2.09	2.70	2.00	−8.10
South Africa	2.1	−2.05	−3.41	−3.35	0.37	8.43

Source: UNU-WIDER (2015).

1998 to 2010. Even more so, Brazilian middle- and upper-middle-income classes have become stronger, while in India there was no significant shift in the national income class distribution.

There have thus first been more dynamics with regard to income-level distribution than gross GINI figures can illustrate. Second, China effectively curbed absolute poverty and inequality appears relatively balanced (given the data provided). In fact, it was not just Brazil that allowed for a more equitable national distribution of wealth, although it featured prominently in the debates on equitable growth. Third, South Africa shifted 8.5% of its national wealth towards the rich. It is hence in danger of becoming a kind of patrimonial capitalism as described by Piketty (2014) if this trend continues. This share of national income does not benefit the South African economy because, as laid out earlier, the rich consume expensive imports rather than local products. Finally, India grew despite there being no significant change in the distribution of income as happened in China. Looking at income classes, "the richest people in India [more than 50 million people] have lower per capita income than the poorest people (as a group) in Germany" (Milanovic 2008, 10). Given the overall low level of per capita income and the fact that the low- and medium-income classes have not grown yet, there seems to be an enormous potential of domestic demand to pursue the SME way in the future. Since this form of capitalism focuses on domestic sources of growth, populations might enjoy a rise in the average standard of living without compromising the 'effectiveness' of the economy as a whole. A 'social face', therefore, must not come at the expense of economic growth. A more severe and looming challenge to state-permeated capitalism comes from the political articulation of social groups within emerging economies.

7.4.2 New middle classes: political challenge to state-permeated capitalism

We have documented how socio-economic inequality is deeply engrained in state-permeated capitalism. While income inequality is less dramatic, we nevertheless identified structural inequalities and asymmetries in the realms of industrial relations and the education and training system. Fragmentation, segmentation and limited upward social mobility usually adhere to social fault lines. But thus far, this inequality has actually served to stabilize complementarities within state-permeated capitalism. However, strong reliance on domestic markets also provides incentives to strengthen mass consumption via social reforms such as increases in worker income and extensions of social security (Cai 2015), as clearly demonstrated in both Brazil and China.

In state-permeated capitalism, however, the development towards poverty reduction and the emergence of new middle classes is not only very salient but also poses a long-term challenge for the central coordination mechanism of this form of capitalism. At the core of this challenge is the upward shift of large parts of the population from absolute poverty into the lower middle classes. Although we outlined earlier that the political connotations of the concept of 'middle class' is not applicable to large emerging economies, there are parallels between the 'old' (Western) and the 'new' (Southern) middle classes regarding the ability to participate in the political realm. In contrast to the very poor, people who are not existentially threatened are better able to organize themselves and to participate in political life (Guarin et al. 2014, 35). This should apply in particular to Brazil, where the lower income classes grew strongly and where the top elite is no longer able to dominate the political arena. It does not, however, mean that these social groups are automatically asking for better political representation or even comprehensive democratization, as assumed by classical and Western modernization theories (Lipset 1959; Easterly 2001; Birdsall 2010; López and Weinstein 2012).[7] Discretionary consumption, in contrast, seems to be a much more important driving force (Therborn 2014, 11). The new middle classes pose a threat to state-permeated capitalism not primarily as citizens, but as consumers. As a consequence, these middle classes become politically vocal when economic growth slows down and limits their consumption possibilities. If these groups demand political influence, it might clash with the social coordination mechanism at the heart of state-permeated capitalism. Furthermore, the state would have to react to these new political demands. Yet, economic programs and tax benefits in favor of new middle classes strain budgets and often establish these groups as constant veto players.

In a nutshell, our observation is as follows: in contrast to the very poor, new middle classes are potentially mobilizing for broad-based political participation. As long as economic growth is strong and steady and people in the middle classes are still improving their individual situations, this mobilization potential usually remains latent. However, if growth slows down or stops, uneasiness with existing economic leadership and demand for participation in economic policymaking increases. These demands pose a potential challenge for the close elite-internal coordination between diverse state agencies and business groups that is central to state-permeated capitalism. In particular, anti-corruption movements pose a major challenge for this coordination mechanism, as they directly address the crucial informal relations between those in power in business and in the state. Comprehensive anti-corruption measures may inhibit a well-working mechanism for economic coordination without replacing it with an effective alternative. For these reasons, anti-corruption movements that aim at large-scale scams[8] have the potential to inhibit the formerly smooth intra-elite coordination mechanisms. This hampers economic policymaking, leading to a further reduction of economic growth and intensified political contestation. The new middle classes are able to mobilize millions of people around issues of corruption and misrepresentation, as diverse and arbitrary as these may be. Developments in the social and political sphere, rather than economic developments, may thus lead to an exhaustion of state-permeated capitalism so that the system becomes a victim of its own success. The social groups that benefited most from state-permeated capitalist trajectories are also those that could be the proverbial nail in state-permeated capitalism's coffin. However, unlike Acemoglu and Robinson (2012), we do not assume that this process is automatically triggered: it becomes triggered only when economic growth slows down considerably.

In the following, we will discuss this in more detail. Arguably, in contemporary Brazil, this process is unfolding with the strongest power. However, these problems are not limited to Brazil; they can also be observed in China, in India and, to a certain degree, in South Africa. Moreover, our illustration will not cover issues that are somewhat idiosyncratic to Brazil, such as the highly fragmented political system (see section 4.3), but will focus on issues that may be applicable for the other countries as well.

State-permeated capitalism has functioned relatively well in Brazil in the 2000s, with satisfactory growth rates that not only benefited the economic elites but also led to an impressive reduction of inequality. Between 2003 and 2008, Brazil's real GDP grew by an annual average of 4.2%. After the financial crisis it rebounded with 7.5% in 2010, but was reduced to an average of 2.1% in 2011–2013 (G20 2014, 2), leading up to a full recession in 2015. In April 2014, the country hit a historical minimum in the open unemployment rate (4.9%), as well as a historical maximum in average monthly real incomes (US$921.82), while the less developed parts of the country such as the northeast gained more than the average.

Of particular importance was the doubling of the minimum wage, which sets the standards for a third of the employed population and also provides the basis for the majority of wage negotiations as well as some important social security standards. Arguably, the increase of the minimum wage was more important than the famous "Bolsa Família" cash transfer program towards poor households and the related social programs such as "Bolsa Escola" and "Bolsa Alimentacao", which amounted to only a small share of less than 1% of GDP (Casanova and Kassum 2014, 30–1; Leubolt 2015, 241–2). Social security, however, certainly helped to stimulate domestic demand. In contrast to China, many households have to save less because Brazil has established a more generous social security and pension system (Jaeger 2013). Because Brazilian households require much less in terms of precautionary savings, additional income flows directly into consumption.

Poverty reduction has thus led to the expansion of new lower middle classes in Brazil. These new middle classes were important supporters of the PT governments during the 2000s because they directly benefited from its redistributive policies. However, when growth slowed down during the mid-2010s, this allegiance wavered quickly. Although Brazil has one of the most capable public administrations in Latin America (Schneider 2013, 177–8), there are very high levels of dissatisfaction with the provision of public services in education and health, in spite of increasing expenditures and high institutional capacity. This indicates a growing degree of impatience in these sections of the population. "The economic progress of recent years and the emergence of a new middle class have raised expectations, and many Brazilians [. . .] now want social progress too" (Melo 2014, 22). Changing these structural features of the Brazilian political economy, however, requires time and resources, which are scarce due to the relatively tight fiscal space of the Brazilian state.[9]

While large populations of the very poor continue to support the state-led development strategy, the middle classes reacted quite severely to growth reduction in the mid-2010s, with a particular focus on issues of corruption, such as those involving oil and gas giant Petrobras.[10] Moreover, the often weak parliamentary majorities for the subsequent Lula and Dilma administrations, combined with the individualistic election system and the private financing of electoral campaigns, have been an important basis for a wave of corruption scandals. A prominent background purpose of these corruption scandals was creating majorities for the government in parliament. This was highlighted during the so-called *mensalão* scandal, which involved monthly payments for congressional deputies in exchange for support of the Lula administration; and during the 2015 Petrobras scandal, in which kickbacks from Petrobras suppliers were used to bolster the finances of political parties, especially the government coalition parties (PT and PMDB). Generally, legislators are very important targets for business lobbying, given their often very powerful role in specific subjects (Schneider 2013, 143–4). Governments thus have to offer strong incentives to convince legislators to support specific legislature and not use their veto power.

These corruption scandals led to aggressive conflicts between the middle classes and the PT government (Anderson 2011; Nowak 2015, 87; Saad Filho 2015). Mass demonstrations in Sao Paulo and other cities were mainly attended by well-educated and relatively prosperous social groups with a great deal of support from the mainstream private media. Participants were unified by a strong opposition to the PT-led government and its corruption scandals, while the original demand of the lower middle classes for more affordable, higher-quality public services quickly became marginalized (Custodio 2014; McKenna 2014; Pitts 2015; Saad Filho 2015); the same applies to the mass strikes by construction workers that have triggered waves of unrest since 2011 (Nowak 2015, 88–94).

Given the fragility of the Brazilian economy, these political turbulences initially triggered by corruption issues contributed significantly to the full-blown recession in 2015. Judicial investigations, which led to the arrest of prominent figures such as the business tycoon Marcelo Odebrecht and Lula da Silva himself, strongly disrupted the well-oiled networks between representatives of state and business. As a direct consequence, investment activity slowed down because protagonists faced uncertainty whether they would have to fear being trapped in a judicial plot. Furthermore, several measures to combat the recession have been blocked in Congress, where opposition to the president became even more powerful than before because of the corruption quagmire. Paralysis of economic decision-making, in turn, prevented the administration from undertaking large economic programs, thereby intensifying the recession.

To wrap up, the boost in income for the lower and lower medium strata during the 2000s seems to have led to an increasing degree of impatience with PT political decision-making in these socio-economic groups, as well as increasing dissatisfaction on the side of the traditional elites. Many demands of the evolving lower middle class still are not met, including access to quality public services in education, health and transportation. Frustration over the slowing dynamic of state-led development has thus led many voters to support presidential and congressional candidates campaigning for a return to the liberal-dependent economic model of the 1990s or even for more authoritarian models. As of 2018, the election of Jair Bolsonaro indicates that the latter might become a realistic option. Thus, somewhat ironically, the socio-economic success of the Lula and Dilma administrations may undermine the long-term stability necessary for a state-led model of catch-up industrialization in Brazil.

In China, the critical political mobilization of the middle classes is limited so far, especially given the high rates of economic growth. Notably, citizens are dissatisfied with lower levels of government that are responsible for providing most public services (Saich 2011, 146–7). They identify a lack of implementation as the most pressing social and political problems. This relates to a comparably high level of general trust in the central government, although it must be acknowledged that protests in China can usually be considered as legitimate only if they are based on a 'lack of implementation' of otherwise laudable policies. Indeed, dissatisfaction is mostly directed toward local governments (Butollo and ten Brink 2012) and rarely toward the central government. The central government maintains a strategy of 'rule by law', as exemplified by attempts to channel conflicts into the bureaucratic and judicial apparatus. Furthermore, increasing inequality has already led to rising political concerns, particularly with regard to the behavior of the very rich and corruptive practices by elite networks including Communist Party officials. This is evidenced by the 2015 Tianjin explosions, in which local politicians and businessmen were partially at fault for setting the stage for dozens of innocent casualties. The massive campaign against corruption forcefully mobilized by President Xi Jinping, however, contributed somewhat to the slowdown of economic growth in the mid-2010s. It negatively affected 'productive cronyism' in local growth alliances, as thickly embedded capitalists shied away from some of their investments and as state officials were more cautious in decision-making. Recentralization efforts in the Chinese economy as part of the anti-corruption campaigns thus acted as a brake on growth and may further restrict intra-elite economic decision-making (Zhu 2018).

In India, the anti-corruption campaigns of the early 2010s have had a modest effect. They were initially a reaction to a giant scam, in which the allocation of mobile telephone spectrum licenses involved heavy bribery by big businesses. In a way similar to Brazil, the campaign managed to quickly mobilize hundreds of thousands for mass rallies against widespread corruption in the commanding heights of the Indian economy and political administration. However, participation in the campaigns dramatically decreased (Nowak 2015, 84). The *Aam Admi Party* (AAP – party of the common men) emerged from the anti-corruption campaign and quickly received considerable support on local levels, but not nationwide. It seems that the anti-corruption campaign erupted and died out quickly. Two reasons why the campaign did not have the same disruptive effect as in Brazil stand out. First, as outlined earlier, the relevant middle classes that would support such a campaign and turn it into a movement are much smaller than in Brazil. The large cities of Delhi, Mumbai and Bangalore are centers for a relatively wealthy upper middle class which is largely detached from the lower income classes. Unlike in Brazil, these upper middle classes are not part of a liberal counter-bloc against state-led development projects. They rather benefit from the exuberance of Indian bureaucracy and therefore have no interest in mobilizing against the major political parties. In fact, middle classes have started to withdraw their support for AAP since 2013 (Times of India 2014). Unless the lower middle classes rise to similar levels as in China or Brazil, their power to challenge state-permeated capitalism will remain very limited. Second, in contrast to Brazil where the PT is in a defensive position with regard to the corruption issue, the BJP under Modi aggressively made the anti-corruption theme a stronghold in its political program. By proactively acknowledging the importance of discontent with corruption, cronyism and bribery, the BJP took on the AAP raison d'etre, albeit from a more trustworthy position with a strong record of effective and successful economic policies, at least in the general public. Modi is also rendered much less vulnerable to potential future challenges that might arise. This strategy is risky, however, because Modi would have to deliver on promises to end corruption while keeping the smooth interpersonal mode of coordination intact. Again, this is easier as long as new social groups do not aim to enter these circles. Additionally, Modi's rather populist style of politics comes closer to the Brazilian *personalismo*, in which strong figures promise benefits that eventually cannot be delivered due to 'bad' circumstances. In sum, India is still much less vulnerable to the deteriorating mechanism that plagues contemporary Brazilian capitalism. This is partly because, first, India lags behind Brazil with regard to the development of middle classes, and second, because India has no capitalist class independent from the state.

Altogether, while we disagree with Western observers who expect an imminent economic collapse of state-permeated capitalism, we see considerable dangers for the long-term stability of this particular type of capitalism evolving from social and political realms. However, in contrast to authors such as Acemoglu and Robinson (2012), we do not expect a necessary degradation due to a lack of "inclusive" institutions, but rather assume that this destabilization can be potentially prevented by continuous economic growth. As long as state-permeated capitalism continues to deliver high levels of consumption, a systemic challenge is highly unlikely (Therborn 2014, 9). Large emerging economies have ample potential to grow based on the mobilization of domestic demand. There are still millions of people waiting to escape poverty and enter the lower middle classes, thereby generating demand for indigenous products. However, this comes with a political dynamic that can lead to destabilization of the state-permeated model.

In a more general perspective, many issues that superficially look purely economic have an important political dimension, and vice versa. This not only pertains to the 'middle-income trap', but also to the sustainability of the central coordination mechanism in state-permeated capitalism in the context of the rise of middle classes and their anti-corruption movements. Hence, we witness a 'tragedy' of state-permeated capitalism: the very success of the model sows the seeds of its own destabilization. Attempts to keep these dynamics down, for example through redistributive means, might actually render the situation even more dramatic. On purely economic grounds, SMEs can thus thrive for a long time, but they become more and more shaky on political grounds. Of course, political dynamics are hard to predict (as are all social dynamics, including economic), but we think there are good reasons to point to mechanisms that can produce path dependencies which large emerging economies can exit only at the cost of politico-economic damage.

Notes

1 Our perspective thus mirrors the concerns articulated by both Albert (1993) and Hall and Soskice (2001) about the potential eroding tendencies for "coordinated" or "Rhenish" capitalism stemming from the global financial markets.
2 A program of bank loans for household purchases to those who had never before had bank accounts, with repayment automatically deducted from monthly wages or pensions.
3 Although Brazil has strongly decreased its foreign currency sovereign debt and has also accumulated substantial foreign currency reserves (see section 3.1.1), it still has substantial and strongly increasing government debt in the Real, as well as a huge volume of foreign currency bonds by state-related companies such as Petrobras. Rating agencies increasingly take a broader perspective on debt repayment by focusing not only on foreign currency sovereign debt (FT 2015). After all, the state could be forced to bail out highly indebted business, as witnessed in Brazil during the 1980s (Bresser-Pereira 2015, 5).
4 This also shows that overcoming the trap is effectively a strategic long-term policy target. Yet, the examples of Singapore, Hong Kong, South Korea and Taiwan succeeding to high-income cannot simply act as role models for today's large emerging economies due to the (smaller) size of these East Asian economies, historical timing and 'exportist' orientations.
5 Usually, these are measured on the household level. However, household data is rare and piecemeal for the countries in focus.
6 The daily income of the bottom 20% as indicated in Table 6.8 roughly matches the 60% of median income level in Table 6.7.
7 See also Handley (2014, 13) for a similarly pessimistic view on the automatic inclination of African middle classes towards democracy.
8 Prominent examples are the 2G scam in India 2011 and the ongoing scandal at Petrobras (see later in this section).
9 The fiscal potential for large-scale investment in institutions and infrastructure is arguably higher in China, but also in India because subnational entities have greater leeway for autonomous policies.
10 Still, we may distinguish Brazil in this regard from many more problematic regimes in other Latin American countries. In contrast to countries such as Mexico, the close collaboration between state and business only rarely degenerates into wasteful rent-seeking (Schneider 2013, 178–81). Furthermore, corruption is not a monopoly of the PT administration but had befallen the Cardoso camp as well (Anderson 2011, 4).

Conclusion

Our research has shown that, first, large emerging economies differ significantly from established Western economies but also share a number of striking institutional communalities. They represent a novel model of capitalism which is characterized by state-permeation and close state-business alliances. Second, a detailed empirical analysis of key institutional spheres has also revealed the main drivers for robust economic growth in these countries. These lies, in particular, in mutual institutional compatibilities, in their large domestic markets in which domestic firms specialize in the production of medium-tech goods, successful developmental policies and beneficial global economic constellations. In this regard, we also point towards differences in their institutional setup that affect their overall economic success. Third, our study has highlighted some substantial challenges of the stability of state-permeated capitalism that are less of an economic but rather of a social and political nature. These achievements not only open further avenues for empirical and theoretical research, but also raise questions for the future of the global economic order.

Empirical research perspectives

Our study is a contribution to the rapidly emerging field of the comparative political economy of emerging economies. We have employed an extended, critical institutionalist CC framework (May and Nölke 2015) to understand and explain the growth of capitalism in large emerging economies, both in a country-specific and a comparative sense. Unlike the pioneering work of Becker (2013a, 2013b), we have been able to compare the four most dynamic large emerging economies in a systematic way. And unlike the path-breaking study by Schneider (2013), which focuses on corporate governance, education and industrial relations, our work takes a broader perspective on the institutions of state-permeated capitalism.

Still, the comparative institutional analysis of emerging economies is far from finished. First, it is uncertain whether our model is applicable to other large emerging economies such as Indonesia, Mexico or Turkey. While there are good reasons to believe that the model does not apply to all developing countries, it is a question of empirical research whether we can find traits of the state-permeated model in other large emerging economies, too – traits that might bring about similar effects as in the countries studied here. Section 4.2.1 has already demonstrated that not all economies studied in this work actually conform to the SME ideal type. But countries like Indonesia might be approaching the model, while more open economies such as Mexico and Turkey, in which the prominent role of foreign industrial and financial capital resembles South Africa, are less likely to fit the model.

Second, the question emerges whether there is a minimum size for state-permeated capitalism to work. A large domestic market is a major precondition for the realization of this model because it serves as a strong base for the development of domestic companies. Likewise, a large domestic market is important for favorable negotiations with foreign capital, because it strengthens the case for the acceptance of conditionalities such as joint ventures. Nonetheless, the question at which size a domestic market is large (and promising) enough to sustain the model of state-permeated capitalism is far from resolved empirically. Furthermore, studies should include the question of whether emerging economies may compensate size through exploiting possibilities on similar, adjacent regional markets, with eventually weaker neighboring states to protect these markets.

A third and related question pertains to the level of economic development necessary to sustain state-permeated capitalism. As discussed earlier, our model has a strong focus on the industrialized regions of large emerging economies and does not cater for a suitable analysis of rural, non-industrialized regions. Still, this raises the question whether a minimal level of industrial structure is necessary for state-permeated capitalism to work properly. Likewise, this issue may be directed towards analyses of macroeconomic development on a middle ground between microeconomic studies (Banerjee and Duflo 2011) and grand development plans such as in modernization theory (Rostow 1990).

Fourth, our analysis can be broadened not only by incorporating additional case studies, but also by looking historically. Our focus was on the institutional setup during a fairly limited period of time, from the 2000s to the early 2010s. Although we highlighted some important historical digressions of the political and economic factors that have led to the current institutional setup, we were unable to systematically study the historical origins of these institutions. Nor were we able to systematically compare contemporary forms of state-permeated capitalism with historical cases of developmentalist, statist or other forms to find out which elements of capitalism are time-specific and which are universal. Arguably, the timing of integration into the world economy has been a major factor in this regard (see section 4.2.1). A comparably late integration, as in China, appears to be favorable for the viability of state-permeated capitalism. Earlier integration, as in Brazil and South Africa, appears to be detrimental. However, the exact meaning of 'early' and 'late' must be elucidated in further studies.

Moreover, the case of Brazil points towards the need of incorporating historical North-South economic power relations in more detail into the analysis, given the important role of the 1980s debt crisis for the denationalization of parts of the Brazilian economy, or for the negative evaluation of import substitution strategies. In addition, it is necessary to analyze the relation between race and capitalism and the impact of racial segregation on the capitalist institutional setting in a historical perspective, not only in South Africa, but elsewhere as well. Finally, the capitalist world economy is not a stable entity, but rather develops in specific historical phases with considerable inter-temporal differences between, e.g., embedded liberalism of the 1950s and 1960s, and financialization since the 1980s. This has substantial repercussions on the opportunities for the emergence and viability of state-permeated capitalisms.

Fifth, although we have incorporated the central mechanism for the coordination in SMEs into the analysis – that is, a close informal coordination between state managers and individual national capitalists – there is ample room for further, empirical elaboration of the link between types of coordination and the domestic power structures that support them. Obviously, informal relations are hard to investigate. Still, recent work on China has highlighted the analytical currency of different approaches towards the study of coordination and the crucial role of capital fractions (Nölke 2015a). However, the study of such fractions mostly remains limited to China, and future research might gauge whether it would be suitable for the analysis of other cases of state-permeated capitalism. Nevertheless, there are strong signs that the study of formal business associations is less relevant for the understanding of state-permeated capitalism than the analysis of informal interpersonal linkages between business and state actors. Similarly, our study has demonstrated – particularly for the cases of Brazil and South Africa – that the dominant state-business relations underpinning SMEs do not come about automatically. Considerably greater party coherence in China – instead of the strongly individualistic or fragmented political parties and capitalist classes in Brazil and South Africa – may be an important factor here, but, on the other hand, this does not seem to be problematic in India. Therefore, further research should aim to identify those political factors which are favorable for such forms of capitalism in a more systematic manner.

Theoretical research perspectives

In a more theoretical vein, our study contributes to a number of issues: First, our work can be considered as belonging to the third generation of CC scholarship.[1] While the classic VoC approach formulated by Hall and Soskice (2001) was the focal point of the first CC generation, its criticism has led to a second generation which highlighted the importance of history and politics, distributive struggles and the role of the state for capitalist development (see section 2.1). Still, this second generation has mostly been preoccupied at supply-side institutions (such as sufficient and stable funds for investment, highly productive labor and substantial investments in research and development) exclusively and to the comparison of models. By incorporating demand-side institutions and the interaction of national capitalisms, the third generation is more heterogeneous. It is also often more critical, as it combines concepts of (post-)VoC with those of (critical) international political economy, focusing on the problematic interdependencies between national varieties of capitalism (e.g. Höpner and Schäfer 2012). It also points towards problems and contradictions within the global political economy arising from a shift of production towards emerging economies (e.g. Bohle and Greskovits 2012; Kalinowski 2013; Nölke et al. 2015). This third generation finds its inspiration not just in (post-)VoC, but also in the regulation approach, dependency theory or post-Kaleckian and post-Keynesian macroeconomics, coming to similar conclusions about the fragile interdependence between national capitalisms (e.g. Stockhammer 2011; Armingeon and Baccaro 2012; Becker 2014; J. Becker 2014b; Gambarotto and Solari 2014; Jessop 2014; Suau Arinci et al. 2015; Johnston and Regan 2016).

In highlighting the importance of large domestic markets for SME development, we connect to such third-generation studies that have identified the need to integrate demand factors into CC analysis. Moreover, our focus on the management of a selective integration into the world economy emphasizes the importance of reflecting on the interaction of different varieties of capitalism, in this case on the tensions between unlimited cross-border financial flows, as propagated mostly by actors from LMEs, and stable long-term development based on national control, as favored by actors from SMEs. Yet, both aspects of domestic demand and international integration have room for further conceptual development in order to integrate these factors more systematically into the institutionalist comparison of contemporary capitalisms. Moreover, the implications of our study are somewhat more cautious about stagnation or the upcoming "end of capitalism" (Streeck 2014b). Given widespread poverty in large parts of emerging economies, there still is potential for triggering processes of economic growth, especially if this demand will be activated by social redistribution or the type of economic growth processes that we have highlighted in the case of state-permeated capitalism.

Second, with respect to other theoretical and disciplinary traditions, our work provides an alternative point of departure for theories of economic development. In contrast to authors such as De Soto (2000) or Acemoglu and Robinson (2012), it does not claim to offer a universal blueprint for the explanation of economic development and underdevelopment. In contrast, it highlights the existence of different types of successful capitalist development, each with their specific institutional complementarities. Thus, while Acemoglu and Robinson predict that China will fail because its lack of "inclusive" and rule-of-law type of institutions (i.e. focusing on the input dimension), we argue that more attention has to be paid to the output side of the system, which has been shown to be absolutely crucial for the legitimacy of capitalisms in the Global South. To be sure, state-permeated capitalism is not the ideal or only way to achieve economic development, but only one among several possible ones. The model of dependent market economies is an important, if less favorable, alternative for emerging economies. These two models, however, do not exhaust the range of options available, and future research may aim to develop alternative models for the sustainable development of late developers.

Third, highlighting alternative paths to economic development also becomes salient if we put our work in relation to different schools of thinking about the state in contemporary capitalism (see section 2.3). By emphasizing the specific features of state-permeation, in contrast to previous waves of state capitalism that featured a stronger role for central state guidance, we call for a more systematic study on the various forms in which the state contributes to economic catch-up (ten Brink and Nölke 2013). This includes decentralized and adaptive instruments of local state support under conditions of local state competition, establishing novel 'coordinative' functions for its interaction with firms and for firm efforts to specialize in domestic product markets. It also includes innovation capacity building via selected local public procurement and subsidies. Moreover, this account has to be balanced against the limits of state support and coordination due to intra-state conflicts, external constraints and uncertainty or diverging preferences among policymakers.

Fourth, our conclusion that neither the state nor the market alone, but rather the stability of interpersonal relations between representatives of business and government is crucial for the success of state-permeated capitalism, points to the necessity to analyze this particular mode of coordination more systematically. We argued that behind multiple forms of 'corruption' in these economies hides an effective mechanism for overall economic coordination: a productive cronyism based on the reciprocity of interpersonal relations that outweighs harmful types of corruption, e.g. rent seeking and bribery. Hence, there are good reasons to conceive of reciprocity as a distinct mode of political-economic coordination. Historically, the mode of reciprocity has been analyzed with regard to the social structure of gifting in traditional and non-Western societies, particularly from sociological and anthropological views (Gouldner 1960; Mauss 1966; Bourdieu 1990). It was Karl Polanyi who took this anthropological view into the comparative analysis of economies. In various writings, he theoretically distinguishes markets, reciprocity and redistribution as distinct modes of coordination (Polanyi 1977, 2001). These mechanisms usually stand in contradiction to each other because each of them, if fully developed, gives rise to fundamentally different economic structures (Polanyi 2001, 49–56). Accounting for reciprocity, interpersonal relations and networks as distinctive principles of economic organization might help to answer the big question why apparently institutionally underequipped economies have been able to grow and prosper. Again, further study would benefit from inter-temporal comparison.

Finally, our contribution calls for a reappraisal of classical approaches to development theory, in particular the debate between various schools of economic liberalism versus different strategies of developmentalism. In this debate, we largely take sides on the latter, as our research has emphasized the connection between long-term national economic growth and a selective insertion into global capitalism, in particular with regard to global financial markets. Nevertheless, in contrast to earlier strategies of import-substitution industrialization (ISI), we stress the importance of keeping strong external competition incentives for domestic companies, either by stimulating domestic competition (e.g. China), or by linking state support to international competitiveness (e.g. Brazil).

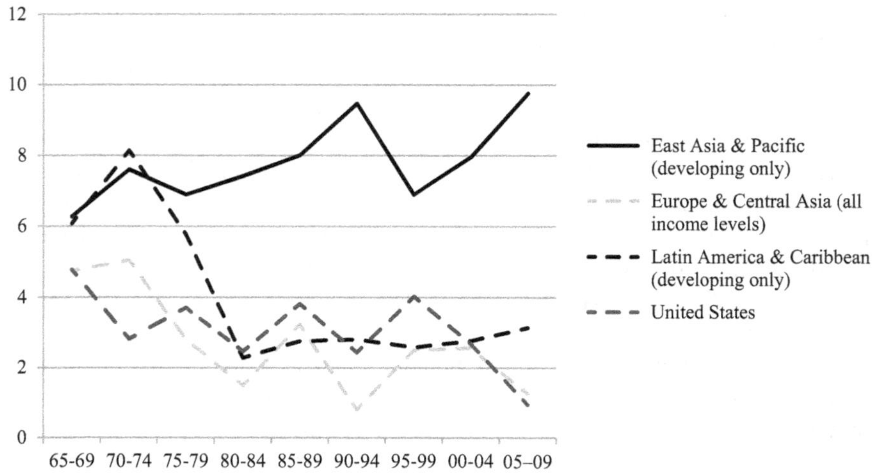

Figure C.1 Selected growth rates, in % of GDP, five-year averages

Source: World Bank.

In retrospect, import substitution may even unjustly appear as a 'failed' strategy because it was overshadowed by the success of East Asian economies that followed a strategy of export-oriented industrialization. Figure C.1 shows that the growth rates of import-substituting Latin American countries, in particular Brazil, were similar to East Asian economies until the end of the 1970s. After the Latin American debt crisis set in, the region descended to the growth rates of developed Western countries. Therefore, what brought Latin American economies down was not necessarily import substitution per se but rather external indebtedness and the specific way it has been resolved (the end of the Bretton Woods regime with fixed exchange rates has been most crucial here). The inward-looking strategies of the preceding period has not just accounted for growth but, perhaps more importantly, established an industrial and corporate structure that helped some countries such as India and Brazil to become inward-oriented while still maintaining economic growth in the 2000s.

Economic policy implications

Perspectives of Comparative Capitalisms do not lend themselves to policy conclusions easily. Against the main thrust of nearly all approaches towards economic policy and development strategy, CC's main message is that there is not 'one best way'. Liberal economies are but one model of economic development among several alternatives. Moreover, due to different institutional complementarities, institutions that have proven successful in one economy cannot be simply transplanted into economies with a different institutional setup. For example, the German system of vocational training ("Duales System") has been a crucial part of many attempts for institutional transfer, but was never as comprehensively established as in Germany because it relies, inter alia, on a coordinated system of industrial relations. Hence, economic policy conclusions based on a CC framework always need to account for the presence or absence of multiple institutional complementarities between different institutional spheres.

Moreover, the fact that economies operating close to the SME ideal type have been successful in terms of economic growth and long-term stability does not necessarily mean that state-permeated capitalism is a desirable economic system. While we think that capitalism is a highly problematic social order from the outset (which should inspire in-depth scientific discussions about conceivable alternatives), we have shown that SMEs still entail considerable income inequality as well as a strong concentration of economic power. We also have omitted environmental concerns in our analysis. If these concerns are taken into account, the success story in terms of manufacturing that is at the core of our SME model looks much less attractive.

Finally, we have to remind readers that the SME model is linked to circumstances in time and space. First, it is a model that presupposes a fairly high level of industrialization. It is therefore hardly suited for analyzing economic processes in rural India or in African economies. Second, it is much better suited for large emerging economies than for smaller ones. Third, the establishment and viability of this model presupposes a certain world economic structure. On one hand, it requires cross-border trade and capital flows as well as substantial amounts of free capital, which is also willing to transfer technology in exchange. On the other, the world economic conjuncture has to allow for a certain degree of national protection against transnational financial flows and other forms of potential domestic destabilization, such as those caused by deep integration (i.e. 'behind the border' liberal trade agreements; see the subsequent section).

However, in spite of these limitations, we still think that our work lends itself to some broad policy-related conclusions, so long as we limit our focus to the creation of economic growth (as immanent to modern capitalism) and assume current global economic conditions as given. First of all, this pertains to the individual countries of our study. In the case of China, it was shown that rising instability of its financial system was at least partially fostered by further or too much liberalization. If it is indeed true that a deepening of liberalization and opening of the financial sector may undermine the SME model in the medium term, including new domestic and international financial actors interested in hollowing out state-permeated capitalism, one policy advice would be to reject the notion that a slowdown in liberal economic reforms will harm the Chinese economy. In our view, a continuation of liberalizing financial markets would endanger growth dynamics in China.

India, in turn, would best be advised to continue its current path. Ceteris paribus, India will likely benefit much more from a state-permeated form of capitalism if several hundred million citizens are lifted from poverty and its young population transforms into a powerful workforce, something that is not too far-fetched. However, to keep up with rising domestic demand, it is necessary to consolidate the status of workers and, correspondingly, the commitment of business to invest in skill development. Furthermore, current and future national governments should refrain from centralizing economic governance too much in order to not inhibit local economic dynamics through burdensome regulations from Delhi. Finally, India would need a kind of 'social compromise' for development to create broad legitimacy for a state-permeated kind of capitalism. Indian politics have the potential to polarize and escalate along the lines of political tensions that arose in Brazil in the 2010s, an outcome that would probably be more severe in India. Again, the main challenge for Indian capitalism is to prevent further political polarization, for it might end up like Brazil. Instead, it is well advised to 'return' to a national development agenda that was characteristic of the period of Congress rule, albeit with a stronger role for social and redistributive policies.

For Brazil, the main implication of our study would be to take the recession of the mid-2010s not as a consequence of too much state capitalism, but rather as a consequence of a haphazard state capitalism. Further moves towards state capitalism seem warranted. This could include more restrictions on capital flows in order to reduce economic volatility. Moreover, Brazil could raise taxes on the rich in order to mobilize sufficient fiscal resources for investments in infrastructures, education and technology, and, after increasing the productive capacity of the Brazilian economy, the further expansion of domestic demand. However, this move would have to overcome massive political opposition not only from financial capital, foreign multinationals, agribusiness elites and the upper middle classes, but also from those that recently have escaped extreme poverty and may prefer the immediate stimulation of domestic demand or the improvement of social services.

Last but not least, the example of South Africa shows that hybrid forms of capitalism in the Global South are quite vulnerable and need to develop more coherent institutional frameworks. In comparison to the other three economies, South Africa follows no common state-led economic development path due to policy incoherence, thorough economic liberalization and enormous social fragmentation. The South African political elites adhere to a state-led economic development strategy on paper only. If the strategy were to be implemented in a more serious manner, the state would be well advised to regulate the openness of the economy more strongly. This would imply stricter limits to foreign capital, financialization and trade. It would also be necessary to increase the institutional coherence of South African capitalism. Corporate governance and investment finance would have to be streamlined with industrial relations, education and innovation as they are currently working in a contradictory manner. Moreover, the state would need to avoid capture by a specific segment of the white and black domestic business elites. Finally, addressing the high inequality between black and white South Africans through redistributive measures would stimulate domestic demand, another crucial precondition for the SME model to work.

In a more general vein, our study still contains some messages that seem to be valid across all of our country cases, even if any successful implementation depends on the pre-existence of the relevant institutional complementarities.

- For the successful establishment of state-permeated capitalism, too much openness towards foreign capital, particularly financial capital, seems to be harmful. A very strong presence of foreign capital complicates domestic economic coordination. Moreover, if technologically advanced sectors of the domestic economy are completely dominated by foreign multinationals, the evolution of domestic companies may be inhibited. Strategies of economic opening thus should be pursued in a cautious manner.

- The state – and not only at the central state level – is indispensable for the development of successful economic strategies for large emerging markets. State-permeation at different administrational levels has proven to be crucial throughout the range of institutions studied in this book. This equally pertains to state control in corporate governance, public development banks, state regulation of labor and education and public funding of research and development. Moreover, the state crucially manages the insertion of the domestic economy into global capitalism.
- Against a widely shared perspective that national configurations of capitalism have to engage in a continuous competition for leadings frontiers in high technologies (Porter 1990), we argue that emerging economies can be economically successful in the medium run with a 'good enough' level of technological innovation. The advice to move up the value chain through technological sophistication (OECD 2013a) has to be qualified.
- Our work also points economic reformers towards the need to reflect upon crucial complementarities when trying to reform individual institutions. From the perspective developed in this study, there is no 'one best way' of developing capitalist institutions. Effective institutions typically provide important support for other institutions, and it is of particular importance to reflect upon these complementarities when reforming institutions.
- Although our work highlights the importance of productive supply-side institutions, it is also imperative to create sufficient demand for domestic production. On the demand side, large and selectively protected domestic markets, as well as the favorable effects of redistribution via social programs, are of high importance.
- In a more political vein, we would warn against the notion that 'corruption' is under all conditions detrimental to economic growth. Practices of 'cronyist' collusion between state and business that look so suspicious to liberal observers in fact often fulfill crucial functions in state-permeated capitalism. Large emerging economy governments – if strongly oriented on GDP growth – are thus well advised to be careful about the widely articulated demands to introduce 'good governance' and to clean up 'corruption'. Such demands not only reflect a "cultural fetish" of Northern observers (Blattman 2012), but also part of neoliberal attempts to fully integrate large emerging markets into the dominant liberal order. Correspondingly, instances of corruption are used in order to discredit alternative development strategies, such as the 'cronyist' model depicted in this book.
- Finally, our work indicates important policy implications with regard to the preferable design of international economic institutions from the perspective of large emerging economies. State-permeated capitalism requires a certain

openness of the global economic order in order to earn sufficient international currency for financing necessary imports, as well as acquiring advanced technologies. However, recent Western initiatives for deepening the global trade order can be detrimental to SME-type economies since these initiatives attempt to transplant LME-style economic institutions globally. 'Behind the border' liberalization under the umbrella of deep integration is quite detrimental for state-permeated capitalism, thereby threatening to disrupt important institutional complementarities within state-permeated capitalism. Thus, large emerging economies may be well advised to protect their domestic institutions against these liberal incursions (Claar and Nölke 2013, 285).

Implications for the global economic order

The rise of state-permeated capitalism in large emerging economies has important consequences for established global economic institutions. In our view, there is an obvious correspondence between the liberal policy outlook of global economic institutions and the domestic economic principles of leading economic powers, as has been plain to see during the (Post-)Washington Consensus under US hegemony. One option for the future of the global economic order lies in adapting the Chinese variety of capitalism to gradually replace Anglo-Saxon liberal capitalism as a general lead model (McNally 2012). However, China alone is neither willing nor powerful enough to challenge the liberal economic order (Lieberthal and Jisi 2012; Chong 2013). Thus, the real contender would rather be an ensemble of large emerging economies from the South. We argue that common economic institutions shared by China, India and Brazil are a more likely alternative to the liberal economic order than the China model alone. The institutionalization of the BRICS group, as witnessed at the annual BRICS Summits, seems to support this claim.

While in the debate on rising powers, many realist IR scholars warn of a coming "threat" (Mearsheimer 2001; Schweller 2011), liberal and constructivist authors foresee a much more harmonious integration of China and other large emerging countries into the international system (Johnston 2007; Ikenberry 2008; Kahler 2013). We argue that an answer to this question has to take the domestic level of emerging countries into account, in particular their internal economic structures. By inquiring into the "externalization of domestic structures" (Katzenstein 1976, 2, 1978a, 1978b) we would be able to add some value to current international relations debates (Narlikar 2010; Stephen 2012, 2014; Ban and Blyth 2013; Gray and Murphy 2013).

If state-permeated capitalism characterizes China, India and Brazil, what would be the contours of their foreign economic strategies? As shown previously, large emerging economies benefit from a selective integration into global economic networks and therefore support global capitalism in general. What is more, an effective challenge to existing liberal global economic governance would not only require considerable administrative capabilities on the sides of the challengers (Kahler 2013, 714), but could also be hampered by a high degree of economic competition between these economies – most notably the threat posed to other emerging economies by Chinese manufactured exports. Finally, any attempt to overturn the liberal global economic order will meet the resistance and counter-strategies of the incumbent powers (Wade 2013).

However, our CC perspective allows us to identify more precisely where preferences of emerging economies are incompatible with the principles of the existing liberal order (see Nölke et al. 2015 for a more detailed discussion). In the sphere of *corporate governance*, liberal international institutions not only insist on the existence of an open market for corporate control, but also on transparency for global investors in accounting. Furthermore, the IMF framework on Reports on the Observance of Standards and Codes (ROSC), designed by the G7 group and adopted by the IMF afterwards, requires the supervision of national corporate governance standards along liberal OECD corporate governance principles. However, this intervention by the IMF in national regulation is hotly contested in the IMF constituency, with Brazil and China refusing to disclose information on corporate governance regulation according to ROSC principles.

The persistence of financial globalization collides with state-capitalist preferences to minimize risk and to preserve economic stability. SMEs regularly erect hurdles against international capital mobility, in particular portfolio capital. Institutional incompatibilities are not only apparent in the area of capital account management, but also in banking regulation. Thus, in the realm of *finance for investment*, a similar picture emerges. The strong role of national development banks in SMEs stands in conflict with the global liberal order because lending by these banks does not merely follow commercial motives, but also national developmental interests. From a liberal perspective, such lending by (de facto) development banks constitutes an ineligible subsidy and therefore collides with WTO rules. We therefore expect a further intensification of conflicts, including punitive tariffs for countries that provide 'unfair' conditions for domestic firms, such as those installed by the Trump administration in 2018.

With regard to *domestic markets* and *international integration*, high levels of market regulation are obviously contrary to liberal principles of free trade. A considerable number of complaints by the European Union and the United States before the WTO Dispute Settlement Body deal with trade practices of Brazil, India and China (May and Nölke 2014). Furthermore, the WTO regime also finds itself in stagnation because the liberalization agenda brought forward by OECD countries includes a range of issues (such as investment regulation and public procurement) which are non-negotiable for emerging economies. The same holds true for monetary politics. Brazil, China and India seek to stabilize their currencies, including the strategic accumulation of reserves, political control of the central bank and, especially for China, a strategy to use the currency beyond its national confines. The latter especially touches upon the role of the US dollar as global currency. Hence, "the currency issue is perhaps the most fundamental point of contention in the economic relationship between China and the United States" (McNally 2012, 758). This is a conflictual issue because other large emerging economies are interested in a stable trading currency next to the US dollar, especially with rising South-South cooperation. If emerging economies would pay their imports increasingly with local currencies (as also discussed at the BRICS Summit in Durban, 2013), more than 20% of world trade would no longer be denominated in US dollars.

Overall, the institutional configuration of state-permeated capitalism differs profoundly from liberal capitalism and the core premises of the Washington Consensus. Since a liberal global economic order does not fully cater for the institutional requirements of firms from large emerging economies, Brazil, China and India will hence see little use in strengthening these institutions. Still, while liberal global institutions are apparently suboptimal for the growth of emerging economies, they are still used by these economies in the absence of better alternatives. This is why, for instance, China has accepted membership in the WTO without subscribing to the deep integration agenda.

In conclusion, the emergence of state-permeated capitalism produces serious global institutional incompatibilities. Will these incompatibilities become stronger? Which conflicts will matter, and which will not? How will Western state managers try to come to grips with this? We conclude that it seems likely that a much closer business-state relationship in large emerging markets may well lead to a less liberal and more 'mercantilist' or neo-Listian global order. Such an international institutional configuration would allow countries to pursue their individual economic strategies with less attention paid to universal liberal principles. Undoubtedly, international economic cooperation will still be important, but this cooperation will take on a more bilateral, reciprocal nature instead of relying on multilateral or even supranational agreements. If the Washington Consensus has been a program for universal liberal regulation, a "State Capitalist Consensus" would clearly call into question many of the former's core principles.

Note

1 This discussion draws in part on Nölke (2016).

Bibliography

Abdel-Latif, Abla, and Hubert Schmitz. 2010. "Growth Alliances: Insights from Egypt." *Business & Politics* 12(4): Art. 4.

ABDI. 2005. *Balanço PITCE*. Brasília: Agência Brasileira de Desenvolvimento Industrial.

Abrol, Dinesh. 2013. "New Science, Technology and Innovation Policy: A Critical Assessment." *Economic and Political Weekly* 48(9): 10–13.

Abu-el-Haj, Jawdat. 2007. "From Interdependence to Neo-Mercantilism: Brazilian Capitalism in the Age of Globalization." *Latin American Perspectives* 34(5): 92–114.

Acemoglu, Daron, and James A. Robinson. 2012. *Why Nations Fail: The Origins of Power, Prosperity, and Poverty*. New York: Crown Publishers.

ACFIC (All-China Federation of Industry and Commerce). 2012. "ACFIC Private Enterprise Ranking." (In Chinese). http://finance.sina.com.cn/hy/20120830/161213002302.shtml (accessed 12 January 2013).

ADB. 2011. *Asia 2050: Realizing the Asian Century?* Manila: Asian Development Bank.

AfricaCheck. 2015. "South Africa's Matric Pass Rate Obscures Dropout Rate." 7 January. https://africacheck.org/spot_check/south-africas-matric-pass-rate-obscures-dropout-rate/ (accessed 19 December 2015).

African News Agency. 2015. "Brics Assists in Ipap Implementation, Says Davies." *Engineeringnews*, 10 July. www.engineeringnews.co.za/article/brics-assists-in-ipap-implementation-says-davies-2015-07-10 (accessed 19 December 2015).

The African Report. 2013. "Top 500 Companies in 2013." www.theafricareport.com/top-500-companies-in-africa-2013.html (accessed 19 December 2015).

Agénor, Pierre-Richard, Otaviano Canuto, and Michael Jelenic. 2012. *Avoiding Middle-Income Growth Traps*. Washington, DC: World Bank.

Aglietta, Michel. 1979. *A Theory of Capitalist Regulation: The US Experience*. London: New Left Book.

Aglietta, Michel, and Antoine Réberioux. 2005. *Corporate Governance Adrift: A Critique of Shareholder Value*. Cheltenham and Northampton, MA: Edward Elgar.

Agrawal, Poonam. 2008. "Emerging Reforms in Vocational Education in India: Focusing on the Indian Qualifications Framework." In *Corporate Human Resource Development and TVET: Scope and Strategies*, edited by InWEnt, 56–61. Bonn: UNEVOC/INWENT.

Aguilera, Ruth, Kabbach de Castro, Luiz Ricardo, Jun Ho Lee, and Jihae You. 2012. "Corporate Governance in Emerging Markets." In *Capitalisms and Capitalism in the 21st Century*, edited by Glenn Morgan and Richard Whitley, 319–44. Oxford: Oxford University Press.

AHK (German Chamber of Commerce in China). 2007. *German Business Expansion in China: 2008–2010*. Shanghai: German Chamber of Commerce in China.

Ahluwalia, Montek Singh. 2002. *Privatization: From Policy Formulation to Implementation. The View from the Inside*. Philadelphia: Center for the Advanced Study of India.

Ahluwalia, Montek Singh. 2007. "Has Gradualism Worked?" In Mukherji 2007a, 87–113.

Aiyar, Shekhar, Romain Duval, Damien Puy, Yiqun Wu, and Longmei Zhang. 2013. "Growth Slowdowns and the Middle-Income Trap." *IMF Working Paper* WP/13/71, Washington, DC: International Monetary Fund.

Albert, Michel. 1993. *Capitalism vs. Capitalism: How America's Obsession with Individual Achievement and Short-Term Profit Has Led It to the Brink of Collapse*. New York: Four Walls Eight Windows.

Allen, Franklin, Rajesh Chakrabarti, Sankar De, Jun 'QJ' Qian, and Meijun Qian. 2010. "Law, Institutions, and Finance in China and India." In *Emerging Giants: China and India in the World Economy*, edited by Barry Eichengreen, Poonam Gupta, and Rajiv Kumar, 125–83. Oxford: Oxford University Press.

Allen, Franklin, Rajesh Chakrabarti, Sankar De, Jun 'QJ' Qian, and Meijun Qian. 2012. "Financing Firms in India." *Journal of Financial Intermediation* 21: 409–45.

Allen, Franklin, Jun Qian, Chenying Zhang, and Mengxin Zhao. 2011. "China's Financial System: Opportunities and Challenges." http://papers.ssrn.com/sol3/papers.cfm?abstract_id=1945259

Altenburg, T., H. Schmitz, and A. Stamm. 2008. "Breakthrough? China's and India's Transition from Production to Innovation." *World Development* 36(2): 325–44.

Alves, Philip, and Lawrence Edwards. 2009. "South Africa." In *The Political Economy of Trade Reform in Emerging Markets: Crisis or Opportunity?* edited by Peter Draper, Philip Alves, and Razeen Sally, 200–38. Cheltenham: Edward Elgar Publishing.

Amable, Bruno, and Karim Azizi. 2011. "Varieties of Capitalism and Varieties of Macroeconomic Policy: Are Some Economies More Procyclical Than Others?" *MPIfG Discussion Paper* 11/6. Cologne: Max Planck Institute for the Study of Societies.

Amable, Bruno, and Stefano Palombarini. 2009. "A Neorealist Approach to Institutional Change and the Diversity of Capitalism." *Socio-Economic Review* 7: 123–43.

Amable, Bruno. 2003. *The Diversity of Modern Capitalism*. Oxford: Oxford University Press.

Amable, Bruno. 2005. "Complementarity, Hierarchy, Compatibility, Coherence." *Socio-Economic Review* 3: 371–3.

AmCham (American Chamber of Commerce). 2005. *American Business in China: 2005 White Paper*. Beijing: The American Chamber of Commerce.

AmCham. 2007. *American Business in China: 2007 White Paper*. Beijing: The American Chamber of Commerce.

AmCham. 2011a. *American Business in China: 2011 White Paper*. Beijing: The American Chamber of Commerce.

AmCham. 2011b. *White Paper on the Business Environment in China*. Guangzhou: The American Chamber of Commerce in South China.

Amin, Samir. 1976. *Unequal Development: An Essay on the Social Formations of Peripheral Capitalism*. New York: Monthly Review Press.

Amsden, Alice H. 1989. *Asia's Next Giant: South Korea and Late Industrialization*. Oxford: Oxford University Press.

Amsden, Alice H. 2007. *Escape from Empire: The Developing World's Journey Through Heaven and Hell*. Cambridge and London: MIT Press.

Anant, T.C.A. 2009. "Revisiting Labour Market Regulation." *The Indian Journal of Labour Economics* 52(2): 195–202.

Anderson, Perry. 2011. "Lula's Brazil." *London Review of Books* 33(7): 3–12.

Andreas, Joel. 2009. *Rise of the Red Engineers: The Cultural Revolution and the Origins of China's New Class*. Stanford, CA: Stanford University Press.

Andreasson, Stefan. 2011. "Understanding Corporate Governance Reform in South Africa: Anglo-American Divergence, the King Reports, and Hybridization." *Business & Society* 50(4): 647–73.

Arbix Glauco. 2008. "Innovation, Internationalization, and Labour: New Strategies of the Brazilian Industrial Elite." Paper presented at the 9th International Symposium on Human Factors in Organizational Design and Management (ODAM), March, Guarujá, Brazil.

Arbix, Glauco. 2010. "Innovation and the Development Agenda." *Economic Sociology: The European Electronic Newsletter* 11(2): 16–23.

Armingeon, Klaus, and Lucio Baccaro. 2012. "Political Economy of the Sovereign Debt Crisis: The Limits of Internal Devaluation." *Industrial Law Journal* 41(3): 254–75.

Armstrong, Phillip, Niel Segal, and Ben Davis. 2005. "Corporate Governance: South Africa, a Pioneer in Africa." *Global Best Practice Report* No.1. Johannesburg: The South African Institute of International Affairs.

Arnason, Johann Pall. 2008. "East Asian Modernity Revisited." In *Irmela Hijiya-Kirschnereit zu Ehren: Festschrift zum 60. Geburtstag*, edited by Judit Árokay, Verena Blechinger-Talcott, and Hilaria Gössmann, 395–407. München: Iudicium.

Arnold, Jens. 2011. "Raising Investment in Brazil." *OECD Economics Department Working Papers* No. 900. Paris: Organization for Economic Cooperation and Development.

Arraya, Monica. 2006. "Exploring Terra Incognita: Non-Financial Reporting in Corporate Latin America." *Journal of Corporate Citizenship* 21: 25–38.

Arrorio, Ana, and Mario Scerri. 2010. "Comparative Report on the Role of Small and Medium Enterprises in the National Innovation System of BRICS." RedSite/Economic Institute: Federal University of Rio de Janerio, Brazil.

Ashman, Sam, and Ben Fine. 2013. "Neo-Liberalism, Varieties of Capitalism, and the Shifting Contours of South Africa's Financial System." *Transformation: Critical Perspectives on Southern Africa* 81–2: 144–78.

Åslund, Anders. 2013. "Why Growth in Emerging Economies Is Likely to Fall." *Working Paper* 13–10, Peterson Institute for International Economics, www.piie.com/publications/wp/wp13-10.pdf

Association for Democratic Reforms. 2014. "Lok Sabha Election Watch." New Delhi.

Atkinson, Michael M., and William D. Coleman. 1989. "Strong States and Weak States: Sectoral Policy Networks in Advanced Capitalist Economies." *British Journal of Political Science* 19(1): 47–67.

Baccaro, Lucio, and Chiara Benassi. 2015. "Throwing Out the Ballast: Growth Models and the Liberalization of German Industrial Relations." Unpublished manuscript.

Baccaro, Lucio, and Jonas Pontusson. 2015. *Rethinking Comparative Political Economy: Growth Models and Distributive Dynamics* (manuscript).

Baek, Seung-Wook. 2005. "Does China Follow the East Asian Development Model?" *Journal of Contemporary Asia* 35(4): 485–98.

Baer, Werner. 1972. "Import Substitution and Industrialization in Latin America: Experiences and Interpretations." *Latin American Research Review* 7(1): 95–122.

Baer, Werner, and Adolfo Figueroa. 1981. "State Enterprise and the Distribution of Income: Brazil and Peru." In *Authoritarian Capitalism: Brazil's Contemporary Economic and Political Development*, edited by Thomas C. Bruneau and Philippe Faucher, 59–83. Boulder, CO: Westview Press.

Bairoch, Paul, and Richard Kozul-Wright. 1996. "Globalization Myths: Some Historical Reflections on Integration, Industrialization and Growth in the World Economy." *Discussion Paper* No. 113. Geneva: UNCTAD.

The Banking Association South Africa. 2014. "The South African Banking Sector Overview." www.banking.org.za/docs/default-source/publication/banking-sector-overview.pdf?sfvrsn=6

Balestro, Moises Villamil. 2014a. "Perspectives of a Developmental State in Brazil." Unpublished manuscript.

Balestro, Moisés Villamil. 2014b. "The Shadowy Social Flipside of the BRICs: Dilemmas of Incorporating Workers Unions in Development Strategies in Brazil." Paper for the Fourth World International Studies Conference (WISC), Frankfurt/Main.

Ban, Corrnel. 2013. "Brazil's Liberal Neo-Developmentalism: New Paradigm or Edited Orthodoxy." *Review of International Political Economy* 20(2): 298–331.

Ban, Cornel, and Mark Blyth. 2013. "The BRICs and the Washington Consensus: An Introduction." *Review of International Political Economy* 20(2): 241–55.

Banerjee, Abhijit, and Esther Duflo. 2011. *Poor Economics: A Radical Rethinking of the Way to Fight Global Poverty*. New York: Public Affairs.

Barbosa, Alexandre de Freitas, and Amilton Moretto. 2013. "Development Pattern, Labour Market and Social Protection in Brazil." In *Aligning Economic and Social Goals in Emerging Economies, Employment and Social Protection in Brazil, China, India and South Africa*, edited by Gerry Rodgers, 27–64. New Delhi: Academic Foundation.

Barbosa-Filho, Nelson H. 2006. "Inflation Targeting in Brazil: Is There an Alternative?" PERI paper, University of Massachusetts, Amherst.

Bardhan, Pranab. 2010. *Awakening Giants, Feet of Clay: Assessing the Economic Rise of China and India*. Princeton: Princeton University Press.

Bardhan, Pranab. 2011. "Notes on the Political Economy of India's Transition." In *Economic Reforms and Growth in India*, edited by Pulapre Balakrishnan, 420–31. Hyderabad: Black Swan.

Basu, Kaushik. 2011. "Why, for a Class of Bribes, the Act of Giving a Bribe Should Be Treated as Legal." Ministry of Finance, Government of India. www.kaushikbasu.org/Act_Giving_Bribe_Legal.pdf

Bawa, Ahmed. 2014. "Higher Education in 2013: At Many Crossroads." In *New South African Review 4 – A Fragile Democracy, Twenty Years On*, edited by Deven Pillay, Gilbert M. Khadiagala, Prishani Naidoo, and Roger Southall, 223–37. Johannesburg: Wits University Press, March.

Bazuchi, Karina Regina Vieira, Suelen Alice da Silva Zacharias, Laurent William Broering, Maria Fernanda Arreola, and Rodrigo Bandeira-de Mello. 2013. "The Role of Home Country Political Resources for Brazilian Multinational Companies." *Brazilian Administration Review* 10(4): 415–38.

BBC News. 2018. "The Guptas and Their Links to South Africa's Jacob Zuma." 2 February. www.bbc.com/news/world-africa-22513410 (accessed 3 December 2018).

Becker, Joachim. 2014a. "Finanzialisierung und globale Peripherie." In *Politische Ökonomie der Finanzialisierung*, edited by Marcel Heires and Andreas Nölke, 181–96. Wiesbaden: Springer VS.

Becker, Joachim. 2014b. "The Periphery in the Present International Crisis: Uneven Development, Uneven Impact and Different Responses." *Spectrum: Journal of Global Studies* 5(1): 21–41.

Becker, Joachim, and Johannes Jäger. 2013. "Regulationstheorie und vergleichende Kapitalismusforschung: Die Europäische Union in der Wirtschaftskrise." In *Vergleichende*

Kapitalismusforschung: Stand, Perspektiven, Kritik, edited by Ian Bruff, Matthias Ebenau, Christian May, and Andreas Nölke, 163–77. Münster: Westfälisches Dampfboot.

Becker, Uwe. 2009. *Open Varieties of Capitalism: Continuity, Change and Performance*. Houndmills: Palgrave Macmillan.

Becker, Uwe. 2013a. "Measuring Change of Capitalist Varieties: Reflections on Method, Illustrations from the BRICs." *New Political Economy* 18(4): 503–32.

Becker, Uwe. (ed.). 2013b. *The BRICs and Emerging Economies in Comparative Perspective*. London: Routledge.

Becker, Uwe. 2013c. "Introduction." In *The BRICs and Emerging Economies in Comparative Perspective*, edited by Uwe Becker, 1–26. London: Routledge.

Becker, Uwe. 2013d. "Institutional Change in the BRICs, Eastern Europe, South Africa and Turkey, 1998–2008." In *The BRICs and Emerging Economies in Comparative Perspective*, edited by Uwe Becker, 27–52. London: Routledge.

Becker, Uwe. 2014. "The Heterogeneity of Capitalism in Crisis-Ridden Europe." *Journal of Contemporary European Studies* 22(3): 261–75.

Becker, Uwe, and Vasileva Alexandra. 2017. "Russia's Political Economy Re-Conceptualized: A Changing Hybrid of Liberalism, Statism and Patrimonialism." *Journal of Eurasian Studies* 8: 83–96. http://dx.doi.org/10.1016/j.euras.2016.11.003

Begley, Thomas M., Naresh Khatri, and Eric W.K. Tsang. 2010. "Networks and Cronyism: A Social Exchange Analysis." *Asia-Pacific Journal of Management* 27: 281–97.

Bell, Daniel. 1973. *The Coming of Post Industrial Society: A Venture in Social Forecasting*. New York: Basic Books.

Bell, Trevor. 1993. "Should South Africa Further Liberalise Its Trade?" In *State & Market: In Post Apartheid South Africa*, edited by Merlie Lipton and Charles Simkins, 81–128. Johannesburg: Westview Press.

Benney, Tabitha. 2014. *Making Environmental Markets Work: The Varieties of Capitalism in Emerging Economies*. London and New York: Routledge.

Benson, John. 2011. "Labour Markets in Japan: Change and Continuity." In *The Dynamics of Asian Labour Markets: Balancing Control and Flexibility*, edited by John Benson and Ying Zhu, 33–60. London: Routledge.

Benson, John, Howard Gospel, and Ying Zhu. 2013. *Workforce Development and Skill Formation in Asia*. London: Routledge.

Bertrand, Marianne, Paras Mehta, and Sendhil Mullainathan. 2002. "Ferreting Out Tunneling: An Application to Indian Business Groups." *The Quarterly Journal of Economics* 117(1): 121–48.

Bhagwati, Jagdish. 2007. "What Went Wrong?" In Mukherji 2007a, 27–51.

Bian, Morris L. 2005. *The Making of the State Enterprise System in Modern China*. Cambridge and London: Harvard University Press.

Bijapurkar, Rama. 2007. *We Are Like That Only: Understanding the Logic of Consumer India*. Gurgaon: Penguin Random House.

Birdsall, Nancy. 2010. "The Indispensable Middle Class in Developing Countries." In *Equity and Growth in a Globalizing World*, edited by Ravi Kanbur and Michael Spenc, 157–87. Washington, DC: World Bank Publications.

Bisseker, Claire. 2013. "Shift to Move More Activist Policy." *Financial Mail*, 11 July. www.financialmail.co.za/fm/Features/2013/04/10/shift-to-move-more-activist-policy (accessed 19 December 2015).

Bizberg, Ilan. 2010. "The Global Economic Crisis as Disclosure of the Existence of Different Types of Capitalism in Latin America." www.ieim.uqam.ca/IMG/pdf/BizbergI2010_crisis-latinamerica-capitalisms.pdf

Bizberg, Ilán. 2014. "Types of Capitalism in Latin America." *Interventions économiques* (49).

Bizberg, Ilán. 2019. *Diversity of Capitalisms in Latin America*. Houndmills: Palgrave Macmillan.

Black, Anthony. 1991. "Manufacturing Development and the Economic Crisis: A Reversion to Primary Production?" In *South Africa's Economic Crisis*, edited by Stephen Gelb, 156–74. Claremont: Zed Books.

Black, Anthony. 2012. "Industrial Policy and Unemployment: Can South Africa Do Better in Labour-Demanding Manufacturing?" www.econ3x3.org/sites/default/files/articles/Black%20Nov%202012%20Industrial%20policy%20FINAL2.pdf (accessed 21 December 2015).

Black, Anthony, and Simon Roberts. 2009. "The Evolution and Impact of Industrial and Competiton Policies." In *South African Economic Policy Under Democracy*, edited by Janine Aron, Brian Khan, and Geeta Kingdon, 211–43. Oxford: Oxford University Press.

Blattmann, Chris. 2012. "Corruption and Development: Not What You Think?" *Chris Blattmann Blog*. November 5. https://chrisblattman.com/2012/11/05/corruption-and-development-not-what-you-think/ (accessed 26 June 2019).

Blyth, Mark. 2003. "Same as It Never Was: Temporality and Typology in the Varieties of Capitalism." *Comparative European Politics* 1: 215–25.

BNDES. 2012. *Annual Report 2011*. Rio de Janeiro, Brazil: Banco Nacional do Desenvolvimento.

BNDES. 2014. *Corporate Presentation Financial Area*. Rio de Janeiro: BNDES.

Bohle, Dorothee, and Béla Greskovits. 2009. "Varieties of Capitalism and Capitalism 'Tout Court'." *Archives de Européennes de Sociologie – European Journal of Sociology* 50(3): 355–68.

Bohle, Dorothee, and Béla Greskovits. 2012. *Capitalist Diversity on Europe's Periphery*. Ithaca: Cornell University Press.

Boschi, Renato. 2011. "State Developmentalism: Continuity and Uncertainty." In *The Brazilian State: Debate and Agenda*, edited by Mauricio Font and Laura Randall, 37–58. Lanham: Lexington Books.

Boschi, Renato. 2012. "Interessengruppen, der Staat und die Beziehung zwischen den Staatsgewalten in Brasilien: Gegenwärtige Entwicklungen." In *Das politische System Brasiliens*, edited by Dana de la Fontaine and Thomas Stehnken, 175–92. Wiesbaden: Springer VS.

Boschi, Renato. 2013. "Politics and Trajectory in Brazilian Capitalist Development." In *The BRICs and Emerging Economies in Comparative Perspective: Political Economy, Liberalization and Institutional Change*, edited by Uwe Becker, 123–43. London: Routledge.

Boschi, Renato, and Flavio Gaitán. 2009. "Politics and Development: Lessons from Latin America." *Brazilian Political Science Review* 3(2): 11–29.

Boschi, Renato, and Carlos Henrique Santana. (eds.). 2012. *Development and Semi-Periphery: Post-Neoliberal Trajectories in South America and Central Eastern Europe*. London: Anthem Press.

Bose, Gautam. 2012. "Aspects of Bureaucratic Corruption." In *The Oxford Handbook of the Indian Economy*, edited by Chetan Ghate, 551–80. Oxford: Oxford University Press.

Bourdieu, Pierre. 1990. *The Logic of Practice*. Stanford: Stanford University Press.

Bowles, Paul, and John Harriss. (eds.). 2010. *Globalization and Labour in China and India: Impacts and Responses*. Houndmills, Basingstoke and New York: Palgrave Macmillan.

Boyer, Robert. 2000. "Is a Finance-Led Growth Regime a Viable Alternative to Fordism? A Preliminary Analysis." *Economy and Society* 29(1): 111–45.

Boyer, Robert. 2005. "How and Why Capitalisms Differ." *MPIfG Discussion Paper* 05/4. Cologne: Max Planck Institute for the Study of Societies.

Boyer, Robert, and Yves Saillard. 2002. "A Summary of Régulation Theory." In *Régulation Theory: The State of the Art*, edited by Robert Boyer and Yves Saillard, 36–44. London and New York: Routledge.

Brainard Lael, and Leonardo Martinez-Diaz. 2009. *Brazil as an Economic Superpower: Understanding Brazil's Changing Role in the Global Economy*. Washington, DC: Brookings Institution Press.

Brandt, Loren, and Eric Thun. 2010. "The Fight for the Middle: Upgrading, Competition, and Industrial Development in China." *World Development* 38(11): 1555–74.

Brandt, Loren, and Eric Thun. 2016. "Constructing a Ladder for Growth: Policy, Markets, and Industrial Upgrading in China." *World Development* 80: 78–95.

Bräutigam, Deborah, Lisa Rakner, and Scott Taylor. 2002. "Business Associations and Growth Coalitions in Sub-Saharan Africa." *The Journal of Modern African Studies* 40(4): 519–47.

Bremmer, Ian. 2010. *The End of the Free Market: Who Wins the War Between States and Corporations?* New York: Portfolio.

Brenner, Robert. 2006. *The Economics of Global Turbulence: The Advanced Capitalist Economies from Long Boom to Long Downturn, 1945–2005*. London: Verso.

Bresnitz, D., and M. Murphree. 2011. *Run of the Red Queen – Government, Innovation, Globalization and Economic Growth in China*. New Haven: Yale University Press.

Bresser-Pereira, Luiz Carlos. 2015. "Brazil's 35 Years-Old Quasi-Stagnation: Facts and Theory." In *Why Latin American Nations Fail: Developmental Strategies in the 21st Century*, edited by Matías Vernengo and Esteban Perez. Berkeley: University of California Press.

Bresser-Pereira, Luiz Carlos, and Yoshiaki Nakano. 2002. "Economic Growth with Foreign Savings?" Paper presented to the Seventh International Post Keynesian Workshop, Kansas City.

Bruff, Ian. 2010. "European Varieties of Capitalism and the International." *European Journal of International Relations* 16(4): 615–38.

Bruff, Ian. 2011. "What About the Elephant in the Room? Varieties of Capitalism, Varieties in Capitalism." *New Political Economy* 16(4): 481–500.

Bruff, Ian, and Matthias Ebenau. 2014. "Critical Political Economy and the Critique of Comparative Capitalisms Scholarship on Capitalist Diversity." *Capital & Class* 38(1): 3–15.

Bruff, Ian, Matthias Ebenau, Christian May, and Andreas Nölke. (eds.). 2013. *Vergleichende Kapitalismusforschung: Stand, Perspektiven, Kritik*. Münster: Westfälisches Dampfboot.

Buchen, Clemens. 2007. "Estonia and Slovenia as Antipodes." In *Varieties of Capitalism in Post-Communist Countries*, edited by David Lane and Martin Myant, 65–89. Houndmills: Palgrave Macmillan.

Buhr, Daniel, and Rolf Frankenberger. 2014. "Spielarten des inkorporierten Kapitalismus." In *Die großen Schwellenländer: Ursachen und Folgen ihres Aufstiegs in der Weltwirtschaft*. Wiesbaden: Springer VS.

Business Insider. 2015. "Credit Suisse: Here's Why the Emerging-Markets Rally May Be About to End." 18 October. www.businessinsider.com/credit-suisse-heres-why-the-emerging-markets-rally-may-be-about-to-end-2015–10?IR=T (accessed 29 November 2015).

Business Standard. 2009. "Business Standard Political Profiles of Cabals and Kings." New Delhi.

Businessworld. 2013. "The BWReal 500." Special Issue, 4 November.

Butollo, Florian, and Tobias ten Brink. 2012. "Challenging the Atomization of Discontent: Patterns of Migrant-Worker Protest in China During the Series of Strikes in 2010." *Critical Asian Studies* 44(3): 419–40.

Butollo, Florian, and Tobias ten Brink. 2018. "Domestic Market Growth and Local State Support in the Upgrading of China's LED Lighting Industry." *Global Networks* 18(2): 285–306.

Cai, Fang. 2015. "Haste Makes Waste: Policy Options Facing China After Reaching the Lewis Turning Point." *China & World Economy* 23(1): 1–20.

Canuto, Otaviano, and Philip Schellekens. 2014. "Three Perspectives on Brazilian Growth Pessimism." *Economic Premise* No. 148. Washington, DC: World Bank.

Cardoso, Fernando Henrique, and Enzo Faletto. 1979. *Dependency and Development in Latin America*. Berkeley: University of California Press.

Carney, Michael, Eric Gedajlovic, and Xiaohua Yang. 2009. "Varieties of Asian Capitalism: Toward an Institutional Theory of Asian Enterprise." *Asia Pacific Journal of Management* 26(3): 361–80.

Carvalho, Flavia, and Andrea Goldstein. 2008. "The 'Making of' National Giants: Technology and Governments Shaping the International Expansion of Oil Companies from Brazil and China." *UNU-MERIT Working Paper* 21.

Casanova, Lourdes, and Julian Kassum. 2013. "Brazilian Emerging Multinationals: In Search of a Second Wind." *Working Paper INSEAD*. Paris.

Casanova, Lourdes, and Julian Kassum. 2014. *The Political Economy of an Emerging Global Power: In Search of the Brazil Dream*. Houndmills: Palgrave Macmillan.

Castoriadis, Cornelius. 1988. "The Relations of Production in Russia." In *Cornelius Castoriadis. Political and Social Writings, Volume 1*, edited by David Ames Curtis, 107–58. Minneapolis: University of Minnesota Press.

CBRC (China Banking Regulatory Commission). 2012. *Annual Report 2011*. Beijing. www.cbrc.gov.cn/chinese/files/2013/8FC77357E36D44D2BD8B3C4BE97F965F.pdf

Cervo, Amando Luiz. 2012. "Brüche und Kontinuitäten im politisch-institutionellen Leben Brasiliens: Vergangene und gegenwärtige Dilemmata der Demokratie." In *Das politische System Brasiliens*, edited by Dana de la Fontaine and Thomas Stehnken, 23–33. Wiesbaden: Springer VS.

Chakrabarti, Rajesh. 2014. "The Financial Sector in India: An Overview." In *The Oxford Handbook of the Indian Economy in the 21st Century: Understanding the Inherent Dynamism*, edited by Ashima Goyal, 846–67. New Delhi: Oxford University Press.

Chakrabarti, Rajesh, William Megginson, and Pradeep K. Yadav. 2008. "Corporate Governance in India." *Journal of Applied Corporate Finance* 20(1): 59–72.

Chalapati Rao, K.S. 2009. "Some Aspects of Corporate Ownership in India: Promoters Versus Public." In *Indian Industrial Development and Globalisation*, edited by S.R. Hashim, K.S. Chalapati Rao, K.V.K. Ranganathan, and M.R. Murthy, 261–310. New Delhi: Academic Foundation.

Chalapati Rao, K.S. 2010. "The Arduous Route to Ensuring Some Minimum Public Shareholding in Listed Companies." *ISID Working Paper* 2010/07. New Delhi: Institute for Studies in Industrial Development.

Chalapati Rao, K.S., and Atulan Guha. 2006. "Ownership Pattern of the Indian Corporate Sector: Implications for Corporate Governance." *ISID Working Paper* 2006/09. New Delhi: Institute for Studies in Industrial Development.

Chan, Anita. (ed.). 2015. *Chinese Workers in Comparative Perspective*. Ithaca and London: ILR Press.

Chan, Anita, and Jonathan Unger. 2009. "A Chinese State Enterprise Under the Reforms: What Model of Capitalism?" *The China Journal* 62(2): 1–26.

Chan, Kam Wing, and Will Buckingham. 2008. "Is China Abolishing the Hukou System?" *The China Quarterly* 195: 582–606.

Chandra, Nirmal Kumar. 2012. "Appraising Industrial Policies of India and China from Two Perspectives: Nationalist and Internationalist." In *Transformation and Development: The Political Economy of Transition in India and China*, edited by Amiya Kumar Bagchi and Anthony P. D'Costa, 95–130. New Delhi: Oxford University Press.

Chase, Bonwen, Thabiso Legoete, and Arend van Wamelen. 2010. "A Seismic Shift in South Africa's Consumer Landscape." McKinsey Insights and Publications. Online. www.mckinsey.com/insights/consumer_and_retail/a_seismic_shift_in_south_africas_consumer_landscape (accessed 21 December 2015).

Chen, Feng. 2009. "Union Power in China: Source, Operation, and Constraints." *Modern China* 35(6): 662–89.

Chen, Minglu. 2015. "From Economic Elites to Political Elites: Private Entrepreneurs in the People's Political Consultative Conference." *Journal of Contemporary China* 24(94): 613–27.

Chen, Zhiwu. 2015. "China's Dangerous Debt." *Foreign Affairs* 94(3): 13–18.

Chenoy, Kamal A.M. 2015. *The Rise of Big Business in India*. New Delhi: Aakar Books.

Chibber, Vivek. 2003. *Locked in Place: State-Building and Late Industrialization in India*. Princeton: Princeton University Press.

Chibber, Vivek. 2005. "The Politics of a Miracle: Class Interests and State Power in Korean Developmentalism." In *Varieties of Capitalism, Varieties of Approaches*, edited by David Coates, 122–38. Houndmills, Basingstoke and New York: Palgrave Macmillan.

Chibber, Vivek. 2014. "The Prospects for Developmentalism: Lessons from India and Korea." Unpublished manuscript.

Chibber, Vivek, and Adaner Usmani. 2013. "The State and the Capitalist Class in India." In *Routledge Handbook of Indian Politics*, edited by Atul Kohli and Prema Singh, 204–10. London: Routledge.

Chong JI. 2013. "Popular Narratives Versus Chinese History: Implications for Understanding an Emergent China." *European Journal of International Relations*, published online before print.

Claar, Simone. 2014. "Handelspolitik als Entwicklungsmotor in Südafrika." In *Die großen Schwellenländer. Ursachen und Folgen ihres Aufstiegs in der Weltwirtschaft*, edited by Andreas Nölke, Christian May, and Simone Claar, 193–208. Wiesbaden: VS-Verlag.

Claar, Simone. 2018. *International Trade Policy and Class Dynamics in South Africa: The Economic Partnership Agreement*. London: Palgrave Macmillan.

Claar, Simone, and Andreas Nölke. 2013. "Deep Integration in North – South Relations: Compatibility Issues Between the EU and South Africa." *Review of African Political Economy* 40(136): 274–89.

Claessens, Stijn, and B. Burcin Yurtogu. 2013. "Corporate Governance in Emerging Markets: A Survey." *Emerging Markets Review* 15(1): 1–33.

Clarke, George R.G., James Habyarimana, Michael Ingram, David Kaplan, and Vijaya Ramachandran. 2007. *An Assessment of the Investment Climate in South Africa*. Washington, DC: World Bank.

Clarke, Simon. 1978. "Capital, Fractions of Capital and the State: 'Neo-Marxist' Analysis of the South African State." *Capital and Class* 5(1): 32–77.

Clarke, Simon, Chang-Hee Lee, and Qi Li. 2004. "Collective Consultation and Industrial Relations in China." *British Journal of Industrial Relations* 42(2): 235–54.

CLB (China Labour Bulletin). 2014. *Searching for the Union: The Workers' Movement in China 2011–13*. Hong Kong: China Labour Bulletin.

Clift, Ben. 2014. *Comparative Political Economy: States, Markets and Global Capitalism*. Houndmills and Basingstoke: Palgrave Macmillan.

Cloete, Nico, Charles Sheppard, and Tracy Bailey. 2015. "South Africa as a PhD Hub in Africa?" In *Knowledge Production and Contradictory Functions in African Higher Education*, edited by Nico Cloete, Peter Massen, and Tracy Bailey, 75–108. African Minds Higher Education Dynamics Series Vol. 1. African Minds: Cape Town. http://chet.org.za/books/knowledge-production-and-contradictory-functions-african-higher-education (accessed 19 December 2015).

CMIE. 2014. *Prowess Database*. Mumbai: Center for the Monitoring of the Indian Economy (accessed January 2014).

Coates, David. 2000. *Models of Capitalism: Growth and Stagnation in the Modern Era*. Cambridge: Polity.

Coates, David. 2014. "Studying Comparative Capitalisms by Going Left and by Going Deeper." *Capital & Class* 38(1): 18–30.

Coates, David. 2015. "Varieties of Capitalism and 'the Great Moderation'." In *New Directions in Comparative Capitalisms Research: Critical and Global Perspectives*, edited by Matthias Ebenau, Ian Bruff, and Christian May, 11–27. Houndmills and Basingstoke: Palgrave Macmillan.

Collins, Colin B., and Roselyn R. Gillespie. 1998. "Educational Renewal Strategies for South Africa in a Post-Apartheid Society." *International Journal of Educational Development* 13(1): 33–44.

Colpan, Asli M., and Takashi Hikino. 2010. "Foundations of Business Groups: Towards an Integrated Framework." In *The Oxford Handbook of Business Groups*, edited by Asli M. Colpan, Takashi Hikino, and James R. Lincoln, 15–66. Oxford: Oxford University Press.

Condé, Eduardo Salomão, and Ignacio Godinho Delgado. 2009. "The Agenda of Difference: State, Varieties of Capitalism, and Economic Governance in Asia and Latin America." Paper presented at the 21st International Political Science Association World Congress of Political Science, July, Santiago, Chile.

Conlé, Marcus. 2011: "The Continuity and Change of China's Capitalism: An Evolutionary Perspective." Paper prepared for the Conference of the Society for the Advancement of Socio-Economics (SASE): Universidad Autónoma de Madrid.

Corbridge, Stuart. 2013. "Corruption in India." In *Routledge Handbook of Indian Politics*, edited by Atul Kohli and Prema Singh, 222–9. London: Routledge.

Corbridge, Stuart, and John Harriss. 2003. *Reinventing India: Liberalization, Hindu Nationalism and Popular Democracy*. New Delhi: Oxford University Press.

COSATU. 2012. "Findings of the COSATU's Workers Survey, 2012." Congress of South African Trade Unions. www.cosatu.org.za/docs/reports/2012/final%20workers%20surveys%20results%20August%202012.pdf (accessed 10 October 2014).

COSATU. n.d. "About: Brief History of COSATU." www.cosatu.org.za/show.php?ID=925 (accessed 19 December 2015).

Cox, Robert. 1987. *Production, Power, and World Order: Social Forces in the Making of History*. New York: Columbia University Press.

Crabtree, James. 2015. "Has Narendra Modi Cleaned Up India?" *Prospect Magazine*, May.

Crouch, Colin. 2005. *Capitalist Diversity and Change: Recombinant Governance and Institutional Entrepreneurs*. Oxford: Oxford University Press.

Crouch, Colin. 2010. "Complementarity." In *The Oxford Handbook of Comparative Institutional Analysis*, edited by Glenn Morgan, John L. Campbell, Colin Crouch, Ove Kaj Pedersen, and Richard Whitley, 117–38. Oxford: Oxford University Press.

Crouch, Colin, and Wolfgang Streeck. (eds.). 1997. *Political Economy of Modern Capitalism: Mapping Convergence and Diversity*. London: Sage.

Cusack, Thomas R., Torben Iversen, and David Soskice. 2007. "Economic Interests and the Origins of Electoral Systems." *American Political Science Review* 101(3): 373–91.

Custodio, Leo. 2014. "The Conflict of the Middle Classes in the Brazilian Youth-Led Protests." Blog.

Dahlman, Carl J. 2009. "Growth and Development in China and India: The Role of Industrial and Innovation Policy in Rapid Catch-Up." In *Industrial Policy and Development: The Political Economy of Capabilities Accumulation*, edited by Mario Cimoli, Dosi Giovanni and Joseph E. Stiglitz, 303–34. Oxford: Oxford University Press.

Dahlmann, Carl J., and Claudio R. Frischtak. 1993. "National Systems Supporting Technical Advance in Industry: The Brazilian Experience." In *National Innovation Systems: A Comparative Analysis*, edited by Richard Nelson, 414–50. Oxford: Oxford University Press.

Daniel, Luke. 2018. "State Owned Enterprises the Biggest Threat to South Africa's Economy." 14 September. www.thesouthafrican.com/state-owned-enterprises-threat-to-economy/ (accessed 3 December 2018).

Dannreuther, Charlie, and Pascal Petit. 2006. "Post-Fordism, Beyond National Models: The Main Challenges for Regulation Theory." *Competition and Change* 10(2): 100–12.

Das Gupta, Chirashree. 2016. *State and Capital in Independent India: Institutions and Accumulation*. Cambridge: Cambridge University Press.

Datz, Giselle. 2013. "Brazil's Pension Fund Developmentalism." *Competition and Change* 17(2): 111–28.

Davies, Rob. 2011. "SACP: Statement by Rob Davies, South African Communist Party Central Committee Member, on the Industrial Policy Action Plan." 5 May. www.polity.org.za/article/sacp-statement-by-rob-davies-south-african-communist-party-central-committee-member-on-the-industrial-policy-action-plan-05052011-2011-05-05 (accessed 21 August 2012).

Debroy, Bibek, and Laveesh Bhandari. 2012. *Corruption in India: The DNA and the RNA*. New Delhi and Seattle: Konark Publishers.

Deeg, Richard. 2007. "Complementarity and Institutional Change in Capitalist Systems." *Journal of European Public Policy* 14(4): 611–30.

Deeg, Richard, and Gergory Jackson. 2007. "Towards a More Dynamic Theory of Capitalist Variety." *Socio-Economic Review* 5(2): 149–79.

Demirbag, Mehmet, and Geoffrey Wood. (eds.). 2018. *Comparative Capitalism and the Transitional Periphery: Firm-Centred Perspectives*. Cheltenham: Edward Elgar.

Department of Trade and Industry (DTI). 2007. "National Industrial Policy Framework (NIPF)." www.dti.gov.za/industrial_development/docs/niPF-3aug.pdf (accessed 17 February 2012).

de Paula, Luiz Fernando Rodrigues. 2003. "The Determinants of Recent Foreign Bank Penetration in Brazil." *CEPAL Review* 79: 159–76.

De Soto, Hernando. 2000. *The Mystery of Capital: Why Capitalism Triumphs in the West and Fails Everywhere Else*. New York: Basic Books.

Deutsche Bank Research. 2011. "BRIC Banking Systems After the Crisis." www.dbresearch.com/PROD/RPS_EN-PROD/PROD0000000000480995/BRIC_banking_systems_after_the_crisis.PDF (accessed 2 February 2018).

Deutsche Bank Research. 2012. "Brazilian Banking Sector – A View from 30,000 Feet." Online. www.dbresearch.com

Deutschmann, Christoph. 2009. "Soziologie kapitalistischer Dynamik." MPI Scholar in Residence Lectures 09/2. Köln: Max-Planck-Institut für Gesellschaftsforschung. www.mpifg.de/aktuelles/SiR/MPIfG-Deutschmann_0902.pdf

de Waal, Mandy. 2012. "Marikana: What Really Happened? We May Never Know." *Daily Maverick*, 23 August. www.dailymaverick.co.za/article/2012-08-23-marikana-what-really-happened-we-may-never-know#.VijmCMv9rTo (accessed 19 December 2015)

Dhume, Sadanand. 2011. "India's Crony Socialism: Capitalists Wield Too Little Influence Over the Country, Not Too Much." *Wall Street Journal*, 6 July.

Diamond, Georg J., and Gavin Price. 2012. "The Political Economy of Corporate Governance Reform in South Africa." *South African Journal of Business Management* 43(1): 57–68.

Dickson, Bruce J. 2007. "Integrating Wealth and Power in China: The Communist Party's Embrace of the Private Sector." *The China Quarterly* 192: 827–54.

Dickson, Bruce J. 2016. *The Dictator's Dilemma: The Chinese Communist Party's Strategy for Survival*. Oxford: Oxford University Press.

Dierckx, Sacha. 2015. "Capital Controls in China, Brazil and India: Towards the End of the Free Movement of Capital as a Global Norm?" PhD diss., University of Gent.

Diniz, Eli, and Luiz Carlos Bresser-Pereira. 2012. "Industrieunternehmertum, Demokratie und politische Macht." In *Das politische System Brasiliens*, edited by Dana de la Fontaine and Thomas Stehnken, 193–208. Wiesbaden: Springer VS.

Djelic, Marie-Laure. 2010. "Institutional Perspectives – Working Towards Coherence or Irreconcilable Diversity?" In *The Oxford Handbook of Comparative Institutional Analysis*, edited by Glenn Morgan, John L. Campbell, Colin Crouch, Ove Kaj Pedersen, and Richard Whitley, 15–40. Oxford: Oxford University Press.

Doner, Richard, and Ben Ross Schneider. 2015. "The Middle-Income Trap: More Politics Than Economics?" Talk given by Ben Ross Schneider at Goethe University, Frankfurt, 30 April.

Dore, Ronald. 2000. *Stock Market Capitalism: Welfare Capitalism: Japan and Germany Versus the Anglo-Saxons*. Oxford: Oxford University Press.

Dowbor, Ladislau. 2009. "Die Krise aus globaler Sicht und ihre Bedeutung für Brasilien." *Nueva Sociedad* Sonderheft, 111–32.

Drahokoupil, Jan, and Martin Myant. 2015. "Putting Comparative Capitalisms Research in Its Place: Varieties of Capitalism in Transition Economies." In *New Directions in Comparative Capitalisms Research: Critical and Global Perspectives*, edited by Matthias Ebenau, Ian Bruff, and Christian May, 155–71. Houndmills: Palgrave Macmillan.

Draper, Peter. 2010. "Trade, Industrial Policy and Exchange Rates in South Africa." Occasional Paper 66, Johannesburg: SAIIA.

DTI. 2007. "Implementation of Government's National Industrial Policy Framework: Industrial Policy Action Plan." August. www.dti.gov.za/industrial_development/docs/IPAP%20-3august.pdf (accessed 19 December 2015).

DTI. 2014. "Industrial Policy Action Plan: Economic Sectors and Employment Cluster. 2014/15–2016/17." www.idc.co.za/images/download-files/IPAP2014.pdf (accessed 19 December 2018)

Dubrovsky, Daniel. 2015. "US Treasury Adjusts Yuan Stance, Sees China Capital Outflows to Increase." *DailyFX*, October 20. www.dailyfx.com/forex/market_alert/2015/10/20/US-Treasury-Adjusts-Yuan-Stance-Sees-China-Capital-Outflows-to-Increase.html (accessed 5 December 2018)

Easterly, William. 2001. "The Middle Class Consensus and Economic Development." *Journal of Economic Growth* 6(4): 317–35.

Ebenau, Matthias. 2013. "Die Globalisierung der Vergleichenden Kapitalismusforschung: ein kritischer Blick auf Stand, Probleme und Herausforderungen." In *Vergleichende Kapitalismusforschung: Stand, Perspektiven, Kritik*, edited by Ian Bruff, Matthias Ebenau, Christian May, and Andreas Nölke, 70–83. Münster: Westfälisches Dampfboot.

Ebenau, Matthias. 2015. "Directions and Debates in the Globalization of Comparative Capitalisms Research." In *New Directions in Comparative Capitalisms Research: Critical and Global Perspectives*, edited by Matthias Ebenau, Ian Bruff, and Christian May, 45–61. Houndmills: Palgrave Macmillan.

Ebenau, Matthias, Ian Bruff, and Christian May. (eds.). 2015. *New Directions in Comparative Capitalisms Research: Critical and Global Perspectives*. Houndmills and Basingstoke: Palgrave Macmillan.

Ebenau, Matthias, and Victoria Liberatore. 2013. "Neodevelopmentalist State Capitalism in Brazil and Argentina." *der modern staat* 6(1): 105–25.

Ebenau, Matthias, Facundo Parés, and Lucía Suau Arinci. 2013. "Zurück in die Zukunft? Dependenzperspektiven in der Analyse der Diversität des Gegenwartskapitalismus." *Peripherie* 130–1: 220–42.

Economic Development Department (EDD). 2010. "The New Growth Path: Framework." www.economic.gov.za/communications/publications/new-growth-path-series (accessed 17 February 2012).

Economic Times. 2010. "Let's Regulate Lobbying." 24 December.

Economic Times. 2015a. "Two Institutes Transferred to Skill Development Ministry." 22 May.

Economic Times. 2015b. "Govt Approves Formation of Indian Skill Development Service." 7 October.

Economist. 1998. "Asian Values Revisited-What Would Confucius Say Now?" 348(8078): 25–7.

The Economist. 2012. "Owning Ideas: Intellectual Property in Brazil." 3 November.

The Economist. 2013a. "Supermarkets in Africa: The Grocers' Great Trec." 21 September. www.economist.com/news/business/21586551-sluggish-home-market-pushing-south-africas-big-retail-chains-northward-grocers-great (accessed 2 January 2014).

The Economist. 2013b. "The End of the Affair: The Fed and Emerging Markets." 15 June. www.economist.com/node/21579461/print (accessed 29 November 2015).

The Economist. 2015a. "Blood at the End of the Rainbow." 25 April. www.economist.com/news/middle-east-and-africa/21649429-south-africas-poor-are-turning-those-even-more-downtrodden-blood-end-rainbow (accessed 19 December 2015).

The Economist. 2015b. "Material Difficulties." 1 August. https://www.economist.com/finance-and-economics/2015/07/30/material-difficulties (accessed 29 November 2015).

Edwards, Lawrence. 2005. "Has South Africa Liberalised Its Trade?" *South African Journal of Economics* 74(4): 754–75.

Edwards, Lawrence, Rashad Cassim, and Dirk van Seventer. 2009. "Trade Policy in South Africa." In *South African Economic Policy Under Democracy*, edited by Janine Aron, Brian Kahn, and Geeta Kingdon, 151–81. Oxford: Oxford University Press.

Edwards, Nick. 2015. "China's Falling FX Reserves Do Not Prove the Case for Capital Flight." *South China Morning Post*, 8 September.

Eichengreen, Barry, Donghyun Park, and Kwanho Shin. 2011. "When Fast Growing Economies Slow Down: International Evidence and Implications for China." *NBER Working Paper* 16919.

Eichengreen, Barry, Donghyun Park, and Kwanho Shin. 2013. *Growth Slowdowns Redux: New Evidence on the Middle-Income Trap*. Cambridge: National Bureau of Economic Research.

Elliott, R., and Y. Zhou. 2013. "State-Owned Enterprises, Exporting and Productivity in China: A Stochastic Dominance Approach." *World Economy* 36(8): 1000–28.

England, Johannes. 2015. "Student Demonstrations Rock South Africa." *Financial Times*, 20 October. www.ft.com/cms/s/0/3460a0fe-7736-11e5-a95a-27d368e1ddf7.html#axzz3pJ1N9z3T (accessed 19 December 2015).

Epstein, Gerald A. 2005. "Introduction." In *Financialization and the World Economy*, edited by Gerald A. Epstein, 3–16. Cheltenham: Edward Elgar.

Erasmus, Pierre. 2009. "Capital Structure and Debt Maturity Choices for South African Firms: Evidence from a Highly Variable Economic Investment." 12th International Conference Proceedings, 28–29 October. www.opf.slu.cz/kfi/icfb/proc2009/pdf/07_Erasmus.pdf (accessed 19 December 2015).

Erawatch. 2007. "Erawatch Database." http://erawatch.jrc.ec.europa.eu/erawatch/opencms/information/country_pages/in/country (accessed 12 July 2013).

Estrin, Saul, and Martha Prevezer. 2011. "The Role of Informal Institutions in Corporate Governance: Brazil, Russia, India, and China Compared." *Asia Pacific Journal of Management* 28(1): 41–67.

Evans, Peter. 1979. *Dependent Development*. Princeton: Princeton University Press.

Evans, Peter. 1989. "Predatory, Developmental, and Other Apparatuses: A Comparative Political Economy Perspective on the Third World State." *Sociological Forum* 4(4): 561–87.

Evans, Peter. 1995. *Embedded Autonomy: States and Industrial Transformation*. Princeton: Princeton University Press.

Evans, Peter, Dietrich Rueschemeyer and Theda Skocpol. 1985. *Bringing the State Back in*. New York: Cambridge University Press.

Faku, Dineo. 2013. "Lonmin Finally Recognises Amcu." *Business Report*, 15 August. www.iol.co.za/business-report/economy/lonmin-finally-recognises-amcu-1562490 (accessed 5 December 2018).

Fan, Peilei. 2011. "Innovation, Globalization, and Catch-Up of Latecomers: Cases of Chinese Telecom Firms." *Environment and Planning A* 43(4): 830–49.

Fan, Ying. 2002. "Questioning Guanxi: Definition, Classification and Implications." *International Business Review* 11: 543–61.

Faucher, Philippe. 1981. "The Paradise That Never Was: The Breakdown of the Brazilian Authoritarian Order." In *Authoritarian Capitalism: Brazils Contemporary Economic and Political Development*, edited by Thomas C. Bruneau and Philippe Faucher, 11–39. Boulder, CO: Westview Press.

FAZ. 2015a. "Brasiliens Anleihen nur noch Ramsch." *Frankfurter Allgemeine Zeitung*, 11 September (online).

FAZ. 2015b. "Schwellenländer schauen gebannt auf die Fed." *Frankfurter Allgemeine Zeitung*, 16 September (p. 23).

FAZ. 2015c. "Die neue Verletzlichkeit der Schwellenländer." *Frankfurter Allgemeine Zeitung*, 11 September (p. 17).

Feldmann, Magnus. 2006. "Emerging Varieties of Capitalism in Transition Countries." *Comparative Political Studies* 39(7): 829–54.

Feldmann, Magnus. 2019. "Global Varieties of Capitalism." *World Politics* 71(1): 162–96.

Fernández Jilberto, Alex E., and Andre Mommen. (eds.). 1996. *Liberalization in the Developing World: Institutional and Economic Changes in Latin America, Africa and Asia*. London: Routledge.

FGV. 2014. "Government Procurement Strategies in Brazil: Auction Theory and 'Big Data'." *FGV Projetos* No. 18, Rio de Janeiro.

FICCI. 2006. *FICCI Survey on the state of Industrial Training Institutes in India*. New Delhi: Federation of Indian Chambers of Commerce and Industry.

Filippetti, Andrea, and Antonio Peyrache. 2015. "Technology or Investment? An Enquiry into the Chinese Model of Growth at the Region Level." *Innovation and Development* 5(1): 39–58.

Financial Mail. 2014. "These Are the Biggest Listed Companies in SA", https://businesstech.co.za/news/general/59253/these-are-the-biggest-listed-companies-in-sa/ (accessed 6 August 2019).

Fine, Ben. 2008. "The Minerals-Energy Complex Is Dead: Long Live the MEC?" In *Amandla Colloquium*. Online. http://eprints.soas.ac.uk/5617/ (accessed 18 August 2012).

Fine, Ben. 2009. "Neo-Liberalism in Retrospect? – It's Financialisation, Stupid." Prepared for Conference on 'Developmental Politics in the Neo-Liberal Era and Beyond', Centre for Social Sciences, Seoul National University. http://eprints.soas.ac.uk/7993/1/seoulart.pdf

Fine, Ben, and Zav Rustomjee. 1996. *The Political Economy of South Africa: From Mineral-Energy Complex to Industrialisation*. London: Hurst and Company.

Fioretos, Orfeo. 2001. "The Domestic Sources of Multilateral Preferences: Varieties of Capitalism in the European Community." In *Varieties of Capitalism: The Institutional Foundations of Comparative Advantage*, edited by Peter A. Hall and David Soskice, 213–44. Oxford: Oxford University Press.

Fischermann, Thomas, Roman Pletter, and Mark Schieritz. 2013. "Das Kapital verlässt das Land." *Die Zeit*, August 29. (p. 23).

Fishwick, Adam. 2013. "Zur Kritik der 'hierarchischen Marktökonomie' Globale Produktion und Arbeiterklassenkonflikte in Argentiniens Automobilindustrie." *Peripherie* 130–1: 287–302.

Fleury, Alfonso, and Maria Tereza Leme Fleury. 2011. *Brazilian Multinationals: Competences for Internationalization*. Cambridge: Cambridge University Press.

Flynn, Matthew. 2007. "Between Subimperialism and Globalization: A Case Study on the Internationalization of Brazilian Capital." *Latin American Perspectives* 34(6): 9–27.

Forte, Jay. 2015. "Informal Economy in Brazil Worth R$826 Billion in 2014." *The Rio Times*, 26 June. http://riotimesonline.com/brazil-news/rio-business/brazils-informal-economy-was-worth-r826-billion-in-2014/ (accessed 13 December 2015).

Fortune Magazine. 2012. "Top 500 companies in the World." (In Chinese), 9 July 2012, http://www.fortunechina.com/fortune500/c/2012-07/09/content_106535.htm (accessed 12 January 2013).

Frankel, Francine. 2005. *India's Political Economy, 1947–2004*. Oxford: Oxford University Press.

Frankel, Jeffrey. 2012. "Will Emerging Markets Fall in 2012?" *Business & Management Journal* 2(2): 119–20.

Frieden, Jeffry A. 1981. "Third World Indebted Industrialization: International Finance and State Capitalism in Mexico, Brazil, Algeria, and South Korea." *International Organization* 35(3): 407–31.

Frieden, Jeffry A. 1991. "Invested Interests: The Politics of National Economic Policies in a World of Global Finance." *International Organization* 45(4): 425–51.

Friedman, Eli. 2014. *Insurgency Trap: Labor Politics in Postsocialist China*. Ithaca and London: ILR Press.

Friedman, Eli, and Ching Kwan Lee. 2010. "Remaking the World of Chinese Labour: A 30-Year Retrospective." *British Journal of Industrial Relations* 48(3): 507–33.

FT. 2015. "Emerging Markets Come Under Heavy Strain." *Financial Times*, 12–13 September. (p. 2).

Fu, X. 2015. *China's Path to Innovation*. Cambridge: Cambridge University Press.

Fu, X., and Y.D. Gong. 2011. "Indigenous and Foreign Innovation Efforts and Drivers of Technological Upgrading: Evidence from China." *World Development* 39: 1213–25.

G20. 2014. "Comprehensive Growth Strategy: Brazil." http://g20.org.tr/wp-content/uploads/2014/12/g20_comprehensive_growth_strategy_brazil.pdf

Gadiesh, O., P. Leung, and T. Vestring. 2007. "The Battle for China's Good-Enough Market." *Harvard Business Review* (September): 80–9.

Gaitán, Falvio, and Renato Boschi. 2015. "State-Business Labour-Relations and Patterns of Development in Latin America." In *New Directions in Comparative Capitalisms Research: Critical and Global Perspectives*, edited by Matthias Ebenau, Ian Bruff, and Christian May, 172–88. Houndmills: Palgrave Macmillan.

Gallagher, Kevin P. 2015. "Emerging Market Dilemma. The Paradox of Global Capital Flows." *The International Economy* (Winter): 52–3.

Gallagher, Mary E. 2004. "'Time Is Money, Efficiency Is Life': The Transformation of Labor Relations in China." *Studies in Comparative International Development* 39(2): 11–44.

Gallagher, Mary E. 2017. *Authoritarian Legality in China: Law, Workers, and the State*. Cambridge: Cambridge University Press.

Gallup. 2013. "Worldwide, Median Household Income About $10,000, Gallup Institute." 16 December. www.gallup.com/poll/166211/worldwide-median-household-income-000.aspx (accessed 12 November 2015).

Galtung, Johan. 1971. "A Structural Theory of Imperialism." *Journal of Peace Research* 8(2): 81–117.

Gambarotto, Francesca, and Stefano Solari. 2014. "The Peripheralization of Southern European Capitalism Within the EMU." *Review of International Political Economy* 22(4): 788–812.

Games, Dianna. 2011. "Doing Business in Post-Conflict and Fragile States: Challenges and Risks." *Development Planning Division Working Paper Series* No. 23. DBSA. www.dbsa.org/EN/About-Us/Publications/Documents/DPD%20No23.%20Doing%20business%20in%20post-conflict%20and%20fragile%20states-%20Challenges%20and%20risks.pdf (accessed 1 December 2018).

Games, Dianna. 2012. "South Africa as Africa's Gateway: A Perspective from Business." *SAIIA Policy Briefing* 46.

Gammeltoft, Peter, Jaya Prakash Pradhan, and Andrea Goldstein. 2010. "Emerging Multinationals: Home and Host Country Determinants and Outcomes." *International Journal of Emerging Markets* 5(3–4): 254–65.

Gelb, Stephen. 1991. "South Africa's Economic Crisis: An Overview." In *South Africa's Economic Crisis*, edited by Stephen Gelb, 1–32. Claremont: Zed Books.

Gentle, Leonard. 2008. "Escom to Eskom: From Racial Keynesian Capitalism to Neo-Liberalism (1910–1994)." In *Electric Capitalism: Recolonising Africa on the Power Grid*, edited by David A. McDonald, 50–72. Cape Town: HSRC.

Gerschenkron, Alexander. 1962. *Economic Backwardness in Historical Perspective: A Book of Essays*. Cambridge: Harvard University Press.

Gerth, Karl. 2010. "The Past, Present & Future of Consumerism in China – Interview with Karl Gerth." http://thechinaobserver.com/2010/08/04/the-past-present-future-of-consumerism-in-china-interview-with-karl-gerth/ (accessed 12 September 2015).

Ghosh, Jayati. 1998. "Liberalization Debates." In *The Indian Economy: Major Debates Since Independence*, edited by Terence J. Byres, 295–334. New Delhi: Oxford University Press.

Gill, Indermit, and Homi Kharas. 2007. *An East Asia Renaissance: Ideas for Economic Growth*. Washington, DC: World Bank.

Gill, Stephen. 1990. *American Hegemony and the Trilateral Commission*. Cambridge: Cambridge University Press.

Gilley, Bruce. 2008. "Legitimacy and Institutional Change: The Case of China." *Comparative Political Studies* 41(3): 259–84.

Gold, Thomas, Doug Guthrie, and David Wank. (eds.). 2002. *Social Connections in China: Institutions, Culture, and the Changing Nature of Guanxi*. Cambridge: Cambridge University Press.

Goldman, Merle, and Roderick MacFarquhar. 1999. "Dynamic Economy, Declining Party-State." In *The Paradox of China's Post-Mao Reforms*, edited by Merle Goldman and Roderick MacFarquhar, 3–29. Cambridge and London: Harvard University Press.

Goldstein, Andrea. 2002. "Embraer: From National Champion to Global Player." *CEPAL Review* 77: 97–115.

Goodspeed, Ingrid. 2012. "The Credit Market." In *Understanding South African Financial Markets*, edited by Wan Wykm, Ziets Botha Karin, and Ingrid Goodspeed, 491–519. Van Shaik: Pretoria.

Goswami, Omkar. 2002. "Corporate Governance in India." In *Taking Action Against Corruption in Asia and the Pacific*, edited by ADB-OECD, 85–106. Manila: Asian Development Bank.

Gouldner, Alvin G. 1960. "The Norm of Reciprocity: A Preliminary Statement." *American Sociological Review* 25(2): 161–78.

Gourevitch, Peter. 1978. "The Second Image Reversed: The International Sources of Domestic Politics." *International Organization* 32(4): 881–912.

Gourevitch, Peter. 1986. *Politics in Hard Times: Comparative Responses to International Economic Crises*. Ithaca and London: Cornell University Press.

Government of India. 2000. *Report of High Level Committee on Competition Policy & Law*. New Delhi: Government of India.

Graf, Patricia, and Thomas Stehnken. 2014. "Innovationssysteme in Brasilien und Mexiko im Vergleich." In *Die großen Schwellenländer: Ursachen und Folgen ihres Aufstiegs in der Weltwirtschaft*, edited by Andreas Nölke, Christian May, and Simone Claar, 153–73. Baden-Baden: Springer VS.

Gramsci, Antonio. 1971. *Selections from the Prison Notebooks*. London: Lawrence and Wishart.

Grant, Laura. 2014. "Research Shows Sharp Increase in Service Delivery Protests." *Mail & Guardian*, 12 February. http://mg.co.za/article/2014-02-12-research-shows-sharp-increase-in-service-delivery-protests (accessed 21 December 2015).

Gray, K., and C.N. Murphy. 2013. "Introduction: Rising Powers and the Future of Global Governance." *Third World Quarterly* 34(2): 183–93.

Gregory, Samantha. 2008. "Intellectual Property Rights and South Africa's Innovation Future." *Trade Policy Brief Report* No. 23. Johannesburg: South African Institute of International Affairs.

Grün, Roberto. 2010. "For a Brazilian Sociology of Finance." *Economic Sociology: The European Electronic Newsletter* 11(2): 10–15.

Gruss, Laura, and Tobias ten Brink. 2016. "The Development of the Chinese Photovoltaic Industry: An Advancing Role for the Central State?" *Journal of Contemporary China* 25(99): 453–66.

Gu, S., B-Å. Lundvall, J. Liu, F. Malerba, and Serger S. Schwaag. 2009. "China's System and Vision of Innovation: An Analysis in Relation to the Strategic Adjustment and the Medium- to Long-Term S&T Development Plan (2006–20)." *Industry and Innovation* 16(4–5): 369–88.

Guan, J., and R. Yam. 2015. "Effects of Government Financial Incentives in Firms' Innovation Performance in China: Evidences from Beijing in the 1990s." *Research Policy* 44(1): 273–82.

Guarin, Alejandro, Mark Furness, Imme Scholz, and Silke Weinlich. 2014. "Wirtschaftliche, politische und soziale Auswirkungen des Aufstiegs neuer Mittelschichten." In *Die großen Schwellenländer: Ursachen und Folgen ihres Aufstiegs in der Weltwirtschaft*, edited by Andreas Nölke, Christian May, and Simone Claar, 21–42. Wiesbaden: Springer VS.

Gumede, William. 2007. *Thabo Mbeki and the Battle for the Soul of the ANC*. London and New York: Zed Books.

Gupta, Nayanee, Christopher Weber, Vanessa Pena, Stephanie S. Shipp, and David Healey. 2013. *Innovation Policies of Brazil*. Alexandria: Institute of Defense Analysis.

Habbard, Pierre. 2010. *Corporate Governance in Brazil: An International Trade Union Perspective*. Paris: Hans-Böckler-Stiftung and Trade Uniona Advisory committee (TUAC) to the OECD.

Habib, Adam. 2009. "Reflections on the Development State for South Africa." *Politiy.org.za*, 15 July. www.polity.org.za/article/reflections-on-the-development-state-for-south-africa-2009-08-13) (accessed 15 February 2012).

Habib, Adam, and Vishnu Padayachee. 2000. "Economic Policy and Power Relations in South Africa's Transition to Democracy." *World Development* 28(2): 245–63.

Haggard, Stephen. 1990. *Pathways from the Periphery*. Ithaca: Cornell University Press.

Haggard, Stephen, and Sylvia Maxfield. 1996. "The Political Economy of Financial Internationalization in the Developing World." In *Internationalization and Domestic Politics*, edited by Robert O. Keohane and Helen V. Milner, 209–41. Cambridge and New York: Cambridge University Press.

Haggard, Stephen, Sylvia Maxfield, and Ben Ross Schneider. 1997. "Theories of Business and State-Buisness Relations." In *Business and the State in Developing Countries*, edited by Ben Ross Schneider and Sylvia Maxfield, 36–60. Ithaca: Cornell University Press.

Haigner, Stefan D., Stefan Jenewein, Friedrich Schneider, and Florian Wakolbinger. 2013. "Driving Forces of Informal Labour Supply and Demand in Germany." *International Labour Review* 152(3–4): 507–24.

Haines, Richard. 2015. "National Planning, Industrial Policy and the New Statism in Contemporary South Africa." In *Economic Planning and Industrial Policy in the Globalizing Economy: Concepts, Experience and Prospects*, edited by Murat Yülek, 149–78. Cham: Springer International Publishing.

Hall, Peter A. 2007. "The Evolution of Varieties of Capitalism in Europe." In *Beyond Varieties of Capitalism: Conflict, Contradictions, and Complementarities in the European Economy*, edited by Bob Hancké, Martin Rhodes, and Mark Thatcher, 39–85. Oxford: Oxford University Press.

Hall, Peter A., and Daniel W. Gingerich. 2004. "Varieties of Capitalism and Institutional Complementarities in the Macroeconomy An Empirical Analysis." *MPIfG Discussion Paper* 04/5. Cologne: Max Planck Institute for the Study of Societies.

Hall, Peter A., and David Soskice. 2001. "An Introduction to Varieties of Capitalism." In *Varieties of Capitalism: The Institutional Foundations of Comparative Advantage*, edited by Peter A. Hall and David Soskice, 1–68. Oxford: Oxford University Press.

Hancké, Bob, Martin Rhodes, and Mark Thatcher. (eds.). 2007. *Beyond Varieties of Capitalism: Conflict, Contradictions, and Complementarities in the European Economy*. Oxford: Oxford University Press.

Handley, Antoinette. 2014. "Varieties of Capitalists? The Middle Class, Private Sector and Economic Outcomes in Africa." *WIDER Working Paper* 2014/101. Helsinki: Word Institute for Economic Development Research.

Hansen, Michael W. 2009. "The Rise of Indian Multinationals: Explaining Outward Foreign Direct Investment from India." In *Institutional Dynamics and the Evolution of the Indian Economy*, edited by Rajesh Kumar and Murali Patibandla, 31–62. Houndmills and Basingstoke: Palgrave Macmillan.

Harriss-White, Barbara. 2003. *India Working: Essays on Society and Economy*. Cambridge: Cambrige University Press.

Hart, Keith, and Vishnu Padayachee. 2013. "A History of South African Capitalism in National and Global Perspective." *Transformation: Critical Perspectives on Southern Africa* 81–2: 55–8.

Hattingh, Damian, Bill Russo, Ade Sun-Basorun, and Arend van Wamelen. 2012. *The Rise of the African Consumer: A Report from McKinsey's Africa Consumer Insights Center*. Johannesburg: McKinsey & Company.

Hazans, Mihails. 2011. *Informal Workers Across Europe: Evidence from 30 Countries*. IZA DP No. 5871, Bonn: Institute for the Study of Labor.

Heilmann, Sebastian. 2008. "Policy Experimentation in China's Economic Rise." *Studies in Comparative International Development* 43(1): 1–26.

Heilmann, Sebastian. 2011. "Making Plans for Markets: Policies for the Long Term in China." *Harvard Asia Quarterly* 13(2): 33–40.

Heires, Marcel, and Andreas Nölke. (ed.). 2013. *Die politische Ökonomie der Finanzialisierung*. Wiesbaden: Springer VS.

Helleiner, Eric. 1994. *States and the Reemergence of Global Finance*. Ithaca: Cornell University Press.

Herd, Richard, Vincent Koen, and Anders Reutersward. 2010. "China's Labour Market in Transition: Job Creation, Migration and Regulation." *OECD Economics Department Working Papers*.

Herr, Hansjörg. 2011. "Perspectives on High Growth and Rising Inequality." In *China's Labor Question*, edited by Christoph Scherrer, 7–27. München and Mering: Rainer Hampp Verlag.

The Hindu. 2014. "Murli Deora: The Longest Serving Petroleum Minister." 24 November.

Hirsch, Alan. 2005. *Season of Hope: Economic Reforms Under Mandela and Mbeki*. Scottsville: University of KwaZulu-Natal Press.

Hirschman, Albert O. 1968. "The Political Economy of Import-Substituting Industrialization in Latin America." *The Quarterly Journal of Economics* 82(1): 1–32.

Hlongwane, Sipho. 2012. "Cyril Ramaphosa's Marikana Email Batters ANC Heavyweight's Reputation." *The Guardian*, 24 October. www.theguardian.com/world/2012/oct/24/cyril-ramaphosa-lonmin-email-reputation (accessed 21 December 2015).

Hobsbawm, Eric J. 1999. *Das imperiale Zeitalter. 1875–1914*. Frankfurt/M.: Fischer.

Hollingsworth, Rogers W., and Robert Boyer. 1997. "Coordination of Economic Actors & Social Systems of Production." In *Contemporary Capitalism: The Embeddedness of Institutions*, edited by Rogers W. Hollingsworth and Robert Boyer, 1–47. Cambridge and New York: Cambridge University Press.

Holmes, Thalia. 2013. "SA Business Is Blooming in Africa." *Mail & Guardian*, 28 June. http://mg.co.za/article/2013-06-28-00-sa-business-is-blooming-in-africa (accessed 21 December 2015).

Höpner, Martin. 2005. "What Connects Industrial Relations and Corporate Governance? Explaining Institutional Complementarity." *MPIfG Discussion Paper*. Köln: Max-Planck-Institut für Gesellschaftsforschung. www.mpifg.de/people/mh/paper/Hoepner%202005%20-%20Explaining%20Complementarity.pdf (accessed 13 October 2011).

Höpner, Martin. 2009. "'Spielarten des Kapitalismus' als Schule der vergleichenden Staatstätigkeitsforschung." *Zeitschrift für Vergleichende Politikwissenschaft* 3(2): 303–27.

Höpner, Martin, and Armin Schäfer. 2012. "Integration Among Unequals: How the Heterogeneity of European Varieties of Capitalism Shapes the Social and Democratic Potential of the EU." *MPIfG Discussion Paper* 12/5. Köln: Max-Planck-Institut für Gesellschaftsforschung.

HSRC/CeSTII. 2014a. "Key Results Summary: Research and Experimental Development (R&D) Survey 2012/13." 3 December. Pretoria. www.hsrc.ac.za/uploads/pageContent/5439/Key%20Results%20Summary%20%20R&D%20Survey%202012-13.pdf (accessed 21 December 2015).

HSRC/CeSTII. 2014b. "National Survey of Research and Experimental Development (2012/13), Results." Presentation, 3 December. Pretoria. www.hsrc.ac.za/uploads/pageContent/5439/RD%20Survey%20Results%202012-13.pdf (accessed 21 December 2015).

Huang, C., and Y. Wu. 2012. "State-Led Technological Development: A Case of China's Nanotechnology Development." *World Development* 40(5): 970–82.

Huang, Yasheng. 2008. *Capitalism with Chinese Characteristics: Entrepreneurship and the State*. Cambridge and New York: Cambridge University Press.

Hung, Ho-Fung. 2008. "Rise of China and the Global Overaccumulation Crisis." *Review of International Political Economy* 15(2): 149–79.

Hurun. 2010. "The Hurun Rich List." www.hurun.net/listreleaseen512.aspx

IDC/Industrial Development Corporation of South Africa Limited. 2014. "Expanding Industrial Capacity for Development." Integrated Report for the Year Ended, 31 March. www.idc.co.za/ir2014/images/pdf/ar2014.pdf (accessed 19 December 2015).

IIF. 2015. "Corporate Debt in Emerging Markets: Where are the Risks?" *CMM Research Note*, 1 June.

Ikenberry, J.G. 2008. "The Rise of China and the Future of the West." *Foreign Affairs* 87(1): 23–37.

ILO. 2012. *Statistical Update on Employment in the Informal Economy*. Geneva: International Labour Organization.

ILO. 2013a. *Global Wage Report: Wages and Equitable Growth*. Geneva: International Labour Organization.

ILO. 2013b. *Women and Men in the Informal Economy: A Statistical Picture*, 2nd Ed., Geneva: International Labour Organization.

ILO. 2015. "LABORSTA Labour Statistics Database, 1998–2015: Lockouts and Strikes."

ILOSTAT. 2015. "ILOSTAT Country Profiles Database."

ILOSTAT. 2016. "Key Indicators of the Labour Market (KILM) Database."

IMF. 2003. *World Economic Outlook: Public Debt in Emerging Markets*. Washington, DC: International Monetary Fund.

IMF. 2012a. *World Economic Outlook: Coping with High Debt and Sluggish Growth*. Washington, DC: International Monetary Fund.

IMF. 2012b. *Brazil: Consumer Credit Growth and Household Financial Stress*. Washington, DC: International Monetary Fund.

IMF. 2013. *Brazil: Selected Issues*. Washington, DC: International Monetary Fund.

IMF. 2015. *World Economic Outlook 2015: Adjusting to Lower Commodity Prices*. Washington, DC: International Monetary Fund.

IMF South Africa. 2012. "Article IV Consultation." IMF Country Report No. 12/247. Washington, DC: IMF. Online. www.imf.org/external/pubs/ft/scr/2012/cr12247.pdf (accessed 21 December 2015).

The Innovation Hub. n.d. "New Study Shows How South African Companies Are Managing Their Innovation." www.theinnovationhub.com/index.php?option=com_content&view=article&id=82:new-study-shows-how-south-african-companies-

are-managing-their-innovation&catid=10:corporate-news&Itemid=80 (accessed 23 June 2015).

International Labor Organisation. 2013. "Global Wage Report 2012/13, Wages and Equitable Growth." Geneva: International Labor Organisation. www.ilo.org/wcmsp5/groups/public/@dgreports/@dcomm/@publ/documents/publication/wcms_194843.pdf (accessed 19 December 2015).

IODASA. n.d. "King Report on Corporate Governance in SA." www.iodsa.co.za. www.iodsa.co.za/?kingIII (accessed 19 December 2015).

Isa, Mariam. 2015. "Uncertainty Makes Firms Reluctant to Invest in South Africa, Survey Shows." *Business Day*, 19 February. www.bdlive.co.za/economy/2013/02/19/uncertainty-makes-firms-reluctant-to-invest-in-south-africa-survey-shows (accessed 21 December 2015).

Ithala. n.d. "Ithala: About Us." www.ithala.co.za/ithala/about-us/history (accessed 21 December 2015).

Jackson, Gregory, and Richard Deeg. 2006. "How Many Varieties of Capitalism? Comparing the Comparative Institutional Analyses of Capitalist Diversity." *MPIfG Discussion Paper* 06/2. Cologne: Max Planck Institute for the Study of Societies.

Jaeger, Markus. 2013. "Time for China to Become More Brazilian." *Deutsche Bank Research Talking Point*, 9 July.

Jäger, Johannes, Bernhard Leubolt, and Lukas Schmidt. 2014. "Alles Extraktivismus in Südamerika? Rohstoffrenten und Politik in Brasilien, Chile und Venezuela." *Journal für Entwicklungspolitik* 30(3): 9–26.

James, Harold. 2008. "Family Values or Crony Capitalism?" *Capitalism and Society* 3(1): Article 5.

Jansen, Jonathan. 2003. "The State of Higher Education in South Africa: From Masification to Merges." In *State of the Nation: South Africa, 2003–2004*, edited by John Daniel, Adam Habib, and Roger Southall, 290–311. Cape Town: HSRC Press.

Jefferson, Gary H., Renai Jiang, and Daniel L. Tortorice. 2014. "Restructuring China's Research Institutes: Impacts on China's Research Orientation and Productivity." http://ssrn.com/abstract=2443546 (accessed 13 October 2015).

Jeffery, Anthea. 2014. *BEE Helping or Hurting?* Cape Town: Tafelberg.

Jenkins, Rhys, and Alexandre de Freitas Barbosa. 2012. "Fear for Manufacturing? China and the Future of Industry in Brazil and Latin America." *The China Quarterly* 209: 59–81.

Jenkins, Rob. 1999. *Democratic Politics and Economic Reform in India*. Cambridge: Cambridge University Press.

Jerschefske, Danielle. 2011. "South Africa Focus: Beyond the BRICs." *Labels and Labeling*, Issue 1 (6 June). www.labelsandlabeling.com/news/features/south-africa-focus-beyond-brics (accessed 21 December 2015).

Jessop, Bob. 2001. "What Follows Fordism?" In *Phases of Capitalist Development: Booms, Crises and Globalizations*, edited by Robert Albritton, Makoto Itoh, Richard Westra, and Alan Zuege, 283–300. Houndmills and Basingstoke: Palgrave Macmillan.

Jessop, Bob. 2002. *The Future of the Capitalist State*. New York and London: Wiley & Sons.

Jessop, Bob. 2014. "Variegated Capitalism, das Modell Deutschland, and the Eurozone Crisis." *Journal of Contemporary European Studies* 22(3): 248–60.

Jessop, Bob. 2015. "Comparative Capitalisms and/or Variegated Capitalism." In *New Directions in Comparative Capitalisms Research: Critical and Global Perspectives*, edited by Matthias Ebenau, Ian Bruff, and Christian May, 65–82. Houndmills and Basingstoke: Palgrave Macmillan.

Jha, Praveen. 2010. "Labour Regulation and Economic Performance: What Do We Know?" *The Indian Journal of Labour Economics* 53(1): 89–111.

Jha, Praveen. 2018. "India's Macroeconomic Policy Regime and Challenges of Employment: Some Reflections on the Manufacturing Sector." *ICDD Working Paper No. 20*. Kassel: The International Center for Development and Decent Work.

Johnson, Chalmers. 1982. *MITI and the Japanese Miracle: The Growth of Industrial Policy 1925–1975*. Stanford, CA: Stanford University Press.

Johnson, Simon, Rafael La Porta, Florencio Lopez-de-Silanes, and Andrei Shleifer. 2000. "Tunneling." *American Economic Review* 90(2): 22–7.

Johnston, Alastair I. 2007. *Social States: China in International Institutions, 1980–2000*. Princeton: Princeton University Press.

Johnston, Alison, and Aidan Regan. 2015. "European Monetary Integration and the Incompatibility of National Varieties of Capitalism." *Journal of Common Market Studies*, advance online publication.

Johnston, Alison, and Aidan Regan. 2016. "European Monetary Integration and the Incompatibility of National Varieties of Capitalism." *Journal of Common Market Studies* 54(2): 318–36.

Jones, Stuart. 2010. "The Banking Sector." In *South African Economy and Policy, 1990–2000*, edited by Stuart Jones and Robert W. Vivian, 197–222. Manchester: Manchester University Press.

Joseph, K.J., and Krian Kumar Kakarlapudi. 2014. "Innovation and Development in India: Changing Paradigms and Trajectories." In *The Oxford Handbook of the Indian Economy in the 21st Century: Understanding the Inherent Dynamism*, edited by Ashima Goyal, 791–821. New Delhi: Oxford University Press.

Kably, Lubna. 2014. "Professionals Step Up Role in Policy-Making." *The Times of India*, 6 December.

Kahler, M. 2013. "Rising Powers and Global Governance: Reforming a Resilient Status Quo." *International Affairs* 89(3): 711–29.

Kalinowski, Thomas. 2013. "Regulating International Finance and the Diversity of Capitalism." *Socio-Economic Review* 11(3): 471–96.

Kaltenbrunner, Annina, and Juan Pablo Painceira. 2015. "Developing Countries' Changing Nature of Financial Integration and New Forms of External Vulnerability: The Brazilian Experience." *Cambridge journal of Economics* 39: 1281–306.

Kang, David C. 2002. *Crony Capitalism: Corruption and Development in South Korea and the Philippines*. Cambridge and New York: Cambridge University Press.

Kang, David C. 2010. "Hierarchy and Legitimacy in International Systems: The Tribute System in Early Modern East Asia." *Security Studies* 19(4): 591–622. DOI: 10.1080/09636412.2010.524079.

Kantha, Sharmily. 2013. *The Big Leap: How Indian Companies Leveraged Reforms for Success*. Noida: Harper Collins.

Kaplan, David. 2009. "Intellectual Property Rights and Innovation in South Africa: A Framwork." In *The Economics of Intellectual Property in South Africa*, 1–14. Geneva: WIPO.

Kathuria, Vinish. 2010. "Does the Technology Gap Influence Spillovers? A Post-Liberalization Analysis of Indian Manufacturing Industries." *Oxford Development Studies* 38(2): 145–70.

Kattel, Rainer, and Annalisa Primi. 2012. "The Periphery Paradox in Innovation Policy: Latin America and Eastern Europe Compared." In *Development and Semi-Periphery: Post-Neoliberal Trajectories in South America and Central Eastern Europe*, edited by R. Boschi and C.H. Santana, 265–304. London, New York and New Delhi: Anthem Press.

Katzenstein, Peter J. 1976. "International Relations and Domestic Structures: Foreign Economic Policies of Advanced Industrial States." *International Organization* 30(1): 1–45.

Katzenstein, Peter J. 1977. "Conclusion: Domestic Structures and Strategies of Foreign Economic Policy." *International Organization* 31(4): 879–920.

Katzenstein, Peter J. (ed.). 1978a. *Between Power and Plenty: Foreign Economic Policies of Advanced Industrial States*. Madison: University of Wisconsin Press.

Katzenstein, Peter J. 1978b: "Conclusion: Domestic Structures and Strategies of Foreign Economic Policy." In *Between Power and Plenty: Foreign Economic Policies of Advanced Industrial States*, edited by Peter J. Katzenstein, 295–336. Madison: University of Wisconsin Press.

Kaushik, Kshama, and Kaushik Dutta. 2012. *India Means Business: How the Elephant Earned Its Stripes*. Oxford: Oxford University Press.

Kay, Cristóbal. 2002. "Why East Asia Overtook Latin America: Agrarian Reform, Industrialisation and Development." *Third World Quarterly* 23(6): 1073–102.

Kennedy, Scott. 2011. "The Business of Lobbying in China." In *Beyond the Middle Kingdom*, edited by Scott Kennedy, 113–35. Stanford, CA: Stanford University Press.

Kew, Janice. 2013. "McDonald's to Bugaboo Gain from South Africa's Black Middle Class." *Mail & Guardian*, 21 June. http://mg.co.za/article/2013-06-21-00-mcdonalds-to-bugaboo-gain-from-south-africa-black-middle-class (accessed 21 December 2015).

Khanna, Tarun, and K. Palepu. 2000. "Is Group Affiliation Profitable in Emerging Markets? An Analysis of Diversified Indian Business Groups." *Journal of Finance* 55(2): 867–91.

Kharas, Homi, and Harinder Kohli. 2011. "What Is the Middle Income Trap, Why Do Countries Fall into It, and How Can It Be Avoided?" *Global Journal of Emerging Market Economies* 3(3): 281–9.

Khumalo, Kabelo. 2018. "Moody's Upgrades Banks Outlook." 12 September. www.iol.co.za/business-report/companies/moodys-upgrades-banks-outlook-17022062

Kidwai, Naina Lal. 2012. *Contemporary Banking in India*. New Delhi: Businessworld Books.

King, Lawrence P., and Iván Szelényi. 2005. "Post-Communist Economic Systems." In *The Handbook of Economic Sociology*, edited by Neil J. Smelser and Richard Swedberg, 205–29. Princeton: Princeton University Press.

Kingstone, Peter R. 1999. *Crafting Coalitions for Reform: Business Preferences, Political Institutions, and Neoliberal Reforms in Brazil*. University Park, PA: Pennsylvania State University Press.

Kochanek, Stanley A. 1974. *Business and Politics in India*. Berkeley: University of California Press.

Kochanek, Stanley A. 1987. "Briefcase Politics in India: The Congress Party and the Business Elite." *Asian Survey* 27(12): 1278–301.

Kochanek, Stanley A. 2007. "Liberalization and Business Lobbying in India." In Mukherji 2007a, 412–40.

Koen, V., R. Herd, and S. Hill. 2013. "China's March to Prosperity: Reforms to Avoid the Middle-Income Trap." *OECD Economics Department Working Papers*, No. 1093. http://dx.doi.org/10.1787/5k3wd3c4219w-en

Kohli, Atul. 2004. *State-Directed Development: Political Power and Industrialization in the Global Periphery*. Cambridge: Cambridge University Press.

Kohli, Atul. 2007. "State, Business, and Economic Growth in India." *Studies in Comparative International Development* 42(1): 87–114.

Kohli, Atul. 2011. "Politics of Economic Growth in India, 1980–2005: The 1980s." In *Economic Reforms & Growth in India*, edited by Pulapre Balakrishnan, 55–77. Hyderabad: Orient Blackswan.

Koyama, Takeshi, and Stephen S. Golub. 2006. "OECD's FDI Regulatory Restrictiveness Index: Revision and Extension to More Economies." *OECD Working Papers on International Investment*, 2006/04. OECD Publishing. http://dx.doi.org/10.1787/112474484663

Krippner, Greta R. 2011. *Capitalizing on Crisis: The Political Origins of the Rise of Finance*. Cambridge and London: Harvard University Press.

Krishnan, Rishikesha T. 2010. *From Jugaad to Systemic Innovation: The Challenge for India*. Bangalore: The Utpreka Foundation.

Krishnan, Rishikesha, and Ganesh Prabhu. 1999. "Creating Successful New Products: Challenges for Indian Industry." *Economic and Political Weekly* 34(31): M114–20.

Kromphardt, Jürgen. 1987. *Konzeptionen und Analysen des Kapitalismus: von seiner Entstehung bis zur Gegenwart*. Göttingen: Vandenhoeck & Ruprecht.

Kruss, Glenda, and Jo Lorentzen. 2009. "The South African Innovation Policies: Potential and Constraint." In *BRICS and Development Alternatives: Innovation Systems and Policies*, edited by José E. Cassiolato and Virginia Vitorino, 163–89. London: Anthem Press.

Kumar, Nagesh. 2015. "Reforms and Global Economic Integration of Teh Indian Economy: Emerging Patterns, Challenges, and Future Directions." In *A Concise Handbook of the Indian Economy in the 21st Century*, edited by Ashima Goyal, 124–60. New Delhi: Oxford University Press.

Kumar, Nirmalya, and Phanish Puranam. 2012. *India Inside: The Emerging Innovation Challenge to the West*. Boston, MA: Harvard Business Review Press.

Kynge, James, and Roger Blitz. 2015. "Surge in Emerging Market Capital Outflows Hits Growth and Currencies." *Financial Times*, 18 August.

Kynge, James, and Jonathan Wheatley. 2015. "Emerging Markets: The Great Unravelling." *Financial Times*, 1 April.

La Porta, Rafael, Florencio Lopez-De-Silanes, and Andrei Shleifer. 1999. "Corporate Ownership Around the World." *Journal of Finance* 54(2): 471–517.

Lall, R. 2012. "From Failure to Failure: The Politics of International Banking Regulation." *Review of International Political Economy* 19(4): 609–38.

Lam, Willy Wo-Lap. 2015. *Chinese Politics in the Era of Xi Jinping: Renaissance, Reform, or Retrogression?* New York: Routledge.

Lane, Christel, and Martin Myant. (eds.). 2007. *Varieties of Capitalism in Post-Communist Countries*. Basingstoke: Palgrave Macmillan.

Lane, Christel, and Geoffrey Wood. 2009. "Capitalist Diversity and Diversity Within Capitalism." *Economy and Society* 38(4): 531–51. DOI: 10.1080/03085140903190300.

Lane, Christel, and Geoffrey Wood. (eds.). 2012. *Capitalist Diversity and Diversity Within Capitalism*. London: Routledge.

Lapavitsas, Costas. 2009. "Financialised Capitalism: Crisis and Financial Expropriation." *Historical Materialism* 17(2): 114–48.

Lardy, Nicholas R. 1998. *China's Unfinished Economic Revolution*. Washington, DC: Brookings.

Lardy, Nicholas R. 2002. *Integrating China into the Global Economy*. Washington, DC: Brookings.

Lardy, Nicholas R. 2016. "No Need to Panic, China's Banks Are in Pretty Good Shape." *Financial Times*, June 1. https://piie.com/commentary/op-eds/no-need-panic-chinas-banks-are-pretty-good-shape (accessed 17 September 2017).

Laubscher, Jac. 2010. "An Evaluation of South Africa's Industrial Policy." *Sanlam Expert Opinions*. Sanlam. www.sanlam.co.za/wps/wcm/connect/Sanlam_EN/sanlam/

media+centre/expert+opinions/an+evaluation+of+south+africas+industrial+policy (accessed 6 September 2013).

Laurenceson, James, and Danielle Rodgers. 2010. "China's Macroeconomic Volatility – How Important Is the Business Cycle?" *China Economic Review* 21(2): 324–33.

Lavinas, Lena. 2018. "The Collateralization of Social Policy Under Financialized Capitalism." *Development and Change* 49: 502–17. DOI: 10.1111/dech.12370.

Lazonick, William, and Mary O'Sullivan. 2000. "Maximizing Shareholder Value: A New Ideology for Corporate Governance." *Economy and Society* 29(1): 13–35.

Lazzarini, Sergio. 2011. *Capitalismo de Lacos: Os Donos do Brasil e suas Conexoes*. Sao Paulo: Campus.

Lazzarini, Sergio, Aldo Musacchio, Rodrigo Bandeira-de-Mello, and Rosilene Marcon. 2011. "What Do Development Banks Do? Evidence from Brazil, 2002–2009." http://ssrn.com/abstract=1969843 (accessed 20 October 2013).

Leahy, Joe. 2015. "BNDES: Lenders of First Resort for Brazil's Tycoons." *Financial Times*, 11 January.

Ledeneva, Alena V. 1998. *Russia's Economy of Favours: Blat, Networking, and Informal Exchange*. Cambridge: Cambridge University Press.

Lee, Ching Kwan. 2016. "Precarization or Empowerment? Reflections on Recent Labor Unrest in China." *Journal of Asian Studies* 75(2): 317–33.

Lee, Il Houng, Murtaza Syed, and Liu Xueyan. 2012. "Is China Over-Investing and Does It Matter?" *IMF Working Paper* WP/12/277. Washington, DC: International Monetary Fund.

Lehmbruch, Gerhard. 1984. "Concertation and the Structure of Corporatist Networks." In *Order and Conflict in Contemporary Capitalism*, edited by John Goldthorpe, 60–80. Oxford: Clarendon Press.

Leibbrandt, Murray, Ingrif Woolard, Hayley McEwen, and Charlotte Koep. 2010. "Employment and Inequality Outcomes in South Africa. – Southern Africa Labour and Development Research Unit (SALDRU) and School of Economics." University of Cape Town. www.oecd.org/employment/emp/45282868.pdf (accessed 19 December 2015).

Lensink, Robert, Remco van der Molen, and Shubashis Gangopadhyay. 2003. "Business Groups, Financing Constraints and Investment: The Case of India." *The Journal of Development Studies* 40(2): 93–119.

Lepsius, M. Rainer. 1995. "Institutionenanalyse und Institutionenpolitik." In *Politische Institutionen im Wandel, Kölner Zeitschrift für Soziologie und Sozialpsychologie, Sonderheft 35*: 392–403.

Lester, Alan, Etienne Louis Nel, and Tony Binns. 2000. *South Africa, Past, Present and Future: Gold at the End of the Rainbow?* New York: Longman.

Leubolt, Bernhard. 2015. *Transformation von Ungleichheitsregimes: Gleichheitsorientierte Politik in Brasilien und Südafrika*. Wiesbaden: Springer VS.

Leung, Chris. 2011. *China: Inflation and Labor Productivity*. Frankfurt am Main: Deutsche Bank. www.lntmf.com/Uploads/Knowledge-Center/cn_21_February_2011.pdf (accessed 20 October 2013).

Lewis, Jeffrey T., and Rogerio Jelmayer. 2015. "Brazilian Inflation and Growth Get Worse." *The Wall Street Journal*, 24 June.

Li, Cheng. 2010. "China's Communist Party-State: The Structure and Dynamics of Power." In *Politics in China: An Introduction*, edited by William A. Joseph, 165–91. New York: Oxford University Press.

Li, Guoping, and Hong Zhou. 2016. "The Systematic Politicization of China's Stock Markets." *Journal of Contemporary China* 25(99): 422–37.

Li, H.B., L.S. Meng, Q. Wang, and L-A. Zhou. 2008. "Political Connections, Financing and Firm Performance: Evidence from Chinese Private Firms." *Journal of Development Economics* 87: 283–99.

Li, Shaomin, and Jun Xia. 2008. "The Roles and Performance of State Firms and Non-State Firms in China's Economic Transition." *World Development* 36(1): 39–54.

Liang, Yan. 2010. "China and the Global Financial Crisis: Assessing the Impacts and Policy Responses." *China & World Economy* 18(3): 56–72.

Lieberthal, K., and W. Jisi. 2012. *Addressing U.S.-China Strategic Distrust*. Washington, DC: Brookings.

Liefner, I., C. Brömer, and G. Zeng. 2012. "Knowledge Absorption of Optical Technology Companies in Shanghai, Pudong." *Applied Geography* 32: 171–84.

Lin, Yi. 2011. "Turning Rurality into Modernity: Suzhi Education in a Suburban Public School of Migrant Children in Xiamen." *The China Quarterly* 206(2): 313–30.

Lipset, Seymour M. 1959. "Some Social Requisites of Democracy: Economic Development and Political Legitimacy." *The American Political Science Review* 53(1): 69–105.

Lipton, Merle, and Charles Simkins. (eds.). 1993. *State and Market in Post-Apartheid South Africa*. Johannesburg: Wits University Press.

López, A. Ricardo, and Barbara Weinstein. (eds.). 2012. *The Making of the Middle Class: Toward a Transnational History*. Durham: Duke University Press.

López Vicente, Fernando, and José Maria Serena Garralda. 2014. "Macroeconomic Policy in Brazil: Inflation Targeting, Public Debt Structure and Credit Policies." *Documentos Ocasionales* No. 1405. Madrid: Banco de Espana.

Lubinski, Christina, Jeffrey Fear, and Paloma Fernandez Perez. (eds.). 2013. *Family Multinationals: Enterpreneurship, Governance, and Pathways to Internationalization*. London: Routledge.

Luo, Siqi. 2011. "Collective Contracts, But No Collective Bargaining." In *China's Labor Question*, edited by Christoph Scherrer, 49–69. München and Mering: Rainer Hampp Verlag.

Lüthje, Boy, Siqi Luo, and Hao Zhang. 2013. *Socio-Economic Transformation and Industrial Relations in China*. Frankfurt and New York: Campus.

Lyons, Thomas P. 1990. "Planning and Interprovincial Co-ordination in Maoist China." *The China Quarterly* 121: 36–60.

Magnus, George. 2013. 1*Hitting a BRIC Wall: The Risk of the Middle Income Trap*. UBS Investment Research Economic Insights, Zurich: UBS Investment.

Maia, Jorge, Lumkile Mondi, and Simon Roberts. 2005. "Industrial Development and Industrial Finance in Brazil and South Africa: A Comparative Assessment." *Annual Forum* 2005.

Mail and Guardian. 2011a. "Black Businesses Opt Out of Business Unity South Africa." 7 September. http://mg.co.za/article/2011-09-07-economic-revolution-black-businesses-quit-busa (accessed 6 September 2013).

Mail and Guardian. 2011b. "Business Unity SA Briefs Zuma on BBC." 27 August. http://mg.co.za/article/2011-09-27-business-unity-sa-briefs-zuma-on-bbc (accessed 19 December 2015).

Majumdar, Sumit K. 2012. *India's Late Late Industrial Revolution*. New Delhi: Cambridge University Press.

Majumdar, Sumit K. 2018. *Lost Glory: India's Capitalism Story*. New Delhi: Oxford University Press.

Makhanya, Mandla S., and Jeanette C. Botha. 2015. "Higher Education in South Africa: A Case Study." In *Democratizing Higher Education International Comparative Perspectives*, edited by Patrick Blessinger and John P. Anchan, 125–40. New York: Routledge.

Mandel, Ernest. 1980. *Long Waves of Capitalist Development*. Cambridge: Cambridge University Press.

Mani, Sunil. 2009. "Is India Becoming More Innovative Since 1991? Some Disquieting Features." *Economic and Political Weekly* 44(46): 41–51.

Mani, Sunil. 2012. "High Skilled Migration and Remittances." In *Growth, Development, and Diversity: India's Record Since Liberalization*, edited by K. Pushpangadan and V.N. Balasubramanyam, 181–210. Oxford: Oxford University Press.

Mani, Sunil. 2013. "The Science Technology and Innovation Policy 2013." *Economic and Political Weekly* 48(10): 16–19.

Mann, Michael. 1998. *Geschichte der Macht, Dritter Band. Teil I: Die Entstehung von Klassen und Nationalstaaten*. Frankfurt and New York: Campus.

Marais, Hein. 2001. *South Africa: Limits to Change: The Political Economy of Transition*. Kenwyn: UCT Press.

Marois, Thomas. 2013. "State-Owned Banks and Development: Dispelling Mainstream Myths." Occassional Paper no. 21. Municipality Service Project. http://eprints.soas.ac.uk/17808/1/OccasionalPaper21_Marois_State-owned_Banks_and_Development_Dec2013.pdf (accessed 19 December 2015).

Marrian, Natasha. 2014. "Cosatu Expels Numsa." *Business Day*, 8 November. www.bdlive.co.za/national/labour/2014/11/08/cosatu-expels-numsa (accessed 21 December 2015).

Masiero, Gilmar, and Luiz Caseiro. 2012. "State Support for Emerging Market Multinationals: The Brazilian and Chinese Experiences." *UC-CIFF-IELAT Working Paper* No. 10. Madrid, Spain: Centro Internacional de FormacioÌn Financiera (CIFF), Universidad de AlcalaÌ.

Masiero, Gilmar, Mario H. Ogasavara, Luiz Caseiro, and Silas Ferreira. 2014. "Financing the Development of Brazilian Multinationals into Europe: The Role of the Brazilian Development Bank (BNDES)." In *Multinational Corporations from Emerging Markets: State Capitalism 3.0*, edited by Andreas Nölke, 130–52. Houndmills: Palgrave Macmillan.

Matsilele, Trust. 2015. "Moody's Downgrades Development Institutions." *Cnbcafrica*, 12 February. www.cnbcafrica.com/news/southern-africa/2014/11/11/idc-dbsa-moodys/ (accessed 19 December 2015).

Mauss, Marcel. 1966. *The Gift: Forms and Functions of Exchange in Archaic Societies*. London: Cohen & West.

Maxfield, Sylvia, and Ben Ross Schneider. 1997. *Business and the State in Developing Countries*. Ithaca: Cornell University Press.

May, Christian, and Andreas Nölke. 2014. "BRIC Capitalism and the New Illiberal Global Order." In *The International Political Economy of Trade*, edited by David A. Deese, 450–70. Cheltenham: Edward Elgar.

May, Christian, and Andreas Nölke. 2015. "Critical Institutionalism in Studies of Comparative Capitalisms: Conceptual Considerations and Research Programme." In *New Directions in Comparative Capitalisms Research: Critical and Global Perspectives*, edited by Matthias Ebenau, Ian Bruff, and Christian May, 83–100. Houndmills and Basingstoke: Palgrave Macmillan.

May, Christian, and Andreas Nölke. 2018. "Dangers of Residual Dependency in State-Permeated Capitalism: The Case of Brazil During Labor Party Rule." *Revue de la Regulation* 24(2): 1–24.

May, Christian, Andreas Nölke, and Michael Schedelik. 2019b. "Institutional Complementarities in Brazilian Industrial Policies: The Case of Finance." In *Untangling Industrial Policy: Ideas and Coordination Between State and business*, edited by Moisés Balestro and Gaitán, Flávio, 102–26. Brasilia: Verbena Publishers.

May, Christian, Andreas Nölke, and Tobias ten Brink. 2019a. *Public-Private Coordination in Large Emerging Economies: The Case of Brazil, India and China*, in print. https://doi.org/10.1080/13569775.2018.1555781

Mazumdar, Dipak, and Sandip Sarkar. 2009. "The Employment Problem in India and the Phenomenon of the 'Missing Middle'." *The Indian Journal of Labour Economics* 52(1): 43–55.

Mazumdar, Surajit. 2008a. "Crony Capitalism: Caricature or Category?" *ISID Working Paper* 2008/02. New Delhi: Institute for Studies in Industrial Development.

Mazumdar, Surajit. 2008b. "Crony Capitalism and India: Before and After Liberalization." *ISID Working Paper* 2008/04. New Delhi: Institute for Studies in Industrial Development.

Mazumdar, Surajit. 2008c: "The Analysis of Business Groups: Some Observations with Reference to India." *ISID Working Paper* 2008/11. New Delhi: Institute for Studies in Industrial Development.

Mazumdar, Surajit. 2010: "Big Business and Economic Nationalism in India." *ISID Working Paper* 2010/09. New Delhi: Institute for Studies in Industrial Development.

Mazumdar, Surajit. 2012. "The Indian Corporate Structure and the 'Theory' of Emerging Market Business Groups." *History and Sociology of South Asia* 6(2): 87–109.

Mazumdar, Surajit. 2013. "Continuity and Change in Indian Capitalism." In *The BRICs and Emerging Economies in Comparative Perspective*, edited by Uwe Becker, 79–99. London: Routledge.

Mazzucato, Mariana. 2013. *The Entrepreneurial State: Debunking Public vs. Private Sector Myths*. London: Anthem Press.

McCartney, Matthew. 2009. *India – The Political Economy of Growth Stagnation and the State, 1951–2007*. Abingdon: Routledge.

McCartney, Matthew. 2010. *Political Economy, Growth, and Liberalisation in India 1991–2008*. Abingdon: Routledge.

McDonald, David A. 2008. "Electric Capitalism: Conceptualising Electricity and Capital Accumulation in (South) Africa." In *Electric Capitalism: Recolonising Africa on the Power Grid*, edited by David A. McDonald, 1–49. Cape Town: HSRC.

McDonald, David A. 2011. "Electricity and the Minerals-Energy Complex in South Africa." *Africa Review* 3(1): 65–87.

McDonald, Hamish. 2010. *Ambani and Sons*. New Delhi: Lotus Collection.

McGrath, Simon, and Akoojee Salim. 2009. "Vocational Education and Training for Sustainability in South Africa: The Role of Public and Private Provision." *International Journal of Educational Development* 29(2): 149–56.

McGregor, Richard. 2010. *The Party: The Secret World of China's Communist Rulers*. New York: HarperCollins.

McKenna, Elizabeth. 2014. "Politics and Protests (and Lack Thereof) in Brazil." Center for Latin American Studies, Berkeley: University of California.

McKinley, Dale. 2003. "Cosatu and the Tripartite Alliance Since 1994." In *Rethinking the Labour Movement in the "New South Africa"*, edited by Tom Bramble and Franco Barchiesi, 43–61. Hants: Ashgate.

McKinsey & Company. 2015. "The China Effect on Global Innovation." Research Bulletin, McKinsey Global Institute.

McKinsey Global Institute. 2015. "Debt and (Not Much) Deleveraging." www.mckinsey.com/insights/economic_studies/debt_and_not_much_deleveraging (accessed 3 February 2016).

McNally, Christopher A. 2011. "State Capitalism Is Dead! Long Live State Capitalism! Rebalancing China's Political Economy." Paper presented at the annual meeting of the Association of Asian Studies. Honolulu, 31 March.

McNally, Christopher A. 2012. "Sino-Capitalism: China's Reemergence and the International Political Economy." *World Politics* 64(4): 741–76.

McNally, Christopher A., and Yin-Wah Chu. 2006. "Exploring Capitalist Development in Greater China: A Synthesis." *Asian Perspective* 30(2): 31–64.

McNally, Christopher A., Hong Guo, and Guangwei Hu. 2007. "Entrepreneurship and Political Guanxi Networks in China's Private Sector." *East-West Center Working Papers: Politics, Governance, and Security Series* 19. Honolulu: East-West Center.

McNally, Christopher A., and Teresa Wright. 2010. "Sources of Social Support for China's Current Political Order: The 'Thick Embeddedness' of Private Capital Holders." *Communist and Post-Communist Studies* 43(2): 189–98.

MDIC. 2011. *Brasil Maior. Inovar para competir. Competir para crescer*. Brasília: Ministério do Desenvolvimento, Indústria e Comércio Exterior.

Mearsheimer, J.J. 2001. *The Tragedy of Great Power Politics*. New York: Norton & Co.

Mehrotra, Santosh, Ankita Gandhi, and Bimal K. Sahoo. 2013. "Estimating India's Skill Gap on a Realistic Basis for 2022." *Economic and Political Weekly*, 30 March: 102–11.

Mehta, Swati. 2011. "Economic Reforms, Technological Intensity and Industrial Development in India." *Economic and Political Weekly* 46(17): 60–6.

Meissner, Mirjam, Lea Shih, Luisa Kinzius, and Sandra Heep. 2015. "Wie Phönix aus der Asche: Reformen sollen Chinas Staatsunternehmen den Rücken stärken." *Merics Web Special*. www.merics.org/fileadmin/templates/art/aktuelles/SOE_Reform/SOE-ReformWeb-Spezial.pdf (accessed 3 February 2016).

Melleiro, Waideli, and Jochen Steinhilber. 2012. "Zur Sonne, zur Freiheit? Gewerkschaftspolitik in Brasilien." In *Das politische System Brasiliens*, edited by Dana de la Fontaine and Thomas Stehnken, 209–29. Wiesbaden: Springer VS.

Melo, Marcus André. 2014. "Political and Institutional Drivers of Social Security Universalization in Brazil." *UNRISD Working Paper* 2014–20. Geneva: United Nations Research Institute for Social Development.

Michailova, Snejina, and Verner Worm. 2003. "Personal Networking in Russia and China: Blat and Guanxi." *European Management Journal* 21(4): 509–19.

Milanovic, Branko. 2008. "Where in the World Are You? Assessing the Importance of Circumstance and Effort in a World of Different Mean Country Incomes and (Almost) No Migration." *Policy Research Working Papers*. Washington, DC: The World Bank.

Minella, Ary Cesar. 2007. "Brazil's Largest Private Banks: An Economic and Sociopolitical Profile." *Sociologias* 18: 100–25.

Modisaotsile, Brenda M. 2012. "The Failing Standard of Basic Education in South Africa." Africa Institute of South Africa, Policy Brief 72. www.ai.org.za/wp-content/uploads/downloads/2012/03/No.-72.The-Failing-Standard-of-Basic-Education-in-South-Africa1.pdf (accessed 3 Feburary 2016).

Mohamed, Seeraj. 2010. "The State of the South African Economy." In *New South African Review 1 Development or Decline*, edited by John Daniel, Prishani Naidoo, Pillay Devan, and Roger Southall, 39–64. Johannesburg: University of Witswaterrand.

Mohamed, Seeraj. 2016. "Financialization of the South African Economy." *Development*, 59(1–2): 137–42. DOI:10.1057/s41301-017-0065-1

Moll, Terence. 1991. "Did the Apartheid Economy 'Fail'?" *Journal of Southern African Studies* 17(2): 271–91.

Moody's Investors Service. 2018. "Moody's Confirms the Baa3 Issuer Ratings of DBSA, IDC and Land Bank; Stable Outlook." 27 March. www.dbsa.org/EN/InvestorRelations/Credit%20Ratings%20Reports/Moody%27s%20-%202018%20March.pdf

Morgan, Glenn. 2005. "Institutional Complementarities, Path Dependency, and the Dynamics of Firms." In *Changing Capitalisms? Internationalization, Institutional Change, and Systems of Economic Organization*, edited by Glenn Morgan, Richard Whitley, and Eli Moen, 414–46. Oxford: Oxford University Press.

Moses, Cheryl, Moses M. Sithole, William Blankley, Demetre Labadarios, Hlamulo Makelane, and Nolitha Nkobole. 2012. "The State of Innovation in South Africa: Findings from the South African National Innovation Survey." *South African Journal for Science* 108(7–8): 1320.

Motshekga, Angie. 2015. "Speech Delivered by Basic Education Angie Motshekga at the Release of NSC Examination Results on Monday 05 January 2015, Department of Basic Education." www.education.gov.za/Newsroom/Speeches/tabid/298/ctl/Details/mid/1749/ItemID/3064/Default.aspx (accessed 21 December 2015).

Mthani, Thanti, and Kalu Olaj, 2016. "Instiutions and Cooperative Governance in South Africa." In *Corporate Governance in Developing and Emerging Markets*, edited by Franklin N. Ngwu, Onyeka K. Osuji and Frank H. Stephen, 125–39. London and New York: Routledge.

Mtshali, Mduduzi N.G., and Radhamany Sooryamoorthy. 2018. "A Research-Inducing Environment at a University of Technology in South Africa: Challenges and Future Prospects." *Futures*. DOI:10.1016/j.futures.2018.06.017

Mukherji, Rahul. (ed.). 2007a. *India's Economic Transition: The Politics of Reforms*. New Delhi: Oxford University Press.

Mukherji, Rahul. 2007b. "Introduction: The State and Private Initiative in India." In Mukherji 2007a, 1–24.

Munusamy, Ranjeni. 2012. "Cyril Ramaphosa: Betrayal Does Not Get More Painful Than This." *The Guardian*, October 25. www.theguardian.com/world/2012/oct/25/cyril-ramaphosa-marikana-email (accessed 21 December 2015).

Murphy, Craig N. 2005. *Global Institutions, Marginalization, and Development*. London and New York: Routledge.

Musacchio, Aldo, and Sergio G. Lazzarini. 2014. *Reinventing State Capitalism: Leviathan in Business, Brazil and Beyond*. Cambridge: Harvard University Press.

Musacchio, Aldo, Sergio G. Lazzarini, and Ruth V. Aguilera. 2015. "New Varieties of State Capitalism: Strategic and Governance Implications." *The Academy of Management Perspectives* 29(1): 115–31.

Myant, Martin, and Jan Drahokoupil. 2011. *Transition Economies: Political Economy in Russia, Eastern Europe, and Central Asia*. Hoboken, NJ: Wiley-Blackwell.

Myburgh, Pieter-Louis. 2017. *The Republic of Gupta: A Story of State Capture*. Cape Town: Penguin.

Mykhnenko, V. 2007. "Strengths and Weaknesses of 'Weak' Co-Ordination: Economic Institutions, Revealed Comparative Advantages, and Socio-Economic Performance of Mixed Market Economies in Poland and Ukraine." In *Beyond Varieties of Capitalism: Conflict, Contradictions, and Complementarities in the European Economy*, edited by Bob Hancké, Martin Rhodes, and Mark Thatcher, 351–78. Oxford: Oxford University Press.

Nagaraj, R. 2017. "Public Sector Employment: What Has Changed?" In *Political Economy of Contemporary India*, edited by R. Nagaraj and Sripad Motiram, 157–78. Cambridge: Cambridge University Press.

Nagaraj, R., and Sripad Motiram. 2017. "From 'Intermediate Regime' to Crony Capitalism." In *Political Economy of Contemporary India*, edited by R. Nagaraj and Sripad Motiram, 1–22. Cambridge: Cambridge University Press.

Narlikar, Amrita. 2010. *New Powers: How to Become One and How to Manage Them*. London and New York: Oxford University Press.

Nassif, André, Carmem Feijó, and Eliane Araújo. 2011. "The Long-Term 'Optimal' Real Exchange Rate and the Currency Overvaluation Trend in Open Emerging Economies: The Case of Brazil." *Discussion Paper* No. 206. Geneva: United Nations Conference on Trade and Development.

Nassif, André, Carmem Feijó, and Eliane Araújo. 2015. "Structural Change and Economic Development: Is Brazil Catching Up or Falling Behind?" *Cambridge Journal of Economics* 39: 1307–32.

National Planning Commission/NPC. 2011. "National Development Plan 2030: Our Future -Make It Work." Republic of South Africa. Pretoria: National Planning Commission, The Presidency.

Nattrass, Nicoli. 2013. "A South African Variety of Capitalism?" *New Political Economy* 19(1): 56–78. DOI:10.1080/13563467.2013.768610

Nattrass, Nicoli, and Jeremy Seekings. 2010. "State, Business and Growth in Post-Apartheid South Africa." *Discussion Paper Series* 34. IPPG Discussion paper.

Naudé, Wim, Adam Szirmai, and Alejandro Lavopa. 2013. *Industrialization Lessons from BRICS: A Comparative Analysis*. Bonn: Forschungsinstitut zur Zukunft der Arbeit.

Naughton, Barry. 2007. *The Chinese Economy: Transitions and Growth*. Cambridge: MIT Press.

Naughton, Barry. 2010. "The Policy Challenges of Post-Stimulus Growth." www.globalasia.org/v5no2/cover/the-policy-challenges-of-post-stimulus-growth_barry-naughton (accessed 3 December 2018).

Naughton, Barry. 2011. "China's Distinctive System: Can It Be a Model for Others?" In *In Search of China's Development Model. Beyond the Beijing Consensus*, edited by S. Philip Hsu, Yu-Shan Wu, and Suisheng Zhao, 67–85. London and New York: Routledge.

Naughton, Barry. 2015a. "Local Debt Restructuring: A Case of Ongoing Authoritarian Reform." *China Leadership Monitor* 47.

Naughton, Barry. 2015b. "Reform Agenda in Turmoil: Can Policy-Makers Regain the Initiative?" *China Leadership Monitor* 48.

Naughton, Barry. 2016. "Supply-Side Structural Reform at Mid-year: Compliance, Initiative, and Unintended Consequences." *China Leadership Monitor* 51.

Naughton, Barry. 2017. "The Regulatory Storm: A Surprising Turn in Financial Policy." *China Leadership Monitor* 53.

Nayar, Baldev Raj. 2007. "The Limits of Economic Nationalism in India: Economic Reforms Under the BJP-Led Government, 1998–9." In Mukherji 2007a, 202–29.

NBS (National Bureau of Statistics of China). 2008. *China Industry Economy Statistical Yearbook*. Beijing: China Statistics Press.

NBS (National Bureau of Statistics of China). 2010. *China Statistical Yearbook 2010*. Beijing: China Statistics Press. www.stats.gov.cn/tjsj/ndsj/2010/indexeh.htm

NBS (National Bureau of Statistics of China). 2012. *China Statistical Yearbook 2012*. Beijing: China Statistics Press. www.stats.gov.cn/tjsj/ndsj/2012/indexeh.htm

Nee, Victor, and Sonja Opper. 2012. *Capitalism from Below: Markets and Institutional Change in China*. Cambridge: Harvard University Press.

Nölke, Andreas. 2010. "A 'BRIC' Variety of Capitalism and Social Inequality: The Case of Brazil." *Revista de Estudos e Pesquisas sobre as Américas* 4(1): 1–14.

Nölke, Andreas. 2015a. "International Financial Regulation and Domestic Coalitions in State-Permeated Capitalism: China and Global Banking Rules." *International Politics* 52: 743–59.

Nölke, Andreas. 2015b. "Rising Powers and Transnational Private Governance: The International Accounting Standards Board." In *Rising Powers and Multilateral Institutions*, edited by Dries Lesage and Thijs van de Graaf, 96–116. Basingstoke and New York: Palgrave Macmillan.

Nölke, Andreas. (ed.). 2015c. "Second Image Revisited: The Domestic Sources of China's Foreign Economic Policies." Special Issue, *International Politics* 52(6).

Nölke, Andreas. 2016. "Economic Causes of the Eurozone Crisis: The Analytical Contribution of Comparative Capitalism." *Socio-Economic Review* 14. DOI:10.1093/ser/mwv031

Nölke, Andreas, and Simone Claar. 2013. "Varieties of Capitalism in Emerging Economies." *Transformation, Critical Perspectives on Southern Africa* 81–2: 33–54.

Nölke, Andreas, Tobias ten Brink, Simone Claar, and Christian May. 2015. "Domestic Structures, Foreign Economic Policies and Global Economic Order: Implications from the Rise of Large Emerging Economies." *European Journal of International Relations* 21(3): 538–67.

Nölke, Andreas, and Arjan Vliegenthart. 2009. "Enlarging the Varieties of Capitalism: The Emergence of Dependent Market Economies in East Central Europe." *World Politics* 61(4): 670–702.

Nowak, Jörg. 2015. "Massenstreiks und Straßenproteste in Indien und Brasilien." *Peripherie* 137(35): 74–102.

Ocampo, José Antonio. 2009. "Die globale Wirtschaftskrise: Auswirkungen und Folgen für Lateinamerika." *Nueva Sociedad* Sonderheft (October): 4–21.

OECD. 2007a. *Staying Competitive in the Global Economy: Moving Up the Value Chain.* Paris: Organization for Economic Cooperation and Development.

OECD. 2007b. *OECD Reviews of Innovation Policy: South Africa.* Paris: Organization for Economic Cooperation and Development.

OECD. 2009. *Guide on Fighting Abusive Related Party Transactions in Asia.* Paris: Organization for Economic Cooperation and Development.

OECD. 2010a. *OECD Science, Technology and Industry Outlook 2010.* Paris: Organization for Economic Cooperation and Development.

OECD. 2010b. *OECD Economic Survey: South Africa.* Paris: Organization for Economic Cooperation and Development.

OECD. 2011a. *OECD Science, Technology and Industry Outlook 2011.* Paris: Organization for Economic Cooperation and Development.

OECD. 2011b. *Economic Survey: India.* Paris: Organization for Economic Cooperation and Development.

OECD. 2011c. "Isic Rev. 3 Technology Intensity Definition." www.oecd.org/sti/ind/48350231.pdf (accessed 3 February 2016).

OECD. 2012. *OECD Science, Technology and Industry Outlook 2012.* Paris: Organization for Economic Cooperation and Development.

OECD. 2013a. *Perspectives on Global Development 2013: Industrial Policies in a Changing World.* Paris: OECD Publishing.

OECD. 2013b. "OECD Economic Surveys South Africa." March. www.oecd.org/eco/surveys/South%20Africa%202013%20Overview%20FINAL.pdf (accessed 19 December 2015).

OECD. 2013c. *OECD Science, Technology and Industry Scoreboard 2013*. Paris: Organization for Economic Cooperation and Development.

OECD. 2014a. *Latin America: Tax Revenues Continue to Rise, But Are Low and Varied Among Countries, According to New OECD-ECLAC.CIAT Report*. Paris: Organisation for Economic Cooperation and Development.

OECD. 2014b. "Social Expenditure Update." November. Paris: Organisation for Economic Cooperation and Development.

OECD. 2014c. "Economic Surveys: India." November. Paris: Organization for Economic Cooperation and Development.

OECD. 2015. "OECD FDI Regulatory Restrictiveness Index Database." http://stats.oecd.org/Index.aspx?datasetcode=FDIINDEX# (accessed 3 February 2016).

OECD/IDB. 2010. *Competition Law and Policy in Brazil: A Peer Review*. Paris: Organisation for Economic Cooperation and Development and Inter-American Development Bank.

Ohno, K. 2009. "Avoiding the Middle Income Trap: Renovating Industrial Policy Formulation in Vietnam." *ASEAN Economic Bulletin* 26(1): 25–43.

Oi, Jean C. 2011. *Going Private in China: The Politics of Corporate Restructuring and System Reform*. Stanford, CA: Walter H. Shorenstein Asia-Pacific Research Center Books.

Olawale, Fatoki, and David Garwe. 2010. "Obstacles to the Growth of New SMEs in South Africa: A Principal Component Analysis Approach." *African Journal of Business Management* 4(5): 729–38.

O'Neill, J. 2001. "Building Better Global Economic BRICs." *Global Economics Paper* No. 66. New York: Goldman Sachs.

Orr, Thomas. 2007. "ICBC Standard Bank Deal Is Only the Beginning." *China Monitor* 24: 4–7. http://www0.sun.ac.za/ccs/wp-content/uploads/2009/04/china_monitor_november_2007.pdf (accessed 14 August 2015).

Orsagh, Matt. 2014. "Women on Corporate Boards: Global Trends for Promotion Diversity." *Market Integrity Insights*, September 24. https://blogs.cfainstitute.org/marketintegrity/2014/09/24/women-on-corporate-boards-global-trends-for-promoting-diversity/ (accessed 12 December 2015).

Ozturk, Aykut, and Leyla Farhan. 2015. "Rethinking Developmentalism: Notes on the Last Decade in Turkey and Brazil." Paper prepared for Warwick IPE Conference, University of Warwick, 12–13 May.

Padayachee, Vishnu. 2008. "Capitalism of a Special Type? South African Capitalism Before and After 1994." *Journal für Entwicklungspolitik* 24(4): 50–77.

Padayachee, Vishnu. 2013a. "Introducing Varieties of Capitalism into the South African Debate: Uses and Limits." *Transformation: Critical Perspectives on Southern Africa* 81–2: 5–32.

Padayachee, Vishnu. 2013b. "Corporate Governance in South Africa: From 'Old Boys Club' to 'Ubuntu'?" *Transformation: Critical Perspectives on Southern Africa* 81–2: 260–90.

Pal, Rupayan, and Bibhas Saha. 2014: "Labour Market: Balancing Freedom and Protection." In *The Oxford Handbook of the Indian Economy in the 21st Century*, edited by Ashima Goyal, 822–45. Oxford: Oxford University Press.

Panagariya, Arvind. 2011. "Growth and Reforms During 1980s and 1990s." In *Economic Reforms & Growth in India*, edited by Pulapre Balakrishnan, 100–30. Hyderabad: Orient Blackswan.

PATRI. 2015. *The Brazilian Tax System*. Brasilia: PATRI.

Paus, Eva. 2012. "Confronting the Middle Income Trap: Insights from Small Latecomers." *Studies in Comparative Industrial Development* 47(1): 115–38.

Pearson, Margaret M. 2011. "Variety Within and Without: The Political Economy of Chinese Regulation." In *Beyond the Middle Kingdom* edited by Scott Kennedy, 25–43. Stanford, CA: Stanford University Press.

Peck, Jamie, and Nik Theodore. 2007. "Variegated Capitalism." *Progress in Human Geography* 31(6): 731–72.

Pei, Minxin. 2016. *China's Crony Capitalism: The Dynamics of Regime Decay*. Cambridge: Harvard University Press.

Pena, Alejandro Milcíades. 2014. "The Political Trajectory of the Brazilian CSR Movement." *Critical Perspectives on International Business* 10(4): 310–23.

Perry, James, and Andreas Nölke. 2006. "The Political Economy of International Accounting Standards." *Review of International Political Economy* 13(4): 559–86.

Phillips, Nicola. 2004. *The Southern Cone Model: The Political Economy of Regional Capitalist Development in Latin America*. London: Routledge.

Piketty, Thomas. 2014. *Capital in the Twenty-First Century*. Cambridge and London: The Belknap Press of Harvard University Press.

Pillai, P. Mohanan. 1979. "Technology Transfer, Adaptation and Assimilation." *Economic and Political Weekly* 14(47): 121–6.

Pillay, Devan. 2011. "The Tripartite Alliance and Its Discontents: Contesting the 'National Democratic Revolution' in the Zuma Era." In *New South African Review 2: New Path? Old Compromises?* edited by John Daniel, Prishani Naidoo, Devan Pillay, and Roger Southall, 31–49. Johannesburg: Wits University Press.

Pilz, Matthias. 2012. *The Future of VET in a Changing World*. Wiesbaden: Springer VS.

Ping, Lv. 2013. "China." In *The Role of the State: BRICS National Systems of Innovation*, edited by Mario Scerri and Helena M.M. Lastres, 188–247. New Delhi: Routledge.

Piramal, Gita. 1996. *Business Maharajas*. New Delhi: Penguin.

Pitcher, Anne. 2012. "Was Privatisation Necessary and Did It Work? The Case of South Africa." *Review of African Political Economy* 39(132): 243–60.

Pitts, Bryan. 2015. "Who's Protesting in Brazil and Why?" https://nacla.org/news/2015/04/09/who%E2%80%99s-protesting-brazil-and-why (accessed 12 December 2015).

Polanyi, Karl. 1977. *The Livelihood of Man*. New York: Academic Press.

Polanyi, Karl. 2001. *The Great Transformation: The Political and Economic Origins of Our Time*. Boston: Beacon Press.

Pollock, Friedrich. 1975. "Staatskapitalismus." In *Friedrich Pollock. Stadien des Kapitalismus*, edited by Helmut Dubiel, 72–100. München: C. H. Beck.

Pons-Vignon, Nicolas, and Miriam Di Paola. 2014. "The South African Labour Market After Eighteen Years: It's Class Struggle, Stupid!" In *New South African Review 4: A Fragile Democracy – Twenty Years on*, edited by Devan Pillay, Gilbert M Khadiagala, Prishani Nai-doo, and Roger Southall, 21–38. Johannesburg: Wits University Press.

Porter, Michael E. 1990. "The Competitive Advantage of Nations." *Harvard Business Review* 3–4: 73–91.

Powell, Lesley. 2012. "Reimagining the Purpose of VET – Expanding the Capability to Aspire in South African Further Education and Training Students." *International Journal of Educational Development* 32(5): 643–53.

Powell, Lesley, and Simon McGrath. 2014. "Exploring the Value of the Capability Approach for Vocational Education and Training Evaluation: Reflections from South Africa." In *Education, Learning, Training: Critical Issues for Development*, edited by

Gilles Carbonnier, Michel Carton, and Kenneth King. International Development Policy Series No. 5. Geneva: Graduate Institute Publications, 126–48. Boston: Brill-Nijhoff.

Prebisch, Raul. 1950. *The Economic Development of Latin America and Its Principal Problems*. Lake Success, NY: United Nations Department of Economic Affairs.

The Presidency. 2009. "Ministerial Clusters Reconfigured to Improve Coordination and Delivery." 19 November. www.thepresidency.gov.za/content/ministerial-clusters-reconfigured-improve-coordination-and-delivery (accessed 6 September 2013).

Prud'homme, Dan. 2016. "Dynamics of China's Provincial-Level Specialization in Strategic Emerging Industries." *Research Policy* 45(8): 1586–603.

Radice, Hugo. 2000. "Globalization and National Capitalisms: Theorizing Convergence and Differentiation." *Review of International Political Economy* 7(4): 719–42.

Radjou, Navi, Jaideep Prabhu, and Simone Ahuja. 2012. *Jugaad Innovation: A Frugal and Flexible Approach to Innovation for the 21st Century*. Noida and London: Random House.

Rajakumar, J. Dennis. 2005. "Corporate Financing and Investment Behaviour in India." *Economic and Political Weekly* 40(38): 4159–65.

Rajan, Raghuram G. 2017. *I Do What I Do: On Reform, Rhetoric and Resolve*. Noida: Harper Business.

Rajput, Jagmohan Singh. 2009. "The Changing Context of TVET for the Workforce in India." In *International Handbook of Education for the Changing World of Work: Bridging Academic and Vocational Learning*, edited by Rupert Maclean and David Wilson, 2417–30. Dordrecht: Springer.

Ramanna, Karthik. 2013. "The International Politics of IFRS Harmonization." *Accounting Economics and Law* 3: 2.

Ramappa, T. 2014. *Competition Law in India: Policy, Issues, and Developments*. New Delhi: Oxford University Press.

Rani, Uma. 2009. "Learning Workshops: Informal Processes of Learning and Skill Acquisition in Auto Components Firms Supplying to Global Production Networks." *The Indian Journal of Labour Economics* 52(4): 671–91.

Ravallion, Martin. 2009. "A Comparative Perspective on Poverty Reduction in Brazil, China and India." *Policy Research Working Paper*. Washington, DC: The World Bank.

Ravenhill, John. 2005. *Global Political Economy*. Oxford: Oxford University Press.

Regan, Aidan. 2013. "Political Tensions in Euro-Varieties of Capitalism: The Crisis of the Democratic State in Europe." *EUI Working Paper* MWP 2013/14. San Domenico di Fiesole: European University Institute.

Rhodes, Robert I. 1971. *Imperialism and Underdevelopment: A Reader*. New York: Monthly Review Press.

Rodrik, Dani, and Arvind Subramanian. 2004. "From 'Hindu Growth' to Productivity Surge: The Mystery of the Indian Growth Transition." *NBER Working Paper* No. 10376. Cambirdge: National Bureau of Economic Research.

Rostow, Walt W. 1990. *The Stages of Economic Growth: A Non-Communist Manifesto*, 3rd Ed. New York: Cambridge University Press.

Rougier, Eric, and Francois Combarnous. 2017. *The Diversity of Emerging Capitalisms in Developing Countries*. Basingstoke: Palgrave Macmillan.

Rüb, Matthias. 2015. "Kanzlerin inmitten brasilianischer Intrigen: Zum Besuch Merkels beschert die Regierung in Brasilia den deutschen Autobauern im Land ein Hilfspaket als Gastgeschenk." *Frankfurter Allgemeine Zeitung*, 21 August (p. 3).

Rudolph, Lloyd H., and Susanne Rudolph. 1987. *In Pursuit of Lakshmi: The Political Economy of the Indian State*. Chicago: University of Chicago Press.

Saad Filho, Alfredo. 2015. "Brazil: Social Change from Import-Substitution to Neoliberalism and the 'Events of June'." *Working Paper*. Nuvole: Turin.

Sachs, Jeffrey D., and Andrew Warner. 1995. "Economic Reform and the Process of Global Integration." *Brookings Paper on Economic Activity* 1.

Sadie, Yolanda. 2006. "Political Parties, Interest Groups and Social Movements." In *Government and Politics in the New South Africa*, edited by Albert Venter and Chris Landsberg, 3rd Ed., 202–32. Pretoria: Van Schaik Publishers.

Sáez, Lawrence. 2004. *Banking Reform in India and China*. Houndmills and Basingstoke: Palgrave Macmillan.

Saich, Tony. 2011. *Governance and Politics of China*. New York and London: Palgrave Macmillan.

SA info reporter. 2015. "Education." http://www.southafrica.info/about/education/education.htm#.Vaz5IIv9rTo (accessed 11 December 2015).

Sake 24. 2010. "SA 'Richest' Country in the World." *fin24.com*, 28 April. www.fin24.com/Economy/SA-richest-country-in-the-world-20100428-2 (accessed 10 December 2015).

Sala-i-Martin, Xavier, BeÑat Bilaboa-Osorio, Jennifer Blacke, Margarete Drzeniek, and Hanouz Thierry Geiger. 2012. "The Global Competitiveness Index 2011–2012: Setting the Foundations for Strong Productivity." World Economic Forum. http://www3.weforum.org/docs/WEF_GCR_Highlights_2011-12.pdf (accessed 19 December 2015).

SAPA. 2012. "Over 2.8m Working Days Lost During Strikes in 2011." *Mail & Guardian*, 8 August. http://mg.co.za/article/2012-08-08-labour-strikes-working-days-lost (accessed 19 December 2015).

Sarkar, Jayati, and Subrata Sarkar. 2012. *Corporate Governance in India*. New Delhi: Sage.

SASAC (State-owned Assets Supervision and Administration Commission of the State Council). 2012. "List of Central Enterprises." (In Chinese). http://www.sasac.gov.cn/n1180/n1226/n2410/n314259/n315134/14666245.html (accessed 12 January 2013).

Saul, John, and Stephen Gelb. 1981. reprinted 1986. "Crisis in South Africa." – "Chapter 2 The Crisis in South Africa: Class defence. Class Revolution." Originally appeared as the July-August 1981 issue of Monthly Review. Zed Books.

Scerri, Mario, and Helena M.M. Lastres. (eds.). 2013. *The Role of the State: BRICS National Systems of Innovation*. New Delhi: Routledge.

Schmalz, Stefan. 2012. "Die brasilianische Wirtschaftspolitik seit dem Ende der Militärdiktatur: Von der Krise der Importsubstitution zum Programa de Aceleração do Crescimento." In *Das politische System Brasiliens*, edited by Dana de la Fontaine and Thomas Stehnken, 265–80. Wiesbaden: Springer VS.

Schmidt, Vivien A. 2002. *The Futures of European Capitalism*. Oxford: Oxford University Press.

Schmidt, Vivien A. 2009. "Putting the Political Back into Political Economy by Bringing the State Back in Yet Again." *World Politics* 61(3): 516–46.

Schmidt, Vivian A. 2010. "Taking Ideas and Discourse Seriously: Explaining Change Through Discursive Institutionalism as the Fourth 'New Institutionalism'." *European Political Science Review* 2(1): 1–25.

Schnabl, Gunther, and Andreas Hoffmann. 2008. "Monetary Policy, Vagabonding Liquidity and Bursting Bubbles in New and Emerging Markets: An Overinvestment View!" *World Economy* 31(9): 1226–52.

Schneider, Ben Ross. 2004. *Business Politics and the State in Twentieth-Century Latin America*. Cambridge: Cambridge University Press.

Schneider, Ben Ross. 2009. "A Comparative Political Economy of Diversified Business Groups, or How States Organize Big Business." *Review of International Political Economy* 16(2): 178–201.

Schneider, Ben Ross. 2013. *Hierarchical Capitalism in Latin America: Business, Labor, and the Challenges of Equitable Development*. Cambridge: Cambridge University Press.

Schneider, Ben Ross. 2015a. "The Developmental State in Brazil: Comparative and Historical Perspectives." *Brazilian Journal of Political Economy* (35)1: 114–38.

Schneider, Ben Ross. 2015b. *Designing Industrial Policy in Latin America: Business-State Relations and the New Developmentalism*, New York: Palgrave Macmillan.

Schneider, Ben Ross, and David Soskice. 2009. "Inequality in Developed Countries and Latin America: Coordinated, Liberal and Hierarchical Systems." *Economy and Society* 38(1): 17–52.

Schrank, Andrew. 2009. "Understanding Latin American Political Economy: Varieties of Capitalism or Fiscal Sociology?" *Economy and Society* 30(1): 53–61.

Schüller, Margot, and Yun Schüler-Zhou. 2015. "China: Die neue Innovationssupermacht?" *GIGA Focus*, January.

Schweller, R. 2011. "Emerging Powers in an Age of Disorder." *Global Governance* 17(3): 285–97.

Sedibe, Kholofelo. 1998. "Dismantling Apartheid Education: An Overview of Change." *Cambridge Journal of Education* 28(3): 269–82.

Seekings, Jeremy, and Nicoli Nattrass. 2005. *Class, Race, and Inequality in South Africa*. Scottsville: University of KwaZulu-Natal Press.

Seekings, Jeremy, and Nicoli Nattrass. 2015. *Policy, Politics and Poverty in South Africa*. Hampshire: Palgrave Macmillan.

Sekhar, C.S.C. 2011. "Economic Growth, Social Development and Interest Groups." In *Economic Reforms and Growth in India*, edited by Pulapre Balakrishnan, 432–51. Hyderabad: Black Swan.

Sen, Kunal. 2011. "When Did the Elephant Start to Trot? India's Growth Acceleration Re-Examined." In *Economic Reforms & Growth in India*, edited by Pulapre Balakrishnan, 131–56. Hyderabad: Orient Blackswan.

Sen, Sandip. 2014. *Neta, Babu & Subsidy*. New Delhi: Vitasta.

Senghaas, Dieter. (ed.). 1972. *Imperialismus und strukturelle Gewalt. Analysen über abhängige Reproduktion*. Frankfurt/Main: Suhrkamp.

Senghaas, Dieter. 1977. *Weltwirtschaftsordnung und Entwicklungspolitik. Plädoyer für Dissoziation*. Frankfurt/Main: Duhrkamp.

Serrano, Franklin, and Ricardo Summa. 2015. *Aggregate Demand and the Slowdown of Brazilian Economic Growth from 2011–2014*. Washington, DC: Center for Economic and Policy Research.

Shambaugh, David. 2016. *China's Future*. Cambridge: Polity Press.

Shao, Sijun, Chris Nyland, and Cherrie Jiuhua Zhu. 2011. "Tripartite Consultation: An Emergent Form of Governance Shaping Employment Relations in China." *Industrial Relations Journal* 42(4): 358–74.

Shih, Victor. 2015. "Can Xi Jinping Turn China's Economy Around? A China File Conversation." 29 July. www.chinafile.com/conversation/can-xi-jinping-turn-chinas-economy-around (accessed 3 February 2016).

Shome, Parthasarathi. 2014. "Government Taxes and Expenditures: Experience and Reform." In *The Oxford Handbook of the Indian Economy in the 21st Century: Understanding the Inherent Dynamism*, edited by Ashima Goyal, 377–414. New Delhi: Oxford University Press.

Shonfield, Andrew. 1965. *Modern Capitalism: The Changing Balance of Public and Private Power*. Oxford: Oxford University Press.

Sibal, David Rajeev. 2014. "Varieties of Capitalism and Firm Performance in Emerging Markets: An Examination of the Typological Trajectories of India and Brazil." PhD diss., London School of Economics and Political Science.

Silva, Eduardo. 1996. "From Dictatorship to Democracy: The Business-State Nexus in Chile's Economic Transformation, 1975–1994." *Comparative Politics* 28(3): 299–320.

Simon, Denis F., and Cong Cao. 2009. *China's Emerging Technological Edge: Assessing the Role of High-End Talent*. Cambridge: Cambridge University Press.

Singh, Amrik. 1999. "Educational Imbalance in India." *Economic and Political Weekly*, 26 June.

Singh, Pragya. 2011. "The Home Alone Boys." *Outlook Magazine*, 10 January.

Sinha, Aseema. 2004. "The Changing Political Economy of Federalism in India: A Historical Institutionalist Approach." *India Review* 31(1): 25–63.

Sinha, Aseema. 2011. "Business and Politics." In *The Oxford Companion to Politics in India*, edited by Niraja Gopal Jayal and Pratap Bhanu Mehta, 459–76. New Delhi: Oxford University Press.

Snowden, Nicholas, and Jesús Munoz. 2012. "Building a BRIC? Stock Market Opening and Investment Finance in India Since Liberalization." *World Development* 40(6): 1109–21.

So, Alvin Y. 2003. "Rethinking the Chinese Developmental Miracle." In *China's Developmental Miracle: Origins, Transformations, and Challenges*, edited by Alvin Y. So, 3–28. Armonk: M. E. Sharpe.

So, Alvin Y. 2005. "Beyond the Logic of Capital and the Polarization Model." *Critical Asian Studies* 37(3): 481–94.

Song, Zheng M., and Xiong Wei. 2018. Risks in China's Financial System. *NBER Working Paper* 24230. http://www.nber.org/papers/w24230 (accessed 17 November 2018).

Sood, Atul, Paaritosh Nath, and Sangeeta Ghosh. 2014. "Deregulating Capital, Regulating Labour: The Dynamics in the Manufacturing Sector in India." *Economic and Political Weekly* 49(26–7): 58–68.

South African Reserve Bank. 2010. "The International Banking Crisis and Domestic Financial Intermediation in Emerging Market Economies: Issues for South Africa." *BIS Papers* No 54. www.bis.org/publ/bppdf/bispap54w.pdf (accessed 19 December 2015).

Srinivasan, Thirukodikaval N., and Suresh D. Tendulkar. 2003. *Reintegrating India with the World Economy*. Washington, DC: Institute for International Economics.

Statistic South Africa. 2015a. *Labour Market Dynamics in South Africa 2014*. Pretoria: Statistics South Africa. Press Statement, April. www.statssa.gov.za/?p=4445 (accessed 19 December 2015).

Statistic South Africa. 2015b. *Labour Market Dynamics in South Africa 2014*. Pretoria: Statistics South Africa.

Statistics South Africa. 2018. "Labour Market Dynamics in South Africa, 2016." Report No. 02–11–02. www.statssa.gov.za/publications/Report-02-11-02/Report-02-11-022016.pdf

Stephen, Matthew D. 2012. "Rising Regional Powers and International Institutions: The Foreign Policy Orientations of India, Brazil and South Africa." *Global Society* 26(3): 289–309.

Stephen, Matthew D. 2014. "Rising Powers, Global Capitalism and Liberal Global Governance: A Historical Materialist Account of the BRICs Challenge." *European Journal of International Relations*, published online before print, 21 May.

Stockhammer, Engelbert. 2004. "Financialization and the Slowdown of Accumulation." *Cambridge Journal of Economics* 28(5): 719–41.

Stockhammer, Engelbert. 2011. "Peripheral Europe's Debt and German Wages: The Role of Wage Policy in the Euro Area." *International Journal of Public Policy* 7(1): 83–96.

Stockhammer, Engelbert. 2013. "Why Have Wage Shares Fallen? A Panel Analysis of the Determinants of Functional Income Distribution." *Conditions of Work and Employment Series* No. 35, Geneva: ILO.

Stockhammer, Engelbert, Cedric Durand, and Ludwig List. 2014. "European Growth Models and Working Class Restructuring." www.boeckler.de/pdf/v_2014_10_30_list.pdf (accessed 6 November 2014).

Strange, Susan. 1986. *Casino Capitalism*. Manchester: Manchester University Press.

Strange, Susan. 1988. *States and Markets*. London: Pinter.

Strange, Susan. 1998. *Mad Money: When Markets Outgrow Governments*. Manchester: Manchester University Press.

Storz, Cornelia, Bruno Amable, Steven Casper, and Sebastien Lechevalier. 2013. "Bringing Asia into the Comparative Capitalism Perspective." *Socio-Economic Review* 11: 217–32.

Streeck, Wolfgang. 1997. "The German Model: Does It Exist, Can It Survive?" *New Political Economy* 2(2): 237–56.

Streeck, Wolfgang. 2010. "E Pluribus Unum? Varieties and Commonalities of Capitalism." *MPIfG Discussion Paper* 10/12. Cologne: Max Planck Institute for the Study of Societies.

Streeck, Wolfgang. 2014a. *Buying Time: The Delayed Crisis of Democratic Capitalism*. New York: Verso.

Streeck, Wolfgang. 2014b. "How Will Capitalism End?" *New Left Review* 87(May–June): 35–64.

Streeck, Wolfgang, and Kathleen Thelen. 2005. "Introduction: Institutional Change in Advanced Political Economies." In *Beyond Continuity: Institutional Change in Advanced Political Economies*, edited by Wolfgang Streeck and Kathleen Thelen, 1–39. Oxford: Oxford University Press.

Suau Arinci, Lucía, Nadia Pessina, and Matthias Ebenau. 2015. "All Varieties Are Equal. . . : Contributions from Dependency Approaches to Critical Comparative Capitalisms Research." In *New Directions in Comparative Capitalisms Research: Critical and Global Perspectives*, edited by Matthias Ebenau, Ian Bruff, and Christian May, 189–206. Houndmills and Basingstoke: Palgrave Macmillan.

Subramanian, T.S.R. 2009. *GovernMint in India: An Inside View*. New Delhi: Rupa & Co.

Talley, Ian. 2016. "Why Emerging Markets Are Melting Down, and Why It Matters, in 10 Charts." *Real Time Economics – Wall Street Journal Blog*, 7 January. http://blogs.wsj.com/economics/2016/01/07/why-emerging-markets-are-melting-down-and-why-it-matters-in-10-charts/ (accessed 16 February 2016).

Taylor, Heather. 2013. "Sector Creation and Evolution: The Role of the State in Shaping the Rise of the Indian Pharmaceutical Sectoral Business System." In *Multinational Corporations from Emerging Markets*, edited by Andreas Nölke, 109–129. Houndmills and Basingstoke: Palgrave Macmillan.

ten Brink, Tobias. 2012. "Perspectives on the Development of the Private Business Sector in China." *China – An International Journal* 10(3): 1–19.

ten Brink, Tobias. 2013a. *Chinas Kapitalismus. Entstehung, Verlauf, Paradoxien*. Frankfurt and New York: Campus.

ten Brink, Tobias. 2013b. "Paradoxes of Prosperity in China's New Capitalism." *Journal of Current Chinese Affairs* 42(4): 17–44.

ten Brink, Tobias. 2018. "A Comparative Analysis of Long-Term Growth in China." In *Capitalism and Capitalisms in Asia*, edited by H.-C. Lim, J. N. Pieterse, and S.-M. Hwang, 265–293. Seoul: Seoul National University Press.

ten Brink, Tobias. 2019. *China's Capitalism: A Paradoxical Route to Economic Prosperity*. Philadelphia: University of Pennsylvania Press.

ten Brink, Tobias, and Andreas Nölke. 2013. "Special Issue on Staatskapitalismus [State Capitalism]." *DMS – Der Moderne Staat* 6(1): 21–32.

Terreblanche, Sampie. 2002. *A History of Inequality in South Africa: 1652–2002*. Scottsville: UKZN Press.

Thelen, Kathleen. 2014. *Varieties of Liberalization and the New Politics of Social Solidarity*. Cambridge: Cambridge University Press.

Therborn, Göran. 2014. "New Masses? Social Bases of Resistance." *New Left Review* 85: 7–16.

Thompson, Lyndon. 2011. "Brazil's Economy: Reaching New Heights." *OECD Observer* (287): 26.

Tilak, Jhandhyla. 2003. "Vocational Education and Training in Asia." In *International Handbook of Educational Research in the Asia-Pacific Region*, edited by John P. Keeves, Ryo Watanabe, Rupert Maclean, Peter D. Renshaw, Colin N. Power, Robyn Baker, S. Gopinathan, Ho Wah Kam, Yin Cheong Cheng, and Albert C. Tuijnman, Volume 11, 673–86. Wiesbaden: Springer VS.

Times of India. 2014. "Grassroots Still with AAP. Middle Class Turning Away." 14 March.

Tsai, Kellee S. 2006. "Adaptive Informal Institutions and Endogenous Institutional Change in China." *World Politics* 59(1): 116–41.

Tshwane, Tebogo. 2018. "Finally: How the Government Plans to Fund Free Education." 21 February. https://mg.co.za/article/2018-02-21-finally-how-government-plans-to-fund-free-education (accessed 11 December 2018).

Tummala, Krishna K. 2015. "India, One Year After Elections: An Impasse in Parliament." *The Governance Blog*, 9 September. http://governancejournal.net/2015/09/09/india-one-year-after-elections-an-impasse-in-parliament/ (accessed 3 December 2015).

Tung, Rossalie L., and Verner Worm. 2001. "Network Capitalism: The Role of Human Resources in Penetrating the China Market." *International Journal of Human Resource Management* 12(4): 517–34.

Tybout, James R. 2000. "Manufacturing Firms in Developing Countries: How Well Do They Do, and Why?" *Journal of Economic Literature* 38(1): 11–44.

UIS Data Centre. 2015. "Public Expenditure on Education as % of GDP." http://data.un.org/Data.aspx?d=UNESCO&f=series%3aXGDP_FSGOV (accessed 19 December 2015).

UNCTAD. 2015. "UNCTAD FDI/TNC Database." (accessed 15 September 2015).

UNESCO Institute of Statistic/UN Data. 2015. "Gross Domestic Expenditure on Research and Development (GERD), as a Percentage of GDP." http://data.un.org/Data.aspx?q=research+and+development&d=UNESCO&f=series%3aST_SCGERDGDP (accessed 19 December 2015).

UNU-WIDER. 2015. "World Income Inequality Database (WIID3c)." September. www.wider.unu.edu/project/wiid-world-income-inequality-database (accessed 3 February 2016).

Vally, Salim. 2007. "From People's Education to Neo-Liberalism in South Africa." *Review of African Political Economy* 111: 39–56.

Valor. 2013a. *Grandes Grupos: 200 Maiores*. Sao Paulo: Valor.

Valor. 2013b. *Valor 1000: 1000 Maiores Empresas*. Sao Paulo: Valor.

van Apeldoorn, Bastiaan. 2002. *Transnational Capitalism and the Struggle Over European Integration*. London and New York: Routledge.

van der Berg, Servaas. 2009. "The Persistence of Inequalities in Education." In *South African Economic Policy Under Democracy*, edited by Janine Aron, Brian Khan, and Geeta Kingdon, 327–54. Oxford: Oxford University Press.

van der Berg, Servaas, and Heleen Hofmeyr. 2018. *Republic of South Africa Systematic Country Diagnostic. An Incomplete Transition: Overcoming the Legacy of Exclusion in South Africa*. Washington, DC: World Bank Group.

van der Linden, Marcel. 2016. "Global Labour: A Not-So-Grand Finale and Perhaps a New Beginning." *Global Labour Journal* 7(2): 201–10.

van der Pijl, Kees. 1998. *Transnational Classes and International Relations*. London and New York: Routledge.

van Tulder Robert. 2010. "Toward a Renewed Stages Theory for BRIC Multinational Enterprises? A Home Country Bargaining Approach." In *Foreign Direct Investments from Emerging Markets: The Challenges Ahead*, edited by Karl P. Sauvant, Geraldine A. McAllister and Wolfgang A. Maschek, 61–74. Houndmills and New York: Palgrave Macmillan.

Vasileva-Dienes, Alexandra and Vivien A. Schmidt. (eds.). 2019. "Capitalism in Crisis." Special Issue, *Contemporary Politics* 25 (in print).

Vegter, Ivo. 2015. "Corruption Is Now Official Policy in South Africa." *Daily Maverick*, 13 October. www.dailymaverick.co.za/opinionista/2015-10-13-corruption-is-now-official-policy-in-south-africa/#.VnhbbBHZrSg (accessed 21 December 2015).

Verhoef, Grietjie. 2009. "Concentration and Competition: The Changing Landscape of the Banking Sector in South Africa 1970–2007." *South African Journal of Economic History* 24(2): 157–97.

Vickers, Edward, and Xiaodong Zeng. 2017. *Education and Society in Post-Mao China*. London and New York: Routledge.

Vishwasrao, Sharmila, and William Bosshardt. 2001. "Foreign Ownership and Technology Adoption: Evidence from Indian Firms." *Journal of Development Economics* 65(2): 367–87.

Vivarelli, Marco. 2015. "Structural Change and Innovation in Developing Economies: A Way Out of the Middle Income Trap?" *LEM Worker Paper Series*, September.

Wade, Robert. 1990. *Governing the Market: Economic Theory and the Role of Government in East Asian Industrialization*. Princeton: Princeton University Press.

Wade, Robert. 2013. "Protecting Power: Western States in Global Organizations." In *Global Governance at Risk*, edited by D. Held and C. Roger, 77–110. Cambridge: Polity Press.

Walder, Andrew G. 1995. "Local Governments as Industrial Firms: An Organizational Analysis of China's Transitional Economy." *American Journal of Sociology* 101(2): 263–301.

Walter, Andrew, and Xiaoke Zhang. 2012. *East Asian Capitalism: Diversity, Continuity, and Change*. Oxford: Oxford University Press.

Walter, Carl E., and Fraser J.T. Howie. 2011. *Red Capitalism: The Fragile Financial Foundation of China's Extraordinary Rise*. Singapore: John Wiley & Sons.

Wank, David L. 1999. *Commodifying Communism: Business, Trust, and Politics in a Chinese City*. Cambridge: Cambridge University Press.

Webster, Edward. 2013. "South Africa's Contested Industrial Relation Path." *Transformation: Critical Perspectives on Southern Africa* 81–2: 208–35.

Wedeman, Andrew. 2004. "The Intensification of Corruption in China." *The China Quarterly* 180: 895–921.

Wheatley, Jonathan, and Sam Fleming. 2015. "Capital Flight Darkens Economic Prospects for Emerging Markets." *Financial Times*, 1 October.

Whitley, Richard. 1992. *Business Systems in East Asia: Firms, Markets and Societies*. London: Sage Publications.

Whitley, Richard. 1999. *Divergent Capitalisms: The Social Structuring and Change of Business Systems*. Oxford: Oxford University Press.

Who Owns Whom. 2013. "South Africa." http://www.whoownswhom.co.za/ ebook/2013_ book. (accessed 14 December 2014).

Williamson, John. 1990. "What Washington Means by Policy Reform." In *Latin American Adjustment: How Much Has Happened?* edited by John Williamson. Washington, DC: Institute for International Economics.

Williamson, John, and Roberto Zagha. 2002. "From the Hindu Rate of Growth to the Hindu Rate of Reform." *Working Paper* 144. Stanford: Stanford Center for International Development.

Williamson, Peter J., and Eden Yin. 2014. "Accelerated Innovation: The New Challenge from China." *MIT Sloan Management Review* 55(4): 27–34.

Windolf, Paul. 2005. "Was ist Finanzmarktkapitalismus?" In *Finanzmarkt-Kapitalismus. Special Issue 45 of Kölner Zeitschrift für Soziologie und Sozialpsychologie*, edited by Paul Windolf, 20–57. Wiesbaden: Springer VS.

Witt, Michael A. 2010. "China: What Variety of Capitalism?" www.insead.edu/faculty research/research/doc.cfm?did=46188

Witt, Michael A. forthcoming. "The Road Ahead for China: Implications from the South Korean Experience." In *Building Innovation Capacity in China: An Agenda for Averting the Middle Income Trap*, edited by Arie Y. Lewin, Martin Kenney, and J. Peter Murmann. Cambridge: Cambridge University Press.

Witt, Michael A., and Gordon Redding. 2013. "Asian Business Systems: Institutional Comparison, Clusters and Implications for Varieties of Capitalism and Business Systems Theory." *Socio-Economic Review* 11: 265–300.

Witt, Michael A., and Gordon Redding. 2014. *The Oxford Handbook of Asian Business Systems*. Oxford: Oxford University Press.

Woetzel, Jonathan, and Jeffrey Towson. 2015. *The One Hour China Consumer Book: Five Short Stories That Explain the Brutal Fight for One Billion Chinese Consumers*. Towson Group: Cayman Islands.

Wolpe, Harold. 1972. "Capitalism and Cheap Labour – Power in South Africa: From Segregation to Apartheid." *Economy and Society* 1(4): 425–56.

World Bank. 2006. *Poverty Reduction and Growth: From Vicious to Virtuous Circles*. Washington, DC: The World Bank Group.

World Bank. 2008. *Skill Development in India: The Vocational Education and Training System*. Washington, DC: South Asia Human Development Sector Series 22.

World Bank. 2009. *World Bank Enterprise Survey for Managers – Brazil Data*. Washington, DC: World Bank (accessed 26 August 2015).

World Bank. 2012. *China 2030. Building a Modern, Harmonious, and Creative High-Income Society*. Washington, DC: World Bank Group.

World Bank. 2013. *Global Development Horizons*. Washington, DC: The World Bank.

World Bank. 2014. "Enterprise Surveys." www.enterprisesurveys.org

World Bank. 2015a. "India Development Update: Towards a Higher Growth Path." *Report* No. 95979, World Bank Group.

World Bank. 2015b. "China Economic Update." June. World Bank Group.

World Bank. 2015c. "World Bank Development Indicators Database." (accessed 4 March 2015).

World Bank. 2015d. "World Bank Development Indicators Database." (accessed 11 October 2015).

World Bank. 2015e. "World Bank Povcalnet Database." (accessed 2 December 2015).

World Bank. 2016. "South African GDP Growth (Annual %) 2016." https://data.worldbank.org/indicator/NY.GDP.MKTP.KD.ZG?locations=ZA

Woronov, Terry E. 2016. *Class Work: Vocational Schools and China's Urban Youth*. Stanford, CA: Stanford University Press.

Xi, Jinping. 2014. *The Governance of China*. Beijing: Foreign Languages Press.

Yadav, Vineeta. 2011. *Political Parties, Business Groups, and Corruption in Developing Countries*. Oxford: Oxford University Press.

Yang, Chun. 2014. "State-Led Technological Innovation of Domestic Firms in Shenzhen, China: Evidence from Liquid Crystal Display (LCD) Industry." *Cities* 38: 1–10.

Yang, Dali L. 2004. *Remaking the Chinese Leviathan: Market Transition and the Politics of Governance in China*. Stanford: Stanford University Press.

Yu, Miaojie, and Wei Tian. 2012. "China's Processing Trade." In *Rebalancing and Sustaining Growth in China*, edited by Huw McKay and Ligong Song, 111–48. Canberra: Australian National University Press.

Zalk, Nimrod. 2014. "Industrial Policy in a Harsh Climate: The Case of South Africa." In *Transforming Economies: Making Industrial Policy Work for Growth, Jobs and Development*, edited by José M. Salazar-Xirinachs, Imgrad Nübler, and Richard Kozul Wright, 327–54. Geneva: ILO.

Zhang, Xiaoke, and Richard Whitley. 2013. "Changing Macro-structural Varieties of East Asian Capitalism." *Socio-Economic Review* 11(2): 301–36.

Zheng, Yinga, and Yuande Zhu. 2013. "Bank Lending Incentives and Firm Investment Decisions in China." *Journal of Multinational Financial Management* 23: 146–65.

Zheng, Yongnian. 2010. *The Chinese Communist Party as Organizational Emperor: Culture, Reproduction, and Transformation*. London: Routledge.

Zhu, Jiangnan. 2018. "Corruption in Reform China: A Multidisciplinary Review." In *The SAGE Handbook of Contemporary China*, edited by W. Wu and M. F. Frazier, 302–22. London: SAGE Publications.

Zysman, John. 1994. "How Institutions Create Historically Rooted Trajectories of Growth." *Industrial and Corporate Change* 3(1): 243–83.

Interviews

Interview AHK (with Executive Director, German Chamber of Commerce South and Southwest China), 3 January 2013.

Interview Brazilian Agency for Industrial Development (ABDI), Brasilia, 26 February 2013.

Interview Brazilian Ministry of Industry and Commerce, Brasilia, 26 February 2013.

Interview Foshan (with two anonymous Deputy Schoolmasters of a Technical School, Foshan, Shunde), 13 December 2012.

Interview Midea (with Lu Juping, Administrative Director, Headquarter, Midea Group, Shunde), 28 December 2012.

Interview PRD (with Qiu Haixiong, Director, Institute for the Development and Reform of the Pearl River Delta, Guangzhou), 30 January 2013.

Interview SYSU (with Lu Jun, Dean, Department of Finance, Sun Yat-Sen University, Guangzhou), 17 December 2012.

Interview SYSU (with Wang Xiaohui, Executive Director, Department of Economics, SYSU, HR Management and Labor Economics), 8 January 2013.

Interview with a Corporate Governance Expert, Johannesburg, 4 April 2013.

Interview with an Economist, BNDES, Rio de Janeiro, 1 March 2013.

Interview with an Economist, Insper, Sao Paulo, 4 March 2013.

Interview with an Economist, Pretoria, 4 April 2013.

Interview with an Independent Consultant, Johannesburg, 17 April 2013.

Interview with Innovation Expert, Stellenbosch, 12 April 2013.

Interview with Innovation Expert 2, Johannesburg, 17 April 2013.

Interview with Representative of FINEP, Rio de Janeiro, 28 February 2013.

Interviews Shunde (with Five Anonymous Officials from Shunde, District of Foshan: Deputy Director General Staff, District Government; First Deputy Director, Economy Promotion Bureau; Official at the Enterprises Registration Department; Official at the Local People's Congress; Deputy Union Chairman in a Development District), end of December 2012/mid-January 2013.

Index

www.ingramcontent.com/pod-product-compliance
Lightning Source LLC
LaVergne TN
LVHW011115300926
849160LV00008B/391